Contents

Energy

Electricity

Waves and radiation

Forces

Acknowledgements

25t, 31, Jim Winkley/Ecoscene; *25l,c*, 107, Martin Bond/Science Photo Library; *25cr*, Chinch Gryniewicz/Ecoscene; *25b*, Ian Pickthall/ Ecoscene; *32l*, 104, Anthony Cooper/Ecoscene; *32r*, David Walker/ Ecoscene; 33, Kevin King/Ecoscene; *34r*, NASA/Science Photo Library; *34l*, 48, 55, 56, 58, 60, 66, 80, 91, 110, *142l*, *156b*, Andrew Lambert; 79, photograph courtesy of IBM UK Labs, Hursley; 81, U.S. Department of Energy/Science Photo Library; 100, 111, 124, Michael Wyndham Picture Collection; *141t*, Takashi Takahara/Science Photo Library; *141b*, George Herringshaw/Associated Sports Photography; *142r*, Dr Jeremy Burgess/Science Photo Library; 144, 174, Sutton Motorsport Images; 146, Arthur Gibson/TRH Pictures; 150, Brown/Ecoscene; 154, TRH Pictures/GMC/Candive Ltd; 155, DEEP FLIGHT/photo by Shirley Richards/SPL; *156t*, Geoff Tompkinson/ Science Photo Library; 160, Luke Dodd/Science Photo Library; 162, Roger Ressmeyer, Starlight/Science Photo Library; 167, 172, NASA/Image Select; *168t*, *168b*, 169, NOAO/Science Photo Library; 170, Pekka Parviainen/Science Photo Library; 171, Science Photo Library; 176, Mike Hewitt/Action Plus; 180, Dave Emerson/Action Plus

Controlling heat transfer in solids

Heat always moves from hot places to cold places. This is called heat **transfer**.

Sometimes you want to make it easy for heat to go from one place to another. Sometimes you want to keep heat in one place. You need to know how it travels.

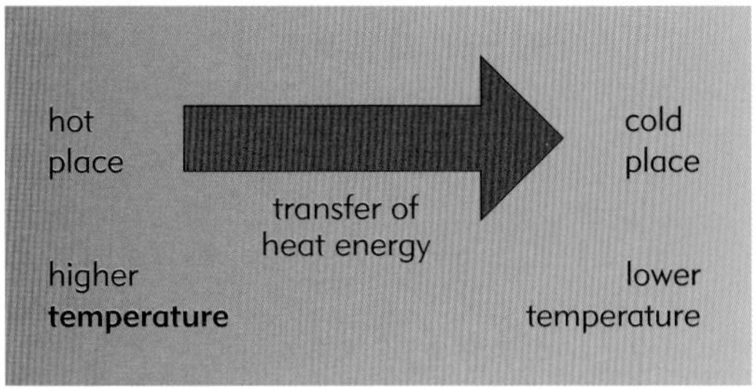

Using solids to control heat

If you put a solid between somewhere hot and somewhere cold, the heat has to travel through the solid. This is called **conduction**.

Heat passes easily through some solids, which we call conductors. Other solids conduct heat badly, and we call these insulators.

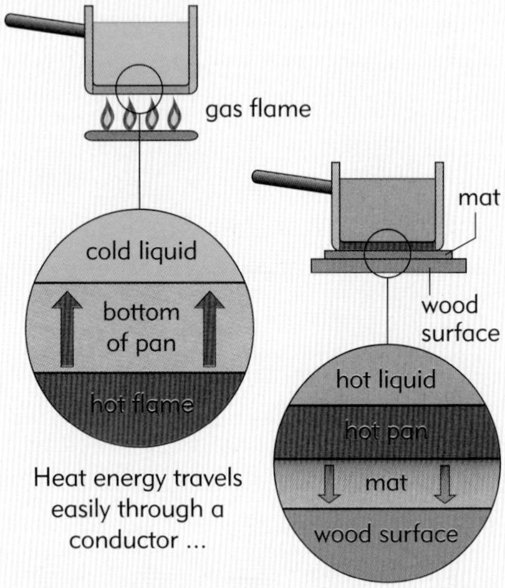

Heat energy travels easily through a conductor ...

... but hardly at all through an insulator.

1 Look at the diagrams.

Copy and complete the table.

	Conductor or insulator?	Reason
bottom of pan		It will help transfer heat from the ____________ to the ____________.
table mat		It will cut down heat transfer from the ____________ to the ____________ surface.

Which solids conduct heat best?

Metals are good conductors. Copper and aluminium transfer heat faster than iron or steel, so they are better conductors than iron or steel.

Non-metals, like plastic, wood, pottery and glass, are good insulators.

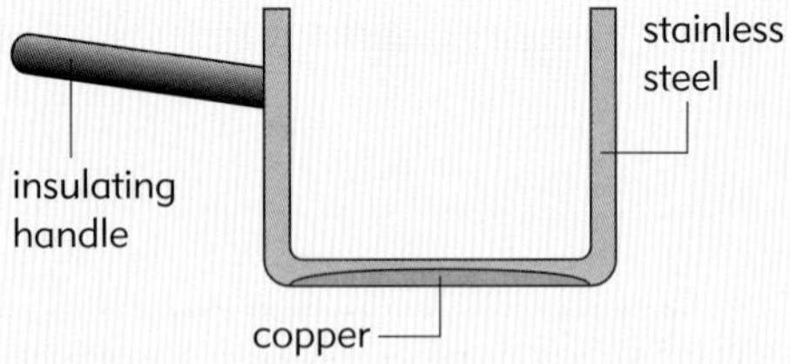

2 (a) Which two metals are used to make the pan in the diagram?

(b) Why are the metals used in different places on the pan?

3 Which material could you use for the pan handle?

4 Why do potatoes bake quicker if you put them on metal spikes?

It takes a long time for baked potatoes to cook right to the middle.

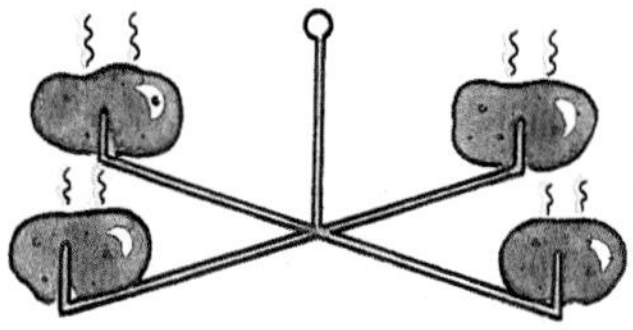

Using aluminium spikes, they cook through in half the time.

Keeping heat where you want it

We often want to stop heat getting into or out of things. To do this we surround the things with **insulation**.

5 Copy the table. Then complete it.

	Why we need to insulate it	What is used for insulation
oven		
fridge		

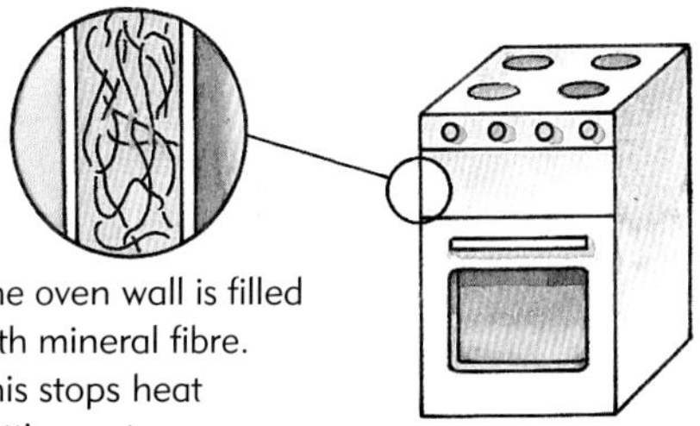

The oven wall is filled with mineral fibre. This stops heat getting out.

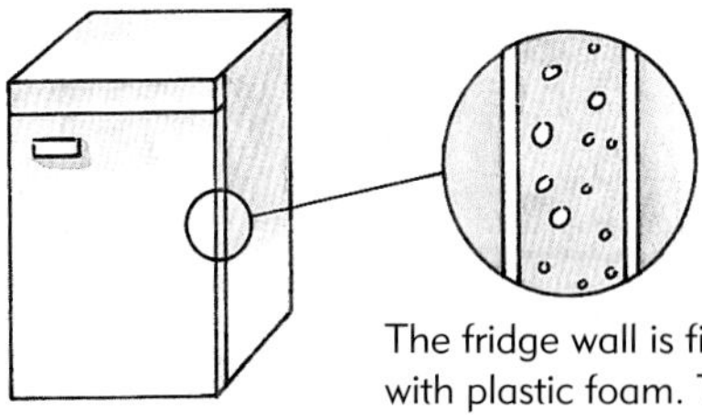

The fridge wall is filled with plastic foam. This stops heat getting in.

Why do handlebars feel so cold?

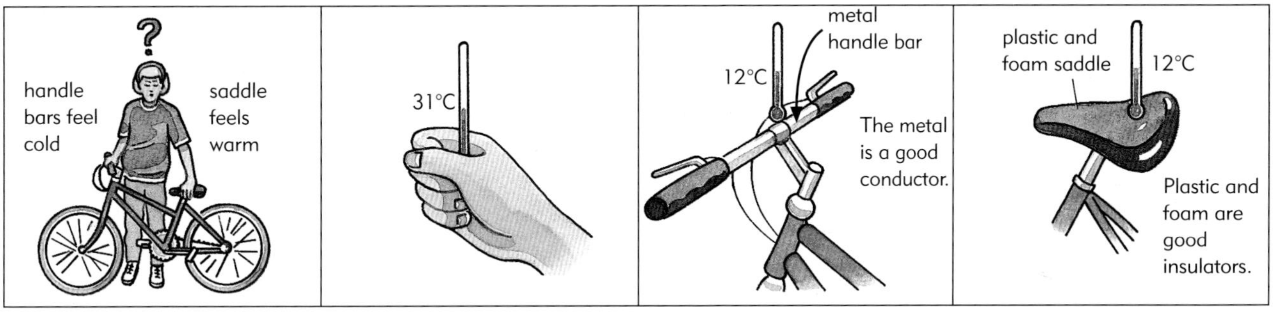

Anna notices that the handlebars of her bicycle feel colder than the saddle.

Anna's science teacher lends her a thermometer. Anna's hand is at 31°C.

Anna measures the temperatures of the handlebars and the saddle. They are both 12°C.

6 (a) Are the handlebars colder than the saddle?

(b) Why do they feel colder to Anna ?

What you need to remember [Copy and complete using the **key words**]

Controlling heat transfer in solids

Heat moves from hot places, where the ________________ is high, to colder places.
This movement of energy is called heat ________________.
Heat is transferred through solids by ________________.
All ________________ are good conductors of heat.
We surround things with ________________ to stop heat getting into or out of them.

How liquids and gases transfer heat

How does all the water in a kettle get hot ?

The water in a kettle is a liquid. **Liquids** can flow. The heating element in an electric kettle is at the bottom, but it still heats up all the water in the kettle.

The diagrams show how it does this.

1 Draw one large diagram of the kettle.

Add arrows to show how hot water rises and cold water falls.

Label them or colour them in. Use red for hot and blue for cold.

Each time the water moves around the kettle it gets a little bit hotter.

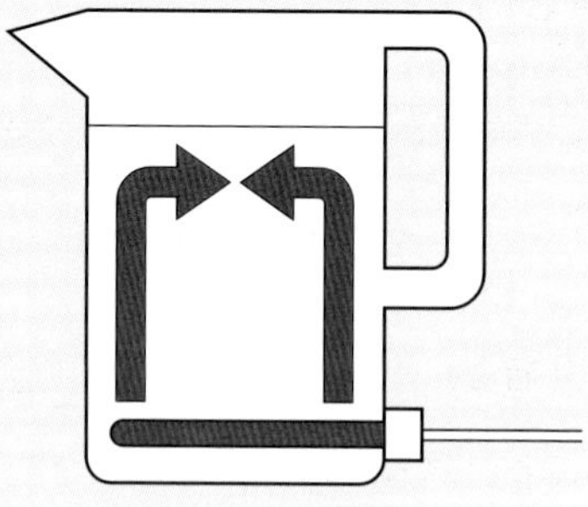

Water next to the heating element gets hotter. This hot water **rises**.

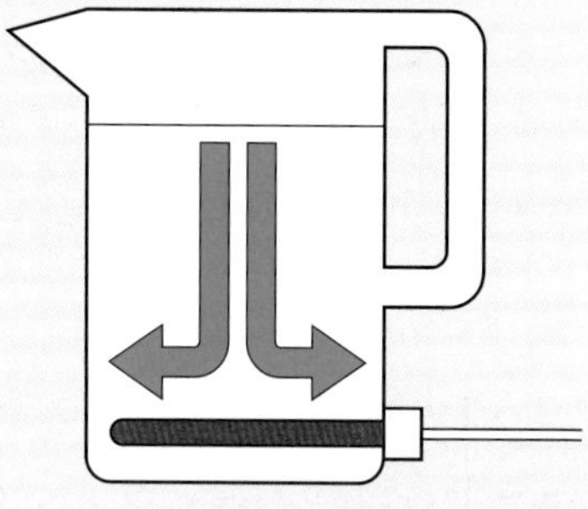

Colder water then **falls** down to take its place.

How does all the air in a room get warm?

The air in a room is a gas. **Gases** can also flow. Heaters are usually near the floor, but the whole of the room gets heated.

The diagrams show how heaters do this.

2 Draw one large diagram of the room and heater.

Draw arrows to show the hot air rising and the cold air falling.

Label or colour the arrows.

Hot liquids and gases will move around and carry their heat with them. This is called **convection**.

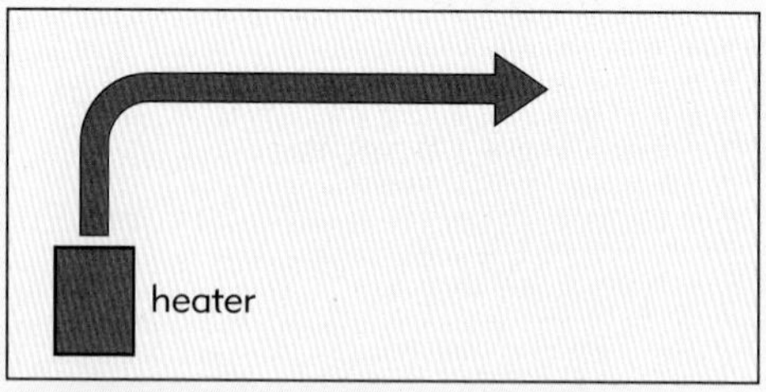

Air next to the heater becomes hotter. This hot air rises.

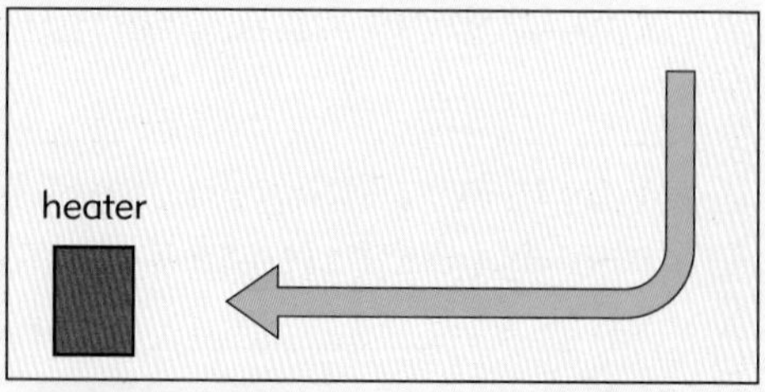

Colder air then falls down to take its place.

How does everywhere inside a fridge get cold?

The diagram shows how the cooling unit cools all the fridge.

3 Copy and complete the following sentences.

The air near the __________ __________ becomes cold.

This cold air will then __________.

Warmer air will then __________ to take its place.

4 Why is the cooling unit at the top of the fridge?

The air moves round and round the fridge. This movement of air is called a **convection current**.

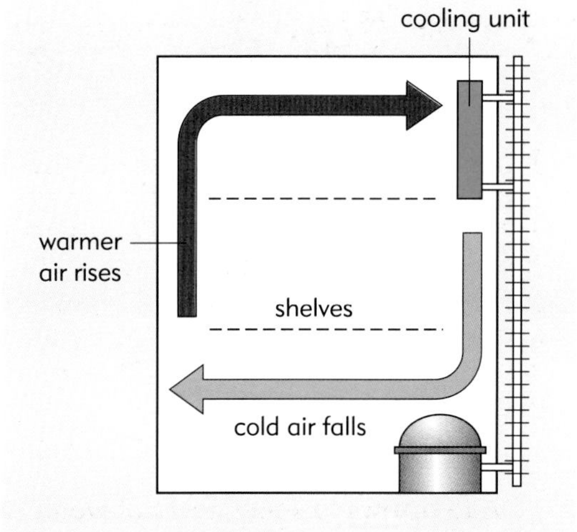

A refrigerator (fridge).

How can you make convection faster?

Sometimes you may want to move heat quicker. You may also want to transfer heat over bigger distances. You can use a pump or a fan to do this.

The diagrams show two examples of using water to convect heat further and faster.

5 Copy and complete the following sentences.

A central __________ system uses water to transfer heat from the __________ to the __________.

A car engine __________ system uses water to convect heat from the __________ to the __________.

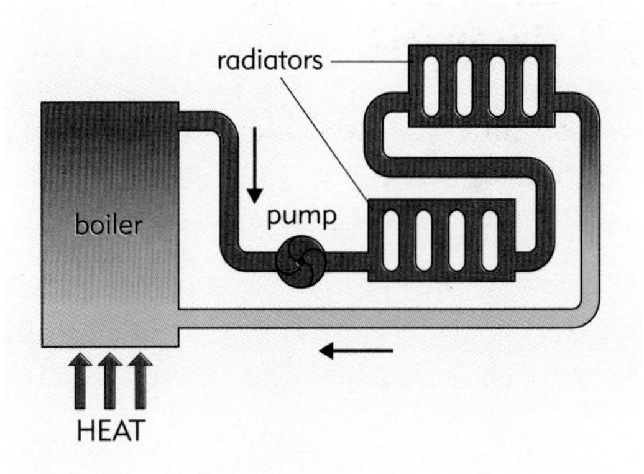

A central heating system.

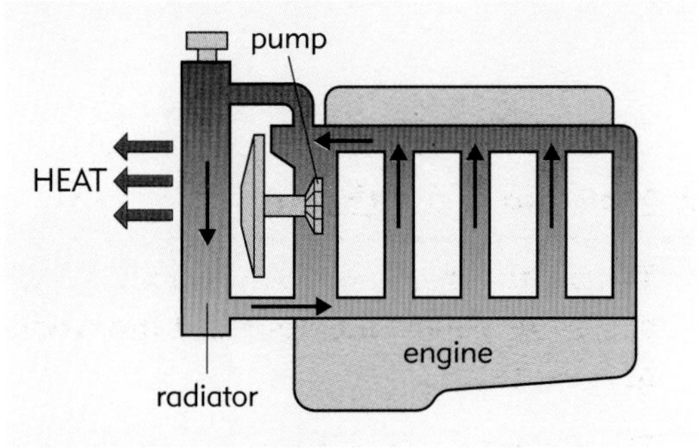

A car engine cooling system.

What you need to remember [Copy and complete using the **key words**]

How liquids and gases transfer heat

______________ and ______________ can both flow.
When part of a liquid or gas is hotter than the rest, it ______________.
When part of a liquid or gas is cooler than the rest, it ______________.
Transferring heat in this way is called ______________.
This movement of a liquid or gas is called a ______________ ______________.

How can heat energy travel through space?

Huge amounts of energy reach the Earth every day from the hot Sun. The 150 million kilometres between the Earth and the Sun are mainly empty **space**. In completely empty space, there isn't even any air or other gas.

REMEMBER

Conduction happens when heat energy travels through a substance.

Convection happens when a hot substance moves and carries heat energy with it.

1 Energy cannot be conducted or convected from the Sun to the Earth.

Explain why.

2 Write down another name for empty space.

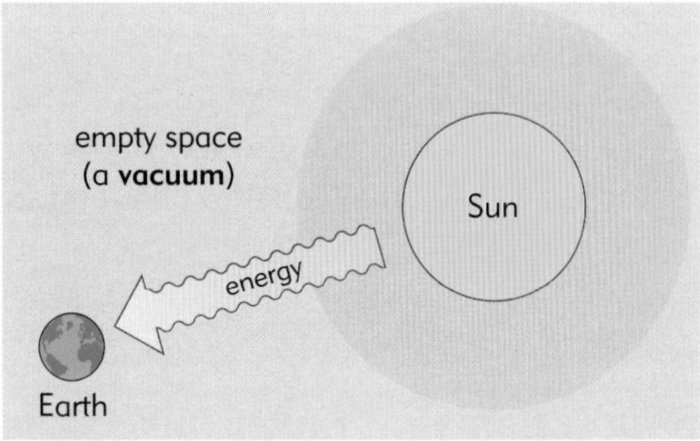

How does energy from the Sun reach the Earth?

The Sun sends out energy as radiation, which can travel through empty space.

Some of the energy is sent as light rays that we can see. Most of the energy is sent as heat, in the form of **infrared** radiation. You cannot see infrared rays, but you can feel them.

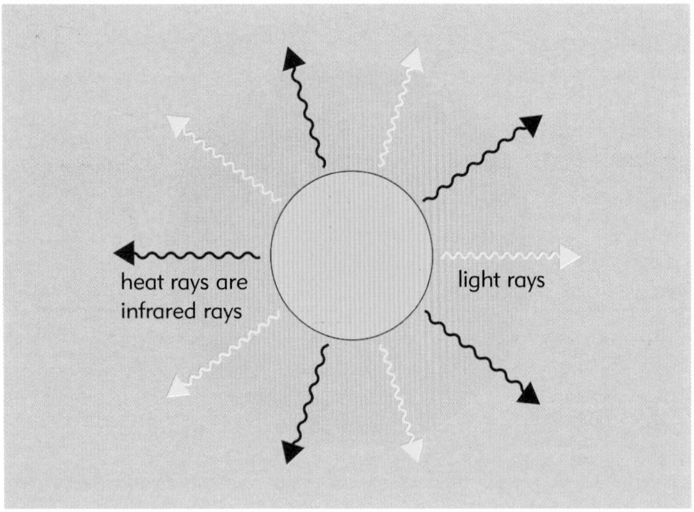

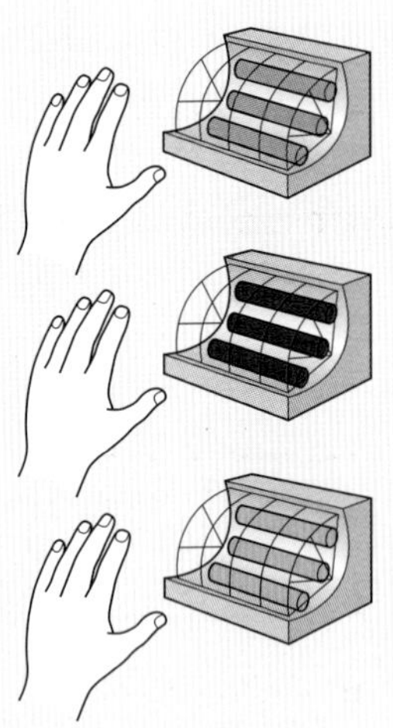

You can feel infrared rays from an electric fire a few seconds after you switch on.
As the fire gets hotter, you can feel **more** infrared radiation.
When the fire is hot enough, it glows orange. It sends out light rays as well as infrared rays.

3 Look at the diagrams. Then copy and complete the following sentences.

Things that are hot give out __________ radiation.

The __________ something is, the more radiation it gives out.

If anything gets hot enough, it gives out __________ rays as well as infrared rays.

How can you capture the energy in heat rays?

A **black** surface is a good **absorber** of heat rays. This means that it soaks up infrared radiation very well.

White or **shiny** surfaces do not absorb heat rays. They are good at reflecting the rays away from them.

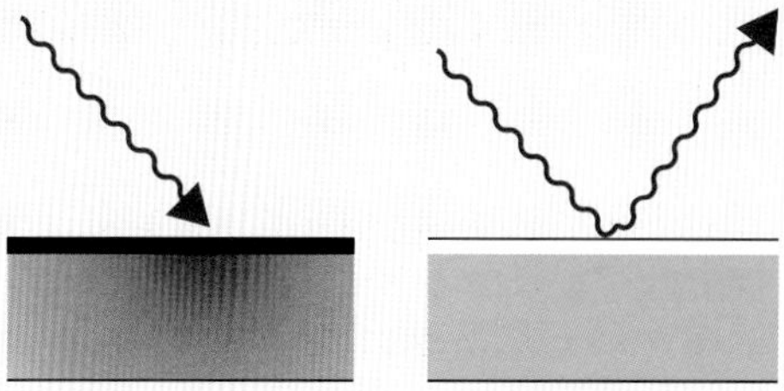

Dark surfaces absorb infrared rays. They get warmer.

A white or shiny surface **reflects** infrared radiation.

4 Look at the pictures below.

Write a sentence to explain each one.

Dark clothes make you feel hot on a sunny day.

Petrol storage tanks and petrol tankers are shiny.

The tar on roads can melt in the summer sun.

Houses in hot countries are often white.

What makes a good radiator?

Black surfaces are better at sending out radiation than white or shiny surfaces.

5 What do the probe readings tell you about the temperatures of the engines?

6 Explain the difference in temperature between the two engines.

Motorcycle with black engine.

Temperature probe reads 175 °C.

Motorcycle with shiny engine.

Temperature probe reads 200 °C.

What you need to remember [Copy and complete using the **key words**]

How can heat energy travel through space?

Heat rays can travel through empty ___________________.
Another name for empty space is a ___________________.
Heat radiation is also called ___________________ radiation.
A ___________________ surface is good at absorbing infrared radiation.
This means that it ___________________ very little radiation.
A ___________________ or ___________________ surface is good at reflecting infrared radiation.
This means that it is not a good ___________________ of radiation.
The hotter something is, the ___________________ energy it radiates.

4 Conduction, convection and radiation – putting it all together

It's useful to know about conduction, convection and radiation. It helps you to understand how things around you work. It also helps you to work out how you can save energy.

You will find five examples in this section. You will have to think of more than one way of heat transfer to answer the questions.

Use the REMEMBER box to remind yourself of what you should know.

REMEMBER

Conduction is how heat is transferred through a solid. The solid does not move. Metals are good conductors, non-metals are poor conductors (they are insulators).

Convection is how heat moves through liquids and gases. The liquids and gases carry the heat with them. Hot gases and liquids rise, cold gases and liquids fall.

Radiation is how heat travels through space (a vacuum). Shiny surfaces reflect infrared rays, so they absorb little heat. Black surfaces reflect little heat and absorb a lot. Hot things radiate heat.

Why do foam and fibres make good insulators?

Air, like all gases, is a very poor **conductor**. But to use it as an insulator, we must stop it moving about.

Look at the diagrams of foam and fibre **insulation**.

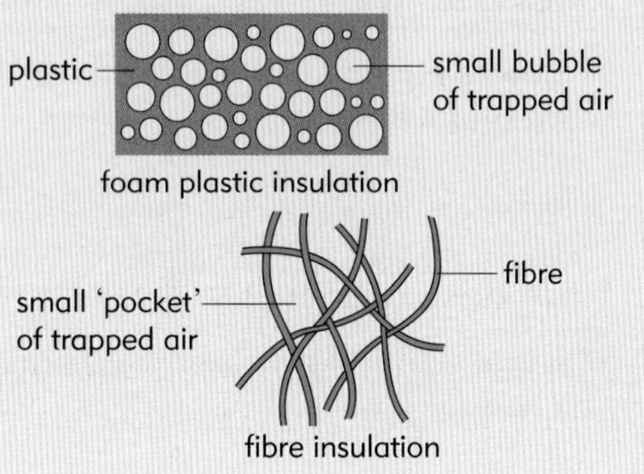

1 Describe how the air is stopped from moving about in the foam and the fibre.

2 Why is it important to stop the air moving about?

How can you heat up part of a tank of water?

Water in houses is often heated using an electric immersion heater. Some heaters can be set to heat just a small amount of water because this is cheaper. The heater that does this is near the top of the tank.

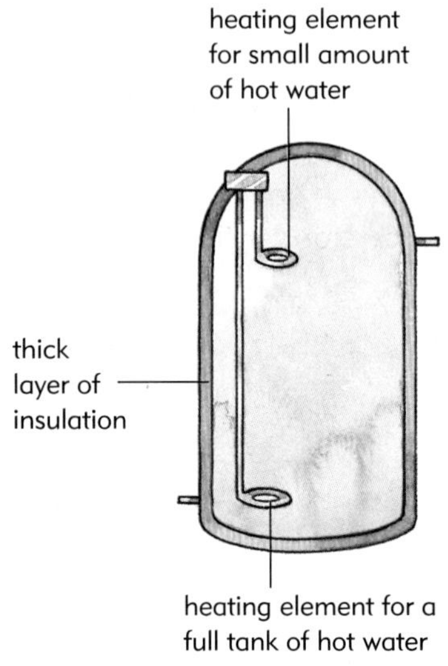

3 Copy the diagram.

Mark on the diagram where there is a convection current made by the top heater.
Use colours to show the parts of the convection current.

4 The rest of the water in the tank stays cold.
Why does the water at the bottom not become hot by conduction through the water?

How can a glider pilot gain height?

To climb higher in the sky, a glider pilot looks for places where air is rising. On a sunny day, the best places are over dark ground such as a ploughed field or a large car park.

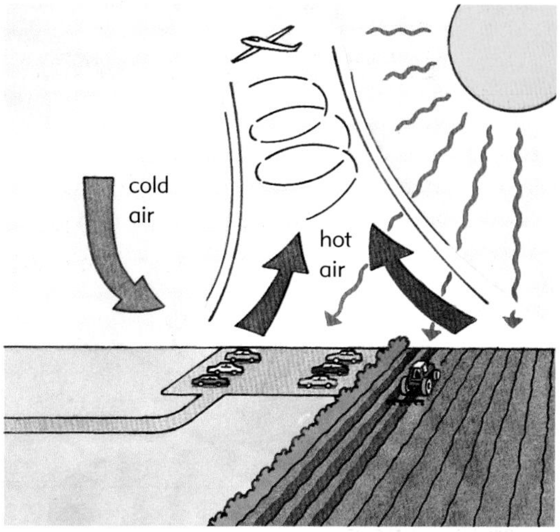

5 Explain as fully as you can why air rises over dark parts of the ground.

Radiators don't just radiate

Look at the diagram.

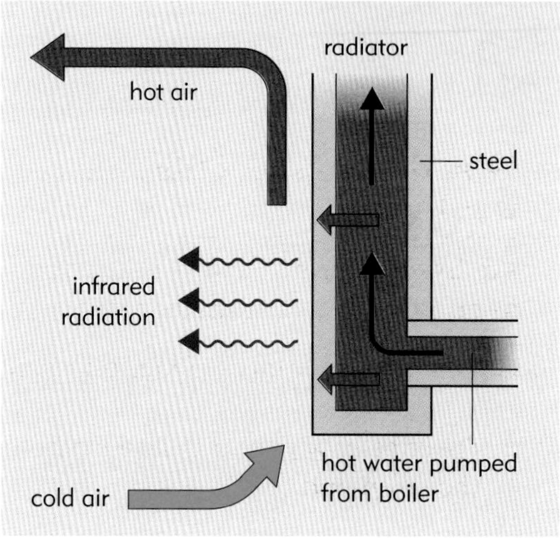

6 How is heat transferred from the boiler to inside the radiator?

7 How is heat transferred from the inside to the outside of the radiator?

8 Only a little energy is radiated into a room by a radiator.

How is most of the heat from the radiator transferred around the room?

How does a thermos flask work?

A thermos flask keeps hot things hot and cold things cold. It has a special inner flask. This transfers very little heat.

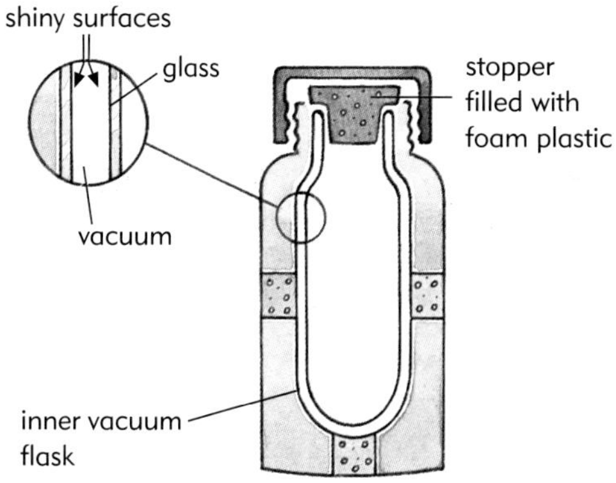

9 Explain how each of the following reduce heat transfer.

(a) The vacuum between the walls of the inner flask.

(b) The shiny surfaces of the walls of the inner flask.

(c) The stopper filled with foam plastic.

What you need to remember [Copy and complete using the **key words**]

Conduction, convection and radiation – putting it all together

Materials that are used for ________________ often contain air.
This air is trapped so it can't move about.
A gas, such as air, is a very poor ________________.

Losing heat from buildings – and how to stop it

■ We're being robbed of our joules!

All buildings lose heat energy in various ways. This costs money and wastes fuel.

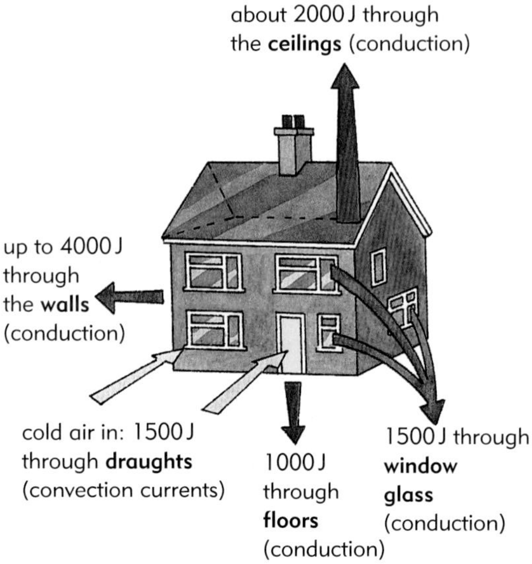

Heat lost each second from a badly insulated house on a cold day.

1 Look at the diagram. Copy and complete the table. (A joule (J) is a unit of energy.)

Part of house	Heat lost each second in J
ceiling	
window glass	
floor	
draughts	
walls	
TOTAL	

2 Copy and complete the following sentences.

Heat moves through walls by ___________.
Draughts are caused by ___________ ___________.
Heat moves up to ceilings by convection and then moves through ceilings by ___________.
Heat moves through window glass by ___________.
Heat moves through the floor by ___________.
The biggest heat loss is through the ___________ .

■ Which home costs less to heat?

Some sorts of homes will lose less heat than others. This is often because they have **fewer** outside walls.

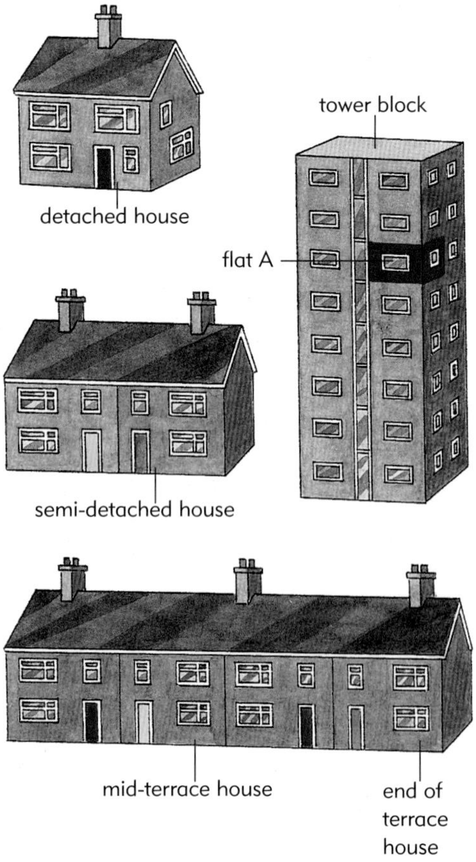

3 Look at the diagrams of the types of homes. Copy and complete the table.

Type of home	Number of outside walls
detached	
semi-detached	3
tower block flat A	
end of terrace	
mid-terrace	

4 Which type of home may cost least to heat? Give a reason.

5 Flat A in the tower block will lose less heat than a flat on the ground floor or the top floor. Why is this?

Energy-saving ideas

Radiators are often placed against outside walls. The heat from the back of the radiator is transferred to the wall by radiation. The heat then moves through the wall by conduction. The diagram shows how to reduce this heat loss.

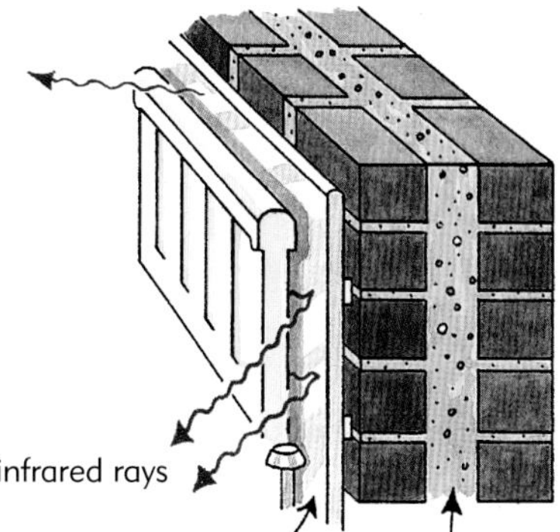

infrared rays
shiny plastic stuck to wall behind radiator reflects infrared
Filling the cavity in the wall with plastic foam **insulation** stops convection. The foam is a bad conductor.
Together this saves $\frac{3}{4}$ of the heat lost through walls.

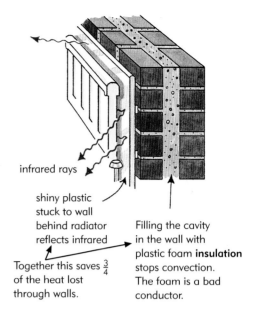

Saving heat lost through the walls.

6 Copy and complete the following sentences.

The shiny surface behind the radiator will __________ the infrared rays back into the room. Plastic foam in wall cavities prevents heat loss by __________.

The foam does not increase heat loss by __________, because foam is an insulator.

7 All the energy-saving ideas on this page are used in the house shown on page 14.

(a) Draw a picture of the house and label the heat losses, now that it is insulated.

(b) What is the total heat loss for the insulated house?

(c) How does this compare with the uninsulated house?

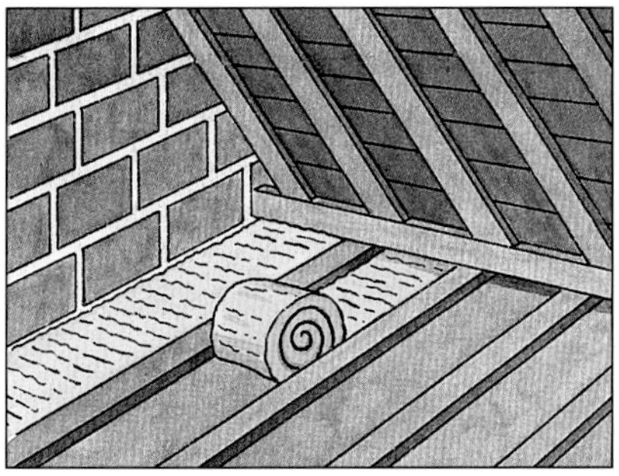

Insulating the loft with 200 mm of glass fibre can save half of the heat lost through the ceiling.

Draught excluders (strips) round doors and windows can save half of the heat lost through draughts.

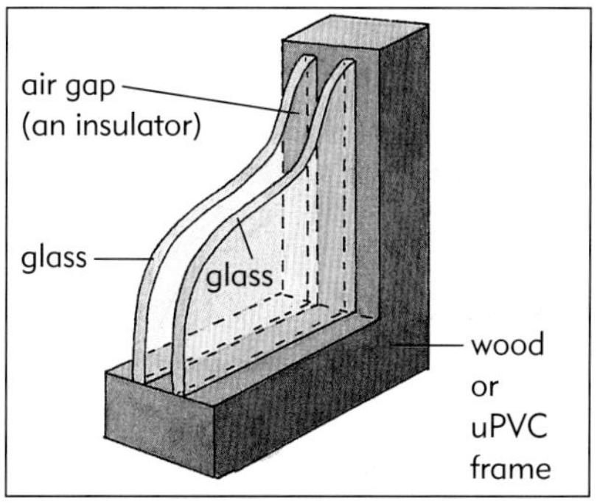

air gap (an insulator)
glass
glass
wood or uPVC frame

Double glazing can save about half of the heat lost through windows.

What you need to remember [Copy and complete using the **key words**]

Losing heat from buildings – and how to stop it

Heat energy can be lost from buildings by conduction through the __________, __________, __________ and __________ __________.

It is also lost by convection because of __________.

Homes lose less heat if they have __________ outside walls.

You can save heat energy by __________ the loft, fitting __________ excluders, putting in cavity wall __________ and __________ __________ windows.

6 Using the Sun's energy to heat your home

Let the Sun shine in!

If your house gets warm from the Sun, you need less fuel.

This saves fossil fuels like coal, oil and gas. You may also use less electricity.

Even in the winter you can get some benefit from the Sun's energy, although the Sun is lower in the sky.

How can we trap energy from the Sun?

The diagram shows how a glass window can trap energy from the Sun inside a house.

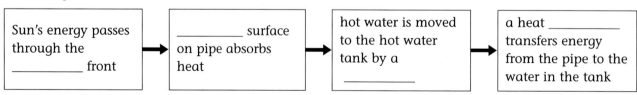

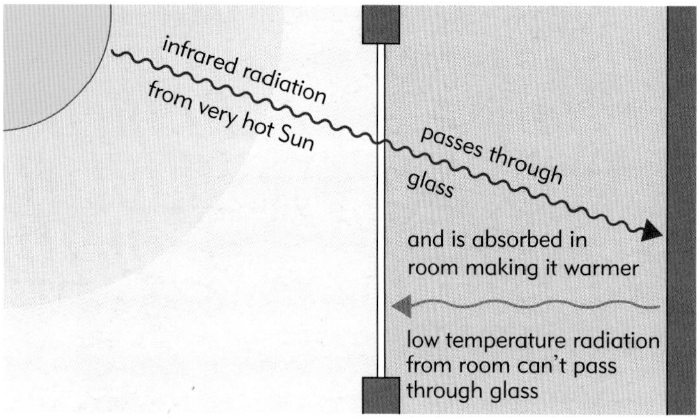
infrared radiation
from very hot Sun
passes through
glass
and is absorbed in
room making it warmer
low temperature radiation
from room can't pass
through glass

1 Explain how the glass window is able to do this.

How does a solar panel work?

Some houses have solar panels in the roof. These use energy radiated by the Sun to heat water. The diagram opposite shows how solar panels work.

2 Copy the series of boxes below. Then fill in the missing words.

Sun's energy passes through the ________ front	→	________ surface on pipe absorbs heat	→	hot water is moved to the hot water tank by a ________	→	a heat ________ transfers energy from the pipe to the water in the tank

3 Why is there a shiny surface behind the water pipes in the solar panel?

4 Explain why there is a layer of insulation at the back of the solar panel.

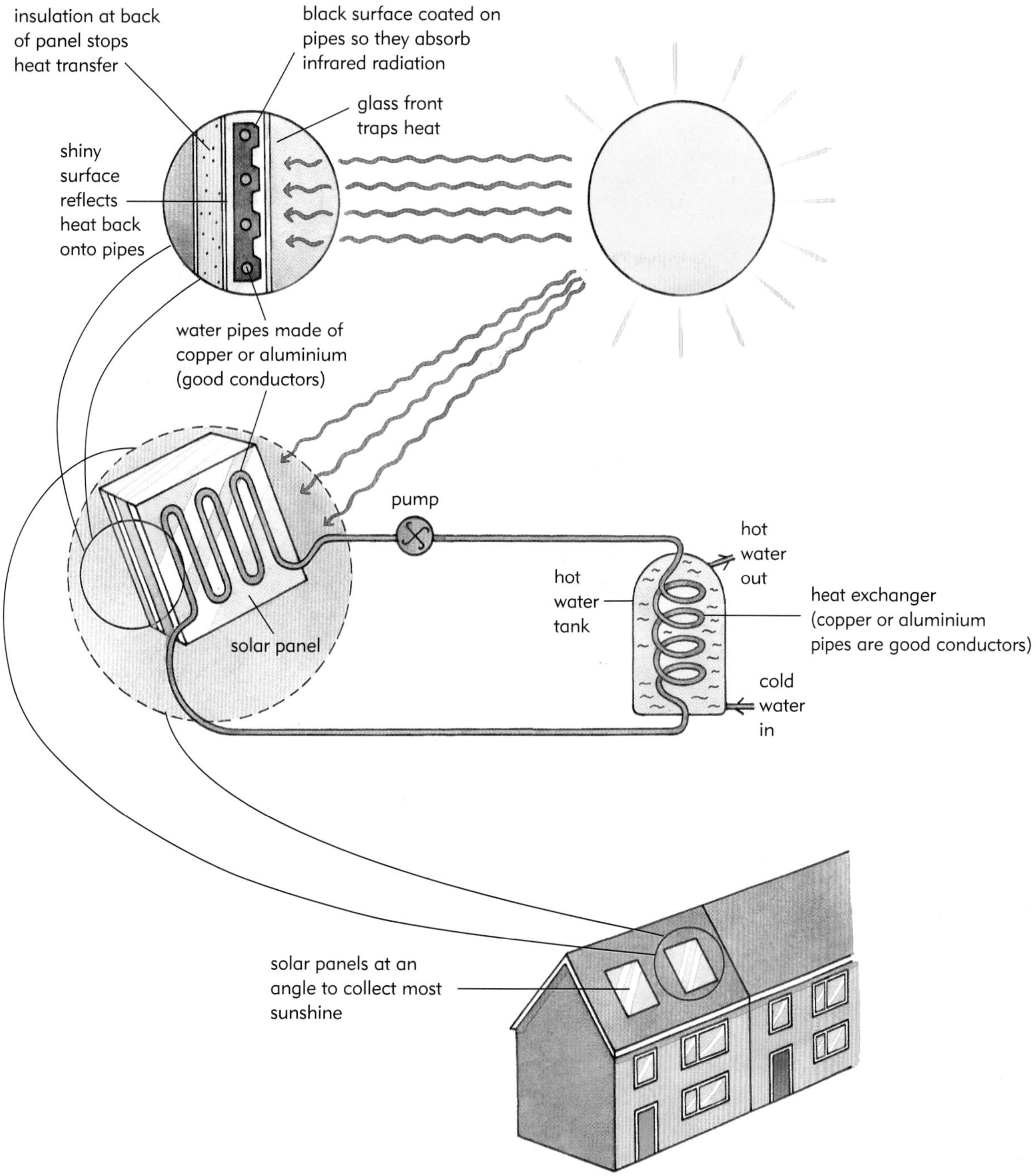

What you need to remember

Using the Sun's energy to heat your home

- There is nothing new for you to remember in this section.
- You are using the ideas you have met earlier.
- You will sometimes be asked questions like these in tests and examinations.

7 Making use of electricity

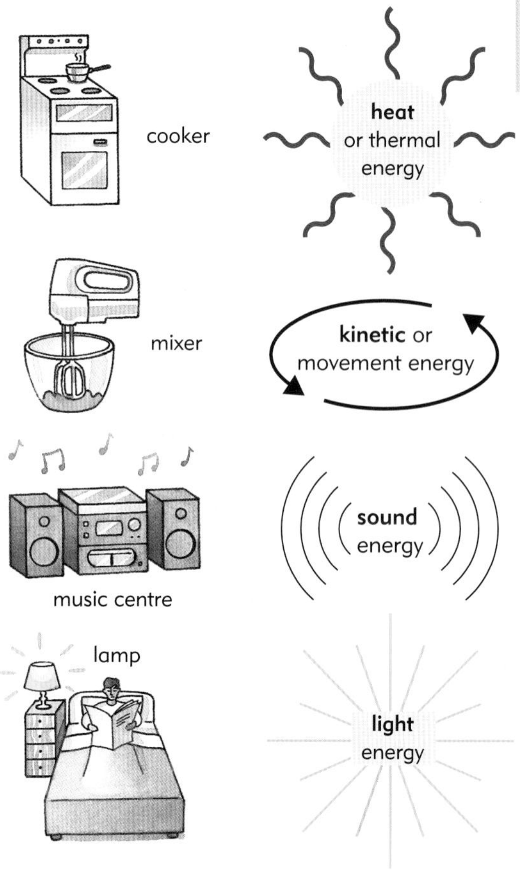

Switched on to electricity

Electricity is a form of **energy**. This means you can make it work for you.

1 Think about the electrical items shown in the diagrams. Copy the table below and fill it in.

Name of electrical item	What we use it for
	to play CDs
	to cook meals
	to read by
	to whip cream

Why is electricity so useful?

We use electricity a lot because it is a very useful sort of energy. Electricity can be easily **transferred** as other kinds of energy. For example, a torch transfers electrical energy as light.

2 Make a new table like the one on the right. Complete it using the names of other sorts of energy on this page.

Name of electrical item	What it transfers electricity as
cooker	heat
mixer	
music centre	
lamp	

Using electricity in industry

Factories and offices also need a supply of energy.

3 Look at the picture of the factory. Copy the sentences and fill in the missing words.

The conveyor belt in the factory uses electricity to make the belt __________.

The fan heater transfers the electricity as two other sorts of energy. It __________ up the air and then makes it __________.

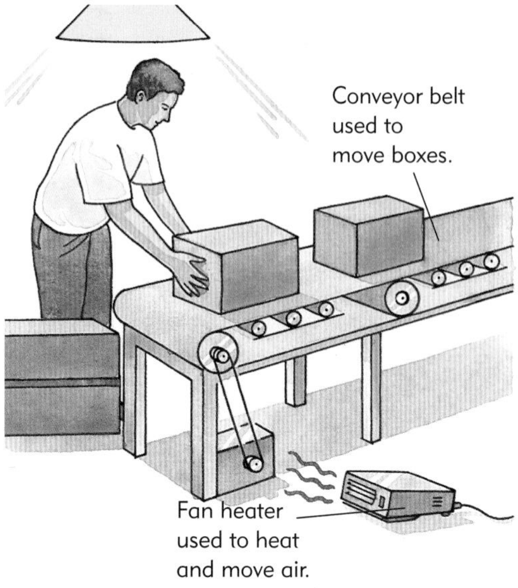

More energy transfers

We design things to get useful energy from electricity. There is usually one main energy transfer we want. For example, a strip light is designed to transfer electrical energy as light.

Here is a way of showing this energy transfer :

electrical energy —strip light→ light

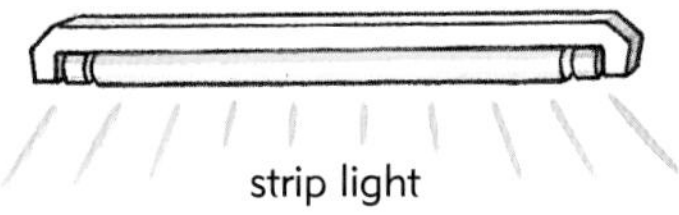

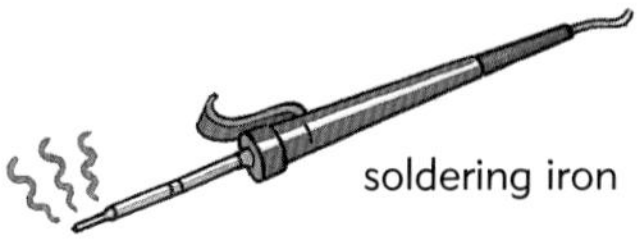

4 Copy these energy transfer diagrams. Then complete them in the same way.

(a) electrical energy —______→ movement

(b) electrical energy —______→ sound

(c) electrical energy —______→ heat

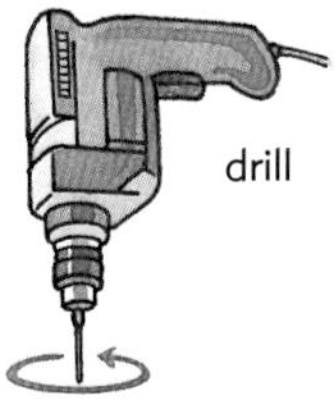

Do you always get what you want?

Very often you do not transfer all the electrical energy into the sort you want. There are other sorts of energy transfers which are not useful.

For example:

- a light bulb produces more heat than light!
- a drill produces sound as well as movement from the motor.
- an electric motor gets hot as well as moving.

5 The electrical energy supplied to the computer is transferred as four different types of energy.

(a) Make a copy of the diagram and label it to show these four different types of energy.

(b) Which three types of energy transfer is the computer designed to make?

(c) Which energy transfer also happens but isn't really wanted?

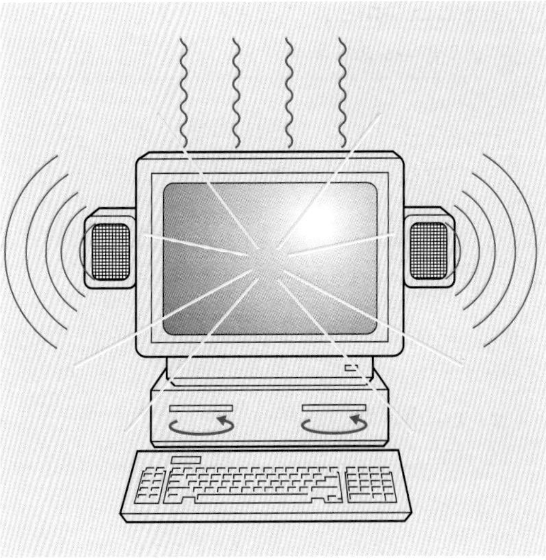

What you need to remember [Copy and complete using the **key words**]

Making use of electricity

We use a lot of electrical ____________ in our homes and in industry.
Electricity can easily be ____________ as other sorts of energy such as ____________, ____________, ____________ and ____________ (or movement) energy.

[You should know what energy transfers electrical appliances are designed to produce.]

8 How much electricity do you use?

Electrical appliances transfer energy. How much energy they transfer depends on how **long** you switch them on for. It also depends on how **fast** they transfer energy.

Look at these light bulbs.

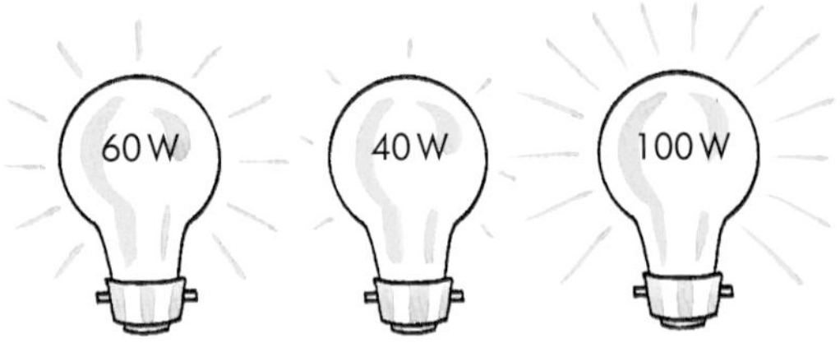

1 Which bulb is the brightest?

2 Which bulb transfers energy the fastest?

How fast something transfers energy is called its **power**.
Power is measured in **watts** (W).
1000 watts is called a **kilowatt** (kW).

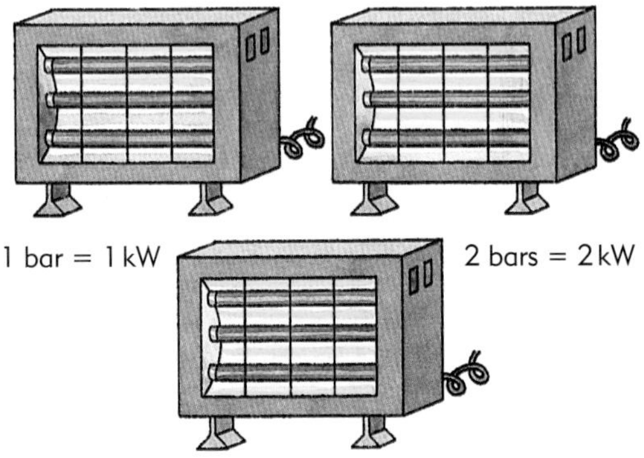

3 Look at the pictures of an electric fire. Copy and complete the table.

Setting of fire	Power	
	watts	kilowatts
1 bar on	1000	
2 bars on		2
3 bars on		

How much do electrical Units cost?

Jed lives in a flat. There is a coin meter for his electricity. He put 30p into the meter one evening. He fell asleep for three hours after leaving the fire on one bar. He had just woken up when the fire went out.

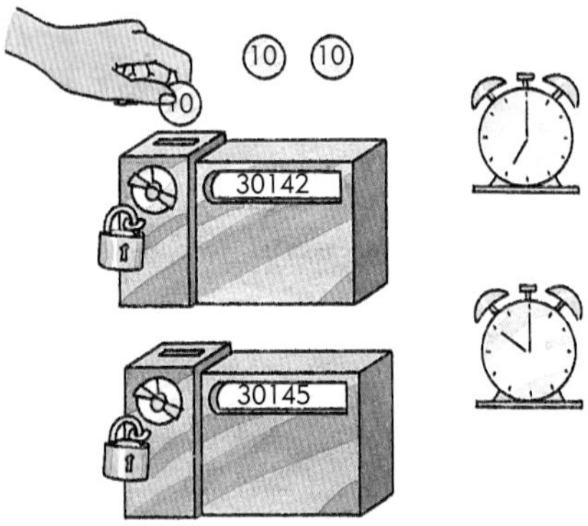

The meter readings show Units used. The difference between the two readings shows how many Units have been used.

Look carefully at the first two meters.

4 How many Units on the meter did one bar of the fire use in three hours?

5 How much did each Unit cost?

It was colder the next night, so Jed put three bars of his fire on. He put 30p into the meter again. A friend arrived to talk to him. He was talking for nearly an hour. When the friend left the fire had just gone out.

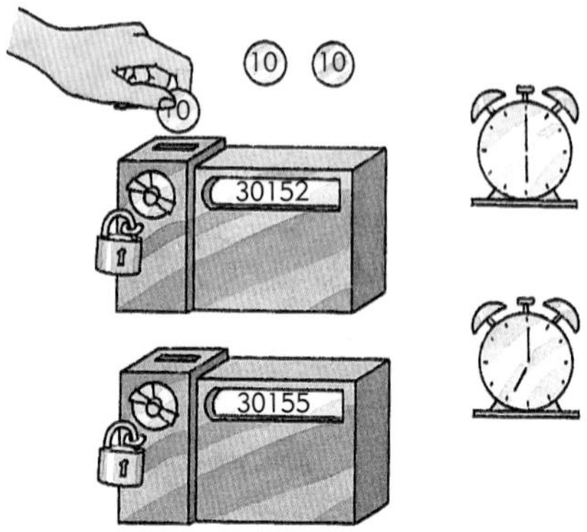

6 How many electrical Units did three bars use in one hour?

How to work out electrical Units

The amount of electrical energy transferred is worked out by multiplying the **power** (in kilowatts) by the **time** (in hours). This gives a **Unit** called the kilowatt–hour (kW h).

energy transferred = power × time

kilowatt–hours = kilowatts × hours
(kW h) (kW) (h)

7 How many Units would two bars of an electric fire use in one hour?

8 Copy the table below and complete it.

The first row has been done for you.

Electrical item	Power in W	Power in kW	Time used	Number of units used in kW × h = kW h
1-bar electric fire	1000	1	2 hours	1 × 2 = 2
2-bar electric fire	2000		2 hours	
light bulb	100		1 hour	
electric drill	500		2 hours	
hair drier	1500		30 minutes	

You may need to change watts into kilowatts, and minutes into hours, before you work out the answer.

100 W = 0.1 kW

500 W = 0.5 kW

1500 W = 1.5 kW

30 minutes = 0.5 hours

What you need to remember [Copy and complete using the **key words**]

How much electricity do you use?

Power is measured in ________________ (W).
The name for 1000 watts is a ________________ (kW).

How much electrical energy is transferred depends on:
- how ________________ an appliance is switched on for
- how ________________ the appliance transfers energy (its ________________).

The energy used in an electrical appliance is worked out by multiplying the ________________ (in kW) by the ________________ (in hours):

energy transferred = power × time
(________________) (kilowatts) (hours)

A kilowatt–hour of electrical energy is called a ________________.

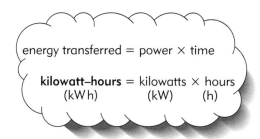

Paying for electricity

REMEMBER

An electrical Unit is a **kilowatt–hour** (kW h).

Counting the cost

To work out how much electricity costs, you need to know:

- how many Units (kW h) have been used
- how much each Unit costs.

total cost for electricity used = **number of Units** used × **cost per Unit**

1 Copy the table below and complete it. Each Unit costs 10p. The first row has been done for you.

Electrical item	Power in W	Power in kW	Time used in hours	Number of Units kW × hours	Total cost Units × 10p
1-bar fire	1000	1	2	1 × 2 = 2	2 × 10p = 20p
2-bar fire			2		
light bulb			2		
electric drill			2		
hair dryer			2		

2-bar fire 2000 W = 2 kW

drill 500 W = 0.5 kW

light bulb 100 W = 0.1 kW

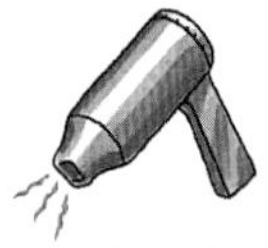

hair dryer 1500 W = 1.5 kW

2 Which item costs the most to use?

Working out electricity bills

It is always worth checking electricity bills, but you need information to do this.

Sometimes you may not be at home when the electricity meter reader calls, so you may get an 'estimated bill'.

MRS. A. CURRENT
42 WALKER ROAD
MAVISTON

MAVISTON
ELECTRICITY
COMPANY

METER READING This Time	METER READING Last Time	UNITS USED	PENCE PER UNIT	AMOUNT £	STANDING CHARGE £	TOTALS £
30340E	29210C	1130	10.0	113.00	14.30	127.30

TOTAL EXCLUSIVE OF VAT 127.30
VAT 10.18

THIS BILL IS ESTIMATED. PLEASE COMPLETE THE ENCLOSED PINK CARD FOR AN AMENDMENT.

YOUR CUSTOMER NUMBER	YOU CAN PHONE US ON	PERIOD ENDING	**AMOUNT DUE NOW**
03 3967 4721 60	00136 247	12 APR	£137.48

E against a meter reading means an estimate
C against a meter reading means it is your own reading

3 Look at the example bill.

(a) What is the 'This Time' reading on the bill?

(b) What does the 'E' after this reading mean?

4 Which reading did Mrs. Current take herself ?

Here is the reading on Mrs. Current's meter when she was sent the bill.

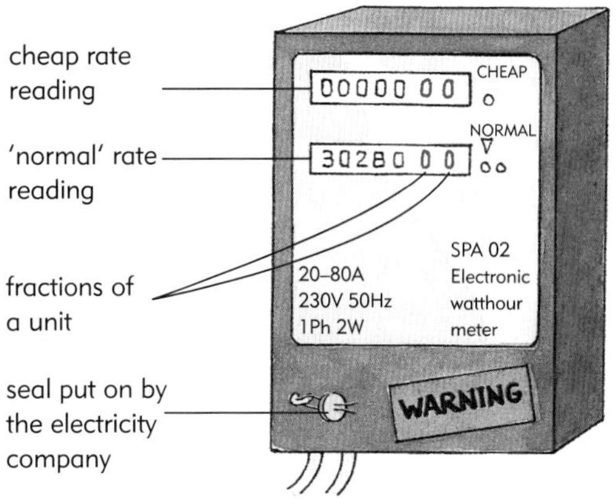

5 Was the estimated reading right?

6 Did Mrs. Current use more or less electricity than it says on the bill?

7 Copy the parts of the bill below. Then fill in all the missing numbers to make it a correct bill.

8 How much less is the new bill?

METER READING This Time	METER READING Last Time	UNITS USED	PENCE PER UNIT	AMOUNT £	STANDING CHARGE £	TOTALS £
	29210C		10.0		14.30	
		TOTAL EXCLUSIVE OF VAT				
		VAT				9.71
						AMOUNT DUE NOW

Half-price electricity

After midnight, most businesses have closed and most people have gone to bed. This means that much less electricity is needed.

However, some power stations cannot be shut down, and they generate more electricity than is needed. The electricity companies sell electricity at a much cheaper price to persuade people to use more. Storage heaters are an example of appliances that use this cheap electricity.

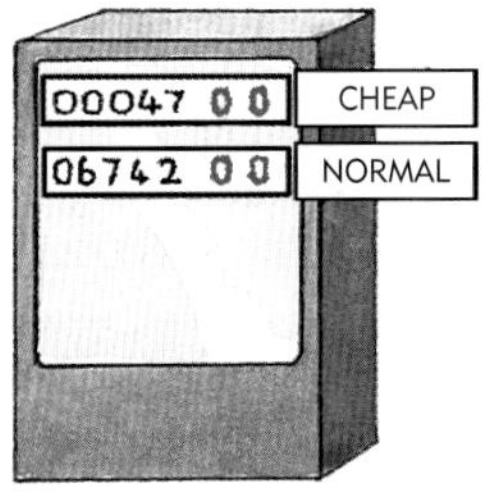

meter reading last time

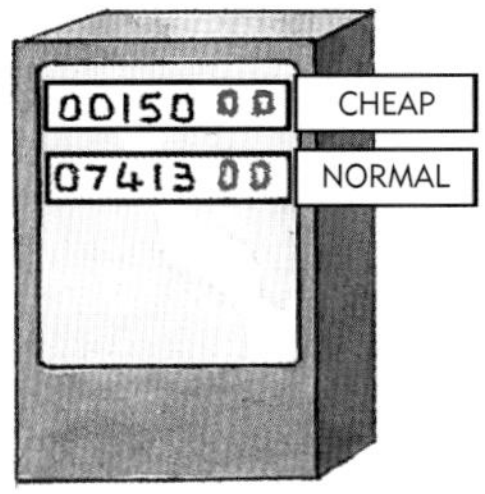

meter reading this time

9 Look at the meter readings. Cheap rate electricity from this company costs 5p per unit. How much would it cost for this electricity on the 'cheap rate' scale?

10 How much would it cost for the same amount of electricity on the 'normal' rate scale (10p per Unit)?

What you need to remember [Copy and complete using the **key words**]

Paying for electricity

An electrical Unit is a ________________–________________ (kWh).

You can work out the cost of electrical energy used by using this equation:

total cost for electricity used = ________________ **of** ________________ used × ________________ **per** ________________

10

Energy to make electricity

Electricity gives us a useful form of energy, which we can transfer as many other types of energy.

Electricity has to be generated, and we need an energy **source** to do this. Because we must generate electricity using some other source of energy, we say that electricity is a **secondary** energy source.

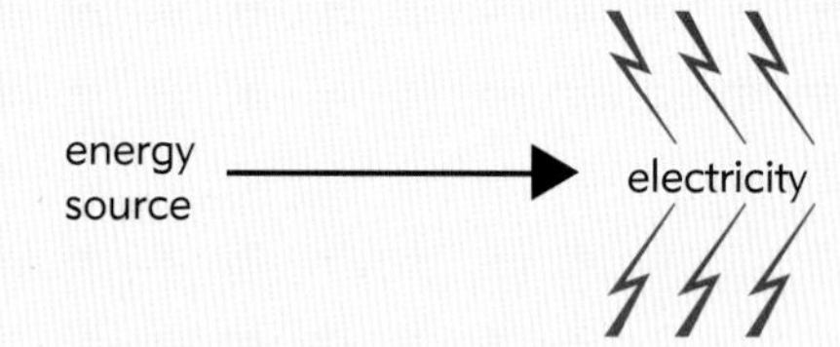

We always need some other energy source to make electricity.

Fuels as energy sources

The diagram shows the four main fuels (primary energy sources) we use to generate electricity.

1 Copy and complete the following sentences.

To generate electricity you need some other __________ of energy.

Fuels like __________, __________, __________ and __________ fuel can be used to generate electricity.

Coal, oil and gas are called __________ fuels.

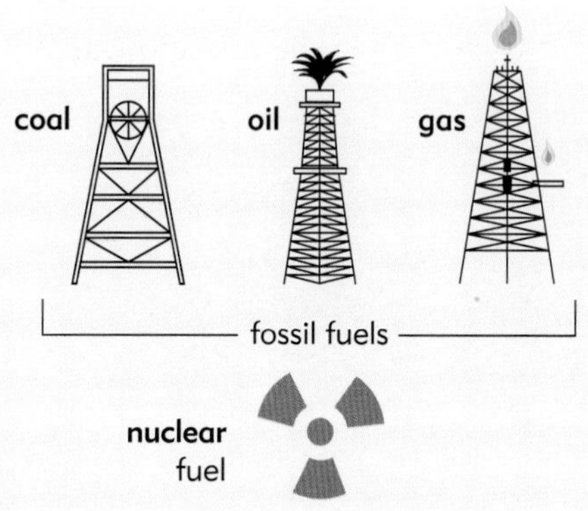

Fuels we use to generate electricity.

How long can fuels last?

Fuels are non-renewable energy sources. This means that once you've used them they cannot be **replaced**.

2 Look at the bar chart of how long primary energy sources will last.

(a) How long will coal, natural gas, oil and nuclear fuel last (at present rates of use)?

(b) Which will last the longest?

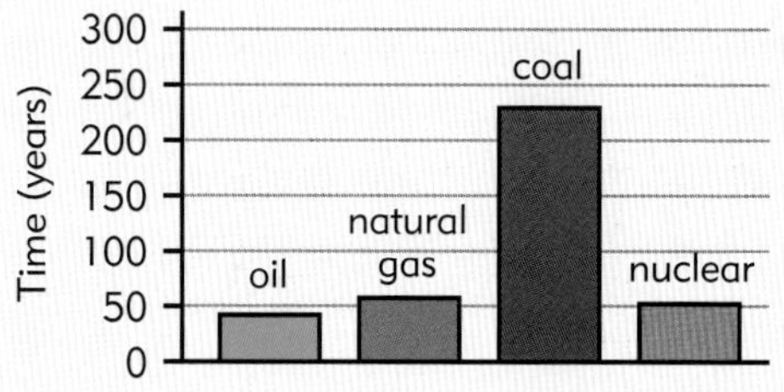

How long fuels will last if we use them at the present rate. (Nuclear fuel will last a lot longer if we use it in fast breeder reactors.)

The pie chart shows the energy sources that are used worldwide to generate electricity.

3 Copy the table headings below. Then complete the table, starting with the highest % and ending with the lowest. The first line has been filled in for you.

Energy source	% of electricity generated
oil	37

4 Which of the energy sources on the pie chart is not a fuel?

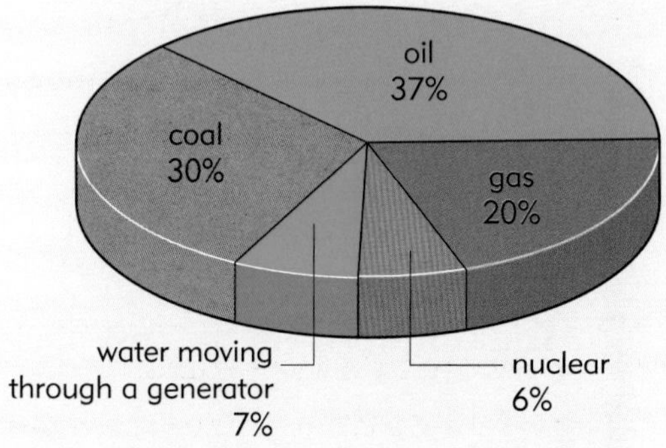

These figures are for the whole world.

Energy sources used to generate electricity.

Renewable energy sources

Fuels like wood are **renewable**. This means that they can be replaced.

Anything that can be grown and used as a fuel is called biomass. Other renewable energy sources are sunlight, the wind, the waves, running water (hydro-electricity) and the tides.

5 Which three ways of generating electricity use moving water?

6 Which renewable energy source

(a) is used by solar cells?

(b) consists of moving air?

The tides moving in and out of this tidal barrage can turn generators.

Waves can turn generators.

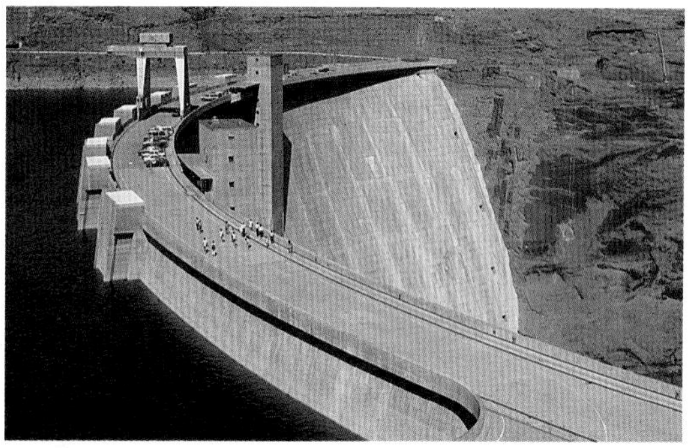

Hydro-electric generators use water falling from behind a dam.

Solar cells change sunlight into electricity.

The wind turns generators.

Energy sources in the future

Fossil fuels and nuclear fuels will eventually run out.

7 What can we do to make fuels last longer before they run out?

8 What energy sources will we eventually have to depend on?

What you need to remember [Copy and complete using the **key words**]

Energy to make electricity

To generate electricity we always need some other energy ________________.
Electricity is a ________________ source of energy.
It is generated from fuels like ________________, ________________, ________________ and ________________ fuel.
These fuels cannot be ________________ once they have been burned. We say they are non-renewable.
Sources of energy like wood, sunlight, wind, waves, running water and the tides are called ________________ energy sources.

Using fuels to generate electricity

Most of the electricity used in Britain is generated using fuels.

Fossil fuels (coal, oil and gas) are burned to transfer energy as heat. Nuclear fuels (**uranium** and **plutonium**) produce heat as the atoms split up in a nuclear reaction.

REMEMBER

Most fuels are non-renewable energy sources. They cannot be replaced.

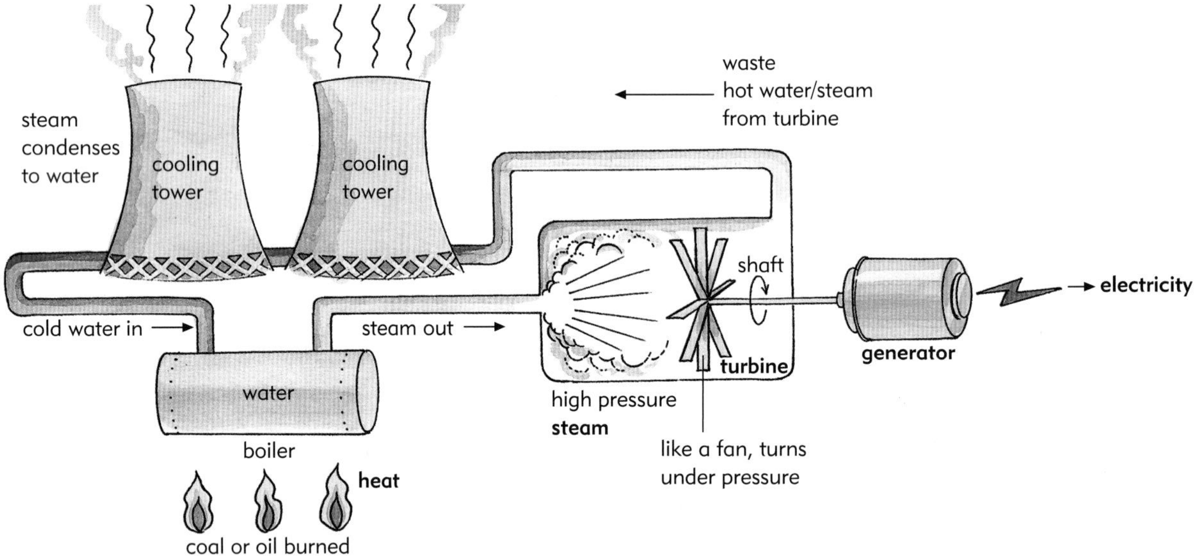

The diagram above shows how the heat released by a fuel is used to generate electricity.

In a nuclear power station, heat from the reactors is used to make steam. The fuel is used up in a nuclear reaction. It does not burn.

1 Write down the following sentences in the right order to explain how the power station works. Start with:

Heat from the fuel is used to boil water.

- The shaft turns the generator.
- Steam from the boiling water builds up a pressure.
- The generator produces electricity.
- A shaft connects the turbine to the generator.
- The pressure turns the blades of the turbine.

2 What happens to the steam after it has been through the turbine?

3 (a) Which type of fuel does not need to be burned to release energy?

(b) What must happen to this fuel for it to release energy?

4 Look at the diagram. What is different about a gas-fired power station?

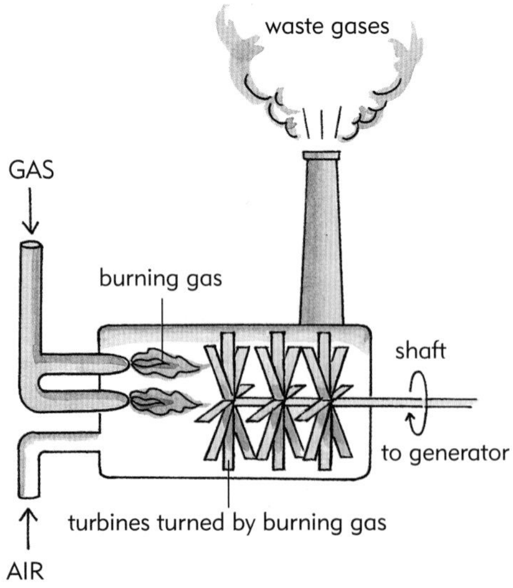

In a gas-fired power station there is no need to use steam. The hot burning gases drive the turbine directly.

What are the problems with using fuels?

Using fuels produces waste.

This can pollute the atmosphere and soil, or may have to be stored until it is safe.

There is only a certain amount of each fuel in the Earth, so they are non-renewable. Once they are used up, they are gone **forever**.

The diagram shows the types of waste from a coal-fired power station.

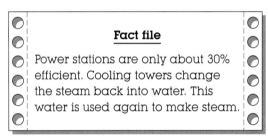

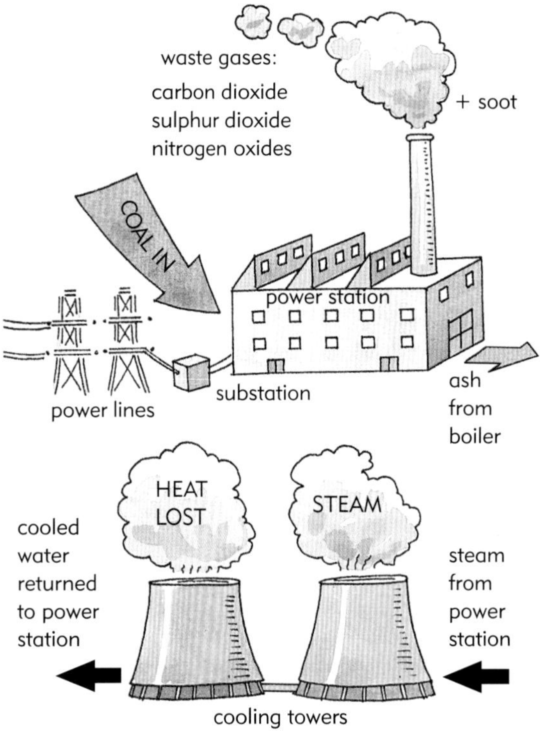

5 (a) Write down one solid waste that has to be put somewhere.

(b) Write down four types of waste that go into the atmosphere.

Look at the information in the box.

6 What are the cooling towers used for?

7 For every 100 tonnes of coal burned in a power station, how many tonnes are usefully transferred as electricity?

Fact file

Power stations are only about 30% efficient. Cooling towers change the steam back into water. This water is used again to make steam.

Why do we use fuels to generate electricity?

The fuels are plentiful (at the moment), but in the 21st century they may start to run out.

Power stations which use fuels can give us electricity at any time and in all sorts of weather.

8 Write down three advantages and three disadvantages of using fuels to generate electricity.

Fact file

Power stations that use fuels can be very big and can spoil the countryside. One power station can generate electricity for over 1 million people. Power stations that use fuels produce pollution.

What you need to remember [Copy and complete using the **key words**]

Using fuels to generate electricity

Coal, oil and gas are called ________________ ________________.
Examples of nuclear fuels are ________________ and ________________.
All these fuels are non-renewable – once they are used up, they are gone ____________.
All non-renewable fuels transfer energy as ________________.
For coal and oil power stations, this energy is used to boil water. This produces ________________, which is used to turn a ________________. This drives a shaft connected to a ________________, which produces ________________.

Comparing fuels for electricity

Using fuels always produces waste. These wastes can pollute the air, the water and the soil. We can reduce some of this pollution, but this makes electricity more expensive.

The diagram and bar charts show some facts about the wastes from different fuels.

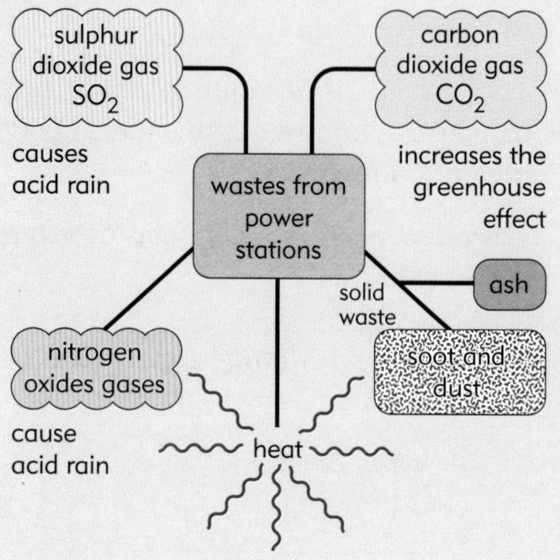

1 Look at the diagram. Copy and complete the table. The first line has been filled in for you.

Name of waste gas	What problem it can cause
sulphur dioxide	causes acid rain

2 Look at the bar charts.

(a) Which type of fuel produces no waste gases and very little solid waste?

(b) Why does this fuel cause a very serious pollution problem?

3 (a) Which fuel produces the most solid waste?

(b) Which fuel – coal, oil or gas – produces the least pollution?

4 (a) Which waste gas increases the greenhouse effect?

(b) Which fuel causes the biggest increase in the greenhouse effect?

5 (a) Which two gases cause acid rain?

(b) Which fuel produces most of the gases that cause acid rain?

6 Look at the amount of sulphur dioxide produced by gas. How many times more sulphur dioxide do coal and oil produce?

Each bar chart shows the waste produced for every thousand million Units of electricity produced.

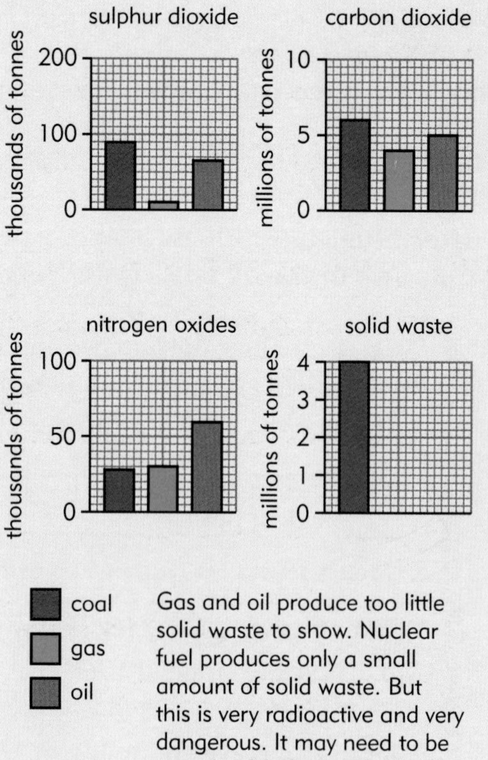

Gas and oil produce too little solid waste to show. Nuclear fuel produces only a small amount of solid waste. But this is very radioactive and very dangerous. It may need to be stored safely for hundreds of years. This is expensive.

Comparing start-up times

The bar chart shows how long it takes to start up different types of power station.

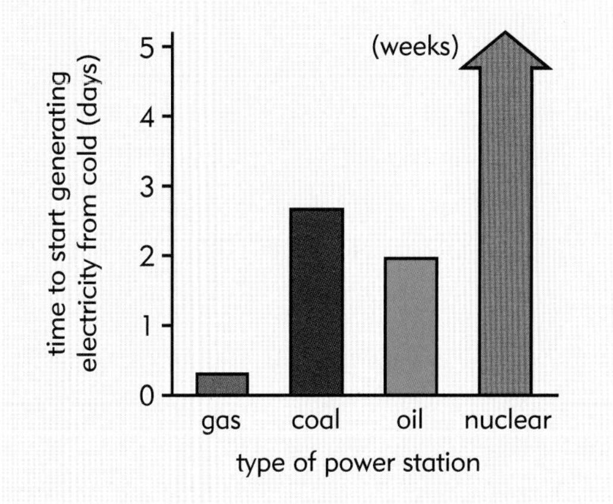

7 Which type of power station takes longest to start up?

This type of power station is usually kept running for very long periods.

More electricity is needed at some times of the day than at other times.

8 Which type of power station can be started quickly, to provide the extra electricity?

How can we cut down air pollution?

Soot and dust are made of tiny particles. These can be removed from chimneys by attracting them using electric charges or by using filters. This makes the electricity a tiny bit more expensive.

Sulphur dioxide can be removed from chimneys by absorbing it in chemicals. This makes the electricity 10% to 20% more expensive. It is far too expensive to remove the huge amounts of carbon dioxide from the waste gases.

Pollutant	How it is removed	Effect on cost of electricity
soot		
sulphur dioxide		

Table for question 9.

9 Copy the table shown above. Then complete it.

Using the waste heat from power stations

The diagrams show how we can use the waste heat from power stations.

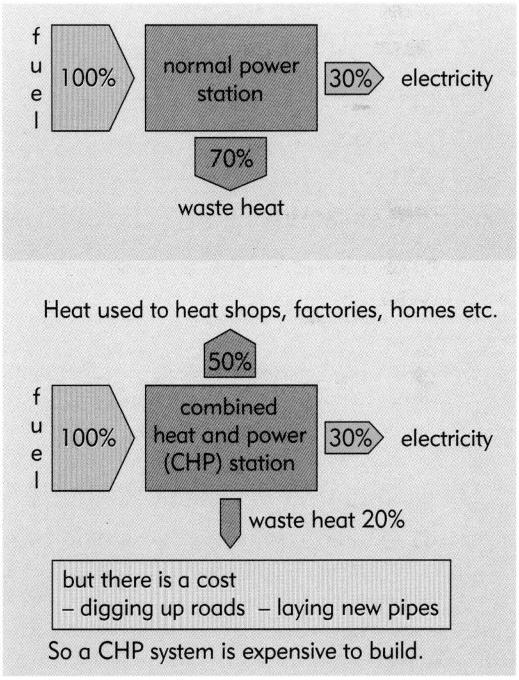

10 Copy and complete the following sentences.

A CHP station reduces waste heat energy from __________% to __________%. But it is __________ to build.

What you need to remember

Comparing fuels for electricity

You should know:

- which types of waste are produced by which fuel
- whether the pollution by each type of waste can be reduced and how this can be done
- how controlling pollution affects the cost of electricity.

Generating electricity with water

Renewable energy sources will never run out – they are always being **replaced**.

Using renewable energy sources means you don't have to buy fuel, and most renewables do not make harmful waste products. But it is expensive to **capture** the energy and transfer it as electricity.

Rain falls on the land and flows to the sea in streams and rivers. Rain keeps on falling because the Sun keeps on evaporating water from the sea.

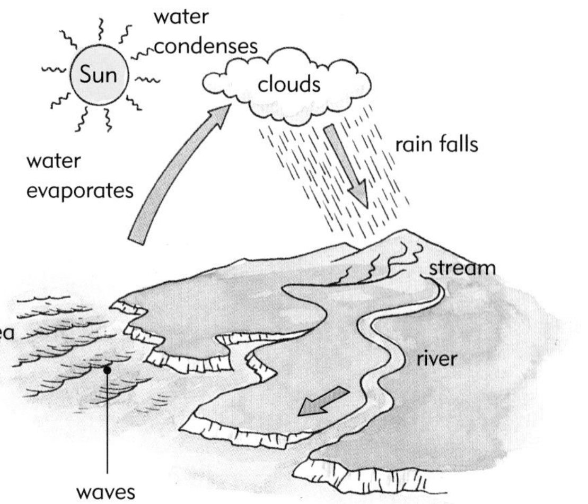

■ Moving water

Water is always on the move.

The diagram shows three types of moving water that we can use to generate electricity.

1 Copy and complete the table. Some boxes have been filled in for you.

Type of moving water	Which way the water moves	Why the movement keeps on happening
waves		the wind keeps on blowing across the sea
rivers	flows along to the sea	
tides		

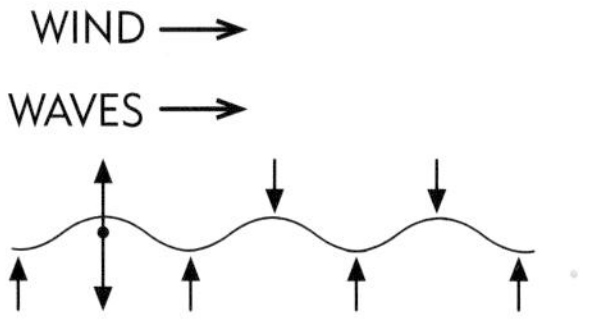

Waves keep forming because the wind keeps blowing across the sea. As waves move along, the water moves up and down.

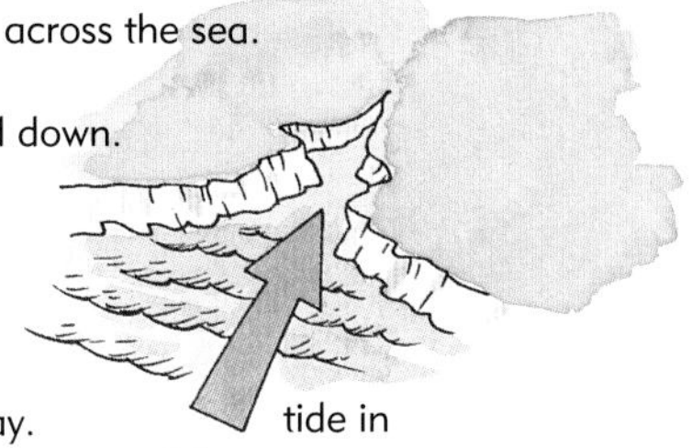

Tides make water flow into estuaries twice a day. Tides keep happening because of the pull of the Moon's gravity as the Earth spins.

■ Hydro-electricity

We build dams across rivers to trap a lot of water. We can use this trapped water to generate electricity whenever we need it.

The diagram shows how we do this.

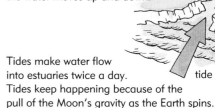

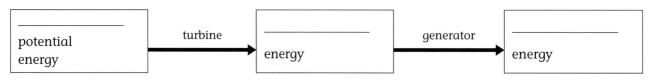

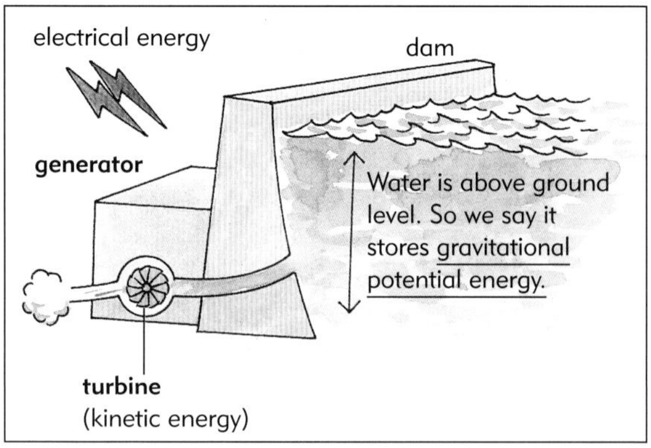

2 Write down the following sentences in the right order. The first one has been done for you.

Water flows out through the bottom of the dam.

- The shaft of the turbine drives a generator.
- The generator transfers kinetic energy as electricity.
- A turbine is turned by the flowing water.

3 Copy and complete the energy flow diagram.

______ potential energy	turbine →	______ energy	generator →	______ energy

Good and bad news about hydro-electricity

Of all the renewable energy sources, at the moment hydro-electricity is the only one that gives us much electricity. But this is still a very small amount compared to the amount we get from fossil fuels.

Land has to be flooded to make reservoirs. **Hydro-electric** generators can be started up in a few seconds.

4 Look at the information on the right. Write down one effect of hydro-electricity on the environment.

5 Hydro-electric generators are very useful if more electricity is suddenly needed. Explain why.

Electricity from tides

Tides make water flow into **estuaries** twice each day. We can trap this water behind a barrage. We can then use it to generate electricity when the tide goes out.

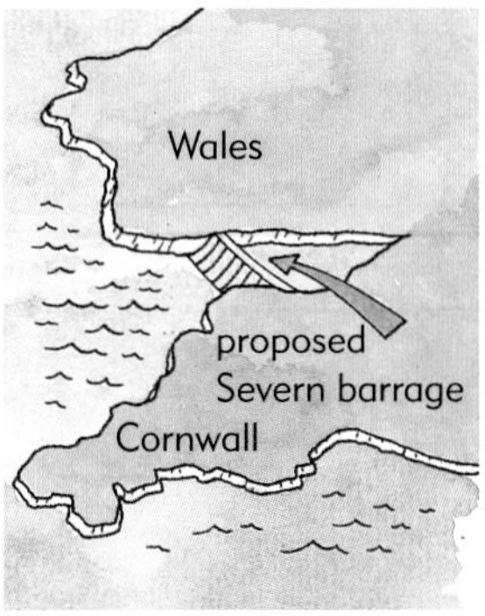

You can only generate electricity at certain times each day.

Large estuaries like the Severn are the only type of habitat for wading birds. Flooding the estuary by using a barrage stops the birds feeding.

6 Where, in Britain, could a large **tidal** power station be built?

7 Write down two disadvantages of generating electricity from tides.

Electricity from waves

The diagram shows a small wave generator. No large generators have yet been made to stand rough seas.

8 What drives the turbine in the wave generator shown in the diagram?

rise and fall of water pushes air through turbine

What you need to remember [Copy and complete using the **key words**]

Generating electricity with water

Renewable energy resources are constantly being ______________.
Energy from these sources is free but it is expensive to ______________.
Water trapped behind dams and barrages can be used to turn a ______________, which then turns a ______________.
You can generate electricity when you need it from a ____________-______________ power station. Reservoirs for these power stations flood ______________.
You can generate electricity only at certain times each day using a ______________ power station. Barrages for these power stations flood ______________, which are the habitats for wading birds.

14 Generating electricity with wind

Wind is a renewable energy resource. It is a regular part of our weather, which is driven by energy from the Sun. So as long as the Sun keeps shining, the wind will keep blowing.

Windmills like this were once used to grind wheat into flour.

The wind has been used to pump water.

Using the wind is an old idea

We have used the energy from the wind for thousands of years. But, during the past 250 years, steam engines, then petrol engines and electricity took over from wind.

1 Write down two ways energy from the wind was used in the past.

We are now using wind energy again. This will help to make our stocks of non-renewable energy sources last longer.

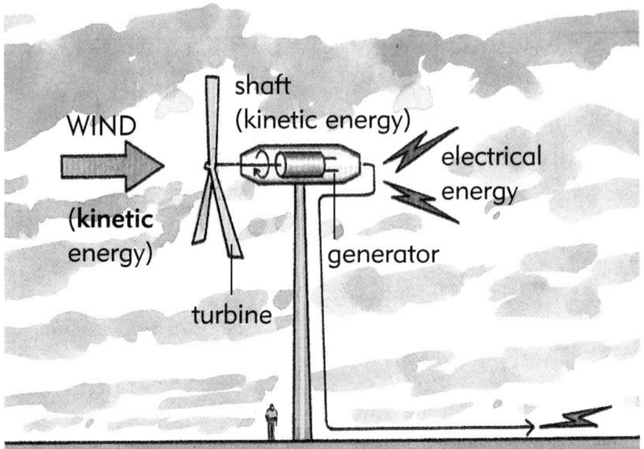

In strong winds the blades of the turbine twist slightly. This slows the turbine down and prevents damage.

A modern wind generator

The diagram shows a modern wind **turbine**. This is used to generate electricity.

2 Copy and complete the energy transfer diagram.

kinetic energy of the wind —turbine→ ________ energy of rotating shaft —generator→ ________ energy

If the wind is too strong it can damage a wind **generator**.

3 How is a wind generator protected against this damage?

Where should we put wind generators?

Large wind generators need a wind of at least 5 metres per second before they generate electricity. So they need to be put in places where there is plenty of **wind**.

Look at this map and the map at the top of the next page.

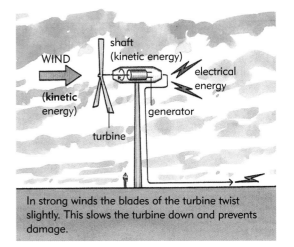

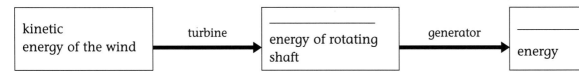

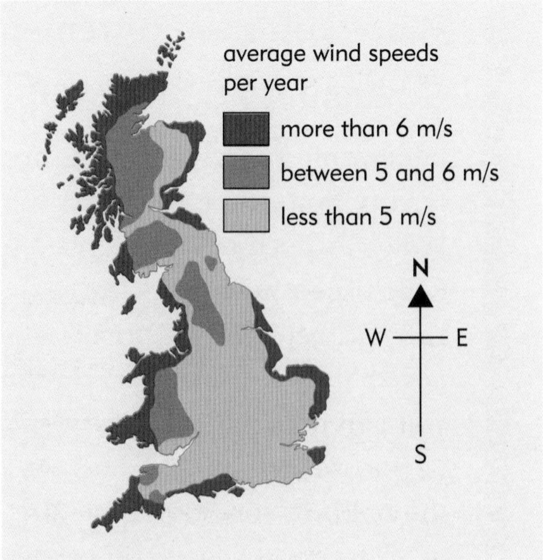

4 Where are the best places for wind turbines in Britain?

Answer in as much detail as you can.

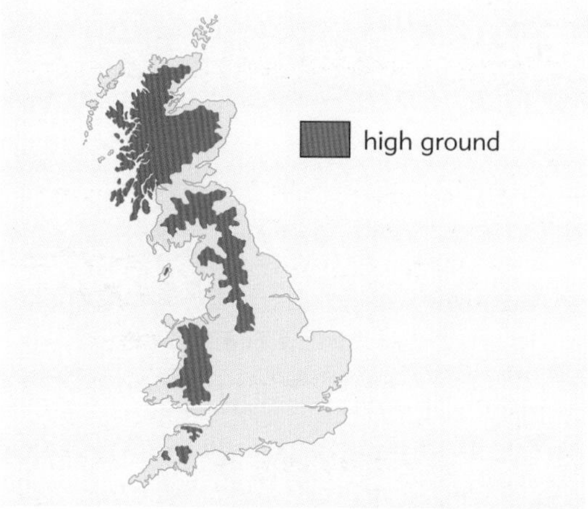

Could wind generators provide all our electricity?

In 1993 there were 21 wind turbine projects in Britain supplying electricity. This is the fastest growing way of using renewables to generate electricity. But this is still only a small amount of electricity.

Many **hundreds** of wind generators would be needed to replace just one power station that uses coal.

Also, the wind doesn't blow all the **time**, even on coasts and hills. When the wind doesn't blow, we need some other way of generating electricity.

Wind farms have lots of wind turbines. Each wind turbine generates about 500 kW. A **coal-fired** power station generates about 1300 MW. (1 MW = 1000 kW.)

5 How many 500 kW wind turbines would be needed to replace a power station that uses coal?

6 Write down two reasons why the wind could not supply all the electricity we need.

Wind generators and the environment

People disagree about whether or not wind **farms** are good for the environment.

Using the wind does not pollute the air.

People like to **visit** unspoilt hills and coasts at weekends and holidays.

You can see wind farms for miles around.

7 Write down one advantage and one disadvantage for the environment of using wind farms to generate electricity.

What you need to remember [Copy and complete using the **key words**]

Generating electricity with wind

We can capture the ________ energy of the wind using a ________.
This then drives a ________, which produces electricity.
Wind generators need to be on hills and coasts where there is plenty of ________.
You need ________ of wind generators to produce as much electricity as a ________-________ power station.
Large groups of wind generators are called wind ________.
These can spoil countryside that people like to ________.
Also, wind generators do not produce electricity all the ________.

15 Generating electricity from the Sun and the Earth

Solar cells

Solar cells are a very simple way of transferring energy from the Sun as electricity. There is only one energy transfer. Light is transferred directly as electricity.

But one problem is that solar cells are a very **expensive** way of making each Unit of electricity.

Another problem is that solar cells will work only if the Sun is shining!

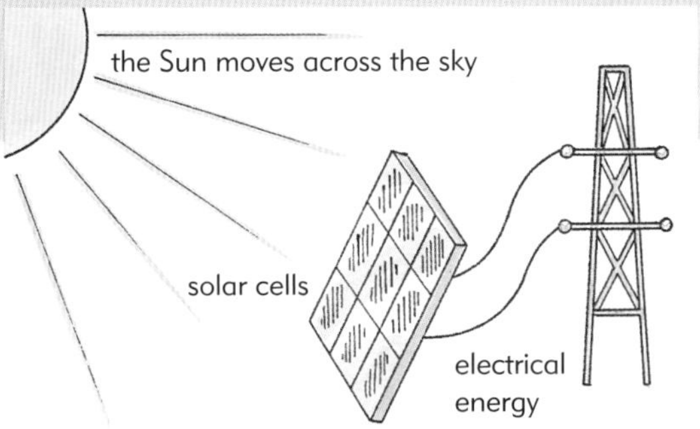

The solar cells must be at the correct angle to collect the most light energy.

1 Complete the energy transfer diagram below for a solar cell.

______ energy	→ solar cell →	______ energy

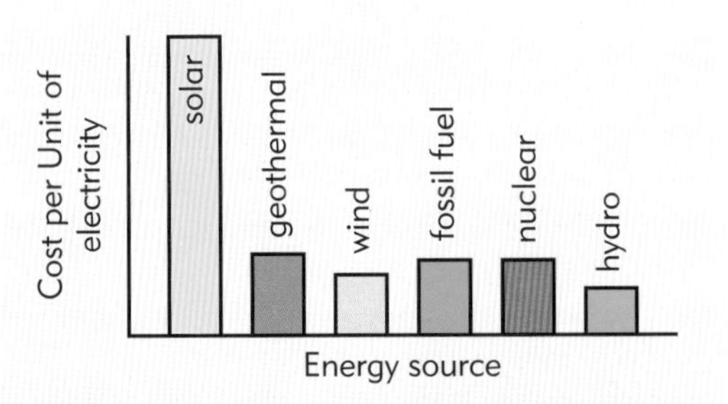

2 Look at the bar chart. To make each Unit of electricity, which source of energy costs

(a) the least?

(b) the most?

3 Write down two disadvantages, apart from the cost, of using solar cells to generate electricity.

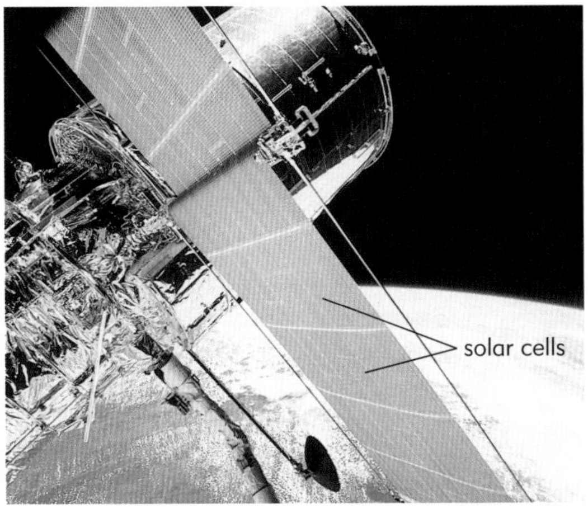

Satellites use solar cells. Solar cells weigh less than batteries and will work for many years.

Why use solar cells?

Although electricity from solar cells is expensive, there are times when they are worth using.

4 Write down two reasons why solar cells are used in satellites.

5 Where would you use a solar-powered pump? Explain why.

6 Why are solar cells suitable for calculators?

Calculators use only a very small amount of electricity. So you can use a very small solar cell instead of batteries.

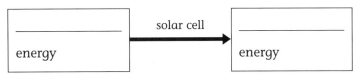

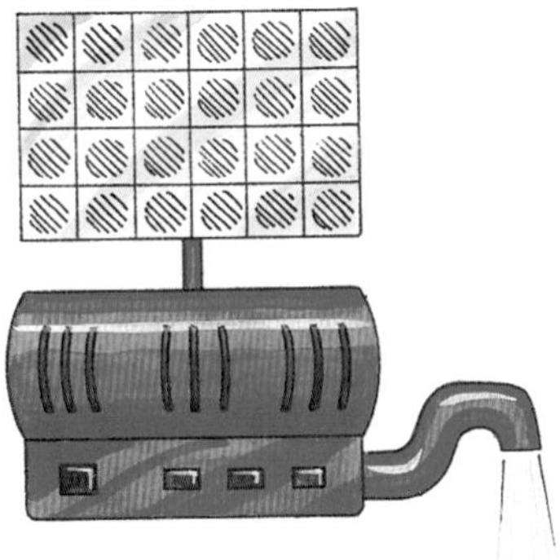

A solar-powered water pump for distant villages. It is often too expensive to put power cables from power stations to **remote** places.

Geothermal energy

'Geo-' means from the Earth and 'thermal' means 'heat'. So geothermal energy is heat from the Earth's rocks.

The rocks in the Earth contain **radioactive** elements like **uranium**. When these elements react, the rocks transfer energy as **heat**. This happens very slowly over billions of years.

There are some places on the Earth where water gets heated up by these reactions, producing **steam** and hot mud.

Natural steam spurting from the Earth is called a geyser.

bubbling mud pools

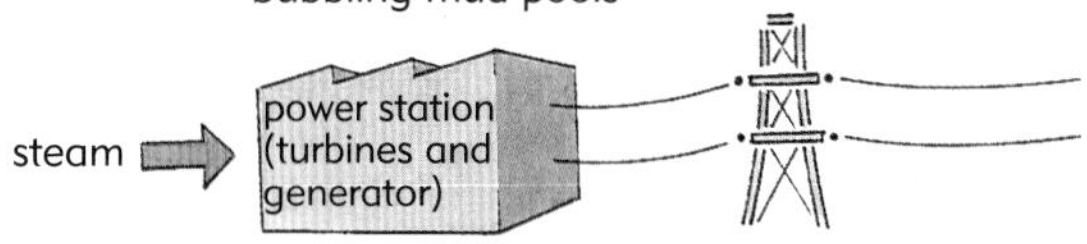
steam
power station (turbines and generator)

Natural steam is used to generate electricity in the USA, Italy, New Zealand and Iceland.

7 What do we call steam that spurts out of the ground?

8 Write down the names of four countries where steam from the ground is used to generate electricity.

Making a heat mine

You can still use geothermal energy even in places where there aren't any geysers. The diagram shows how you can do this.

A heat mine.

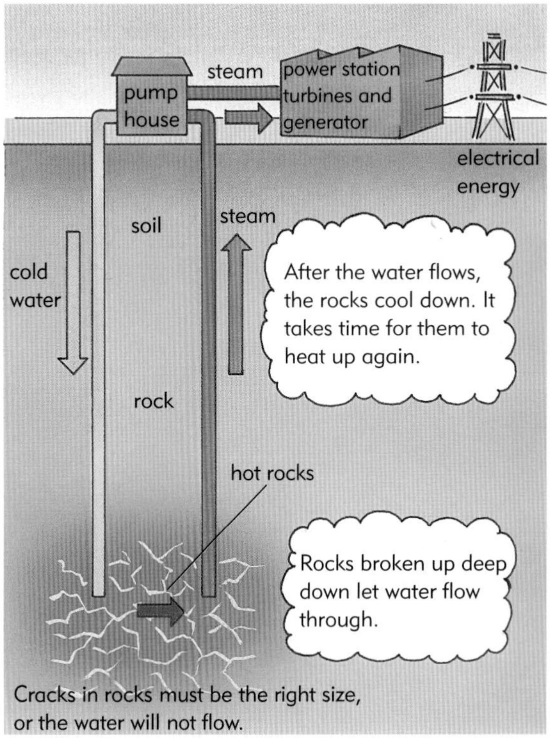
pump house
steam
power station turbines and generator
electrical energy
soil
steam
cold water
After the water flows, the rocks cool down. It takes time for them to heat up again.
rock
hot rocks
Rocks broken up deep down let water flow through.
Cracks in rocks must be the right size, or the water will not flow.

9 Copy and complete the following sentences.

In a 'heat mine', __________ water is pumped deep down into the ground.

It passes through tiny cracks in __________ rocks and is turned into steam.

This steam is used to generate __________ energy.

10 Write down two problems in using geothermal energy to generate electricity.

What you need to remember [Copy and complete using the **key words**]

Generating electricity from the Sun and the Earth

Energy from the Sun can be transferred as electricity using __________ __________.
Each Unit of electricity from a solar cell is very __________.
But solar cells will work for many years and are useful in __________ places on Earth and on __________.
They are also useful in things that need very little electricity, such as __________.
Geothermal energy is produced by the reactions of __________ elements (like __________) in the Earth's rocks.
The __________ released can be used to change water into __________, which can then be used to generate electricity.

A review of renewable energy sources

Many people think that we should use renewable energy sources instead of non-renewable fuels.

1 Why are renewable energy sources thought to be 'better' for the environment than non-renewable fuels?

But there are problems with using renewable energy sources, as well as advantages. The boxes show some of these.

2 Match each of the renewable energy sources below with the statements in the boxes.

The numbers in the brackets tell you how many boxes you must match with each energy source. You will need to use some of the boxes more than once.

(a) Tidal barrages (4)

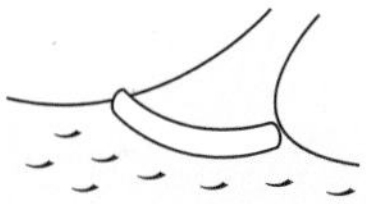

(b) Hydro-electric power stations (6)

(c) Wave generators (3)

(d) Geothermal (2)

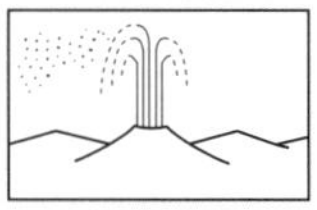

(e) Solar cells (2)

(f) Wind turbines (2)

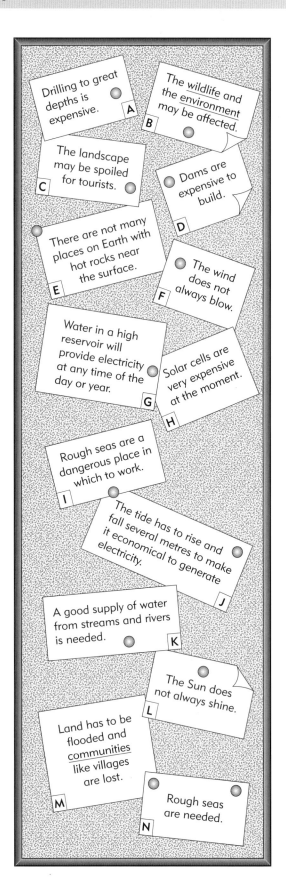

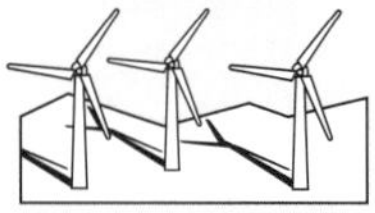

3 Which renewable energy source would you choose to generate electricity in these situations:

(a) in a desert region, for pumping water?

(b) in a mountainous region with many streams?

(c) in a country with many volcanoes and geysers?

A Drilling to great depths is expensive.

B The wildlife and the environment may be affected.

C The landscape may be spoiled for tourists.

D Dams are expensive to build.

E There are not many places on Earth with hot rocks near the surface.

F The wind does not always blow.

G Water in a high reservoir will provide electricity at any time of the day or year.

H Solar cells are very expensive at the moment.

I Rough seas are a dangerous place in which to work.

J The tide has to rise and fall several metres to make it economical to generate electricity.

K A good supply of water from streams and rivers is needed.

L The Sun does not always shine.

M Land has to be flooded and communities like villages are lost.

N Rough seas are needed.

Choosing the best renewables for the job

Study the map of Arbril and read the 'Fact File' carefully. Then answer the questions.

Fact file on Arbril Island

- Arbril is in the Antarctic ocean between the Falklands and the South Pole.
- There is sunlight for six months of the year and then darkness.
- The seas around the island are very rough, which sometimes makes it impossible to travel to Arbril.
- The tides only rise and fall by less than a metre.
- Port Herbert is the main town, which relies on fishing as its main industry. This is on a sheltered part of the island.
- Soil is poor quality but rainfall is high during the year.
- There are hot springs on the south-west of the island, but they are difficult to reach over very high mountains.

Port Herbert is in need of a reliable electricity supply. The old power station is coming to the end of its useful life. It uses coal, which is very expensive to import.

4 Suggest four renewable energy sources which could be used.

5 For each energy source, suggest at least one problem to be solved.

6 (a) Copy the map. Then show on your map where you would build the new power station for each of your suggestions.

(b) Give a reason for your choice of site in each case.

What you need to remember

A review of renewable energy sources

There is nothing new to remember on these pages.
You have been applying ideas you have met before.
You may be asked to do this in tests and examinations.

Lifting things with electricity

Up and down

Getting the cars up a roller coaster needs energy. The force of **gravity** pulling downwards makes this hard, so an electric **motor** pulls the cars to the top against the force of gravity.

When the cars get to the top of the slope they are ready to run down the other side. The cars are pulled down by gravity because of their **height**. We say they have **gravitational potential** energy.

Electrical energy from motor pulls cars up.

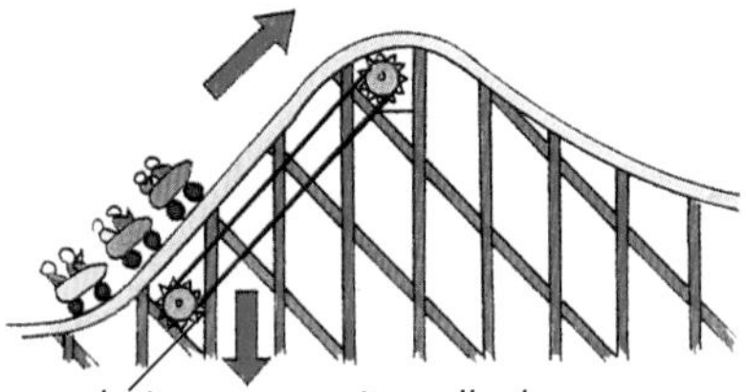

1 Copy and complete the following sentences.

__________ pulls down on things. We can use __________ energy to lift things up against gravity.

When you raise things to a __________ above the ground they store __________ potential energy.

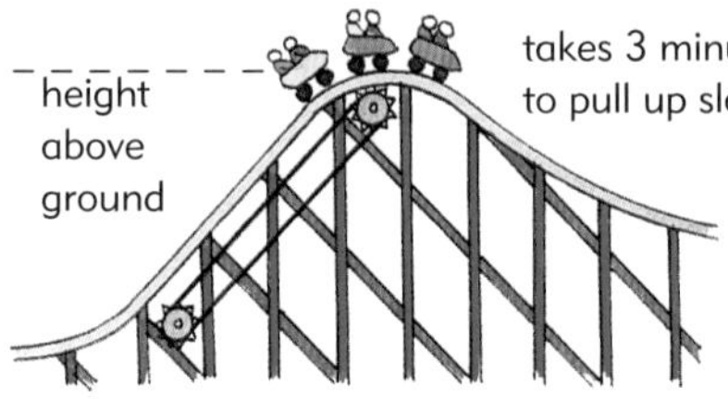

Cars store gravitational potential energy at top.

When the cars are running down the slope they transfer potential energy as movement. This is called kinetic energy.

2 How much of their gravitational potential energy have the cars transferred when they are halfway down the slope?

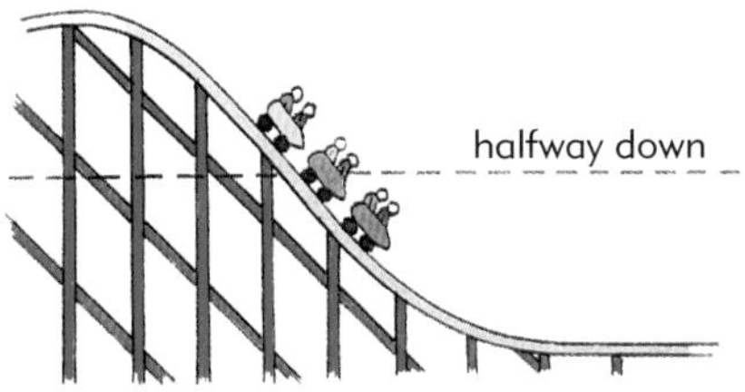

Cars have transferred half their potential energy to kinetic energy.

Higher still

The cars are then pulled up a slope that is twice as high.

3 How much more gravitational potential energy will the cars have at the top of this slope than at the top of the first slope?

4 How much electrical energy do you think would be needed to pull the cars to the top of this slope? Would it be:

A the same amount as before

B half as much as before

C twice as much as before

D six times as much as before?

5 How long will it take the same motor to pull the cars up this slope?

This slope is twice as high as the first, so the gravitational potential energy of the cars at the top will be twice as much. More electrical energy must be transferred to lift the car to the top. The electric motor must be switched on for a longer time.

6 Copy the energy transfer diagram below. Then fill it in.

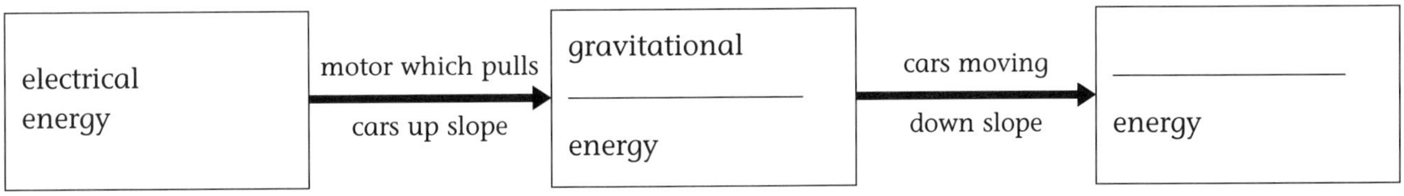

Lift off!

Lifts move people and objects up and down buildings. They have to work against the pull of gravity to do this.

The diagrams show two different lifts.

Both lifts need the same amount of energy to reach the same height, but the electric motors in the lifts do not supply this energy at the same rate.

How fast a motor transfers energy is called its **power**.

The 'standard' lift moves slowly.

7 Which electric motor will have to supply energy faster?

8 Which electric motor will have to be the more powerful?

The 'express' lift moves faster. It transfers energy quickly.

Power is measured in **watts** (W) or in **kilowatts** (kW).

1 kW = 1000 W

9 The standard lift has a 5 kW motor.

The express lift moves twice as fast.

How powerful must the electric motor of the express lift be?

What you need to remember [Copy and complete using the **key words**]

Lifting things with electricity

The force that pulls things down is called ____________.
When you lift something up to a ____________ above the ground it stores energy.
This stored energy is called ____________ ____________ energy.
To lift things up using electrical energy, you can use a ____________.
If a motor works faster it has more ____________.
Power is measured in ____________ (W) or in ____________ (kW).
1 kW = 1000 W

18 Measuring power and energy

REMEMBER

Power is a measure of how fast energy is transferred.

If the power is greater then more energy is transferred in a certain time.

Athletic power

Athletes train so that their muscles become more powerful. This means that they can transfer energy more quickly. They can then run faster, jump higher or throw further.

1 Copy and complete the following sentences.

A more powerful athlete transfers more __________ in a certain time.

Power is a measure of how __________ energy is transferred.

Athletes transfer energy. Energy is measured in **joules** (J).

Who's working hardest?

Look at the weight trainers.

2 Who is working harder?

3 Who has transferred more energy to the weights in one minute?

4 Who is producing more power?

Both lift their weights 10 times in 1 minute. Lifting a bigger weight needs more energy.

Jane lifts the whole of her school bag, loaded with books, on to the bench in one go. Joanne takes out her books one by one and puts them on the bench.

5 Who takes longer to move the books?

6 Who is transferring energy faster?

7 Who is producing more power?

Both girls have the same number of books (of the same mass) in similar bags.

How much energy?

The unit of energy is the **joule** (J).

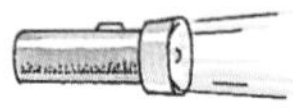

The 1 watt bulb in this torch transfers 1 joule of energy every second.

1 joule of energy is transferred to the apple when it is lifted onto the table.

8 Look at the diagrams above. Write down two examples of transferring one joule of energy.

How much power?

Power measures how fast energy is transferred, so you can work out power like this:

$$\text{power (watts)} = \frac{\text{energy transferred (joules)}}{\text{time taken (seconds)}}$$

(this line means 'divided by')

So one watt is one joule of energy transferred every **second**.

watts (W) = joules per second (J/s)

9 Look at the diagram of the person running up stairs. What is the power produced by this person running up these stairs?

How much energy?

You can rearrange the power formula to find out how much energy an electric lamp or kettle uses.

energy transferred = power × time

Look at the diagrams.

10 How much energy has the lamp transferred?

11 How much energy has the kettle transferred?

(Remember 1 kW = 1000 W)

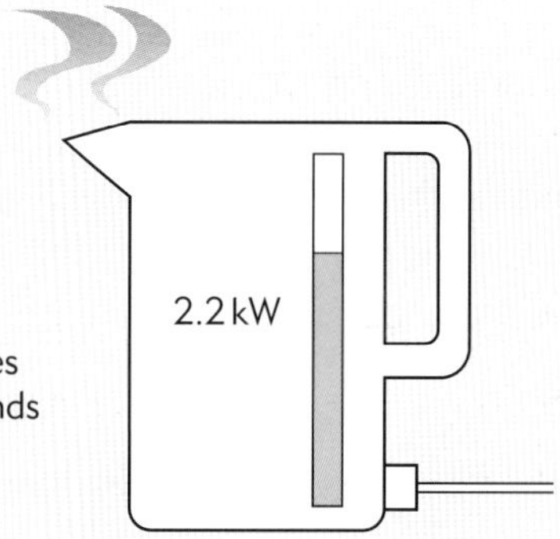

What you need to remember [Copy and complete using the **key words**]

Measuring power and energy

Energy is measured in ______________ (J). Power is measured in ______________ (W).
One watt is one ______________ of energy transferred every ______________.

$$\underset{\text{(watts)}}{\text{\_\_\_\_\_\_\_\_\_\_}} = \frac{\text{energy transferred (joules)}}{\text{time taken (seconds)}}$$

______________ ______________ = power × time
(joules) (watts) (seconds)

Energy where you want it

Which kettle is best?

The owner of a hotel wants kettles for her rooms. She tests three different kettles. The results are shown on the right.

1 Which kettle transferred the most energy to boil 1 litre of water?

2 Which one would you choose to put in guest rooms if you ran the hotel?
Give a reason for your choice.

3 How was the test made a 'fair test'?

Why are some kettles better than others?

An electric kettle is designed to transfer electrical energy as heat energy.

4 Copy the energy change diagram below and fill it in.

______ energy	— kettle →	______ energy

We want the energy transferred by the kettle to heat the water.

5 Look at the diagrams. What <u>two</u> other things get heated up besides the water in the kettle?

Only the energy that is transferred to the water is **usefully** transferred. Energy transferred to anything else is **wasted**.

6 Which kettle wastes most energy, a plastic kettle or a metal one?

7 Look again at the kettles that the hotel owner tested. Which kettle usefully transfers most energy?

The best kettle transfers most heat to the water. We say that this kettle transfers energy in the most **efficient** way.

8 Which kettle is most efficient?

REMEMBER

energy transferred (joules) = power (watts) × time (seconds)

AQUAHEAT MODEL W

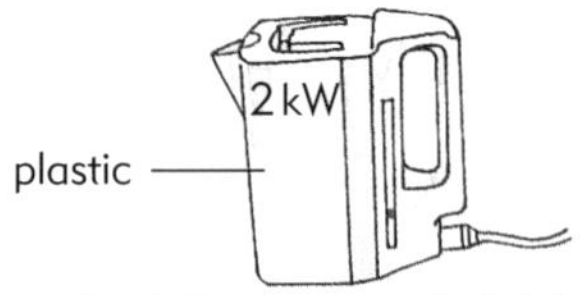

Took 3 minutes to boil 1 litre.

PIGEON MODEL 17

Took 4 minutes to boil 1 litre.

RUNCORN MODEL 5D

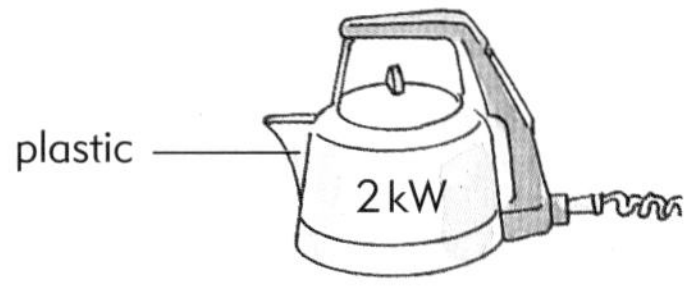

Took 3 minutes 10 seconds to boil 1 litre.

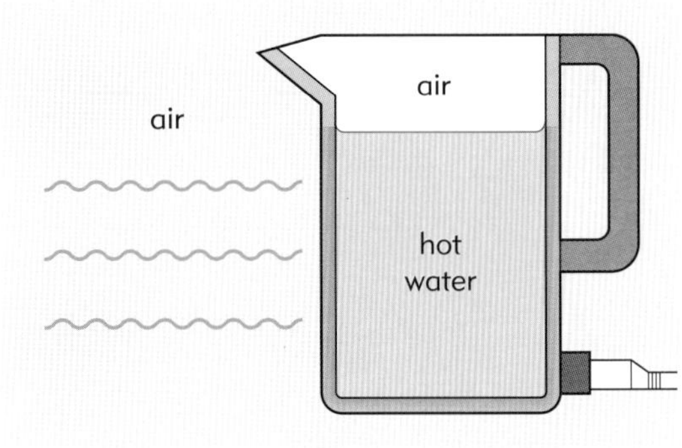

Plastic is a poor conductor of heat. It is an insulator.

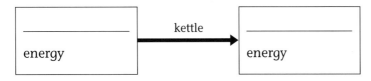

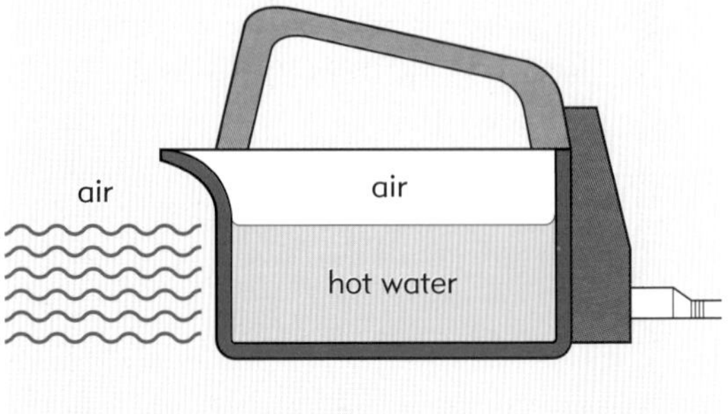

Metal is a good conductor of heat.

Using lamps effectively

A lamp is effective if it sends light to where we want it.

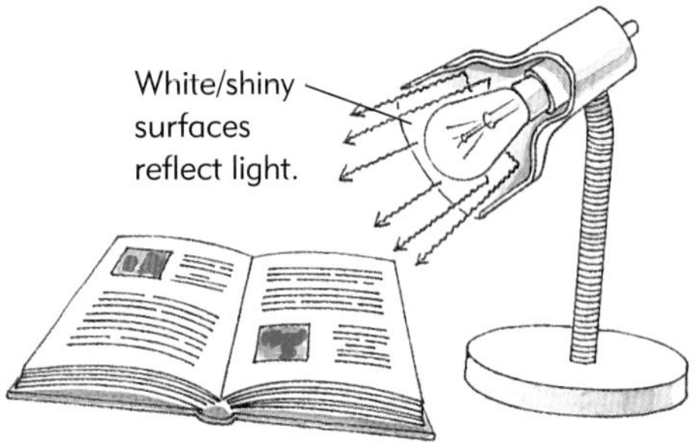

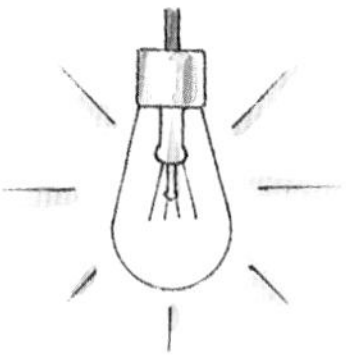

A light bulb sends out light in all directions.

9 Look at the pictures of the lamps. Which is the most effective way of using a light bulb

(a) for reading?

(b) for lighting the whole room?

Give reasons for your answers.

Heating food efficiently

An efficient oven is one which transfers as much energy as possible to food.

10 Study the microwave and electric oven diagrams. Then copy and complete the following sentences.

The microwave oven transfers electrical energy as __________, __________, __________ and __________ energy. It does not waste much energy because only the __________ gets heated up.

The electric oven transfers electrical energy only as __________ energy. But lots of heat energy gets lost by being __________, __________ and __________ through the sides and top.

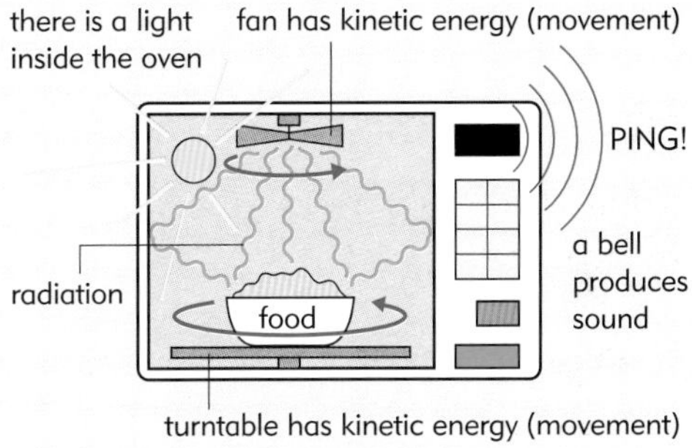

A microwave oven.

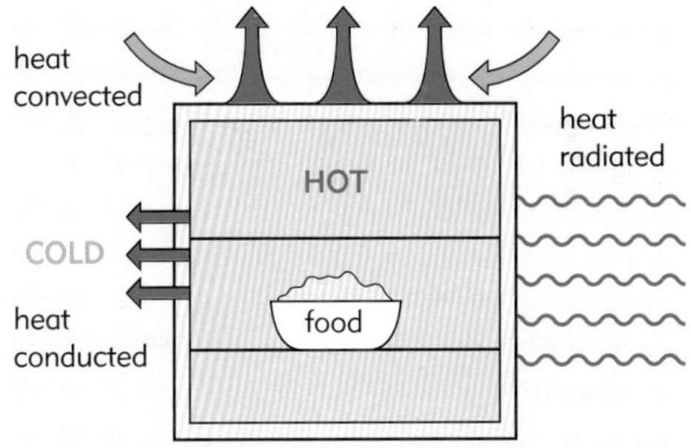

An electric oven.

What you need to remember [Copy and complete using the **key words**]

Energy where you want it

We try to use energy in the most __________ way.
This means that more of the energy we use is __________ transferred.
Any energy that is not transferred usefully is __________.

[You should be able to apply these ideas to everyday electrical appliances, just like you have on these pages.]

Energy of the sort you want

You use many devices to transfer energy in the form you want. For example, a radio transfers electrical energy as sound.

1 Copy the crossword shape (use a piece of graph paper). Then read the clues and complete the crossword.

ACROSS
1 The form of energy you transfer to a bicycle when you pedal.
2 The form of energy you want from a battery.

DOWN
3 The main form of energy you want from a CD player.
4 The main form of energy you want from a torch.
5 The main form of energy you want from an electric fire.

You don't always get what you want

When you transfer energy you don't get only the form of energy you want.

Usually other energy transfers also happen, which you don't want and can waste energy. This reduces **efficiency**.

2 Look at the TV set. Copy the table and complete it.

Energy put in	Useful forms of energy given out	Waste forms of energy given out
____________	____________ and ____________	____________

3 The TV is designed to let the waste energy get out easily. How is this done?

Friction wastes energy

Machines that have moving parts waste energy because of **friction**. The moving parts rub together and produce a lot of **heat** and a little sound.

4 Copy the diagrams of the bicycle and the skateboard. Mark with an 'X' the places where friction between moving parts can waste energy.

5 How would you cut down the wasteful energy transfers on the bicycle and the skateboard?

REMEMBER

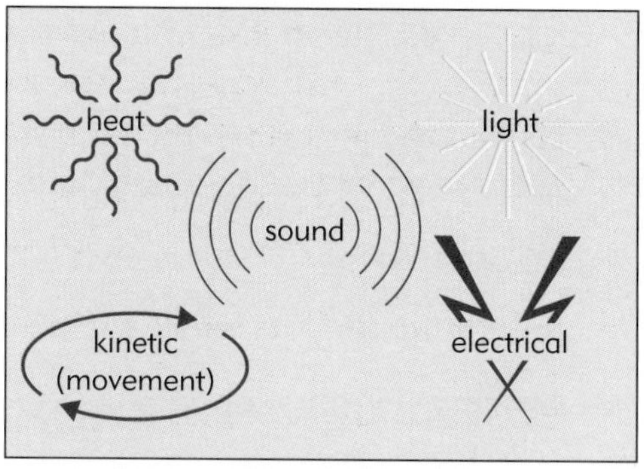

Different forms of energy.

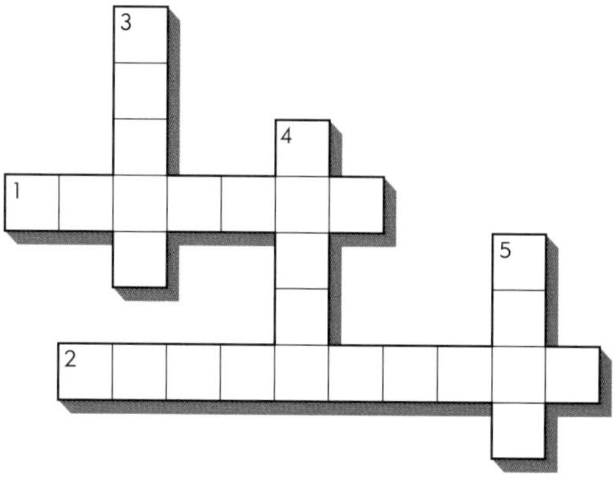

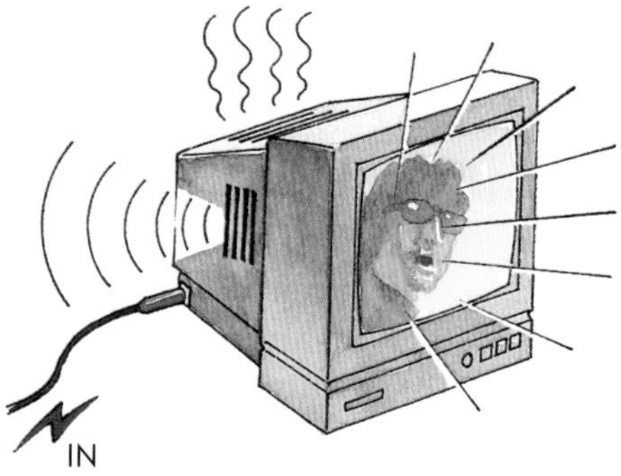

lubrication reduces friction

What do you want from an engine?

When you use an engine, you want it to do some sort of job for you. You also want it to use most of its energy in doing that job. You don't want it to waste any energy.

If an engine is 100 per cent efficient, it means that it is transferring all its energy as **useful work**.

Look at the engines in the diagrams.

6 Which engine is the most efficient?

7 What two sorts of 'waste' energy do all the engines produce?

8 Railways changed from steam engines to diesel engines and then to electric trains.

Why did this happen?

9 Imagine that you used 100 litres of petrol on a long car journey. How many litres would be doing useful work?

REMEMBER

'Per cent' (%) means 'out of 100.'

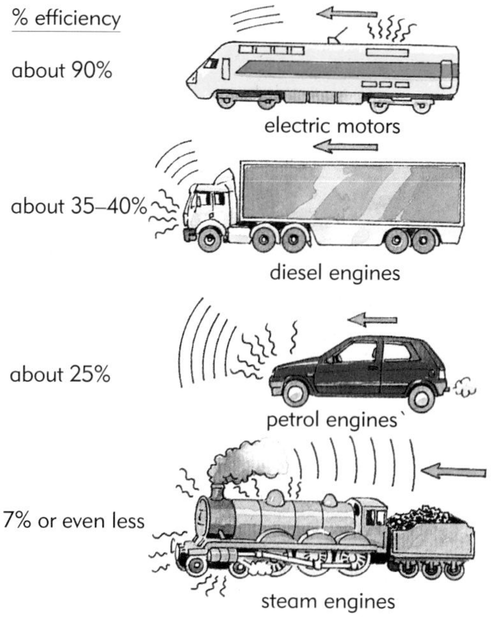

Which lamps are most efficient?

A lamp can't produce light without also producing heat. The efficiency of a lamp is the fraction (or percentage) of energy that is transferred as light.

10 Copy the table. Then complete it for the rest of the lamps, using the information in the diagrams.

Type of lamp	Energy transferred as light (%)	Energy transferred as heat (%)	Efficiency (%)
Filament	4	96	4

11 Write down the three types of lamp in order, starting with the most efficient and ending with the least efficient.

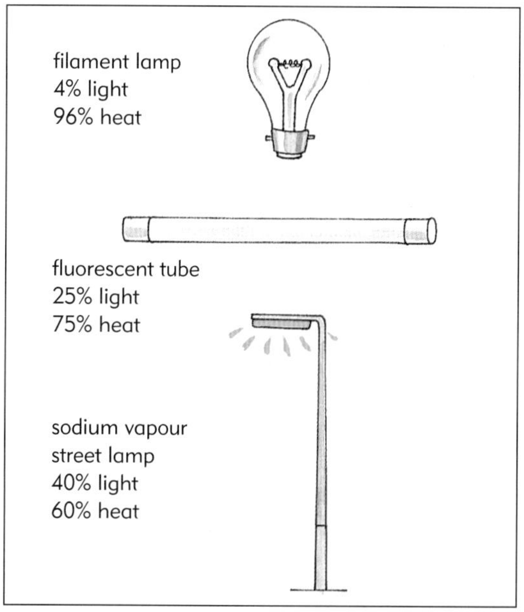

What you need to remember [Copy and complete using the **key words**]

Energy of the sort you want

Wasting energy reduces ________________.
Energy is most often wasted as ________________ energy.
In machines, moving parts rub together and waste energy because of ________________.
An engine with 100 per cent efficiency transfers all its energy as ________________ ________________.

21 What happens to all the wasted energy?

Adding it up

Energy doesn't disappear, it just gets changed from one type of energy to another.

Some of the types of energy are what you want, others are just **wasted**. No energy gets lost – the total amount of energy you end up with is always **exactly** the same as the amount you started with.

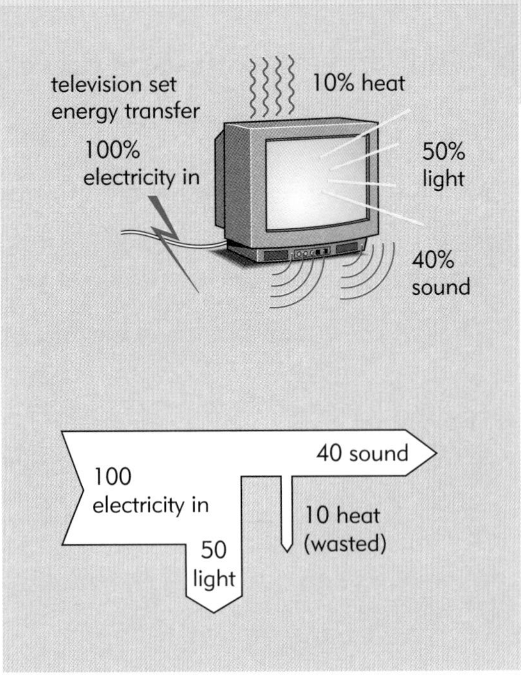

How the television set transfers energy.

1 Copy and complete the following sentences.

The energy put into the television set is __________ % electricity. The useful energy transferred is 50% as __________ and 40% as _____. There is __________% wasted as heat.

The arrows on the diagram show how the television set transfers energy. The thickness of each arrow shows how much energy is transferred in that particular way.

The wasted and **useful** energy always add up to 100%.

2 Copy and complete the energy transfer diagrams below.

(a) Filament lamp

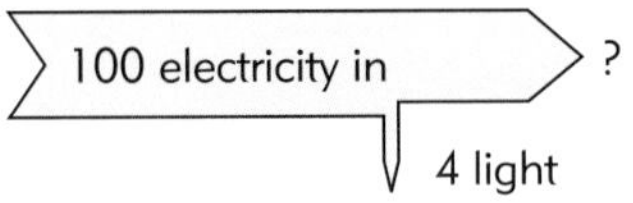

(b) Fluorescent tube

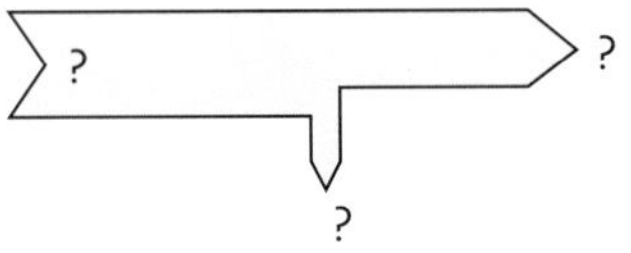

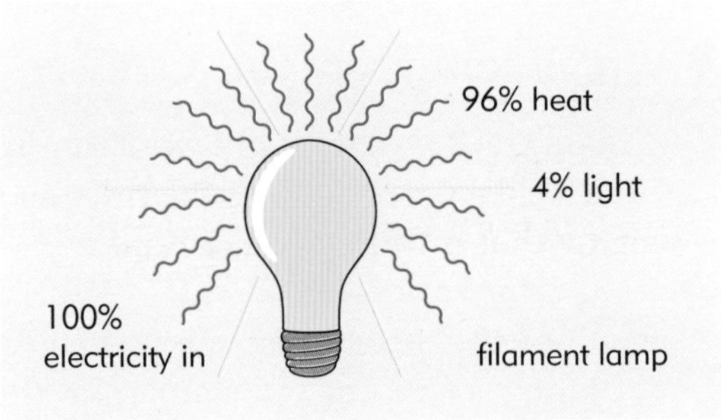

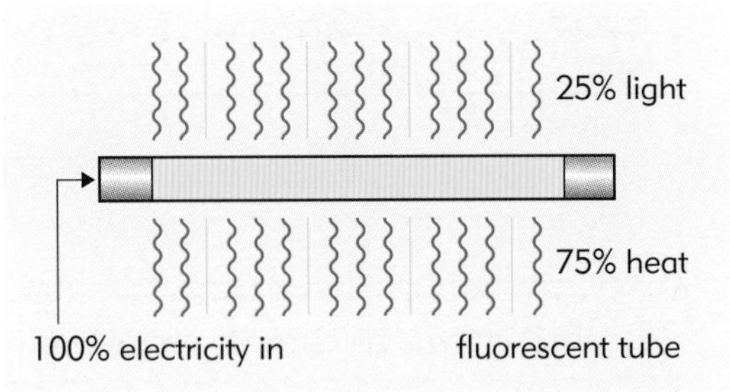

Everything ends up as heat

The light from the television set is used by you to see the picture, but much of it will not go into your eyes. It is soaked up by everything in the room.

When this happens it makes the room a little bit **warmer**. The same thing happens to the sound vibrations. The energy ends up as **heat** and **spreads** out.

This makes it more difficult for you to do anything useful with it.

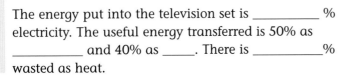

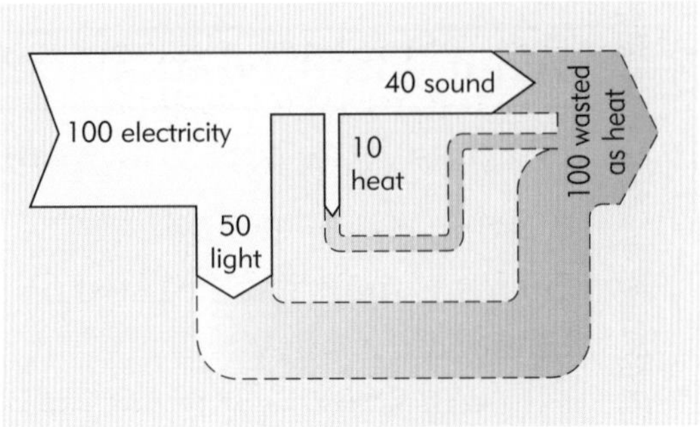

All the energy from the television set gets spread out and wasted as heat in the end.

3 Copy the table of energy transfers and complete the spaces.

		Transferred energy		
Machine	Energy in	heat	movement	sound
electric motor	100	5	90	
diesel engine	100			
petrol engine	100		25	10
steam engine	100	73	7	

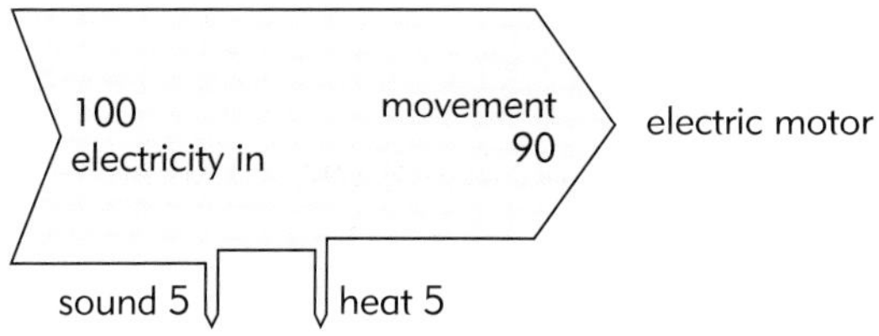

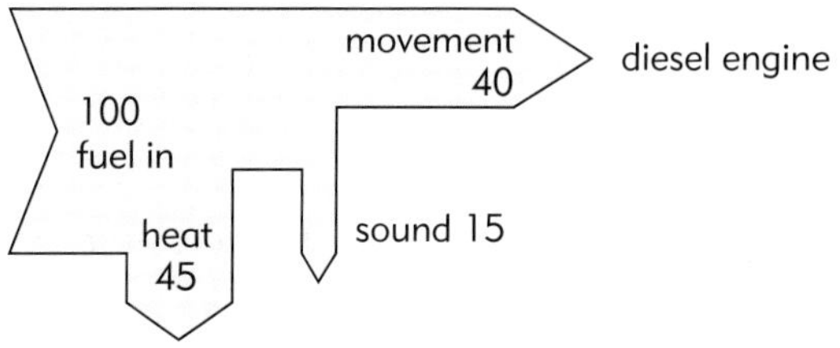

4 Draw a diagram showing the energy transfers for the petrol engine. (Use a piece of squared paper.)

5 Which produces more waste heat energy, a petrol engine or a diesel engine?

Can you use wasted energy for anything?

Sometimes you can make use of 'wasted' energy.

Look at the diagram.

6 How can you use the wasted heat from a car engine?

If a building is well insulated, the waste heat from television sets, lamps, cookers and freezers can also help to keep it warm.

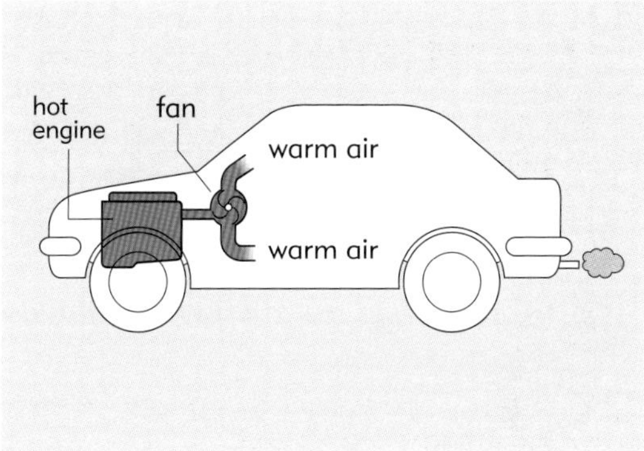

You can use waste heat from a car engine to heat the inside of the car.

What you need to remember [Copy and complete using the **key words**]

What happens to all the wasted energy?

Some of the energy you put into a device will be transferred in a ________________ way but some of it will be ________________.
The useful energy plus the wasted energy always adds up ________________ to the energy you put in.
All the energy eventually ends up as ________________, which makes everything a bit ________________.
But this energy ________________ out, which makes it more difficult to transfer in a useful way.

1 Are you a conductor or an insulator?

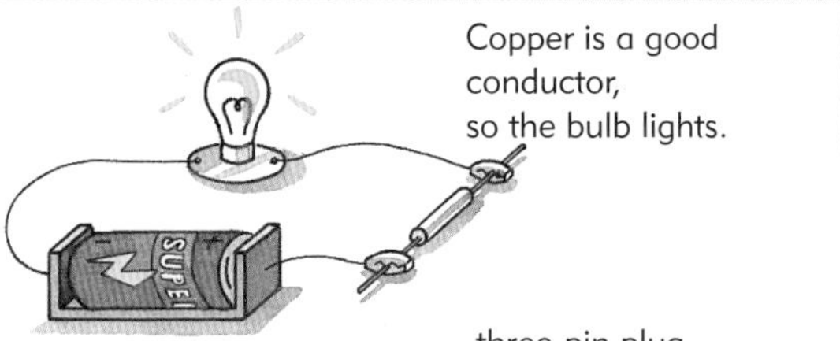

Copper is a good
conductor,
so the bulb lights.
SUPER

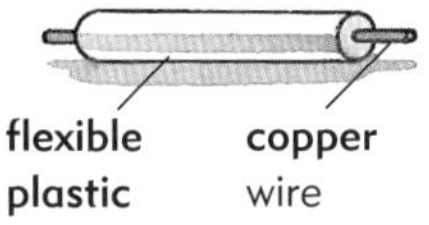

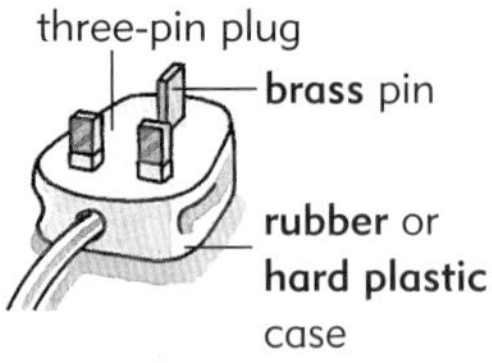

How to test for good conductors

Some materials let electricity pass through them very easily. A material like this is called a good **conductor**. You can find out which materials are good conductors. The diagram shows you how.

1 What happens if you test a good conductor?

The table shows the results of some tests.

Material	Does bulb light?
flexible plastic	no
copper	yes
hard plastic	no
rubber	no
brass	yes

2 Write down the materials that are good conductors.

If you tested your body in the same way, the bulb would not light.

3 What does this tell you about your body?

How to test for good insulators

You can do the same tests with a sensitive electrical meter instead of a bulb. A good **insulator** does not let any electricity pass through it. So the meter stays at zero. The table shows the results of some tests.

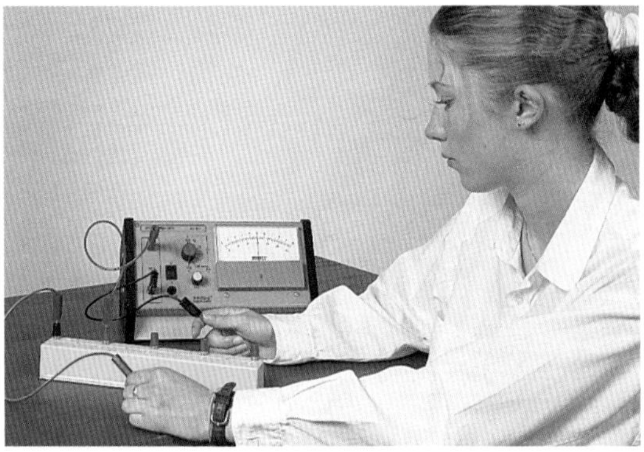

Material	Meter reading
flexible plastic	zero
body (hands dry)	small
body (hands wet)	larger
hard plastic	zero
rubber	zero

4 Which materials are good insulators?

5 Is your body a good insulator? Answer as carefully as you can.

Why can mains electricity kill?

The average voltage of the mains electricity in Europe is **230** volts. This is much higher than the voltage of a battery. The 230-volt mains can send an electric current through your body that is big enough to **kill** you.

6 Make a copy of the table below. Then use the information from the diagram to complete the table.

Size of current	Effect on body
below 7 mA	
	can't let go; painful but won't kill you
	may kill you
over 30 mA	

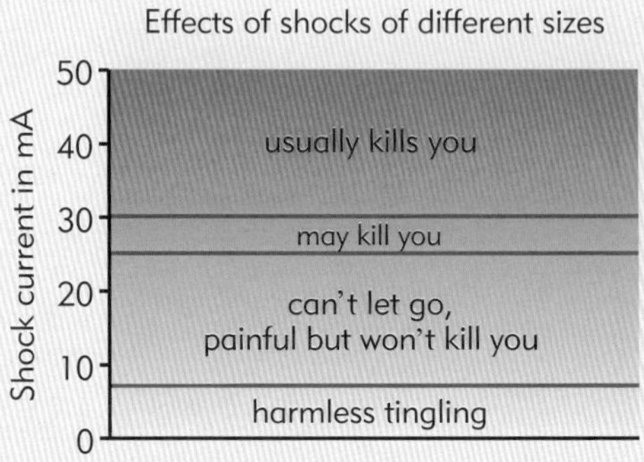

1 milliamp (1 mA) is a thousandth of an amp.

What makes an electric shock bigger?

You get a shock if electricity flows through your body to the earth. The size of the shock depends on how easily electricity can pass into and out of your body.

7 Why are you less likely to get a shock that kills you:

(a) if your hands are dry?

(b) if you are wearing shoes or boots with rubber soles?

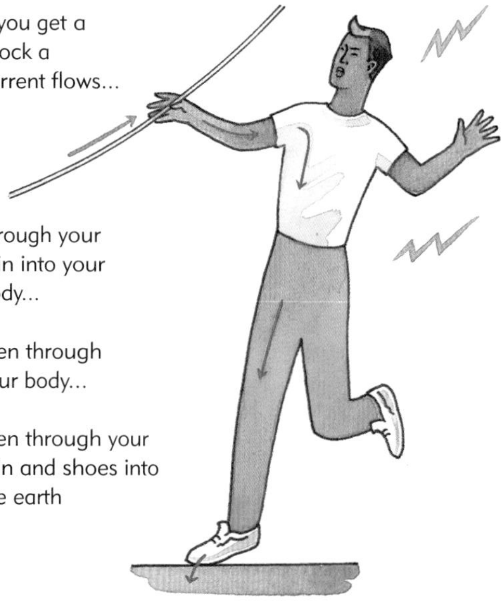

The 230-volt mains can kill you.

How is mains electricity kept safe?

In the UK, more than 50 million people use mains electricity every day.

Plugs and **cables** are covered with insulators, so we can't touch any of the metal parts that are conducting electricity. This makes plugs and cables **safe** to use.

Fewer than a hundred people are killed by mains electricity in Britain each year.

What you need to remember [Copy and complete using the **key words**]

Are you a conductor or an insulator?

The European mains electricity supply is about ________ volts.
This is big enough to ________ people.
Electrical appliances are usually connected to the mains using ________ and three-pin ________.
These are made from the materials shown on the diagrams, so that they work well and are ________.

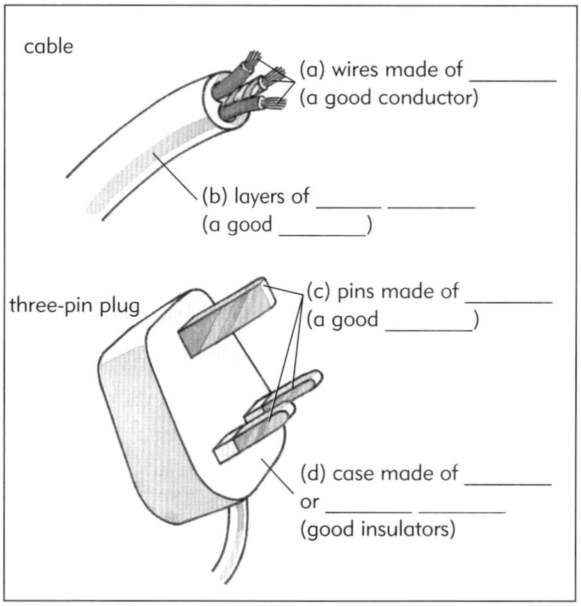

Wiring a three-pin plug

> **REMEMBER**
> - Copper and brass are good conductors.
> - Plastic is a good insulator.

Mains electricity of 230 volts can kill you. So you must be able to wire up plugs safely.

Which colour wire goes to which pin?

The diagram shows a correctly wired plug.

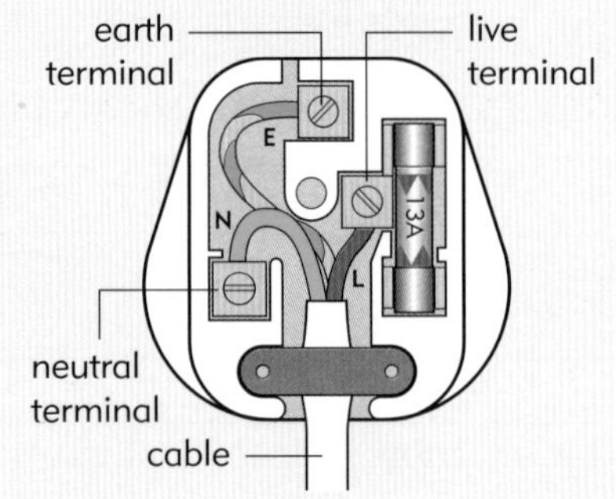

1 Make a copy of the table below.

Then complete it using the information from the diagram.

Letter by terminal	Name of terminal	Colour(s) of wires
E		
L		
N		

How should the wires be connected to the terminals?

The diagram shows how to connect a wire to its terminal.

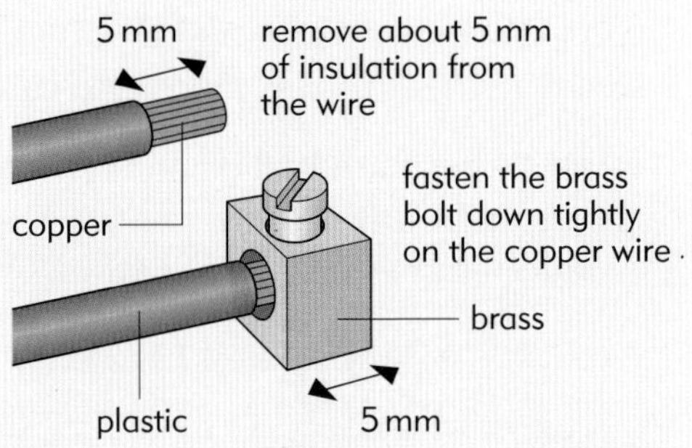

2 Why do you remove some of the plastic insulation from a wire before you connect it?

3 Why do you remove only about 5 mm of insulation from each wire?

Why does a plug have three pins?

The **live** and **neutral** pins of a plug carry the electric current to and from the mains supply.

The earth pin is there for **safety**. It is very important when using electrical equipment that has a **metal** case. It can help to stop you getting a shock if something goes wrong.

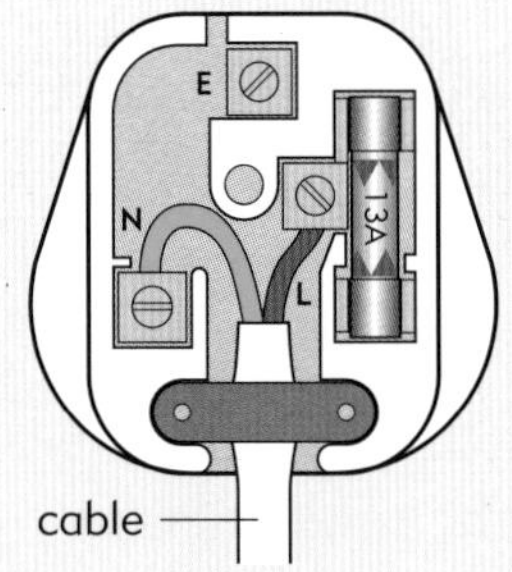

4 The diagram of the three-pin plug shows a cable that has only two wires inside it.

Which terminals are these wires connected to?

5 The next diagram shows two light fittings. One is made of plastic and the other of metal.

(a) What other difference can you see?

(b) Why do you think there is this difference?

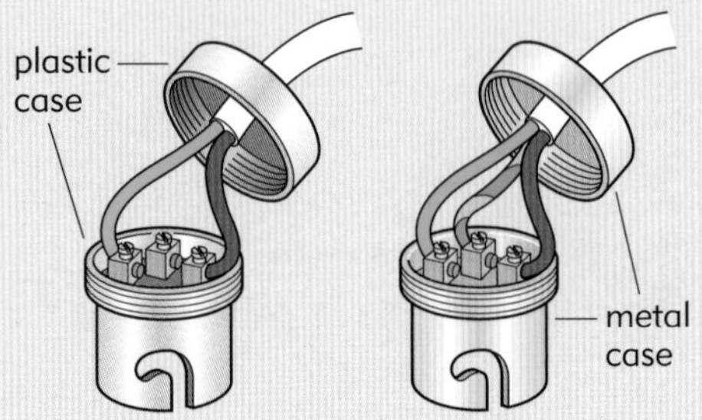

Why is the cable grip important?

The cable connected to a plug often gets pulled. The **cable grip** means that the whole of the cable takes the strain. Without a cable grip, the copper wires take the strain instead. These are not so strong and can easily break.

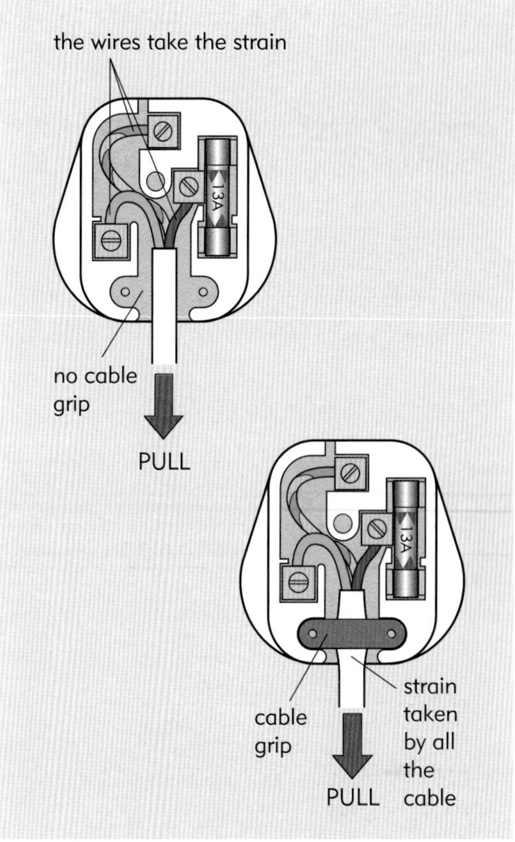

6 Copy the table. Then complete it to show what happens if one of the wires inside the plug breaks.

	Brown	Blue	Green + yellow
Will the appliance work?			
Is it safe?			

What's wrong?

The following diagrams show plugs that are unsafe.

7 For each diagram:

- say why the plug is unsafe;
- say what you can do to make it safe.

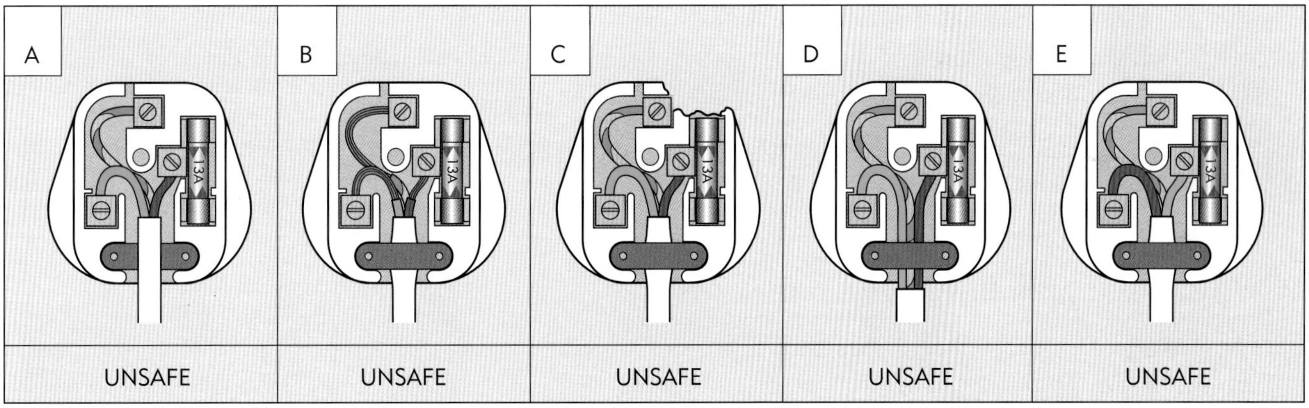

What you need to remember [Copy and complete using the **key words**]

Wiring a three-pin plug

The current to an electrical appliance is supplied through the ________________ and ________________ pins.
The earth pin is there for ________________.
Appliances with ________________ cases are usually earthed.
To prevent strain where the copper wires are connected to the terminals, we use a ________________ ________________.

Some 'do's' and 'don'ts' that could save your life

You must have plugged things into the mains thousands of times. We use mains electricity a lot. So it's very easy to get careless about it. This is dangerous. You can be killed if you use mains electricity carelessly.

REMEMBER

- The mains supply is 230 volts. Higher voltages are even more dangerous.
- You will get a worse shock if your skin is wet.

1 An electricity company is making some safety posters for junior schools. The artist has already drawn the posters. She needs some words to finish them off. What words would you add to each of the posters?

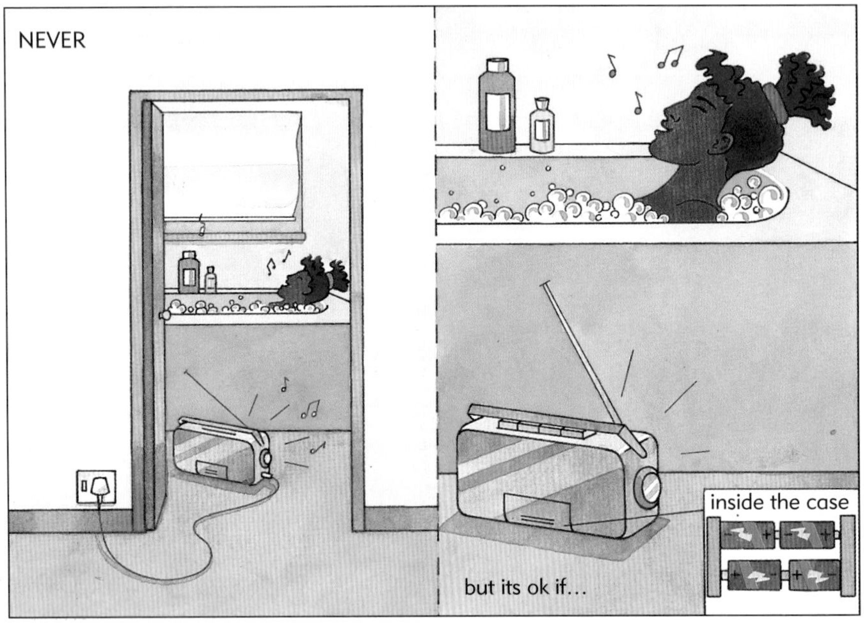

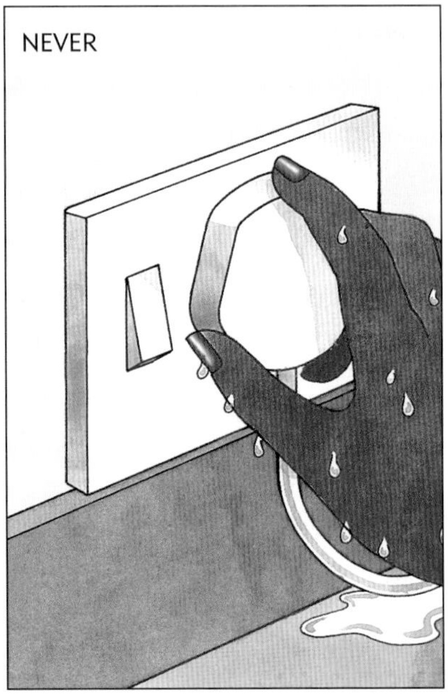

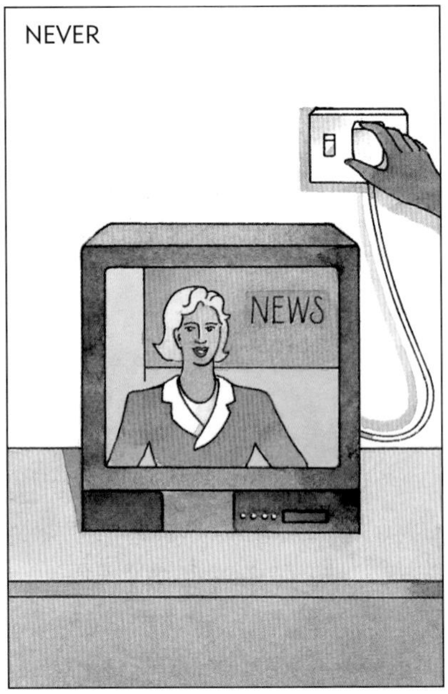

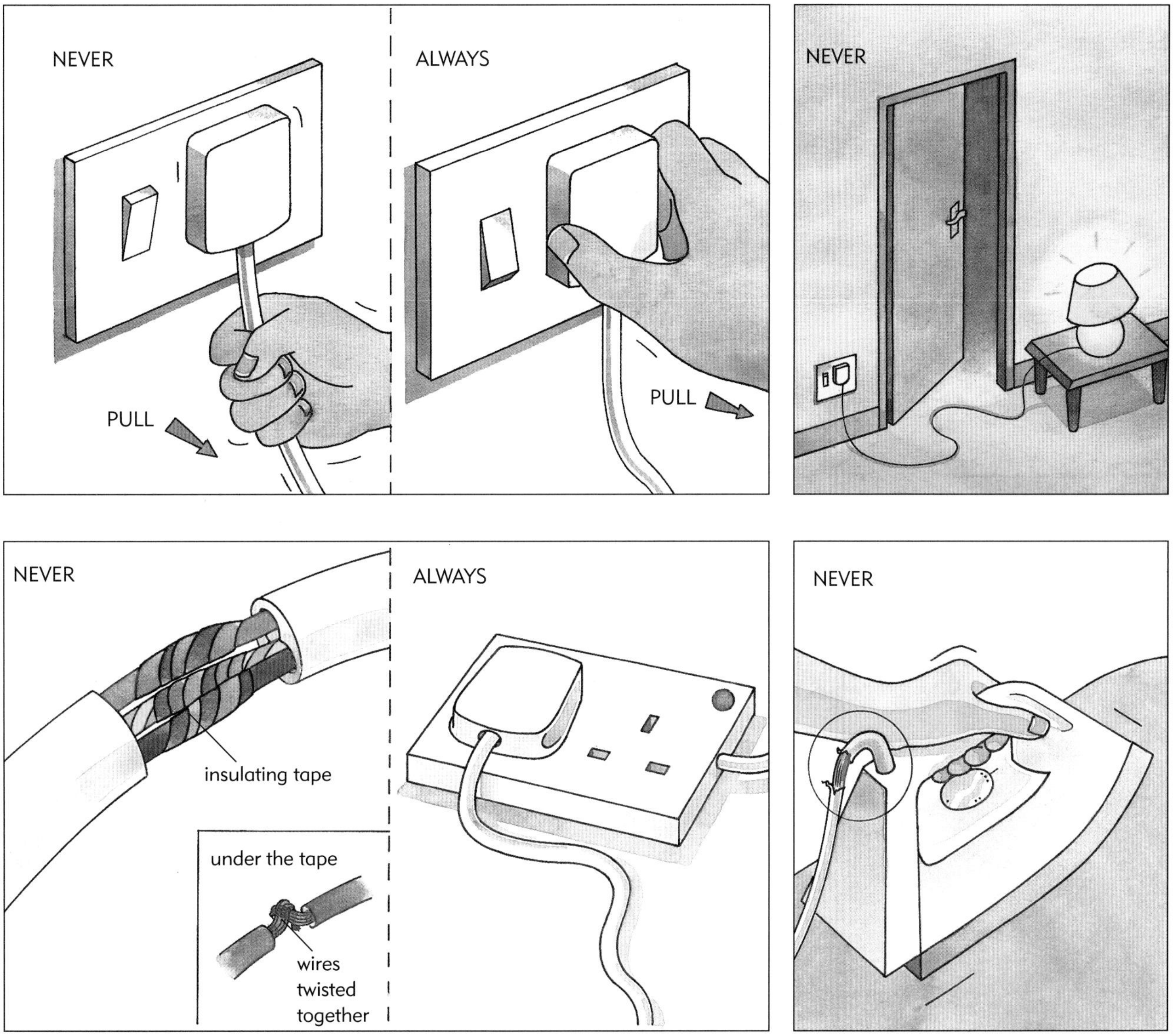

2 Think of another thing that it is dangerous to do with mains electricity.

Make a safety poster about it. Do a drawing, then add the words.

What you need to remember

Some 'do's' and 'don'ts' that could save your life

You should be able to spot whenever mains electricity is being used dangerously. You will find more examples on pages 51, 54–55 and 87.

Why do plugs have fuses?

Sometimes the **fuse** inside a plug 'blows'. You then have to replace it or the plug won't work.

> **REMEMBER**
> - Metals are good conductors.
> - Most non-metals are insulators.

Why won't a plug work without a fuse?

Electricity won't pass through a plug unless it is fitted with a fuse.

The diagrams show you why.

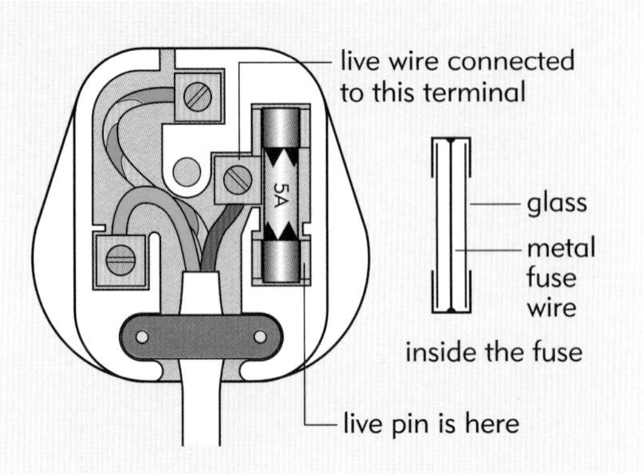

1 How does a current get from one end of a fuse to the other?

2 What two parts of a plug does the fuse connect?

3 A plug won't supply a current unless a fuse is fitted. Why not?

What are fuses for?

Sometimes the current through a circuit becomes too big. The diagrams show why this can be dangerous.

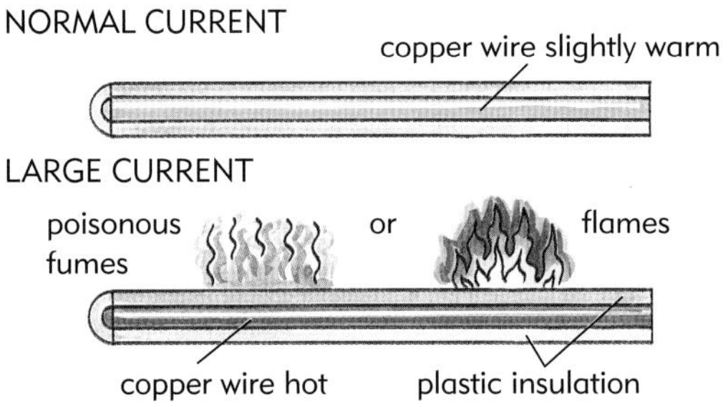

4 Copy and complete the following sentences.

If the current flowing through a cable gets too big, the wires get __________. This can make the plastic insulation give off poisonous __________. If the wire gets hot enough, the insulation might burst into __________.

Electrical appliances can also be damaged by a current that is too big.

The fuse makes a circuit **safer**. The fuse **cuts off** the current if the current becomes too big.

How does a fuse do its job?

The diagrams show how a fuse does its job.

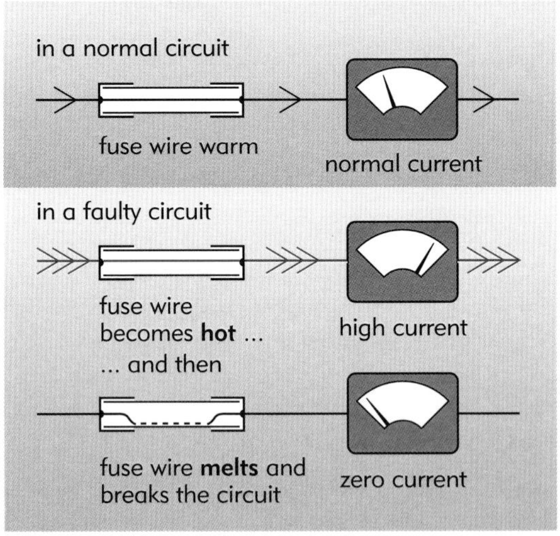

5 Copy the table. Then use the information from the diagrams to complete the table.

Current to the fuse wire	What happens to the fuse wire
normal	__________
much bigger than normal	__________ and then __________

6 Copy and complete the sentences.

If the fuse wire melts it __________ the circuit. There is then __________ current.

Choosing the right kind of wire for the job

Look at the information in the table.

Metal	Melting point in °C
aluminium	about 900
copper	about 1350
tin	about 500

7 Why is tin a suitable metal for fuse wire?

8 People sometimes replace a blown fuse with aluminium foil or copper wire. This makes the plug work but it is very dangerous. Explain why.

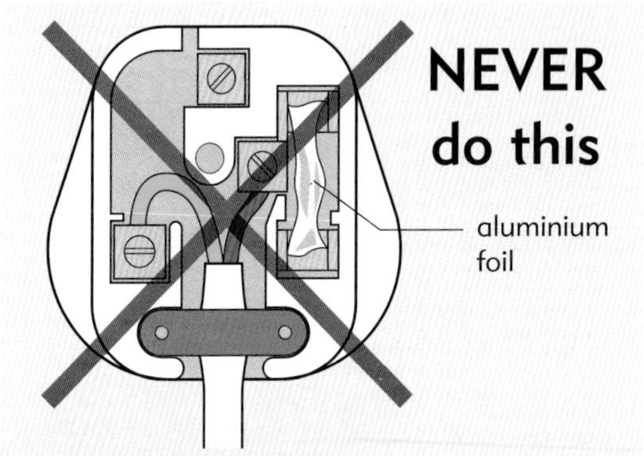

What size of fuse should I use?

The picture shows the three most common types of fuse.

When you replace a fuse you should use the type recommended by the makers of the **appliance**. The correct type of fuse will already be fitted in the plug when you buy an appliance. So you should replace a fuse with one of the **same** type.

The information in the photograph tells you another way of choosing the right fuse for an appliance.

9 Which type of fuse would you use for the hair dryer? Say why the two other types of fuse would not be right.

Circuit breakers can also be used to do the same job as fuses. You can read about them on page 65.

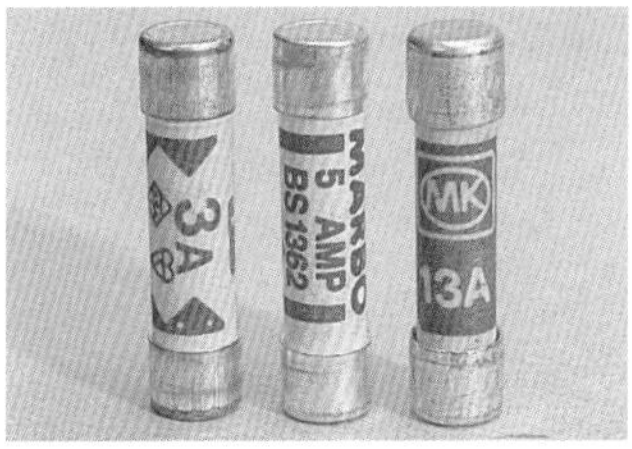

A = amperes

A 3A fuse will melt if a current of more than 3A passes through it.

A fuse mustn't melt with the normal current, but it must melt if the current is bigger than normal.

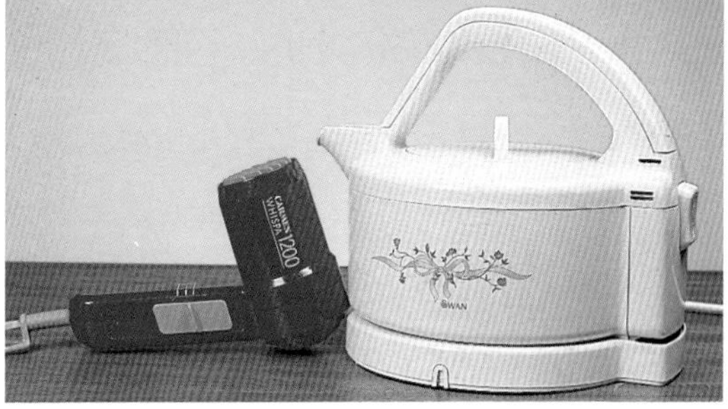

normal current 4A
fuse ?

normal current 11A
fuse 13A

Choosing the right fuse.

What you need to remember [Copy and complete using the **key words**]

Why do plugs have fuses?

A three-pin plug won't work unless it is fitted with a __________.
If the current becomes too big, the fuse becomes __________ and then __________.
This ______ ______ the current. Fuses make circuits much __________.
You should always replace a fuse with the type recommended by the makers of the __________. This will normally be the __________ type as the fuse you are replacing.
Dangerous currents can also be switched off using __________ __________.

5 V/a.c./d.c./Hz What do they all mean?

Electrical appliances have lots of letters and numbers printed on them. It's important for you to know what these letters and numbers mean. If you don't, you could easily damage the appliances or harm yourself.

What does the V mean?

Look at the diagrams of the light bulbs. **V** stands for **volts**.

1 Copy and complete the following sentences.

A 12 V bulb should be used with a _______ supply.
A _______ bulb should be used with a 230-volt supply.

What does d.c. mean?

The diagram shows a battery pushing a current through a circuit.

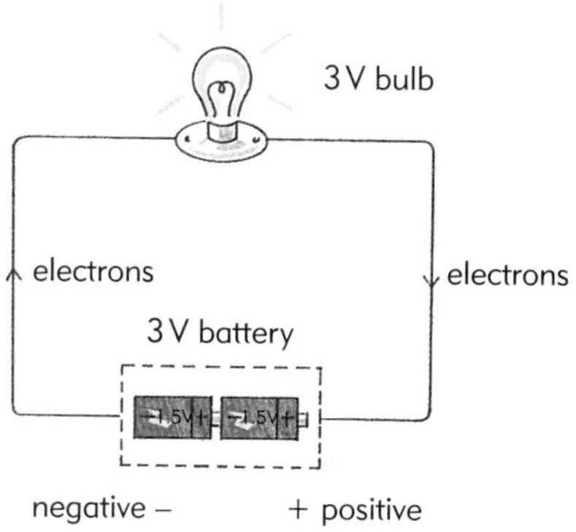

An electric current.

2 Copy and complete the following sentences.

When an electric current flows, _________ are moving round the circuit. They move from the __________ side of the battery, then through the wires and bulb, and then back to the __________ side of the battery.

The **electrons** always flow in the same **direction**. This is called a **direct current**, or **d.c.** for short.

3 The battery is connected to the bulb the opposite way round. Draw a diagram to show which way the electrons move now.

How can you see the direction of a current?

You can use an oscilloscope to draw a graph of the current. The pictures show the current from a battery.

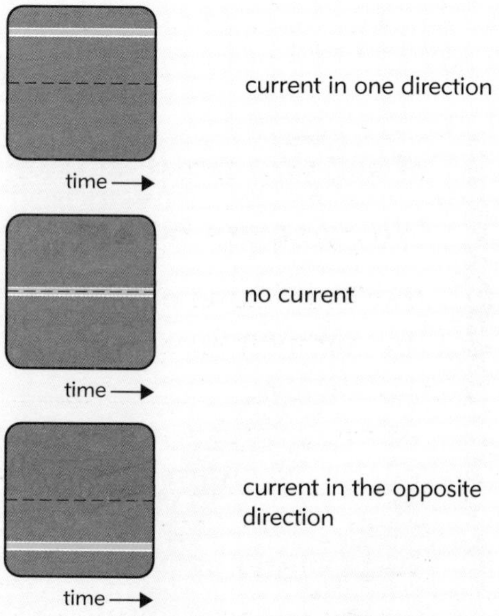

Oscilloscope pictures of a direct current.

4 Copy and complete the following sentences.

When the current is in one direction, the graph is __________ the centre line.
When the current is in the opposite direction, the graph is __________ the centre line.
When there is no current, the graph is
the centre line.

What does a.c. mean?

The diagram shows the same bulb connected to a 3 V a.c. supply. The bulb lights up just like it did with the 3 V battery.

The picture shows the current from the a.c. supply.

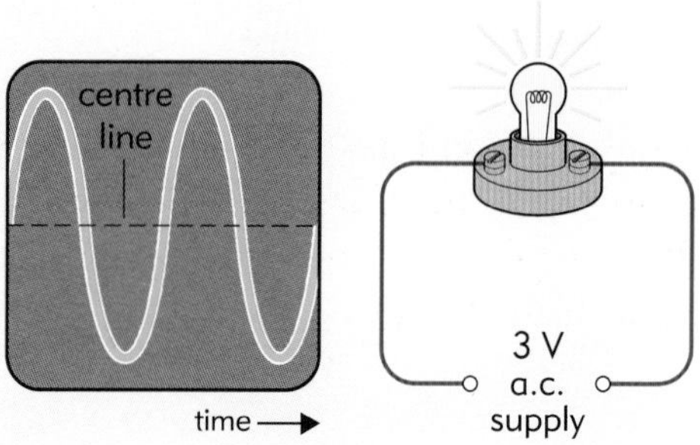

5 What does the picture tell you about the direction of the current?

A current that keeps on changing its direction is called an **alternating** current, or **a.c.** for short.

What does Hz mean?

The picture shows the graph of an alternating current. A time scale has now been added.

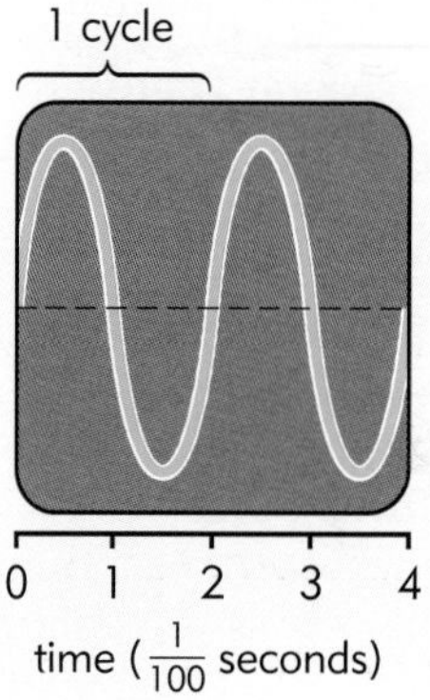

6 How long does it take for the current to change direction and back again?

This is called a cycle.

7 How many cycles will there be in one whole second?

The number of **cycles** per second is called the frequency. In Europe, mains electricity has a frequency of 50 cycles per second or 50 **hertz** (Hz for short).

8 The diagrams show the information on the back of two electrical appliances. Explain, as fully as you can, what this information tells you.

~220–240 V. 50 Hz	UK
110 V a.c. 60 Hz.	USA

~ = a.c.

What you need to remember [Copy and complete using the **key words**]

V/a.c./d.c./Hz What do they all mean?

An electric current through a wire is, in fact, a flow of ________________.
The current from a battery always flows in the same ________________.
It is called a ________________ current, or ________________ for short.
A current that constantly changes direction is called an ________________ current, or ________________ for short.
Mains electricity is an a.c. supply. In Europe, it has a frequency of 50 ________________ per second, or 50 ________________ (Hz for short).
The mains supply in Europe is about 230 ________________, or 230 _______ for short.

6 Why is mains electricity a.c? Why is it 230 volts?

REMEMBER

An alternating current (a.c.) keeps changing direction.

A direct current (d.c.) flows the same way all the time.

The a.c. mains supply often has to be changed to d.c. before it can be used.

1 Write down the names of <u>two</u> appliances that need d.c. to work.

Also, electricity at 230 volts is high enough to kill. So why do we use an a.c. mains electricity supply of 230 volts?

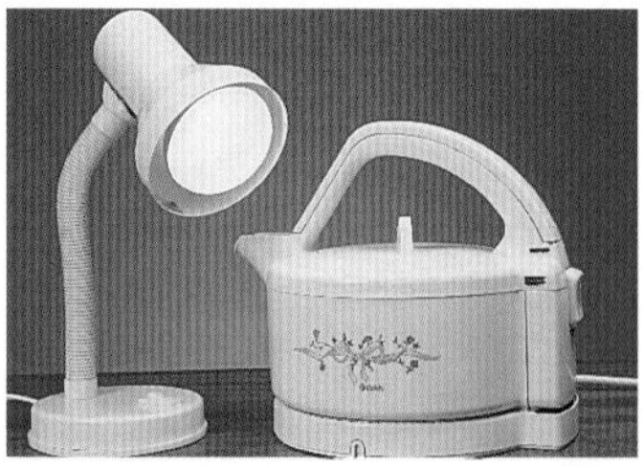

Bulbs and kettles can use a.c. or d.c.

Radios and televisions will only work using d.c.

Why mains electricity is a.c.

Different electrical appliances need different voltages to work properly. It is easy to change the **voltage** of a.c. using a **transformer**. Transformers do not work with d.c.

To increase the voltage of an a.c. supply you need a **step-up** transformer. To reduce the voltage of an a.c. supply you need a **step-down** transformer.

2 Copy and complete the table.

	Voltage needed	What is used to produce this voltage from the mains?
personal stereo		step-______ transformer
television		step-______ transformer

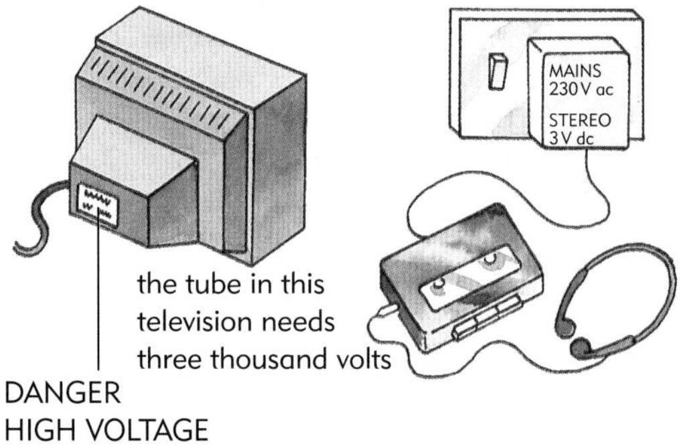

Why mains electricity is 230 volts

We use copper cables to conduct electricity. The higher the voltage we use, the less energy we waste in the cables. But low voltages are much **safer**.

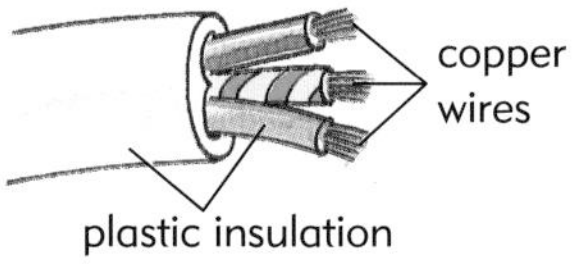

The copper wire in cables is a very good conductor, but it gets slightly warm when a current flows through it. The longer the wire is, the more **energy** gets wasted as heat.

3 Why is 230 volts better in our homes

(a) than 2300 volts?

(b) than 23 volts?

4 In the USA the mains voltage is 110 volts. Do you think this is better or worse than 230 volts? Explain your answer.

5 How is electrical energy wasted in copper cables?

6 Cars use a 12-volt electrical system. Write down <u>two</u> reasons why this low voltage is suitable for cars.

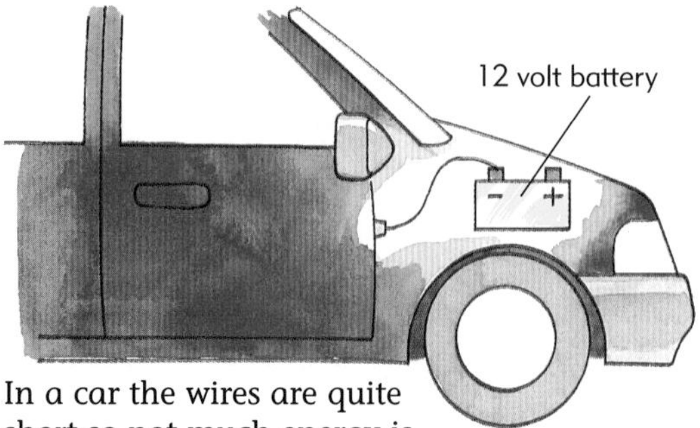

In a car the wires are quite short so not much energy is wasted. Components are connected to one side of the battery through the body of the car, so the voltage must be low to make sure the passengers are safe.

How electricity reaches your home

Electricity is generated in power stations. It is then sent to towns and cities through a network of cables called the **National Grid**.

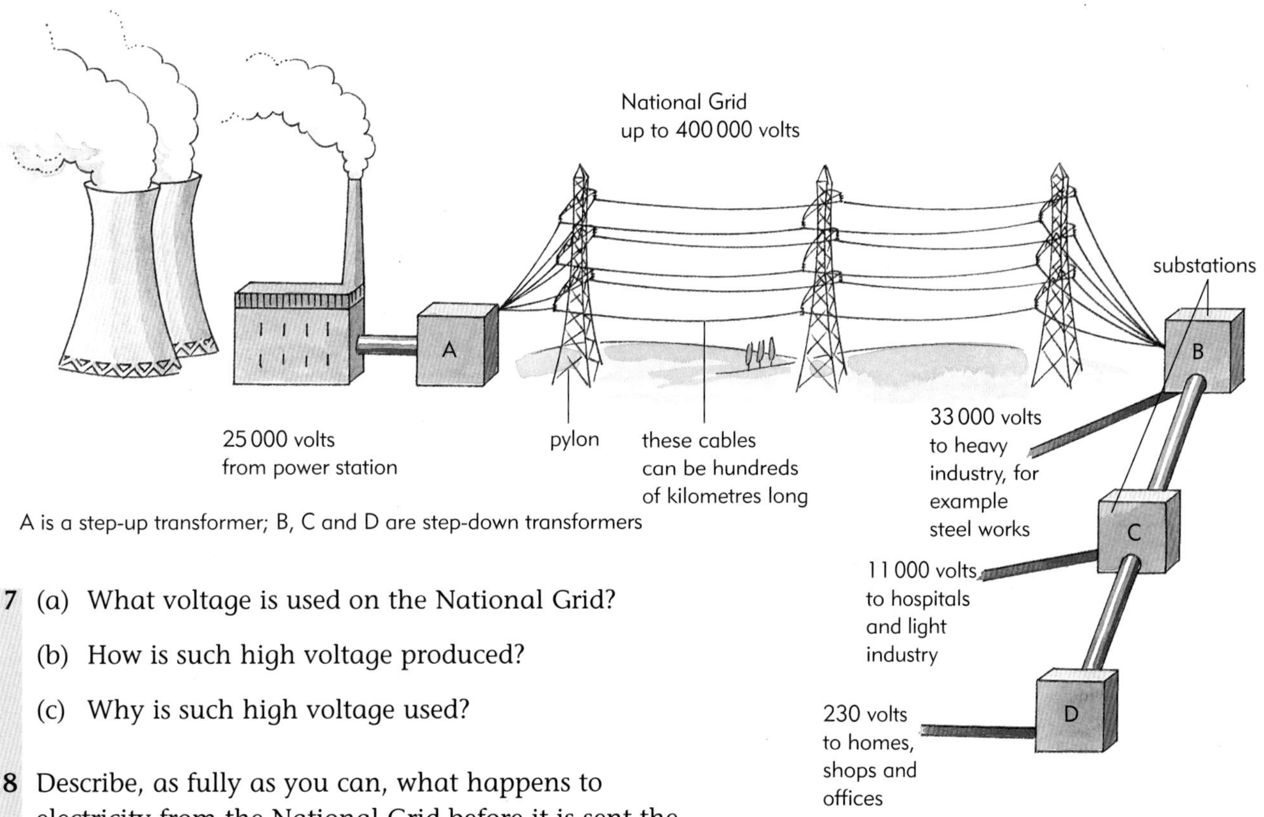

A is a step-up transformer; B, C and D are step-down transformers

7 (a) What voltage is used on the National Grid?

(b) How is such high voltage produced?

(c) Why is such high voltage used?

8 Describe, as fully as you can, what happens to electricity from the National Grid before it is sent the people who use it.

What you need to remember [Copy and complete using the **key words**]

Why is mains electricity a.c? Why is it 230 volts?

You can change the voltage of an a.c. supply using a ________________.
Electricity from power stations reaches us through the ________________ ____________.
Electricity is sent through the Grid at a very high ________________.
This is produced using a ________________ transformer and means that less ________________ is wasted.
Before it reaches homes and factories, the voltage is reduced using a ________________ transformer. This makes the electricity ________________ to use.

Doing things with magnets

Making things stick without glue

Magnets will stick to things made of **iron** or **steel**. A force pulls the magnet and the iron or steel together. The magnet and the iron or steel **attract** each other.

Look at the pictures.

1 (a) You can fasten L-plates with magnetic strips to a car.

Why is this better than sticky-back L-plates?

(b) Some cars have plastic or aluminium bodies.

Why can't you stick L-plates with magnetic strips on these cars?

2 A fridge door is held shut with a magnetic strip.

Explain why this works.

3 How can you use a magnet to hold a wooden door shut?

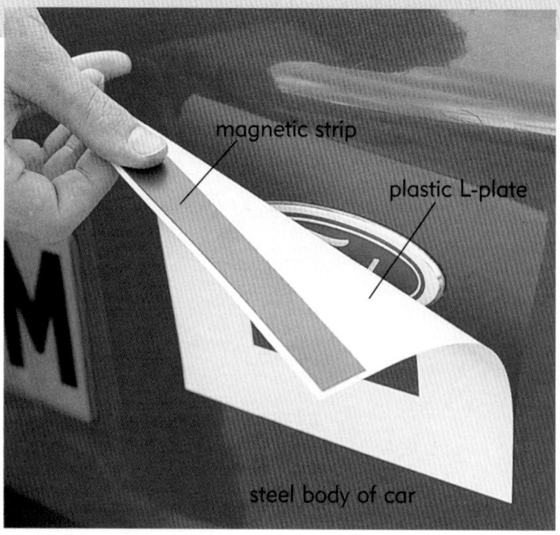

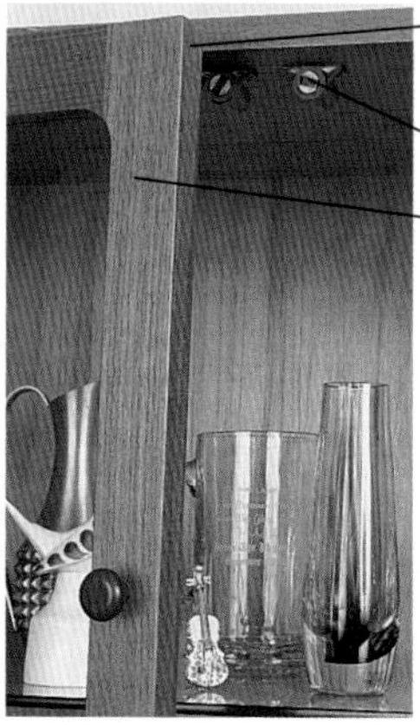

Finding which way to go

Hills are often covered in mist. People walking on the hills can't see where they are going and they might get lost. They can use a magnetic compass to find their direction.

4 Copy and complete the following sentences.

The needle of a magnetic compass always comes to rest pointing __________ and __________.

The end of the magnetic needle that points south is called the __________-__________ pole.

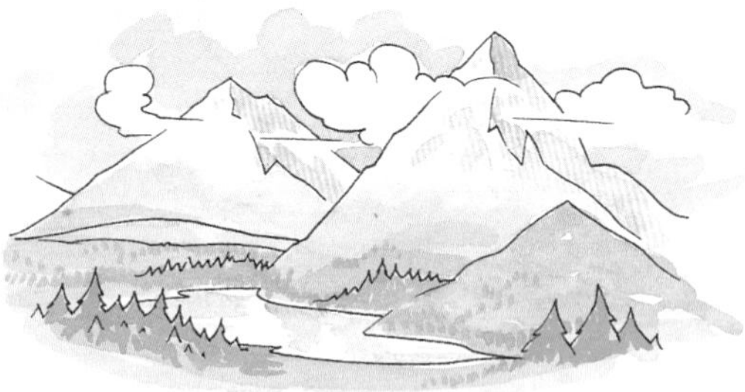

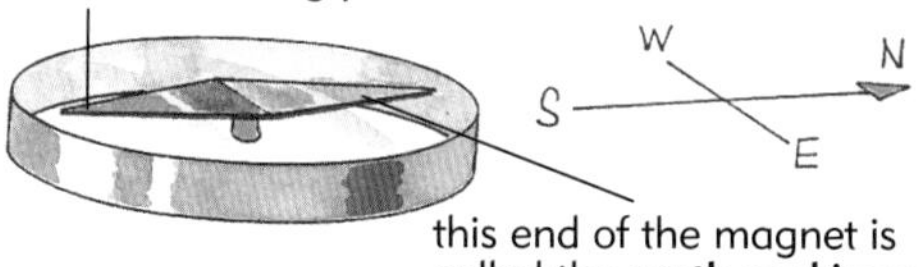

The needle of the compass is a magnet that can rotate. It comes to rest pointing north and south.

Making a magnetic compass

You can make a magnetic compass with any magnet. All you have to do is to make sure the magnet is **free** to **move**.

5 If you put a bar magnet on to a table it won't act as a compass. Explain why.

6 Write down two ways of making the bar magnet into a magnetic compass.

7 The magnets in the diagrams are marked with the letters N and S.

Why are these letters marked on the magnets?

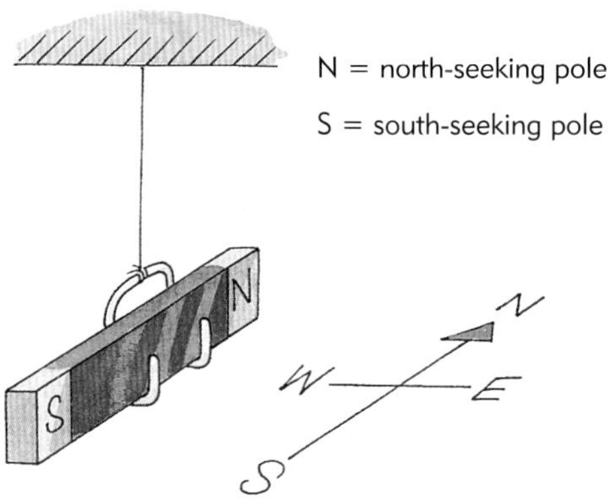

If a magnet is free to move, it ends up pointing north and south.

You can't always trust a compass

A magnetic compass doesn't always point north and south. The diagrams explain why.

8 Write down two places where you cannot trust a magnetic compass.

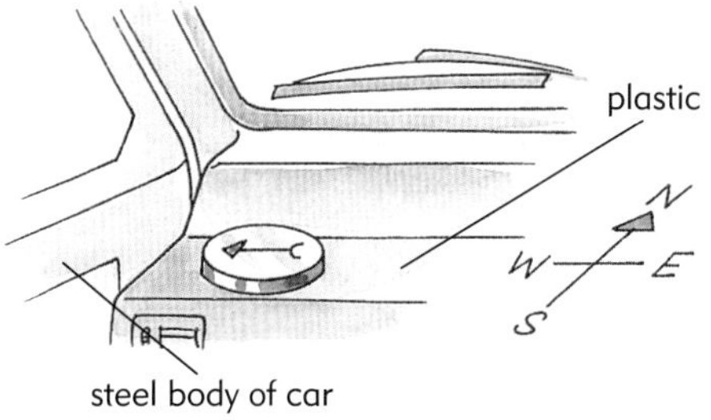

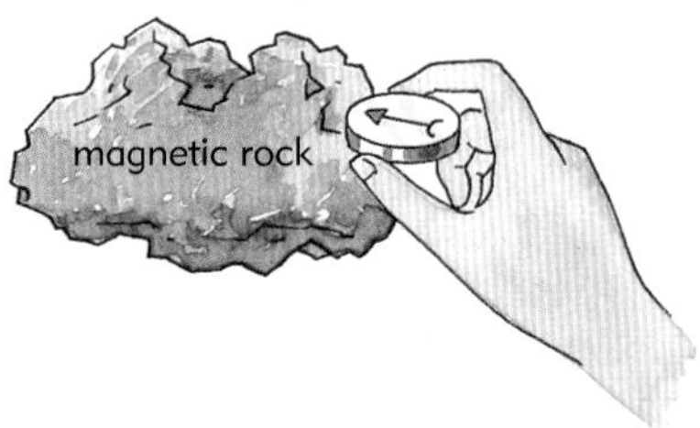

What you need to remember [Copy and complete using the **key words**]

Doing things with magnets

A force pulls together a magnet and anything made from ________________ or ________________.

We say they ________________ each other.

If a magnet is ________________ to ________________, it will come to rest pointing north and south.

The part of the magnet that points north is called the ________________**-seeking** ________________.

8

What do magnets do to each other?

Magnets can attract each other

As well as attracting things made from iron or steel, magnets can also attract each other.

Look at the diagram.

1 Which parts of the magnets attract each other?

REMEMBER

N = north-seeking pole of a magnet.

S = south-seeking pole of a magnet.

These magnets pull towards each other.

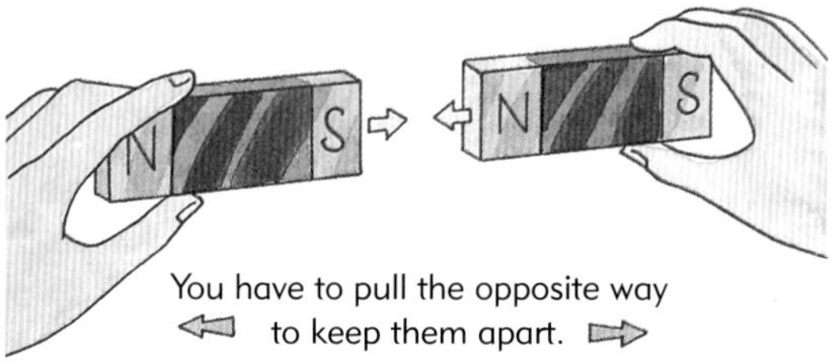

What happens if you turn one of the magnets round?

Two magnets are attracting each other. If you turn one of them round, they push each other away. We say that the magnets **repel**.

2 Which parts of the magnets repel each other?

3 Copy and complete the following sentences.

A south-seeking pole and a north-seeking pole __________.

Two south-seeking poles __________.

Two north-seeking poles __________.

Here is a simple way to remember what happens: **like** poles repel; **unlike** poles attract.

These magnets push each other away.

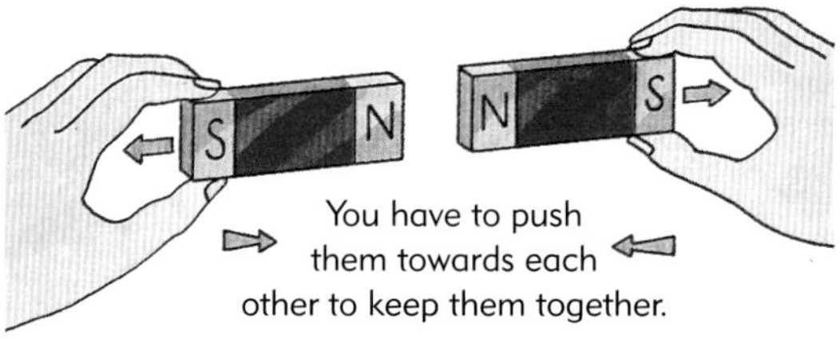

These magnets also repel.

Exploring magnets with a compass

A magnetic compass doesn't just tell you where north is. It can also tell you a lot about another magnet.

4 Look at the diagram. Then copy and complete the following sentences.

End A of the magnet attracts the __________-seeking pole of the compass and repels the __________ -seeking pole.
So end A must be a __________-seeking pole.

End B of the magnet does the opposite. So end B must be a __________-seeking pole.

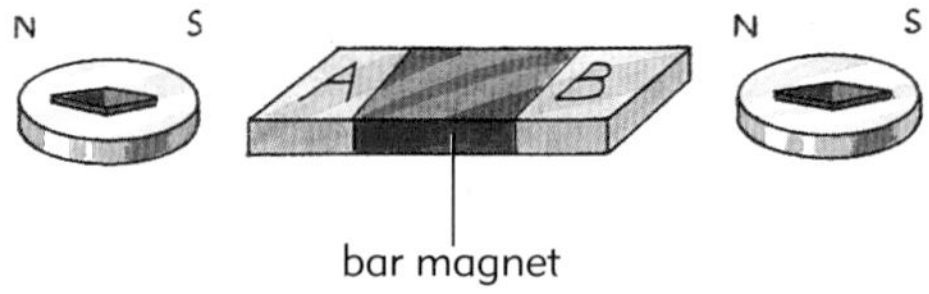

We can also draw a compass like this:

the arrowhead is the north-seeking pole.

Making maps of magnetic fields

A magnet affects a compass that is <u>anywhere</u> near the magnet. We say that there is a **magnetic field** around the magnet. You can use a magnetic compass to find out about the shape of a magnetic field.

5 Look at the diagram. Then copy and complete the following sentences.

We can use a magnetic compass to draw the lines of magnetic __________ around a magnet. These lines show us the shape of the magnet's magnetic __________.

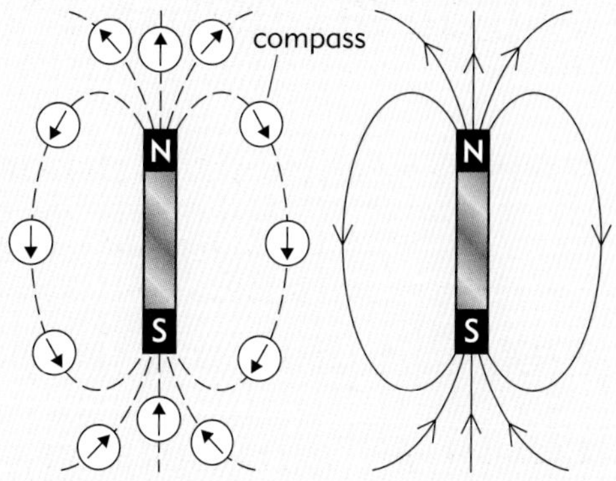

There is a magnetic field all around a magnet.

We can show a magnetic field by lines of magnetic force.

Magnets with unusual shapes

The poles of a magnet are not always at the ends.

Look at the diagrams.

6 One of the disc magnets 'floats' above the other.

Where are the poles of these magnets?

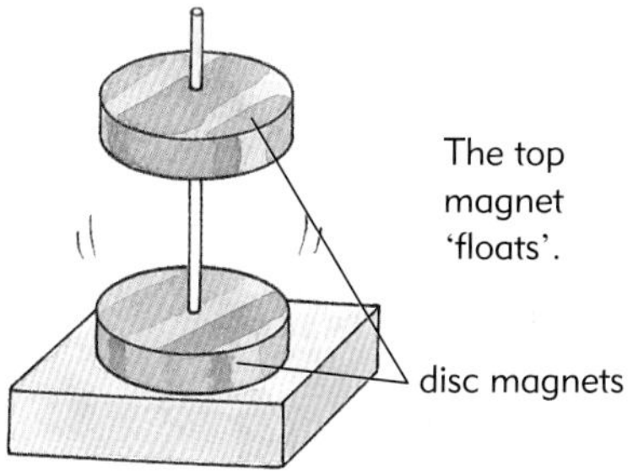

7 The poles of a magnetic strip are on the long flat faces.

Copy the diagram and complete it to show which way the compasses will point.

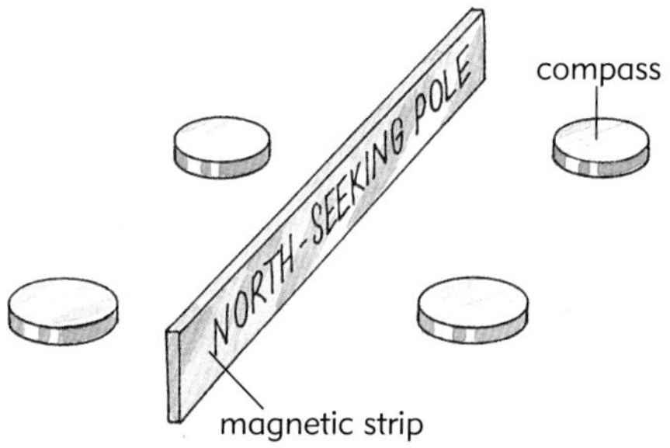

What you need to remember [Copy and complete using the **key words**]

What do magnets do to each other?

Two magnets may attract each other.
If one of them is then turned round they will __________.
Two poles that repel each other must be the same; they are __________ poles.
Two poles that attract each other must be different; they are __________ poles.
The area around a magnet that affects other magnets and pieces of iron or steel is called a __________ __________.

Using magnets to lift things

If you drop a box full of pins, you can pick them up with a **magnet**. If you have a strong enough magnet, you can use it to pick up a car.

1 Why can magnets pick up pins and cars?

A magnet that stays magnetised all the time is called a permanent magnet.

2 What's the problem with using a permanent magnet to pick up pins or scrap cars?

Magnets you can switch off

After you have picked up pins or scrap cars, you want to be able to drop them somewhere else. A permanent magnet can't do this. You need a magnet you can **switch** off.

You can make one by passing an electric current through a coil of wire. This is called an **electromagnet**. The coil has a **north-seeking pole** at one end and a **south-seeking pole** at the other end, just like a bar magnet.

3 Look at the diagram opposite. Copy and complete the table for when a current flows through the coil.

End of coil	Effect on magnetic compass	What this tells you
left	attracts ______-seeking pole repels ______ -seeking pole	this end of the coil is a ______-seeking pole
right	attracts ______-seeking pole repels ______ -seeking pole	this end of the coil is a ______-seeking pole

How can you make a stronger electromagnet?

An electromagnet must be strong enough for the job it has to do. To lift scrap cars it has to be very strong indeed.

The diagrams show three different ways to make an electromagnet **stronger**.

4 Write down three ways of making an electromagnet stronger.

REMEMBER

Magnets attract things made of steel. The north-seeking pole of a magnet:

- attracts a south-seeking pole
- repels another north-seeking pole.

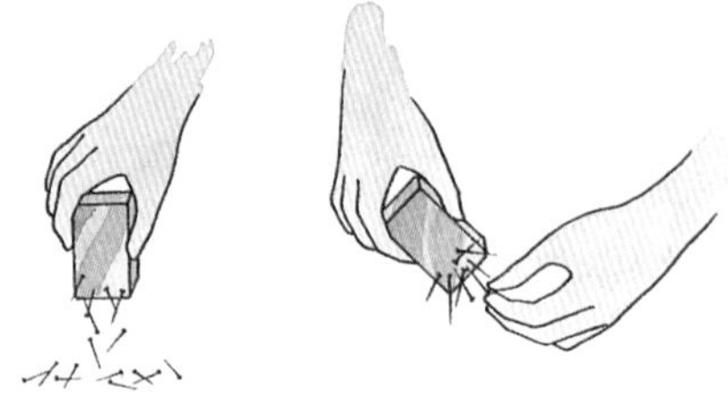

It's easy to pick up pins with a magnet. But it's not so easy to take them off.

You can pick up scrap cars with a very strong magnet. But you need to be able to drop them again.

A coil of copper wire does not move a compass needle. When a **current** flows through the coil, the compass needle moves.

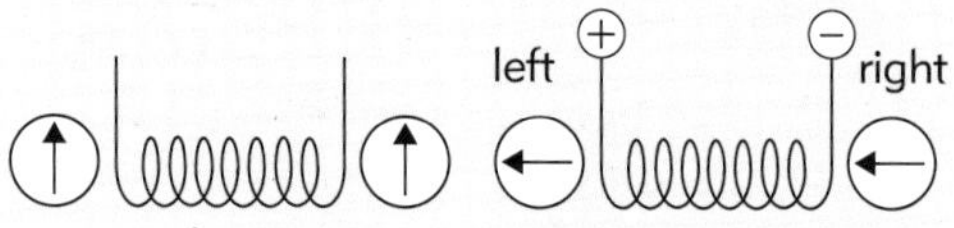

The coil is not a magnet. The coil is just like a bar magnet.

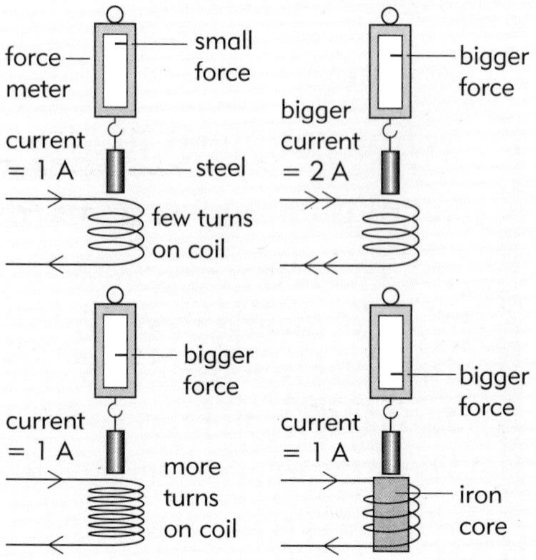

How a circuit breaker works

A circuit breaker breaks a circuit if the current is too large. Look at the diagrams of a circuit breaker.

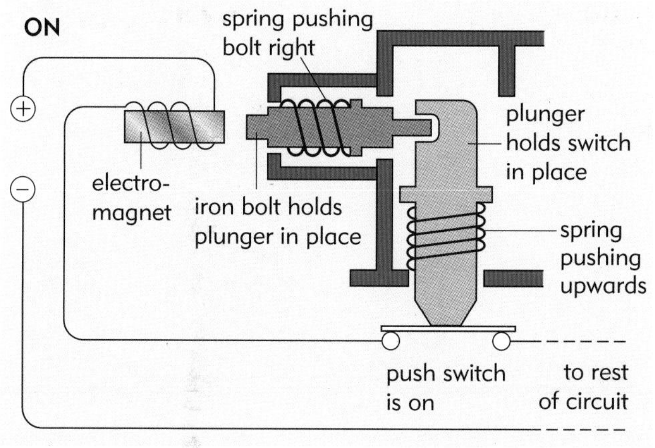

Normal current.

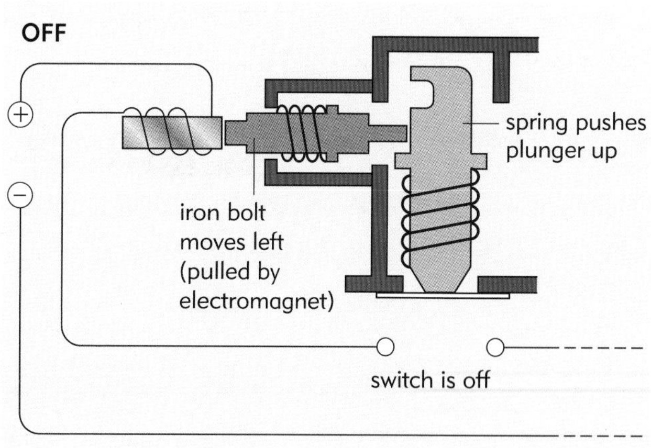

If the current is too big.

5 Use the following sentences to explain how the circuit breaker works. Write them down in the right order. The first sentence has been done for you.

A current that is bigger than normal makes the electromagnet stronger than normal.

- The plunger can then move up.
- To re-set the circuit breaker you push the plunger down.
- The push switch then goes to off.
- A stronger electromagnet pulls the iron bolt further to the left.

What you need to remember [Copy and complete using the **key words**]

Using magnets to lift things

When an electric ________________ flows through a coil of wire it acts like a bar ________________.
It has a **north-**________________ ________________ at one end and a ________________**-seeking pole** at the other end.
This type of magnet is called an ________________.
Electromagnets are useful because you can ________________ them off.
More turns, an iron core and a bigger current are three ways of making an electromagnet ________________.

[You won't be expected to draw a circuit breaker but you should be able to describe how it works.]

How do loudspeakers work?

Our lives wouldn't be the same without loudspeakers. Most of us spend a lot of hours each day listening to the sounds they make.

1 Write down three things that produce sounds using loudspeakers.

To understand how a loudspeaker works you need to know how it is built.

Loudspeakers make sounds.

How a loudspeaker is built

The diagrams show the main parts of a loudspeaker.

2 Copy and complete the following sentences.

A loudspeaker has a stiff cone made of __________ or __________.

The cone has a __________ edge so that it can move backwards and forwards.

A __________ is fixed to the centre of the cone at the back. Behind this is a strong __________.

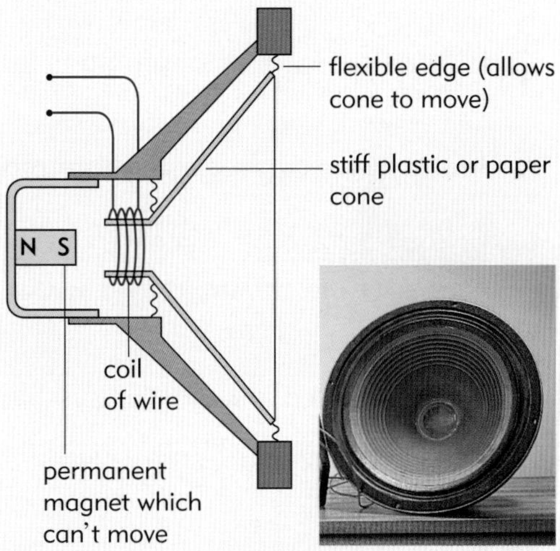

What happens when an electric current passes through the coil?

When an electric current passes through the coil it becomes a magnet.

3 Look at the diagram, then copy and complete the following sentences.

The left-hand end of the coil becomes a __________ -seeking pole.

This is __________ by the south-seeking pole of the permanent magnet.

So the cone of the loudspeaker moves to the __________.

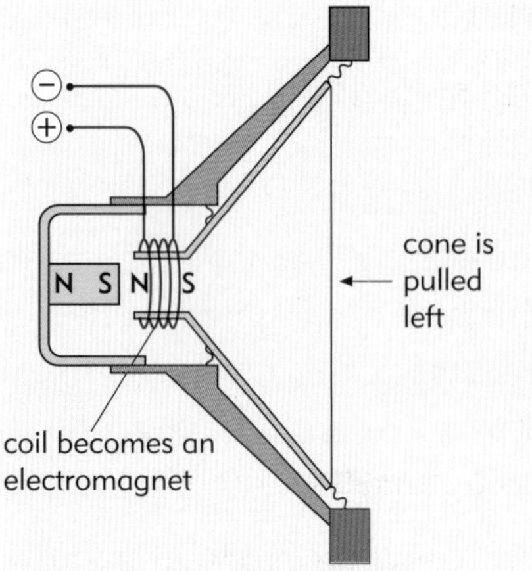

The permanent magnet attracts the electromagnet. So the cone moves to the left.

How can you make the cone move the opposite way?

The diagram shows how you can make the cone move back again to the right.

4 Copy and complete the following sentences.

To make the cone move the opposite way, you must send a current the __________ way through the coil.

The left-hand end of the coil then becomes a __________ -seeking pole.

It is then __________ by the permanent magnet so the cone moves to the __________.

How does a loudspeaker make sounds?

To produce a sound, the cone of the loudspeaker must move backwards and forwards over and over again. It must **vibrate**. To make the cone vibrate, the direction of the current must be changed over and over again.

5 What type of current keeps changing direction?

Look at the diagram.

6 Copy and complete the following sentences.

The cone of the loudspeaker __________ in time with the alternating current that goes through the coil. This means that the frequency of the sound is the same as the frequency of the __________ __________.

The loudspeaker makes a louder sound if the current is increased.

REMEMBER

An alternating current is a current that keeps on changing direction.

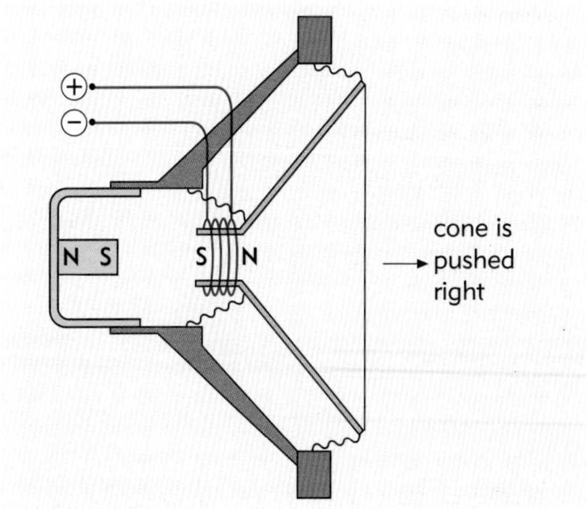

If you reverse the current, the poles of the electromagnet reverse. So the permanent magnet repels the electromagnet, and the cone moves to the right.

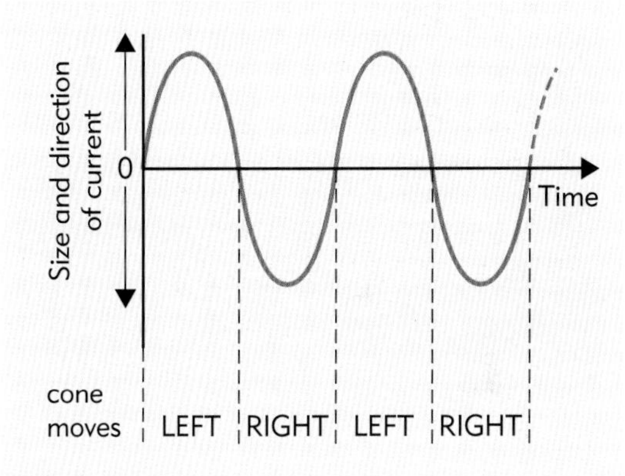

The cone vibrates in time with the **alternating** current. It has the same **frequency**.

What you need to remember [Copy and complete using the **key words**]

How do loudspeakers work?

To reverse the poles of an electromagnet, you need to __________________ the direction of the current that flows through it. This idea is used to make the cone of a loudspeaker __________________ and produce a sound.
An __________________ current is fed into the coil of the loudspeaker. This produces a sound with the same __________________ as the a.c.

[You won't be expected to draw the parts of a loudspeaker. But you may be given a drawing and be asked to explain how it works.]

11 How do electric motors work?

Many of the things we use every day use magnets to make things move. They usually have an electric **motor** inside them. The electric motor uses electricity to produce movement.

1 Write down six things that use electricity to produce movement.

> **REMEMBER**
>
> Like poles repel. Unlike poles attract.

All these things use electric motors.

How does an electric motor move?

An electric motor uses the force between magnets to produce movement. Look at the diagrams of an electric motor.

2 Copy and complete the following sentences.

In the electric motor, there is an electromagnet called the ___________.

This is on an ___________ so that it can spin.

It is placed between the poles of a ___________ magnet.

When a current flows through the **armature** it becomes a magnet.

The north- and south-seeking poles of the armature are shown in the diagram.

3 Copy and complete the following sentences.

The north-seeking pole of the armature is next to the ___________-seeking pole of the permanent magnet. So they will ___________.

The ___________-seeking poles of the two magnets will also repel.

This means that the armature will ___________ until it faces the opposite way.

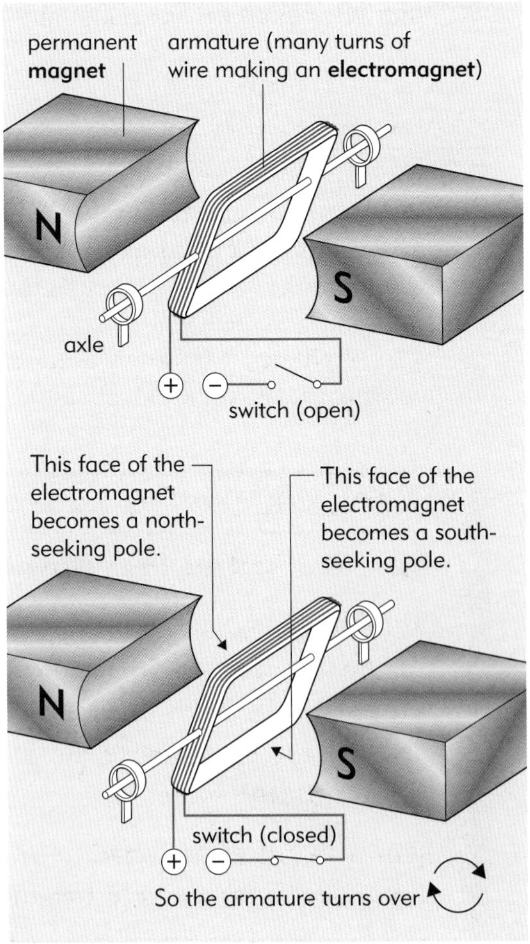

How does a motor keep on turning?

The armature of an electric motor doesn't just turn over and then stop. It keeps on turning. The diagrams show how you can make it do this.

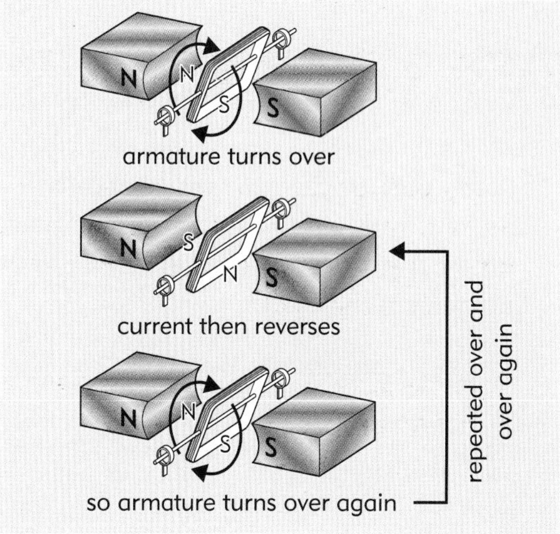

4 Use the following sentences to explain what happens. Write them down in the right order.

- The poles of the armature are once again repelled by the permanent magnet.
- Each time the armature turns over the current is reversed.
- So the armature turns over again.
- This reverses the poles of the armature.

You don't have to sit there and keep **reversing** the current yourself. A split ring on the axle does this automatically each time the armature turns over. Electricity reaches the armature through graphite brushes which rub against the split ring.

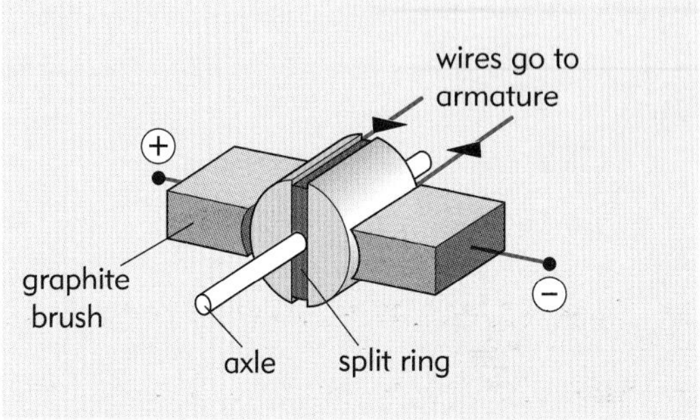

Sending electricity like this stops the wires to the power supply getting twisted.

5 What other problem does this solve?

How to make a more powerful motor

An electric motor must be powerful enough for the job it has to do. To make a more powerful motor, you need a bigger force between the permanent magnet and the armature.

6 Write down <u>four</u> things you could do to make this force bigger.

REMEMBER

To make an electromagnet stronger:

- increase the current
- increase the number of turns in the coil
- use an iron core.

What you need to remember [Copy and complete using the **key words**]

How do electric motors work?

An electric ________________ uses electricity to produce movement.
The forces between a permanent ________________ and an ________________ are used to produce this movement. The electromagnet is called an ________________.
The armature of a motor keeps on turning because the current is ________________ over and over again.

[You will not be expected to draw an electric motor, but you might be given a drawing and be asked to explain how it works.]

How to make a magnet move a copper wire

A magnet only attracts certain metals. It has no effect on things made from copper. But it does have an effect on a copper wire if an electric **current** is flowing through it.

The diagram shows this effect.

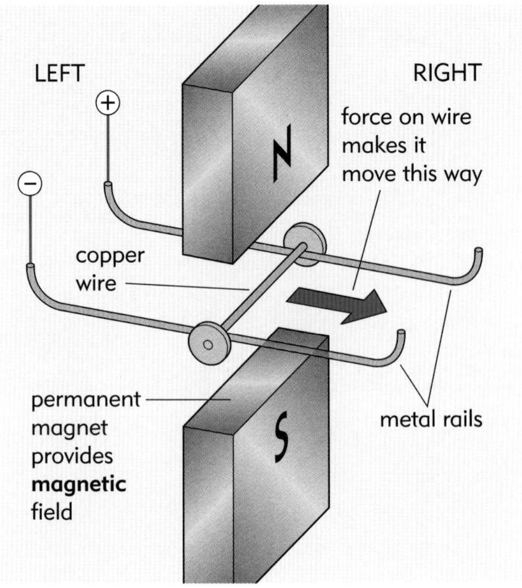

1 Copy and complete the following sentences.

When a current is flowing, the copper wire rolls to the __________.

This shows that a __________ is pushing it in this direction.

What happens if you reverse the current?

You can **reverse** the current by swapping the + and − connections to the power supply. The diagram shows what then happens.

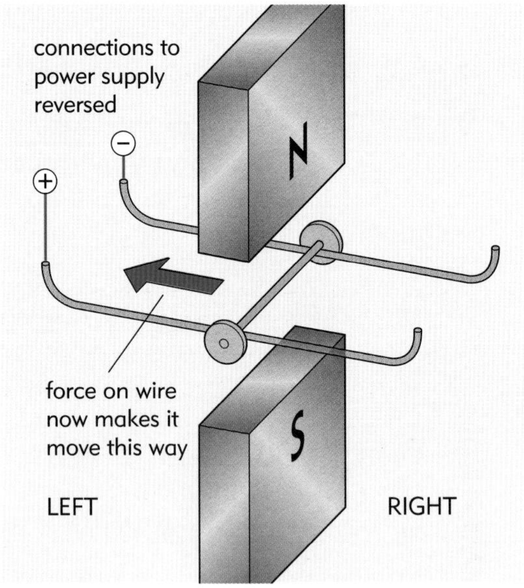

2 Copy and complete the following sentences.

The copper wire now rolls to the __________.

Reversing the current reverses the direction of the __________ that acts on the wire.

There is something else you can do to make the wire move the opposite way. You can swap round the **poles** of the permanent magnet.

Another way of explaining electric motors

The diagram shows a very simple electric motor.

3 Look at the diagram. Then copy and complete the following sentences.

The wire at the top of the coil is pushed to the __________.

The current in the wire at the bottom of the coil is in the opposite direction.

So this wire is pushed to the __________.

These two forces make the coil __________ in an __________ direction.

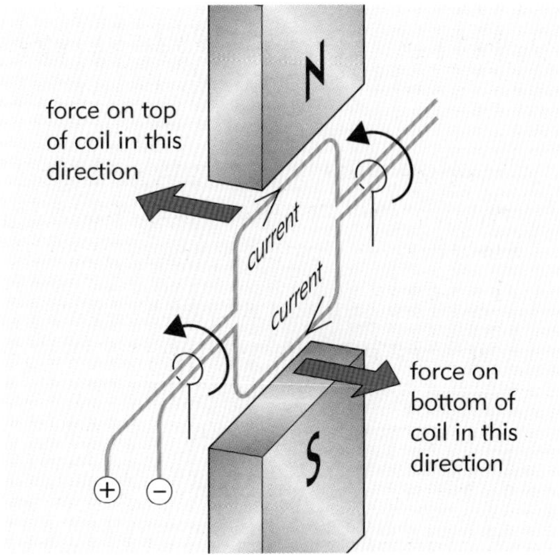

The forces on the top and bottom of the coil are in opposite directions, so the coil turns (anticlockwise).

Making a more powerful motor

A motor with only one coil is very weak.
To make it stronger you need to have lots of coils of wire.

4 Write down at least two other ways of making the motor more powerful.

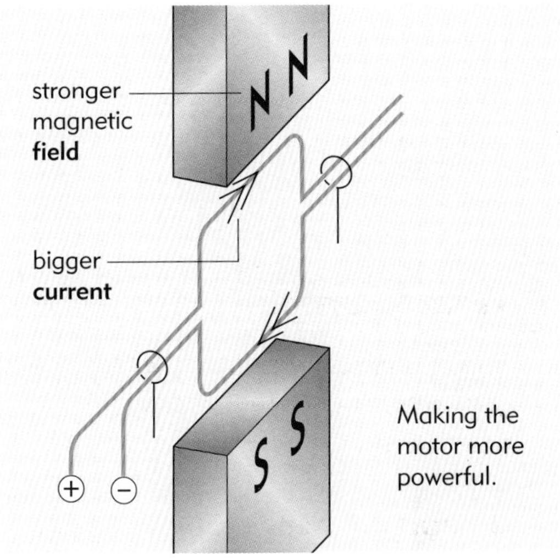

Making the motor more powerful.

What you need to remember [Copy and complete using the **key words**]

How to make a magnet move a copper wire

A __________ field will only move a copper wire if an electric __________ flows through the wire.

To make the wire move the opposite way you can:

- __________ the direction of the current
- reverse the __________ of the permanent magnet.

The size of the force acting on a wire can be increased:

- by increasing the size of the __________ through the wire
- by increasing the strength of the magnetic __________.

[You will not be expected to draw a diagram of the electric motor. But you might be given a diagram and be asked to explain how it works.]

13 Electricity that can make your hair stand on end

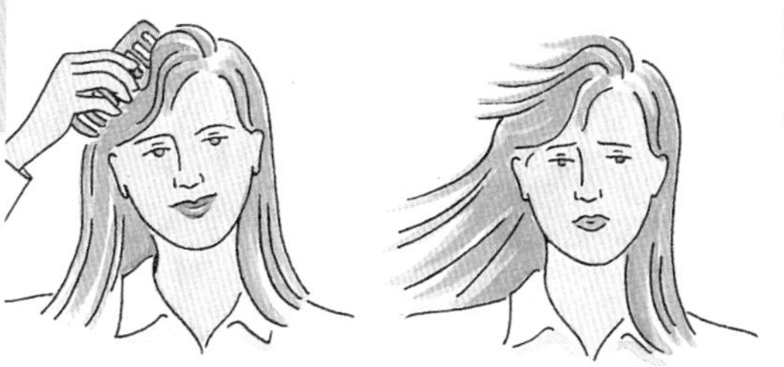

Combing your hair produces static electricity.

Your hairs then push each other away. They **repel**.

Electricity doesn't always flow through circuits. Electricity can also stay just where it is. This is called **static** electricity.

You can produce static electricity by rubbing together two **different** materials. We say that we have **charged** the materials with electricity.

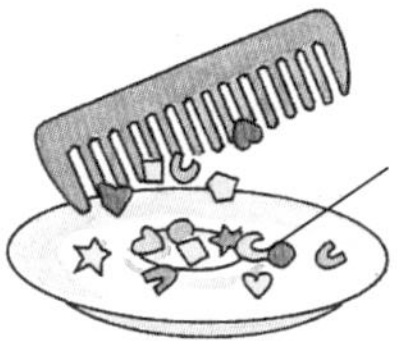

Your comb will also then **attract** small bits of dust or paper.

1 Combing your hair can produce static electricity.

(a) Why does this happen?

(b) Write down two ways in which you can tell when it happens.

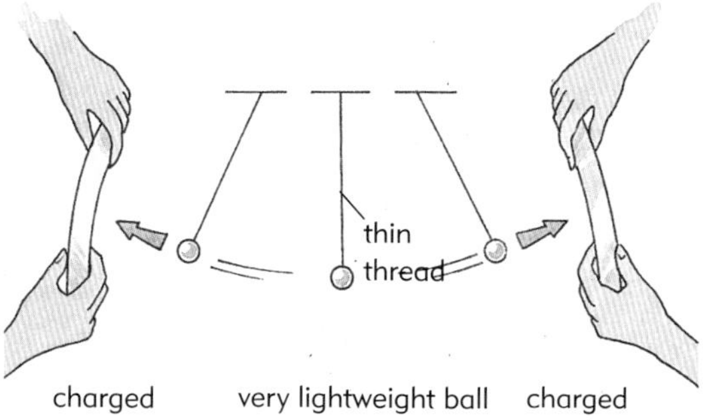

Is all static electricity the same?

You can rub two strips of plastic with a cloth. This charges them with static electricity. The diagrams show what the charged strips of plastic will then do.

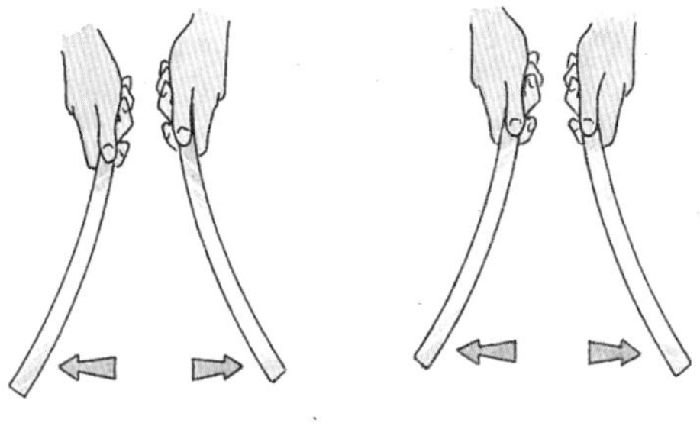

two charged polythene strips

two charged acetate strips

2 Copy the sentences. Then use the words attract and repel to complete them.

Two charged strips made from the same plastic __________ each other.

A charged polythene strip and a charged acetate strip __________ each other.

Both charged strips will also __________ light objects that do not have a charge.

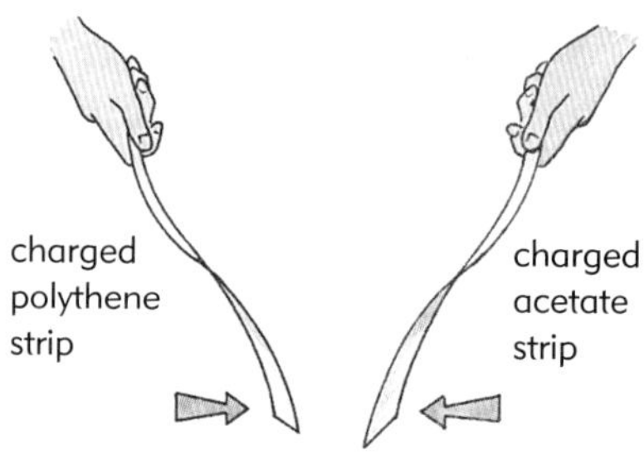

Charged objects sometimes attract and sometimes repel.

This means that there must be different types of electrical charge.

Two types of charge

Two polythene strips that are rubbed with the same cloth must have the same kind of charge. These charges repel.

Two acetate strips rubbed with the same cloth must have the same kind of charge. These charges also repel.

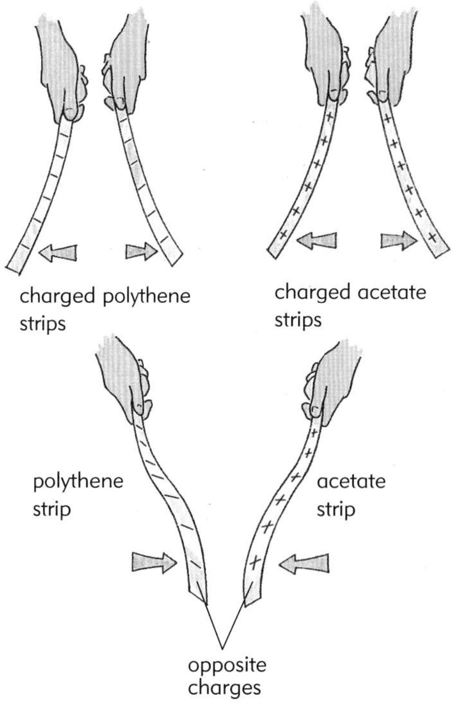

3 Copy and complete the following sentences.

Objects that have the __________ type of electrical charge repel each other.

So if two charged objects attract each other they must have __________ electrical charges.

Here is a simple way to remember what happens:
like charges repel; **unlike** charges attract.

The charge you get on a polythene strip when you rub it is called **negative** (–).

The charge you get on an acetate strip when you rub it is called **positive** (+).

4 Copy and complete the table.

Charge		Do the strips attract or repel?
First strip	Second strip	
+	+	
+	–	
–	–	

Really making hair stand on end

You can use an electrostatic machine to make hair really stand on end.

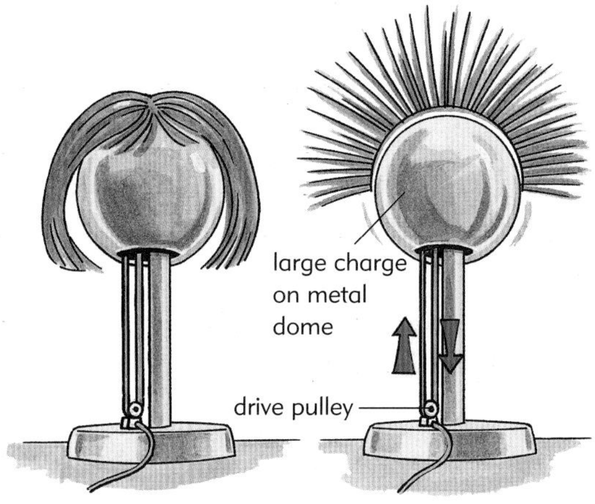

Electrostatic generator. The belt becomes charged as it rubs against the drive pulley. The charge on the belt rubs off on the dome.

5 Explain how this happens, as fully as you can.

What you need to remember [Copy and complete using the **key words**]

Electricity that can make your hair stand on end

When you rub two ________________ materials together they become ________________ with electricity. This is called ________________ electricity.
There are two types of charge, called ________________ (+) and ________________ (–).
Charges of the same type ________________ each other.
Charges of different types ________________ each other.
We say: ________________ charges repel; ________________ charges attract.

14 Why rubbing things together produces electricity

It's all down to electrons

When you rub two different materials together, **electrons** are rubbed off one material and on to the other. These electrons are very tiny. Each electron carries a small electrical charge.

If you rub two pieces of the *same* material together, electrons don't move.

To start with, a cloth and a polythene strip have no overall charge.
When you rub them together, you make electrons move.

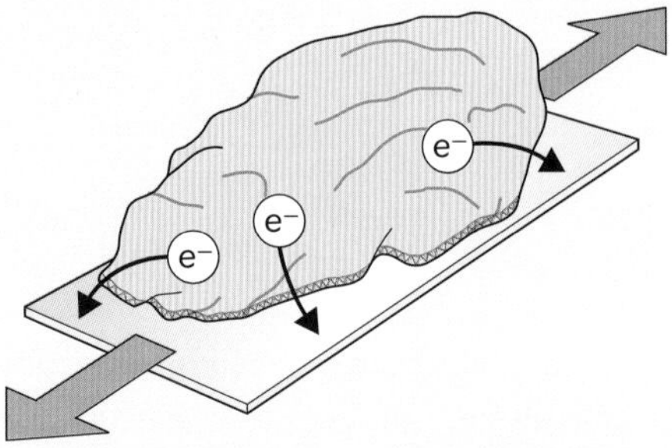

(e⁻) = electron

Each electron carries a small, **negative** electron charge.

1 When you rub two different materials together they become charged. Why?

2 What type of electrical charge does each electron carry?

Why rubbing polythene gives it a negative charge

The diagrams show what happens when you rub polythene with a cloth.

The cloth loses electrons. So it ends up with a positive charge.

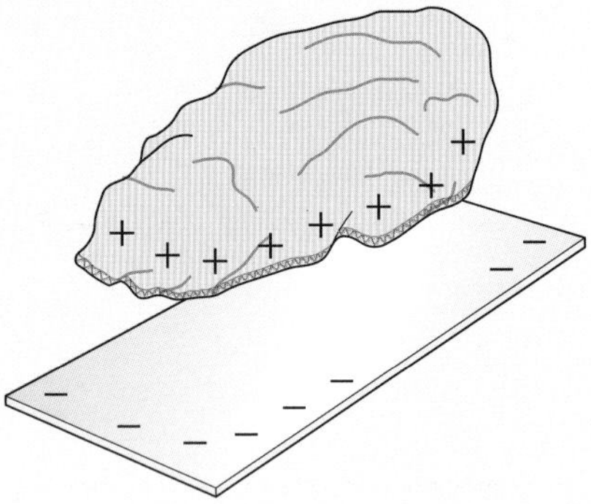

The polythene gains electrons. So it ends up with a negative charge.

3 Copy and complete the following sentence.

When you rub a piece of polythene with a cloth you make electrons move from the __________ to the __________.

4 Explain the following, as fully as you can.

(a) Why the polythene ends up with a negative charge.

(b) Why the cloth ends up with a positive charge.

5 The negative charge on the polythene is exactly **equal** to the positive charge on the cloth. Why is this?

Why rubbing acetate gives it a positive charge

When you rub a piece of acetate with a cloth, the acetate becomes positively charged.

6 (a) What type of charge do you get on a cloth when you rub a piece of acetate with it?

(b) What happens to electrons as you rub the acetate with a cloth?

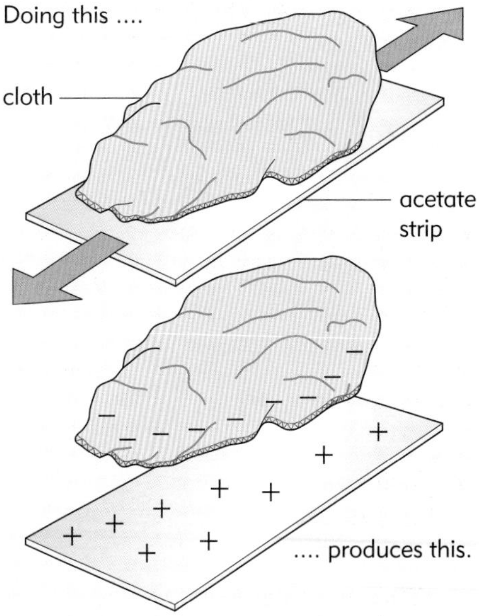

Peeling things apart

Peeling two different materials apart has the same effect as rubbing them together.

Electrons are transferred from one material to the other.

7 Copy and complete the following sentence.

When you peel different materials apart, one of them becomes __________ charged and the other becomes __________ charged.

8 When you peel some sticky tape from a roll it often tries to go back on again.

Explain, as fully as you can, why it does this.

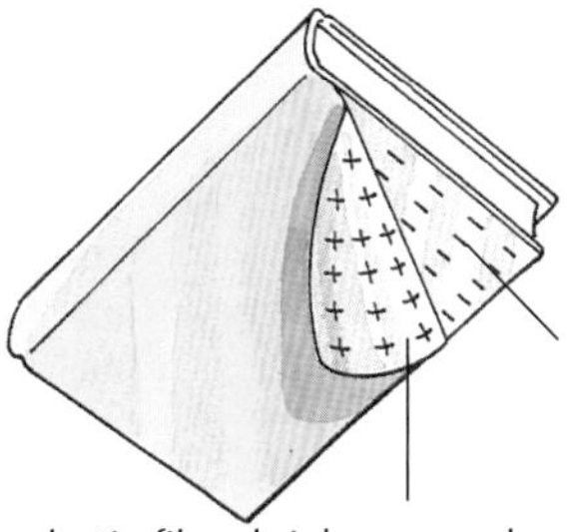

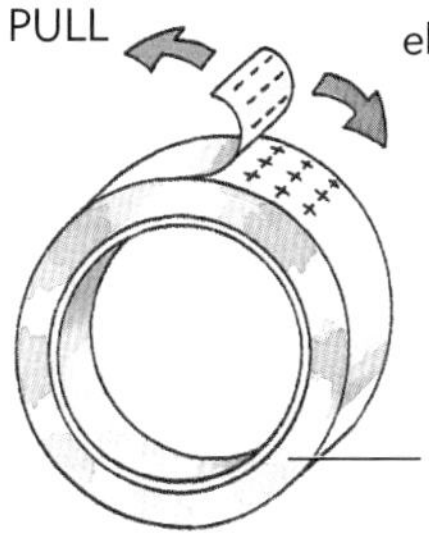

What you need to remember [Copy and complete using the **key words**]

Why rubbing things together produces electricity

When two different materials are rubbed together, __________ are rubbed off one material and on to the other.
Each electron carries a small, __________ electrical charge.
The material that gains electrons becomes __________ charged.
The material that loses electrons becomes __________ charged.
These two charges are exactly __________ in size.

Making use of static electricity

We can use static electricity in many different ways to do useful jobs.

1 Write down four different uses for static electricity.

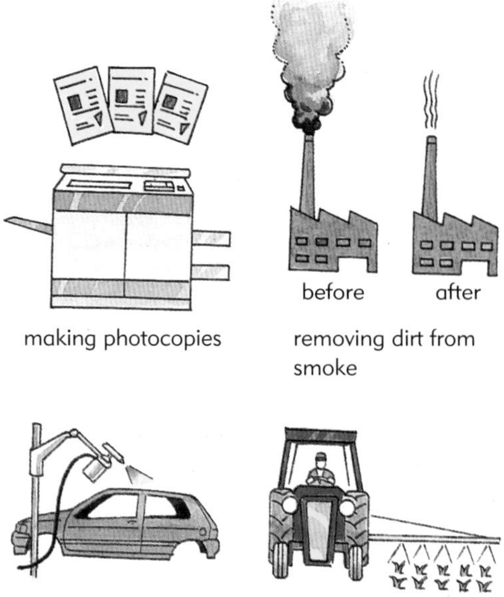
before
after
making photocopies
removing dirt from smoke
spraying car bodies
spraying crops
Using static electricity.

How a photocopier works

We take photocopiers for granted, but schools and offices could not manage without them.

The diagrams below show, step by step, how a photocopy is made.

2 Look carefully at the diagrams. Then use the following sentences to explain how a photocopy is made. Write the sentences down in the right order. The first one is in the right place.

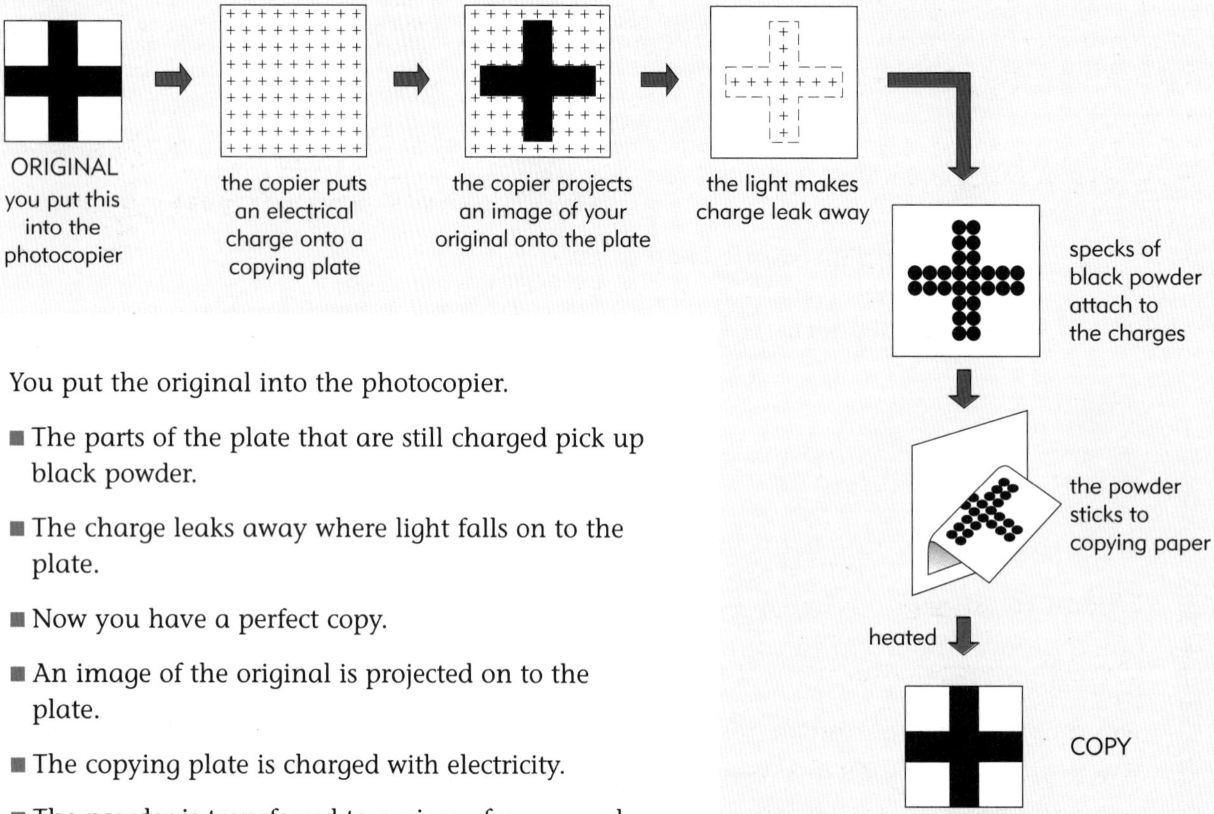
ORIGINAL
you put this into the photocopier
the copier puts an electrical charge onto a copying plate
the copier projects an image of your original onto the plate
the light makes charge leak away
specks of black powder attach to the charges
the powder sticks to copying paper
heated
COPY

You put the original into the photocopier.

- The parts of the plate that are still charged pick up black powder.
- The charge leaks away where light falls on to the plate.
- Now you have a perfect copy.
- An image of the original is projected on to the plate.
- The copying plate is charged with electricity.
- The powder is transferred to a piece of paper and heated so that it sticks.

How to remove the dirt from smoke

Smoke contains lots of tiny bits of dirt. This dirt falls on houses and gardens. If people breathe in the dirt, it can damage their lungs.

The diagram shows how the dirt can be removed from factory chimneys.

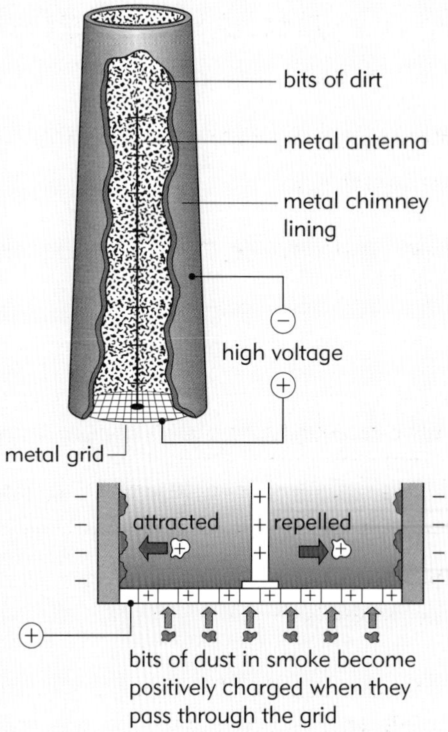

3 Copy and complete the following sentences.

A metal grid and antenna are connected to the positive side of a high __________ supply.

The metal chimney is connected to the __________ side of the supply.

Tiny bits of dirt pick up a __________ charge as they pass through the grid. They are then __________ by the antenna and __________ by the chimney.

So the dirt collects on the inside of the __________ and is removed every so often.

How to make a spray hit its target

When a liquid is sprayed out of a nozzle, it becomes electrically charged. Sprays can be made to charge the droplets as much as possible. The diagrams show how this helps the spray to find its target.

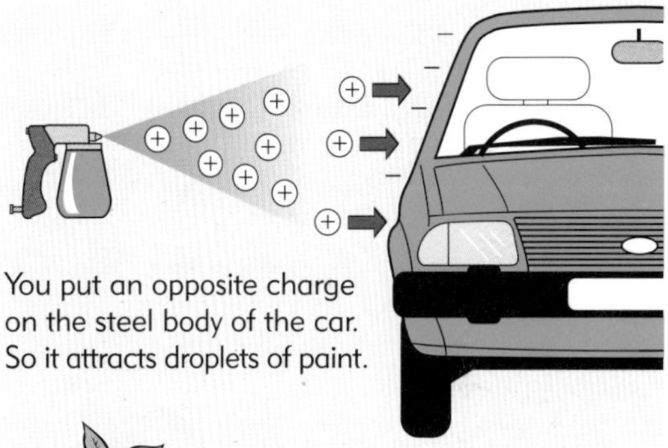

You put an opposite charge on the steel body of the car. So it attracts droplets of paint.

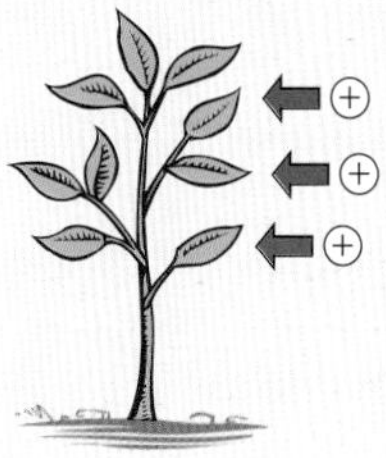

Charged droplets of pesticide are tiny enough to be attracted to the leaves (like dust to a comb). So less falls to the ground.

4 Explain why a pesticide spray works better if it charges the droplets of pesticide.

5 Car makers want most of the paint from a spray to end up on a car body. What can they do to the car body to make sure this happens?

What you need to remember

Making use of static electricity

You may be asked to choose your own example of using static electricity and explain how it works. You may also be given some information about an example and then be asked to explain what is happening, just like on this page.

Danger from sparks

Static electricity can produce sparks. Often these sparks are very small. But sometimes they are huge.

1 Look at the pictures. Then copy and complete the table.

	Size of sparks (large or small)	How the static charge is produced
television screen		
lightning		
taking off a sweater		

Large sparks such as lightning can kill people. But even quite small sparks can be very dangerous.

Clouds rubbing together produce huge static electrical charges. These may cause lightning.

A sweater rubbing on a shirt produces static electricity. You sometimes see and hear lots of small sparks.

In a TV tube electrons are fired at the screen. The screen may become charged.

Small sparks may then jump from the screen onto your hand.

■ Fire hazards with petrol tankers

Petrol is very flammable. A very small spark can cause a serious fire when petrol or petrol vapour is open to the air.

At filling stations, petrol is transferred from tankers to underground tanks. There must be no sparks while this is being done.

2 In what <u>two</u> ways can petrol tankers produce static electricity?

3 Write down <u>two</u> things that are done to prevent sparks.

A static charge can build up on a petrol tanker because of the tyres rubbing on the road.

A static charge can also build up as petrol flows through a pipe.

Metal strap. This is connected to the tank before the tank is opened.

from tanker

petrol

underground metal tank connected to earth

■ Preventing explosions at flour mills

Flour is made by grinding wheat to a very fine powder. The bits of flour make the air very dusty. This mixture of flour and air can be very dangerous. Just a tiny spark can make it explode.

Look at the diagrams.

4 There a danger of a spark between the pipe and the container. Explain why.

5 How can such a spark be avoided?

metal pipe

flour

metal vat

metal strap

conductor to earth

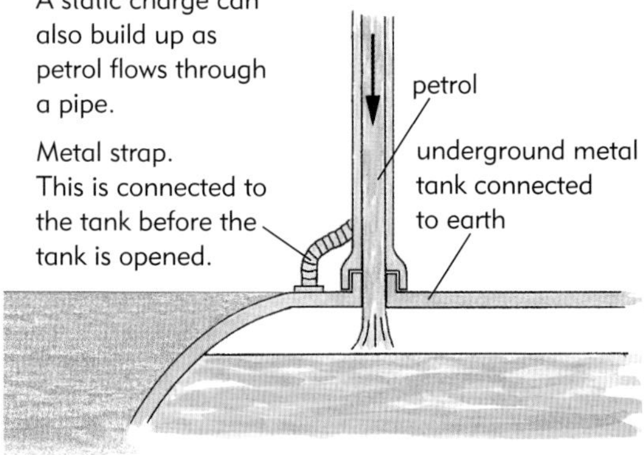

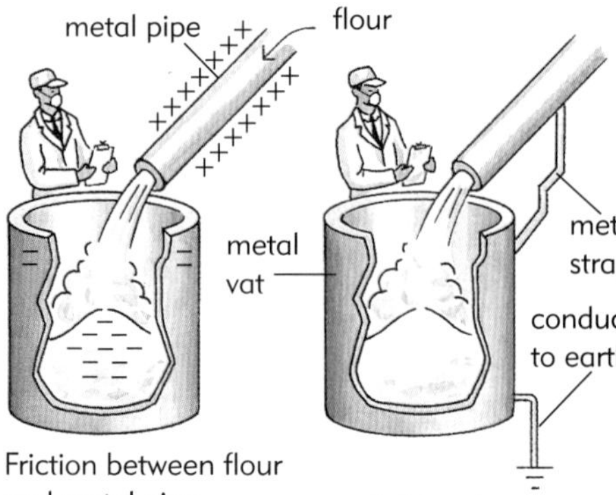

Friction between flour and metal pipe produces static charges.

Solving the problem.

Handle chips with care

People who put electronic chips into circuits have special mats on their workbenches. These mats conduct electricity and are connected to earth. The people sometimes also wear wrist straps connected to earth.

6 Explain, as fully as you can, why these precautions are needed.

An electronic chip is easily damaged by static electricity.

Why does earthing work?

To earth something, you must connect it to the **earth** with a **conductor**. The conductor allows electrons to flow through it. This is a current of electricity. The diagrams show how earthing works.

7 Look at the diagrams, then copy and complete the following sentences.

When a negatively charged, conducting object is earthed, __________ move from the object to earth.

When a positively charged object is earthed, electrons move from the __________ to the __________.

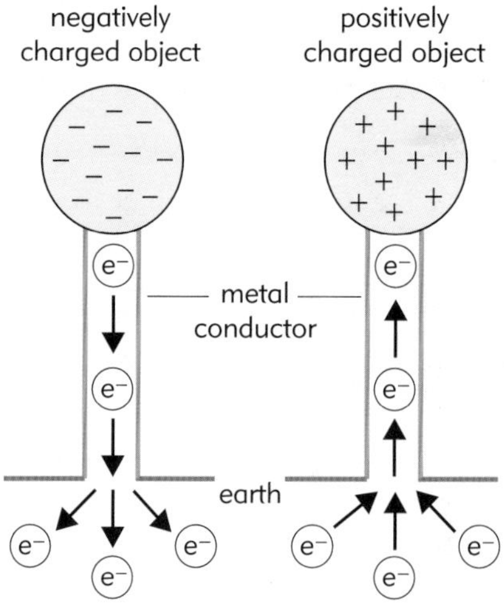

Electrons move until the object is discharged.

What you need to remember [Copy and complete using the **key words**]

Danger from sparks

A charged conductor can be discharged by connecting it to the ______________ with a ______________.

[You must be able to describe an example of where static electricity can be dangerous and explain how the danger can be avoided. You may also be given information about an example and be asked to explain it.]

17 How to produce an electric current

REMEMBER

An electric current that keeps changing direction is called an alternating current (a.c. for short).

Static electricity is useful. For example, we can use it to make photocopies. But most of the electrical appliances we use need an electric current.

1 A photocopier needs an electric current as well as static electricity.

What does it need an electric current for?

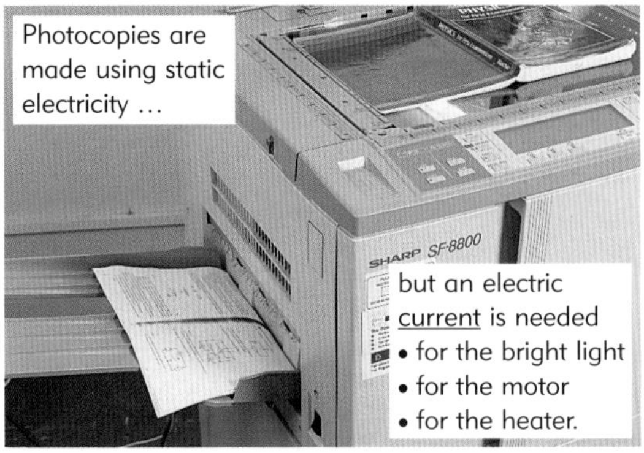

Photocopies are made using static electricity …
but an electric current is needed
• for the bright light
• for the motor
• for the heater.
SHARP SF-8800

A home-made generator

All you need to produce an electric current is a **magnet** and a coil of wire. The diagrams show you what to do.

2 Make a copy of the table. Then complete it.

What you do with the magnet	What the meter tells you
move it into the coil	
hold it still inside the coil	
move it out of the coil	

3 What difference does it make if the N and S poles of the magnet are the other way round?

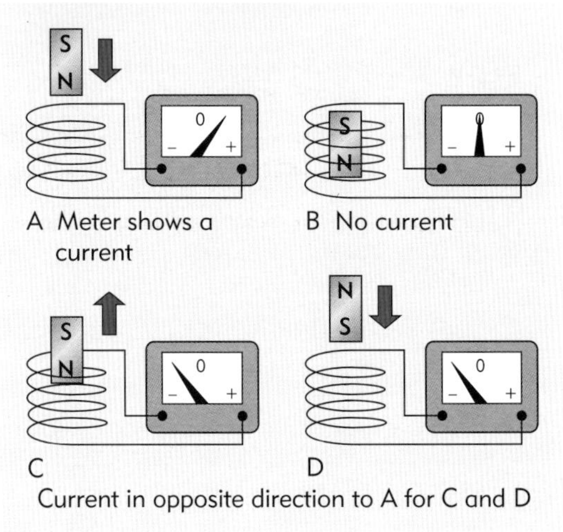

S
N
0
A Meter shows a current
B No current
C
D
Current in opposite direction to A for C and D

How can you produce a bigger current?

When we produce an electric current using a magnet and a coil of wire, we say we have **induced** the current.

4 Look at the diagrams.

Write down three things you can do to induce a bigger current.

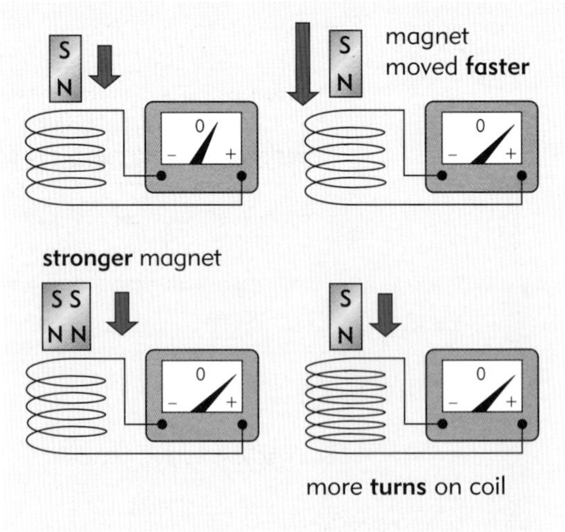

magnet moved **faster**
stronger magnet
more **turns** on coil

How can you keep on producing a current?

To keep on producing a current you can keep on moving a magnet into and out of a coil.

5 Look at the diagram. What kind of electric current is produced by moving a magnet into and out of a coil?

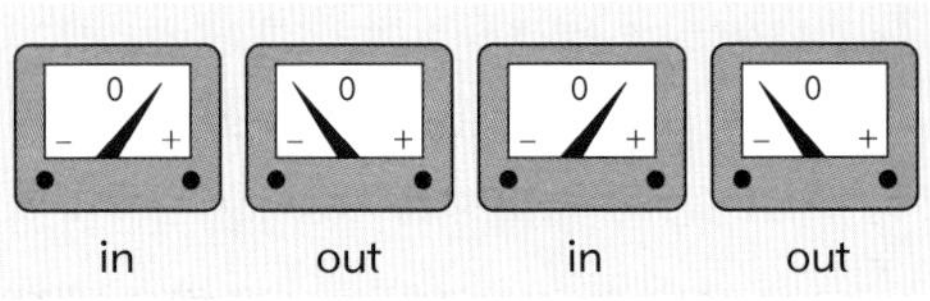

in
out
in
out

You also get an alternating current when a magnet **spins** inside a coil. This is how a cycle dynamo works.

6 The lights on a cycle sometimes work from a dynamo. Explain each of the following.

(a) The lights go off when the cyclist stops at some traffic lights.

(b) The lights are brighter when the cyclist is going downhill.

7 A dynamo spins but is not connected to any lamps.

Copy and complete the following sentences.

There isn't a ________ circuit without a lamp. So the dynamo produces a voltage but not a ________.

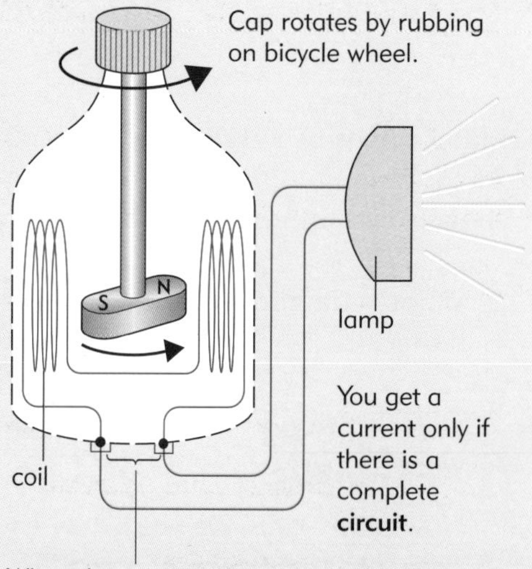
Cap rotates by rubbing on bicycle wheel.
S
N
lamp
coil
You get a current only if there is a complete **circuit**.

When the magnet rotates, you always get a **voltage** across the ends of the coil.

Generators in power stations

The generators in power stations are very large. They need very powerful magnets.

8 What makes the magnets work in a large generator?

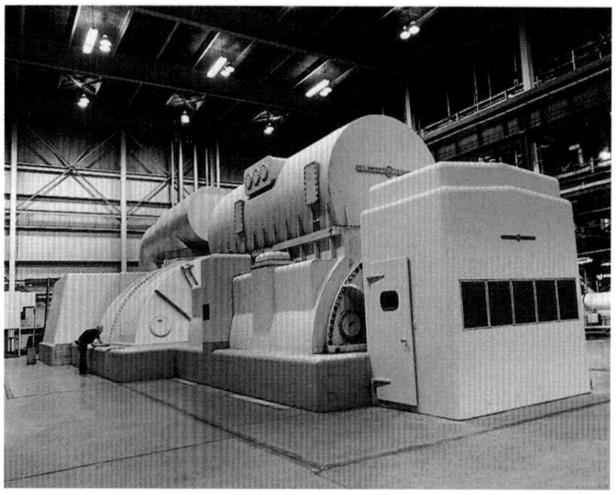

These generators use large electromagnets which work from a d.c. supply.

What you need to remember [Copy and complete using the **key words**]

How to produce an electric current

You can produce an electric current by moving a ________ into a coil of wire. We say that the current has been ________.

If you move the magnet <u>out</u> of the coil or move the <u>opposite end</u> of the magnet into the coil, you get a current in the ________ direction.

To induce a bigger current you can:

- use a ________ magnet;
- move the magnet ________;
- have more ________ on the coil of wire.

In a generator, a magnet ________ inside a coil of wire.

This induces a current if the coil is connected to a complete ________.

Otherwise it induces a ________ but not a current.

How many batteries do I need?

Many things need electricity to work. Some of these things plug in to the mains electricity. The diagram shows some things that work from batteries.

1 What is the proper name for what we often call a battery?

2 Different things need different numbers of cells to work properly.

How many cells are needed by each of the things shown in the diagram?

cycle lamp bulb with two **cells**

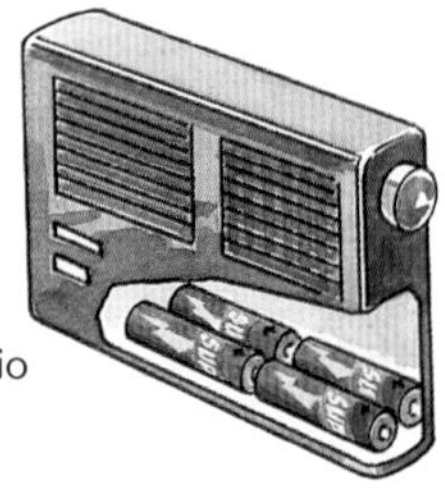

Why does a cycle lamp need two cells?

For a cycle without a dynamo, the cells in a cycle lamp provide the push that forces an electric current through the bulb. The lamp needs two cells connected **in series** (in line) to provide enough push to make it light properly.

Electrical push is called **voltage**. Voltage is also called **potential difference.**

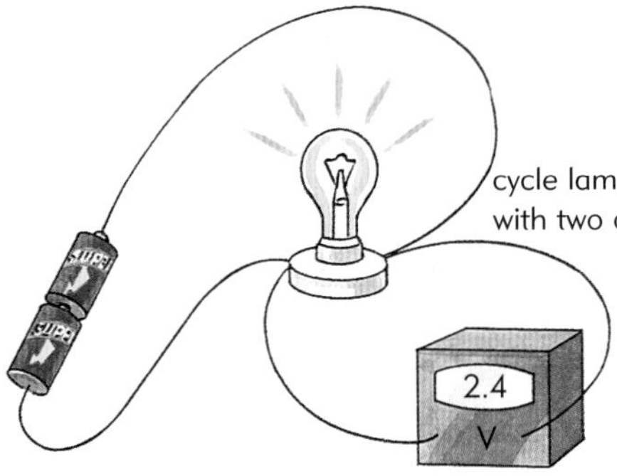

The bulb lights normally.

How to measure voltage

You can measure voltage using a **voltmeter**. To measure the voltage that is pushing a current through a bulb, you connect the voltmeter across the bulb. The diagram shows you how to do this. We say the voltmeter is connected **in parallel** with the bulb.

Voltage is measured in **volts** (**V** for short).

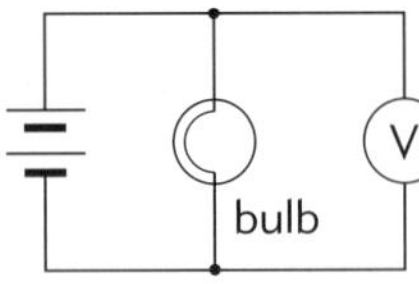

3 What voltage do the two cells supply to the cycle lamp bulb?

4 The diagram shows two cells connected the opposite way round.

What voltage do these two cells give? Give a reason for your answer.

These cells are pushing in opposite directions. Their total voltage is zero.

What happens if you use the wrong number of cells?

Cycle lamp bulb with one cell.

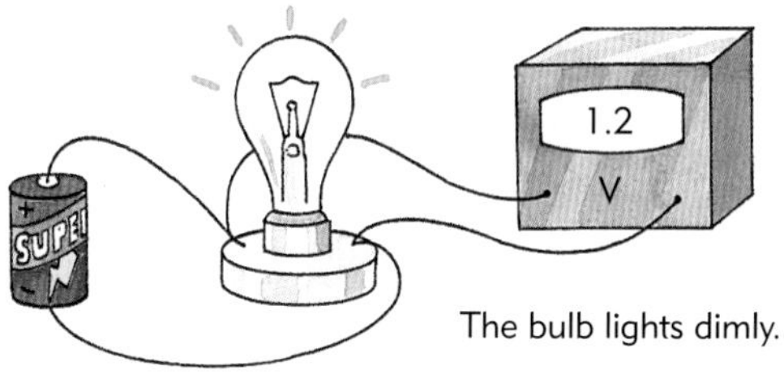

The bulb lights dimly.

Cycle lamp bulb with three cells.

The bulb lights very brightly but does not last long.

5 Copy the table. Then use the information from the diagrams to complete it.

The diagram for two cells is on page 82.

Number of cells (connected in series)	Total voltage
1	
2	
3	

6 What pattern do you see in the voltages when you connect cells together?

7 What voltages do the cycle lamp, radio and clock from question 2 need to work properly?

What is a battery?

A **battery** is made up of two or more **cells** joined together. When you connect cells in series you can **add** their voltages to get the total.

8 What voltage does each cell in the car battery provide?

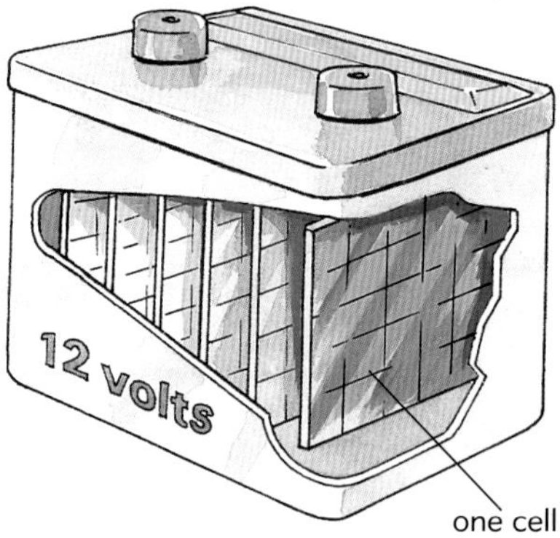

What you need to remember [Copy and complete using the **key words**]

How many batteries do I need?

To make an electric current flow through a bulb there must be a ________________ (also called a ________________ **difference**) across it.
We measure voltage in units called ________________ (______ for short) using a ________________.
This meter is connected **in** ________________ with the bulb.
To get a bigger voltage, you can connect more than one cell **in** ________________.
This is called a ________________.
To find the total voltage of a battery, you should ________________ the voltages of the ________________.

19

Making a current flow

REMEMBER

You can connect cells together in series to get a higher voltage.

1.3 V 2.6 V 3.9 V

Different types of cells give slightly different voltages.

To make a bulb light up you must send an electric current through it. You can do this by putting a voltage across its ends.

1 Look at the diagrams below. Then copy and complete the following sentences.

To make the bulb light you must press the __________.

There is then a __________ across the ends of the bulb.

This makes a __________ flow through the bulb.

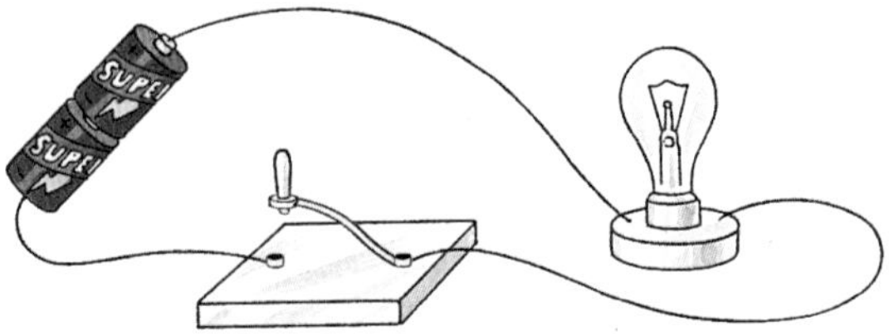

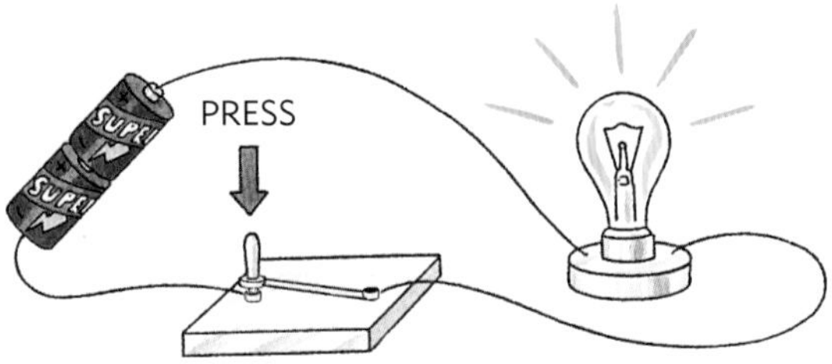

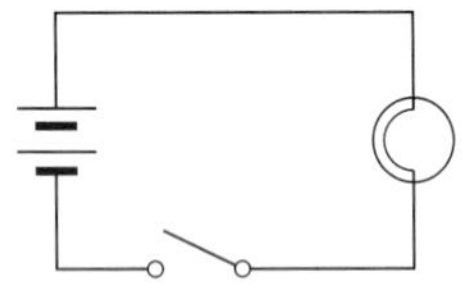

Switch open (off). So no voltage across bulb, no current through, bulb doesn't light.

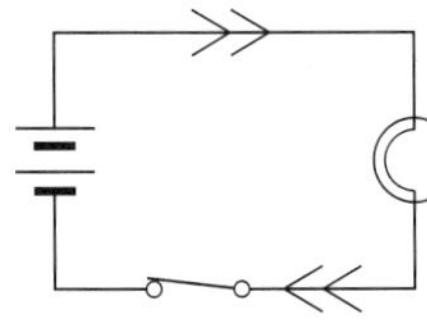

Switch closed (on). So voltage across bulb, current through bulb, bulb lights brightly.

Getting the right current

The diagram shows what happens if you connect a smaller voltage across the same bulb.

2 Look at the diagram. Then copy and complete the following sentences.

The bulb only lights up __________. This is because there is a smaller __________ across the bulb. So the __________ through the bulb is also smaller.

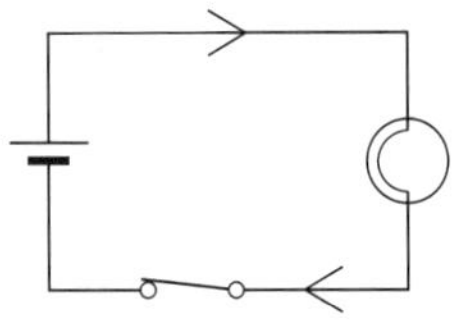

Smaller voltage across bulb. So smaller current through bulb, bulb lights dimly.

How to measure current

You can measure an electric current using an **ammeter**. The diagram shows how you connect an ammeter to measure the current through a bulb. The current that flows through the bulb must also flow through the ammeter. We say that the ammeter is connected **in series** with the bulb.

Current is measured in **amperes** (**A** for short).

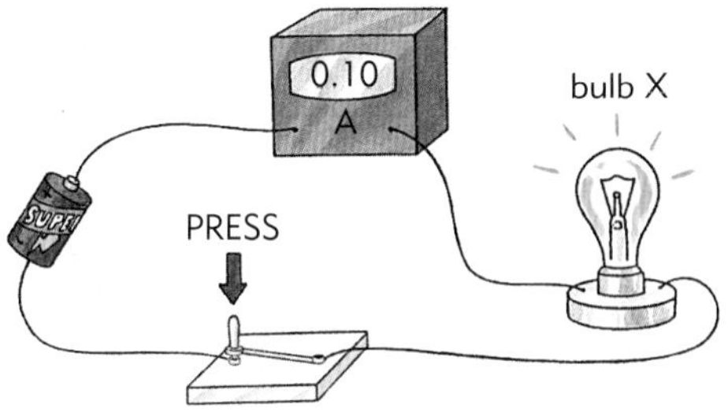

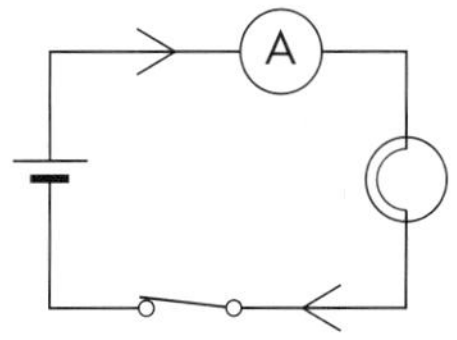

3 What current flows through bulb X:

(a) when you connect it to just one cell?

(b) when you connect it to two cells to get a bigger voltage?

A voltage pushes a current through a bulb. The bulb **resists** this current. We say that it has a resistance.

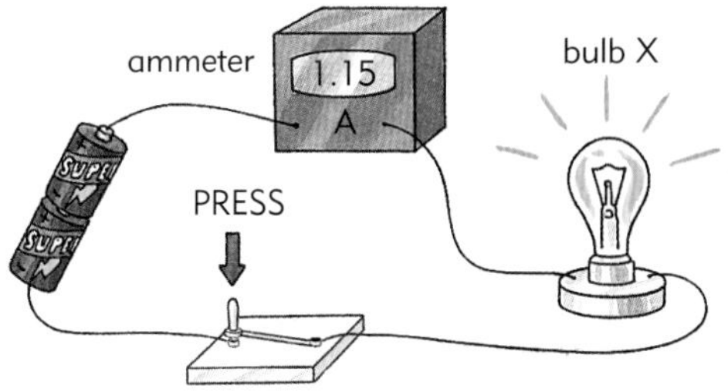

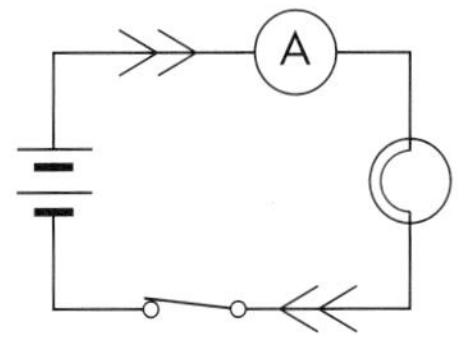

Comparing resistance

Some bulbs resist a current more than others, so they have a bigger resistance. You need a bigger **voltage** to push the same current through a bigger resistance.

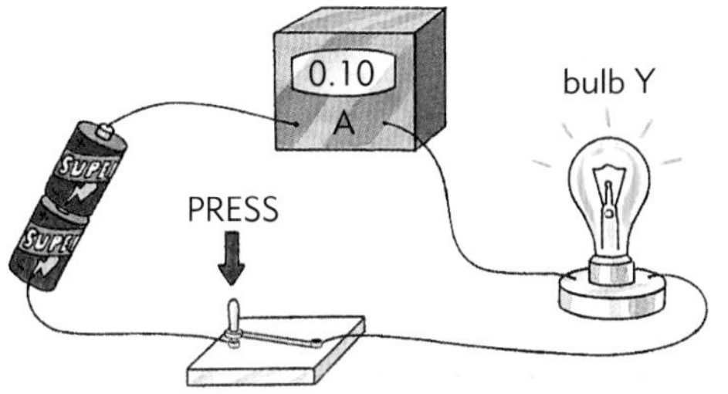

4 (a) Which has the bigger resistance, bulb X or bulb Y?

(b) Give a reason for your answer.

5 How can you make bulb Y light brightly?

Explain your answer as fully as you can.

What you need to remember [Copy and complete using the **key words**]

Making a current flow

We measure electric currents in units called ________________ (__________ for short) using an ________________.

To measure the current through a bulb, you must connect the ammeter **in** ________________ with it.

A bulb ________________ a current flowing through it.

The bigger the resistance of a bulb, the bigger the ________________ you need to send a particular current through it.

20 Connecting several things to the same supply

> **REMEMBER**
>
> To make a bulb light, you must send a big enough current through it. You can do this by putting a big enough voltage across the bulb.

A bulb lights brightly when you connect it as shown in the diagram below.

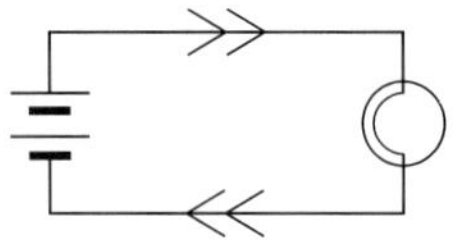

You can connect another bulb to the same battery so that both bulbs light brightly. The diagram on the right shows how you can do this.

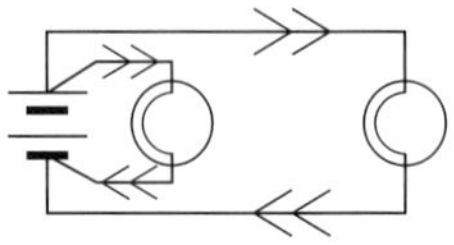

The full voltage is applied across each bulb. A current flows separately through each bulb. We say the bulbs are connected in parallel.

1 Copy and complete the following sentence.

The two bulbs are connected in __________.

2 Why do both bulbs light brightly?

3 Suppose one bulb breaks or you take it out.

How will this affect the other bulb?

The two bulbs in the diagram are connected to the two cells by separate wires. But this isn't the only way to connect things in parallel.

Connecting things in parallel

Connecting wires let electricity flow through them very easily. They have hardly any resistance.

Look at the two circuits. Each bulb is connected directly to both sides of the battery. In each circuit the two bulbs are connected in parallel.

4 Copy and complete the following sentences.

In these parallel circuits, the current from the battery to both bulbs flows through the __________ wire. Then the current splits and flows through each bulb __________. Then the current joins back up and flows back to the battery through the __________ wire.

The bulbs in these circuits are also connected in parallel.

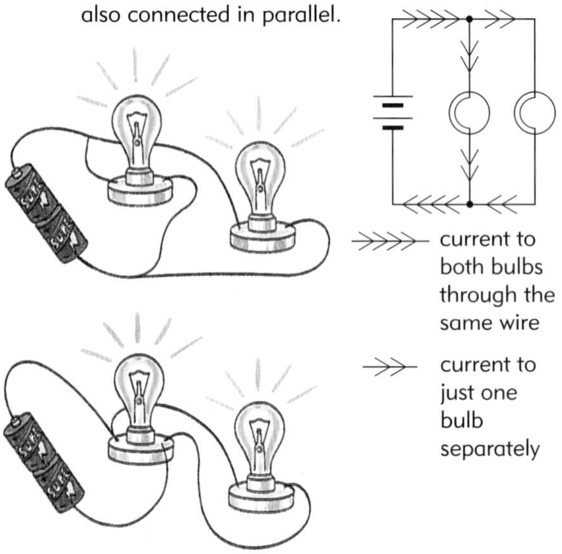

Measuring currents in parallel circuits

When bulbs are connected in parallel there is exactly the same **voltage** across each bulb. So if one bulb has a smaller **resistance**, a bigger current will flow through it.

5 Look at the diagram.

(a) What is the current through bulb X?

(b) What is the current through bulb Y?

(c) Which bulb has the bigger resistance? Give a reason for your answer.

6 (a) What is the total current supplied by the battery to the two bulbs? This is shown by meter A_1.

(b) How does this current compare to the separate currents through bulb X and bulb Y?

In a parallel circuit, the total current from the supply is the same as the currents through the separate branches added together. It is the **sum** of these separate currents.

> **REMEMBER**
>
> To measure the current through a bulb, you must connect an ammeter in series with it.

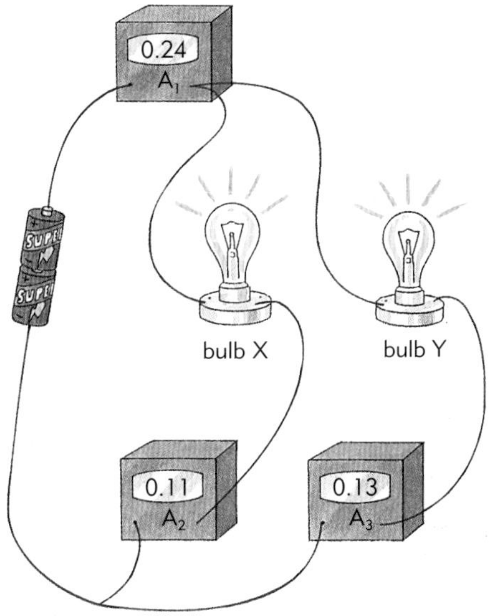

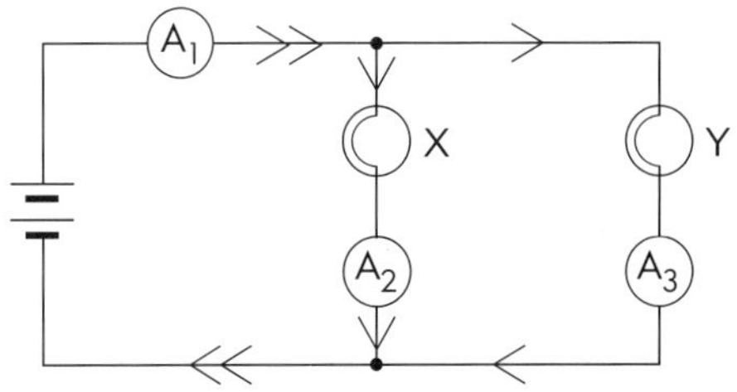

Safety when connecting things in parallel

When we plug things into the mains supply we are connecting them in parallel. But it isn't safe to take more than 13 A of current from one mains socket. So we need to be very careful about what we plug into it.

7 Copy and complete the table.

Appliances	Total current	Safe to connect in parallel?
heater + large TV	12 A + 2 A = 14 A	no
lamp + CD player		
small TV + hair dryer		

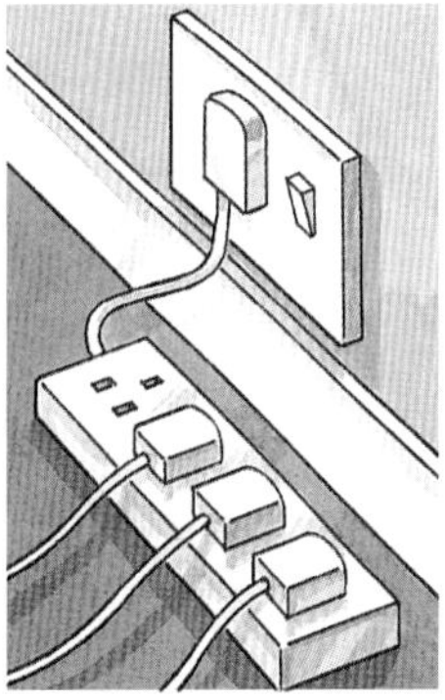

How much current?	
room heater	12 A
hair dryer	3 A
large TV	2 A
small TV	1 A
CD player	1 A
lamp	0.5 A

Parallel connections to the mains.

> ### What you need to remember [Copy and complete using the **key words**]
>
> **Connecting several things to the same supply**
>
> When bulbs (or other components) are connected in parallel:
>
> - the full ________________ of the supply is connected across each component;
> - the current through each component depends upon its ________________;
> - the total current from the supply is the ________________ of the currents through the separate components.

Different ways of connecting things in circuits

In our homes, lights, power sockets and appliances are usually connected in parallel.

1 Write down two reasons for connecting things to the mains supply in parallel.

In the diagram the switch for each bulb is connected differently. It is connected in series with its bulb.

2 The diagram shows an important component connected in series with all of the bulbs and switches in the circuit. What is this component?

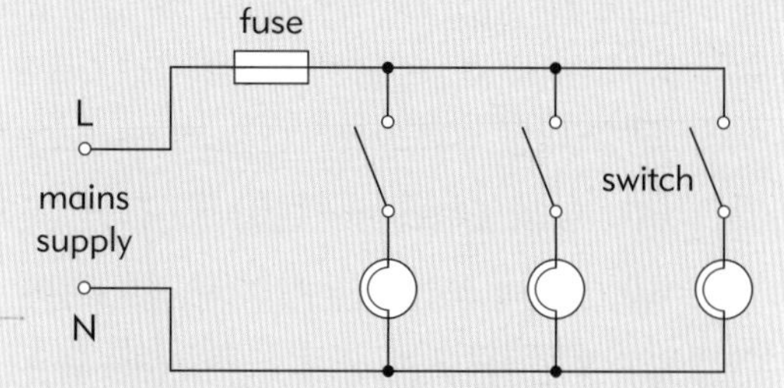

The lights in a house are connected in parallel.

This means:
- they all get the full 230 volts
- they can all be switched on and off separately.

Connecting things in series

The bulb in the first diagram is shining brightly.

The second diagram shows what happens when you connect another bulb in series with it.

3 Copy and complete the following sentence.

The current that flows through a series circuit is exactly the __________ in each part of the circuit.

4 (a) What happens to the brightness of the bulbs when the second bulb is connected?

(b) Explain, as fully as you can, why this happens.

When bulbs are connected in series their total resistance is the same as their separate resistances added together. It is the **sum** of their separate resistances.

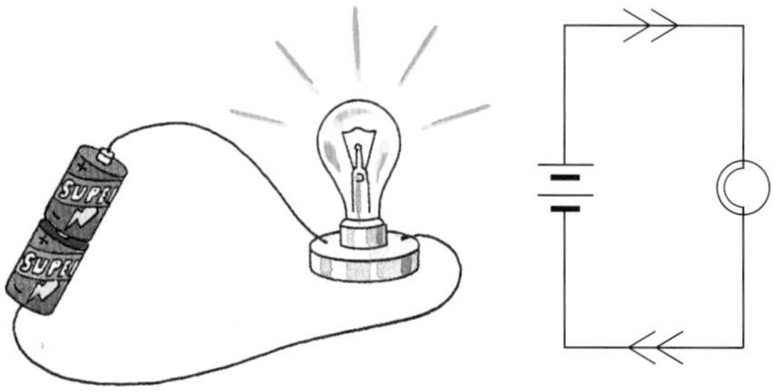

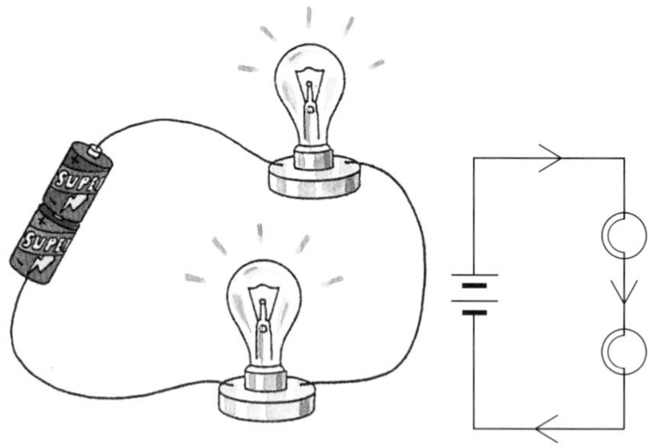

The **same** current flows through one bulb and then through the other. So we say they are connected in series.
The two bulbs are dimmer than with one bulb by itself.
So we know that:
- the current is smaller
- the resistance of the two bulbs is bigger than the resistance of one bulb.

Measuring voltages in a series circuit

The diagram shows the voltages across the cells and the bulbs in a series circuit.

REMEMBER

To measure the voltage across a component, you must connect a voltmeter in parallel with it.

5 (a) What is the voltage across bulb X?

(b) What is the voltage across bulb Y?

(c) Copy and complete the following sentences.

The same current flows through both bulbs.
But bulb X needs a bigger __________ to push this current through it.
So bulb X must have a __________ resistance.

6 (a) What is the voltage across the two cells?

(b) How does this voltage compare with the separate voltages across the bulbs?

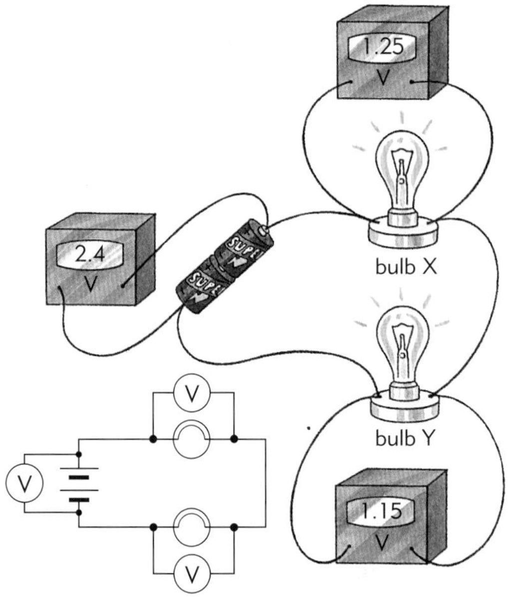

In a series circuit, the total voltage of the supply is the same as the voltage across the separate components added together. It is the **sum** of the voltages across the separate components.

Using resistors to control currents

We can put a resistor in series with a component. This reduces the current through the component. The diagrams show two examples.

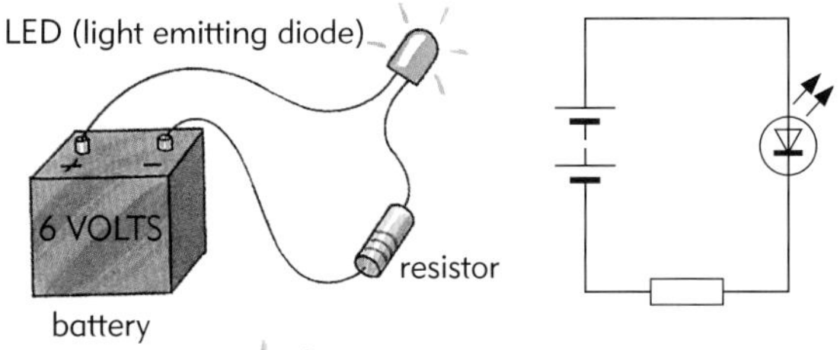

7 (a) You can't connect an LED to a 6 V battery. The current will be too big and it will damage the LED. How can you protect an LED against this?

(b) Putting a resistor in the circuit reduces the voltage across the LED to 2 V. What is the voltage across the resistor?

8 The lamp starts to glow when there is 0.8 V across it. This happens when there is 1.7 V across the variable resistor. What is the voltage across the two cells?

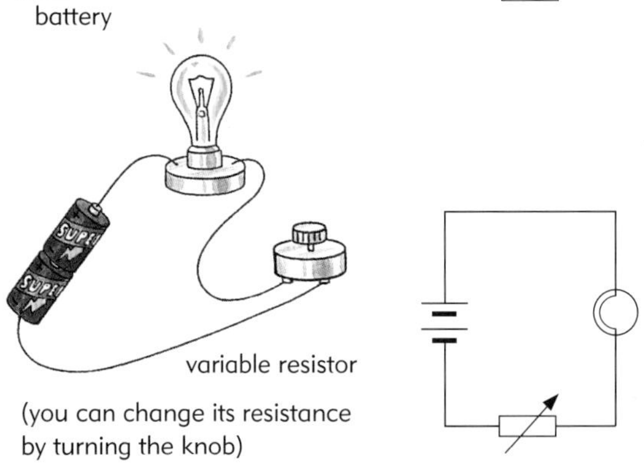

(you can change its resistance by turning the knob)

What you need to remember [Copy and complete using the **key words**]

Different ways of connecting things in circuits

When bulbs (or other components) are connected in series:

- the total resistance is the ________________ of the separate resistances;
- exactly the ________________ current flows through each component;
- the supply voltage is the ________________ of the voltages across each component.

22

Electric circuits and energy transfer

The diagram shows the electrical symbols that have been used on the past eight pages. These symbols make it easier to draw diagrams of electric circuits.

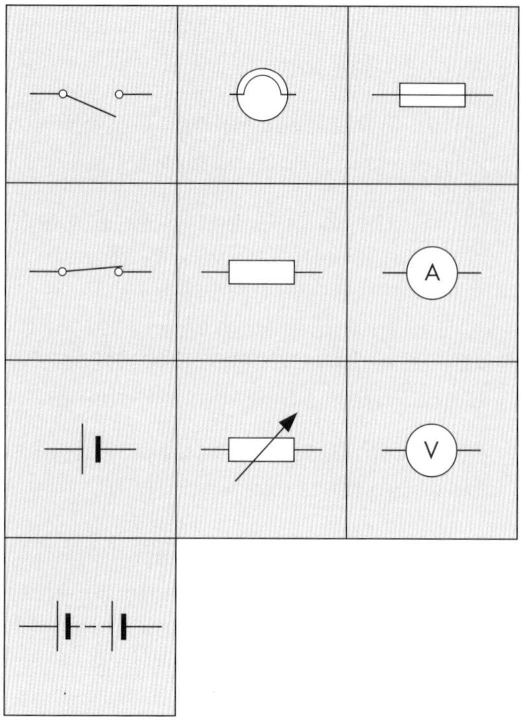

1 Copy the diagram. Then write the correct name under each symbol.

Choose the names from the list below. (Look back at pages 82–89 if you need to.)

ammeter	battery	cell
fuse	lamp	resistor
switch (closed)	switch (open)	variable resistor
voltmeter		

Drawing circuit diagrams

You should be able to draw a circuit diagram from looking at a circuit.

2 Draw the circuit diagram for each of the two circuits shown.

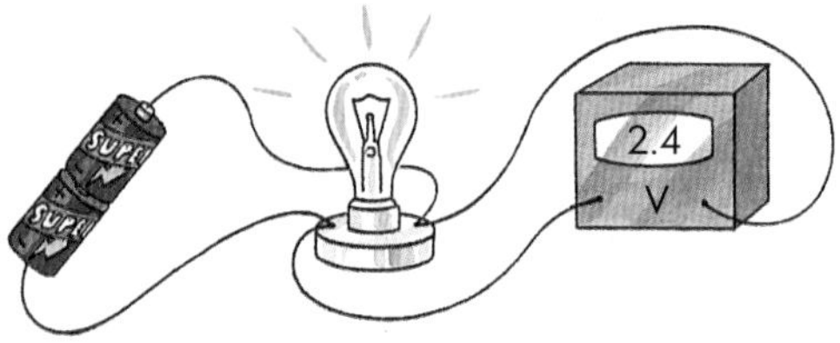

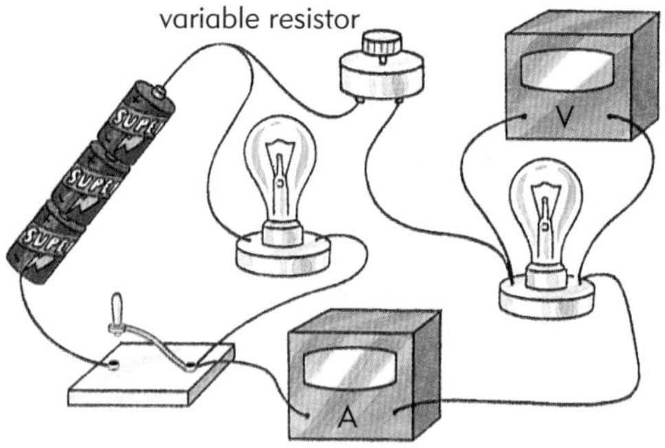

Interpreting circuit diagrams

You should be able to understand, from a circuit diagram, how components are connected.

3 Look at the diagram.

Then copy and complete the following sentences.

X and Y are both __________.

Connected in series with X and Y there is a __________ and a __________.

Connected in parallel with X there is a __________, which is __________.

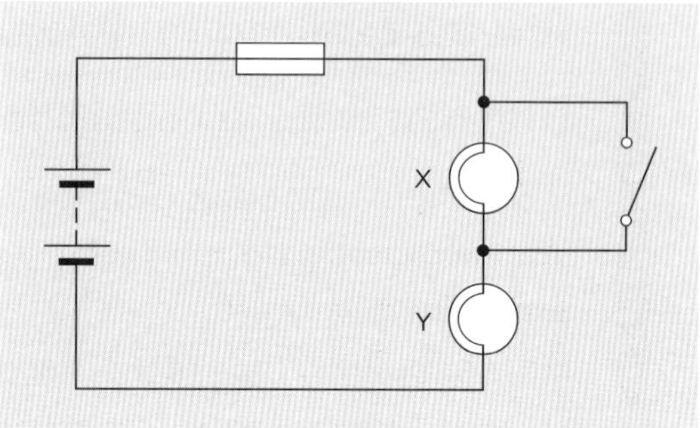

What happens when a current flows?

The diagram shows a current flowing through a circuit.

4 What is actually moving round a circuit when a current flows?

5 (a) What happens as an electric current flows through a resistance?

(b) Where does the energy that is transferred in an electric circuit come from?

A current is a flow of negatively charged **electrons**.

How fast is energy transferred?

The wattage, or power, of an electrical appliance tells you how fast it transfers energy. It is measured in watts (W for short).

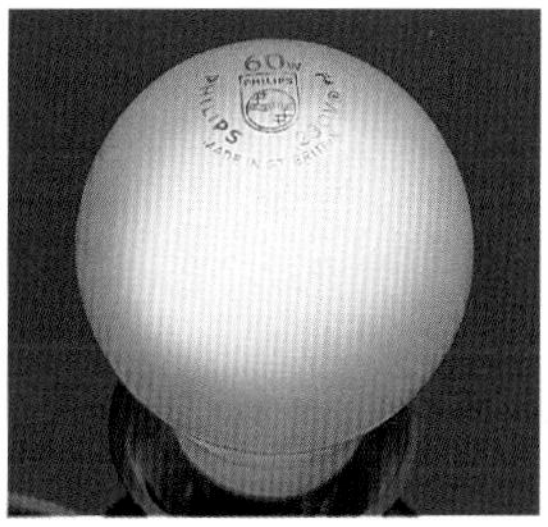

A 60-watt bulb transfers 60 joules of energy a second.

6 How fast does a 100-watt light bulb transfer energy?

What's the connection between watts, amperes and volts?

You can work out the power of an electrical appliance like this:

power (**watts**) = **potential difference** (p.d.) (volts) × **current** (amperes)

7 Look at the diagrams of electrical appliances.

In each case work out the missing figure.

Kettle  230 volts 10 amperes ? watts Power = p.d. × current = 230 volts × 10 amperes = 2300 watts	Headlight bulb 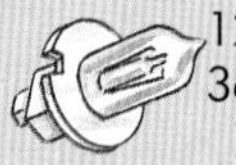 12 volts 36 watts ? amperes Current = power ÷ p.d. = 36 watts ÷ 12 volts = 3 amperes
Hair dryer  230 volts 3 amperes ? watts	TV and video  230 volts 345 watts ? amperes

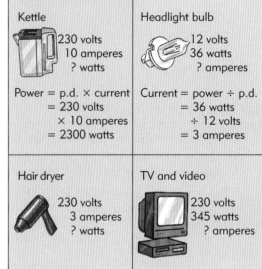

What you need to remember [Copy and complete using the **key words**]

Electric circuits and energy transfer

An electric current is a flow of negatively charged ________________.

When a current passes through a resistance, electrical energy is transferred as ________________.

How fast an electrical appliance transfers energy is given by

power (in ________) = ________________ ________________ (in volts) × ________________ (in amperes)

[You should be able to understand circuit diagrams that use any of the electrical symbols on page 90.

You should also be able to use any of the symbols to draw circuit diagrams.]

How does current change with voltage?

The current through a bulb depends on the voltage you apply across it. It is the same for any other electrical component.

You can use the circuit shown on the diagram to find out how current changes with voltage.

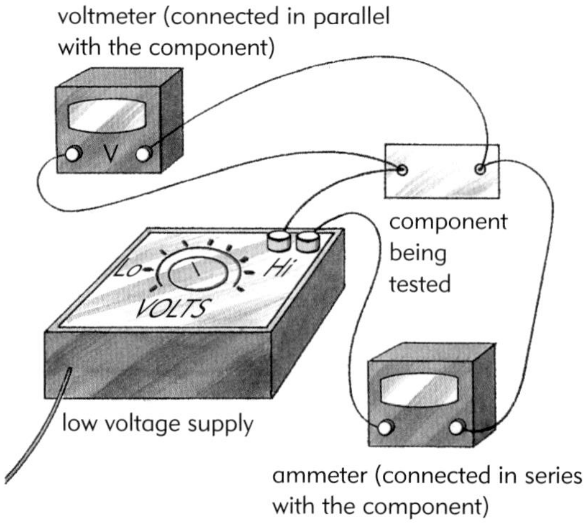

1 Copy and complete the following sentences.

Current is measured using an __________.

This is connected in __________ with the component.

Voltage is measured using a __________.

This is connected in __________ with the component.

Different components give different results. You can show these results on a current–voltage graph.

Current–voltage graph for a resistor

The graph shows how the current through a resistor changes when you change the voltage across it. The graph is like this only if the resistor does not get hot. So you must keep the current through the resistor quite small.

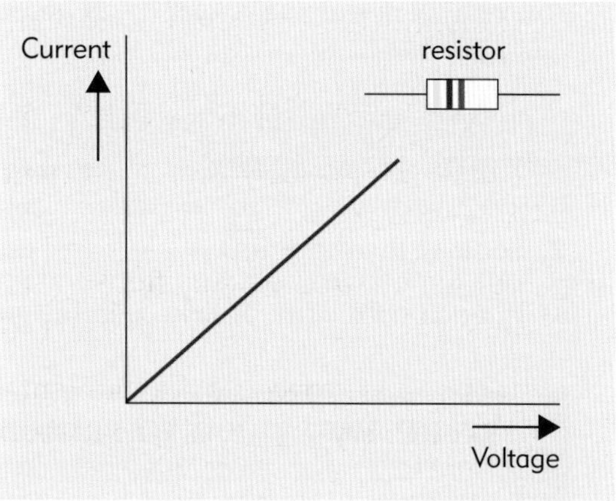

2 Describe, as carefully as you can, how the current through the resistor changes as you increase the voltage.

It sometimes matters which way round you connect a component to the supply. You can check this by connecting it the other way round.

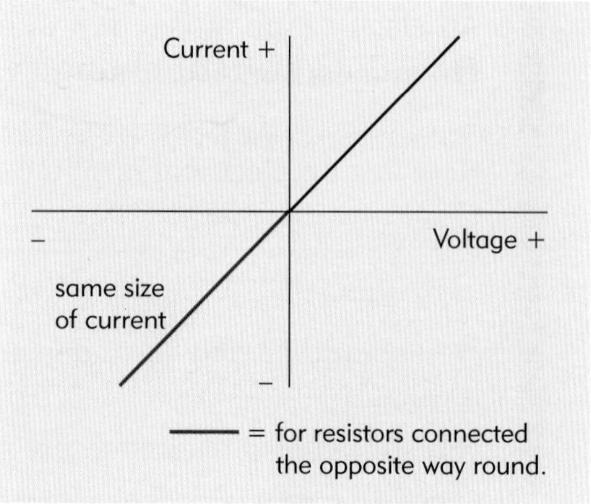

3 Look at the second graph. Copy and complete the following sentence.

When you connect a resistor the other way round, the <u>size</u> of the current that flows through it is the __________.

Current–voltage graph for a diode

Some circuits use a component called a diode. The current–voltage graph for a diode shows that it behaves differently from a resistor.

4 Does it matter which way round you connect the diode?

Explain your answer as fully as you can.

5 Write down one other difference between the diode and a resistor.

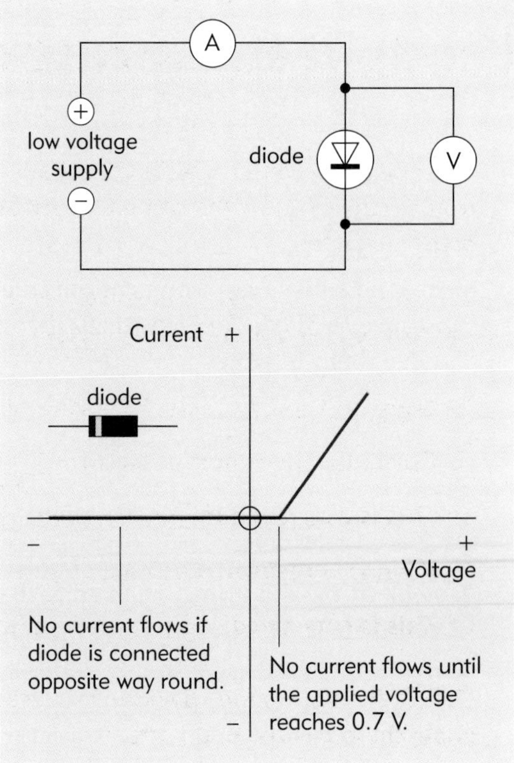

Current–voltage graph for a filament lamp

A bulb has a filament that gets very hot. A bulb is sometimes called a filament lamp. Look carefully at the current–voltage graph for a filament lamp.

6 Does it matter which way round you connect the lamp?

Explain your answer as fully as you can.

7 Copy and complete the following sentences.

As the voltage increases, the current through the filament __________.

But the graph gradually flattens out. This tells you that the __________ is increasing less and less.

This happens because the filament of the lamp becomes very __________ so its resistance increases.

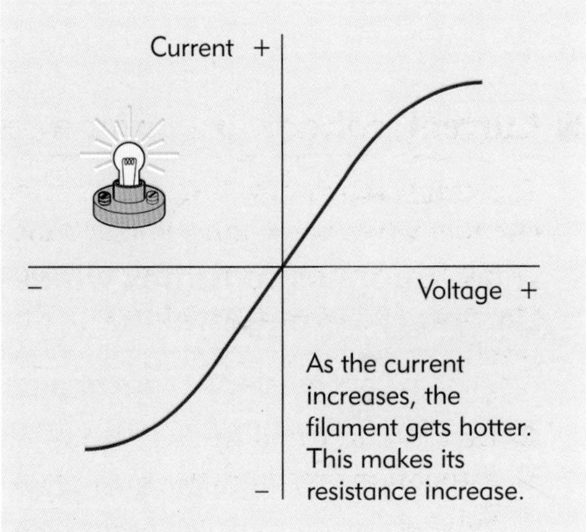

What you need to remember [Copy and complete the graphs]

How does current change with voltage?

The current–voltage graphs for a resistor, a diode and filament lamp are as shown:

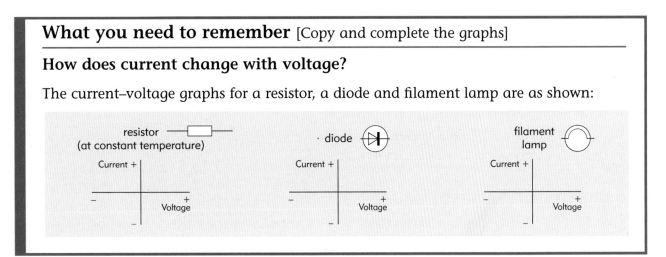

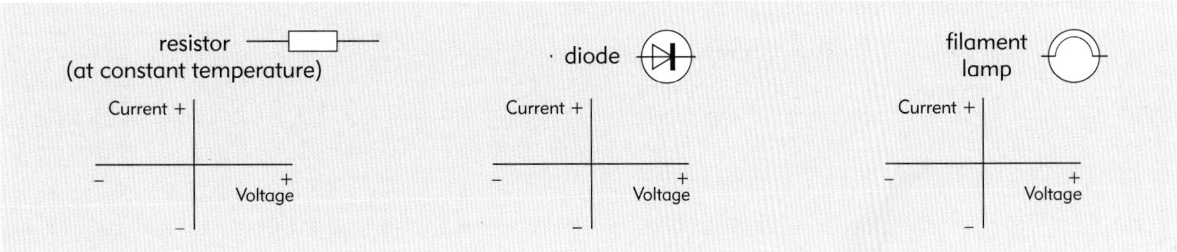

24 Using electricity to split things up

REMEMBER

Metals and graphite conduct electricity. Other solid substances are insulators.

Most solid substances won't conduct electricity. But some substances will conduct electricity if you melt them or dissolve them in water.

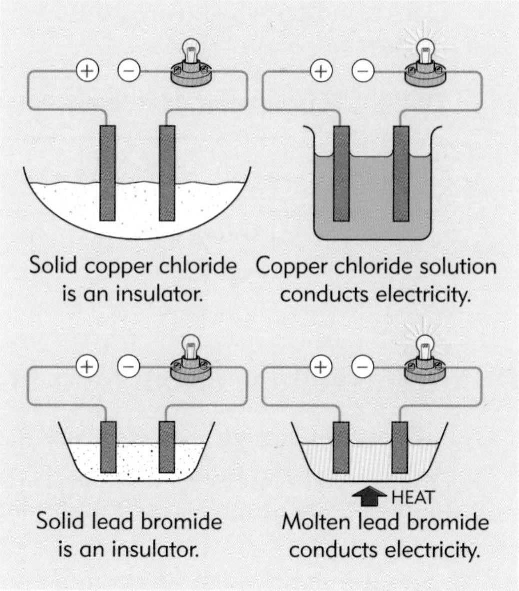

Solid copper chloride is an insulator.
Copper chloride solution conducts electricity.
HEAT
Solid lead bromide is an insulator.
Molten lead bromide conducts electricity.

1 Which solid substances will conduct electricity?

2 Look at the diagrams. Then copy the table and complete it. The first box has been filled in for you.

Insulators	Conductors
solid copper chloride	copper chloride ________
________ lead bromide	________ lead bromide

What happens to things when you pass electricity through them?

When you pass an electric current through a metal it gets warmer. The same happens with graphite.

But something else also happens when you pass electricity through a melted or dissolved substance. The substance gets split up into **simpler** substances. This is called **electrolysis**.

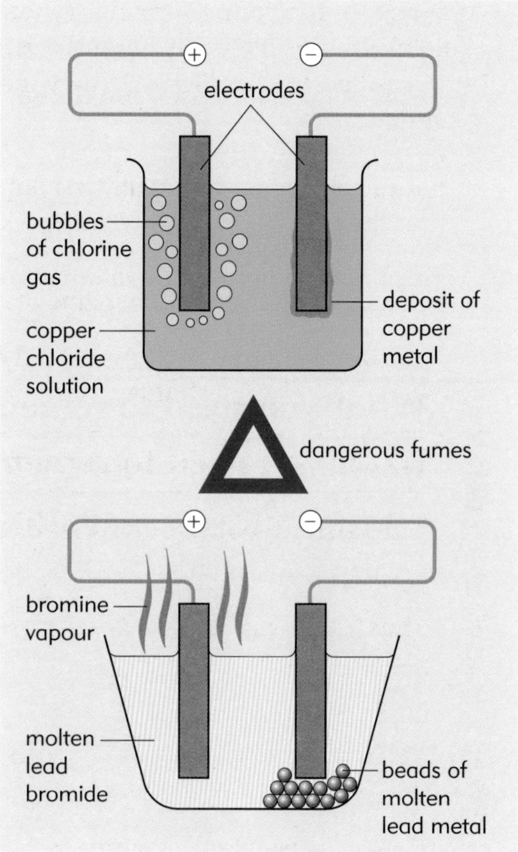

3 Look at the diagrams.

Then copy and complete the following sentences.

Electrolysis of copper chloride solution produces:

- ________ at the positive (+) electrode
- ________ at the negative (–) electrode.

Electrolysis of molten lead bromide produces:

- ________ at the positive (+) electrode
- ________ at the negative (–) electrode.

How does electrolysis work?

Some substances are made of electrically charged particles called **ions**. When the substance is **melted** (molten) or **dissolved**, these ions can move about. These are the substances that you can split up by electrolysis.

4 Look at the diagrams.

Then copy the table and complete it.

Substance	Ions that move to the + electrode	Ions that move to the – electrode
copper chloride solution	chloride ions	
molten lead bromide		

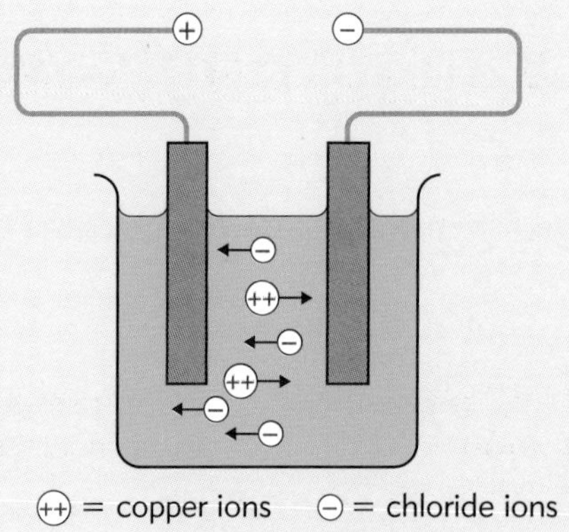

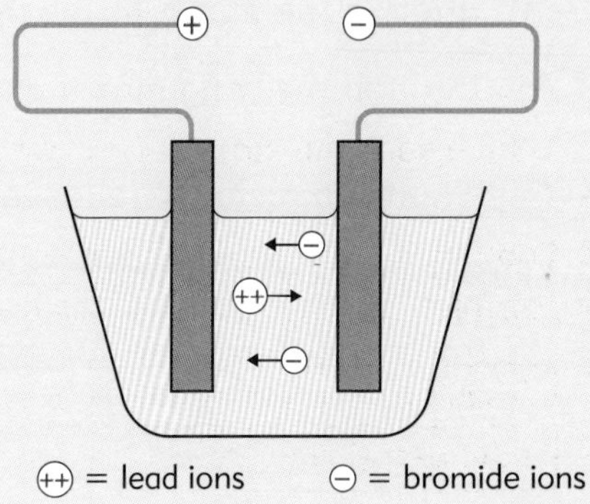

Negatively charged ions move to the **positive** (+) electrode.
Positively charged ions move to the **negative** (–) electrode.

What is an electric current?

An electric current is always a flow of electrical charges. In solids, like copper connecting wires and most electrical components, an electric current is a flow of negatively charged electrons. But during electrolysis, different sorts of charged particles called ions carry the current through the liquid.

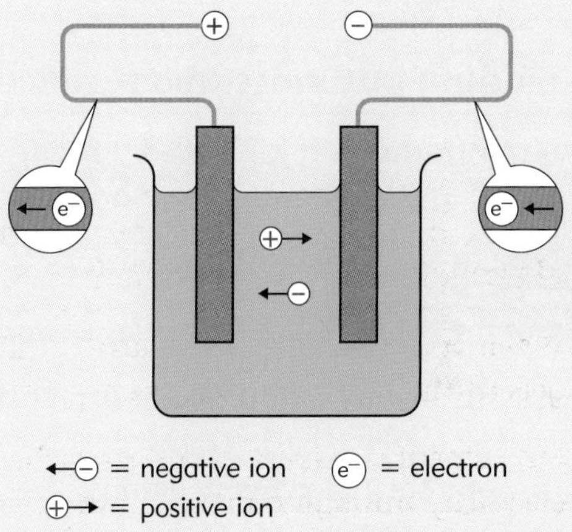

5 Copy and complete the following sentences.

In the wires the current is a flow of __________.

In the liquid the current is a flow of __________.

Some of these have a __________ charge and others have a __________ charge.

What you need to remember [Copy and complete using the **key words**]

Using electricity to split things up

Some substances are made of electrically charged particles called __________.
These ions can move about if the substance is __________ or __________.
Negatively charged ions move to the __________ electrode.
Positively charged ions move to the __________ electrode.
The substance gets split up into __________ substances.
This is called __________.

1 Doing things with mirrors

We use mirrors to do many useful things.

1 Look at the diagrams.

Write down <u>two</u> common uses for mirrors.

2 What does the car driver see:

(a) through the mirror inside the car?

(b) through the wing mirror outside the car?

3 Copy and complete the following sentences.

Light bounces off a mirror.

We say that a mirror __________ light.

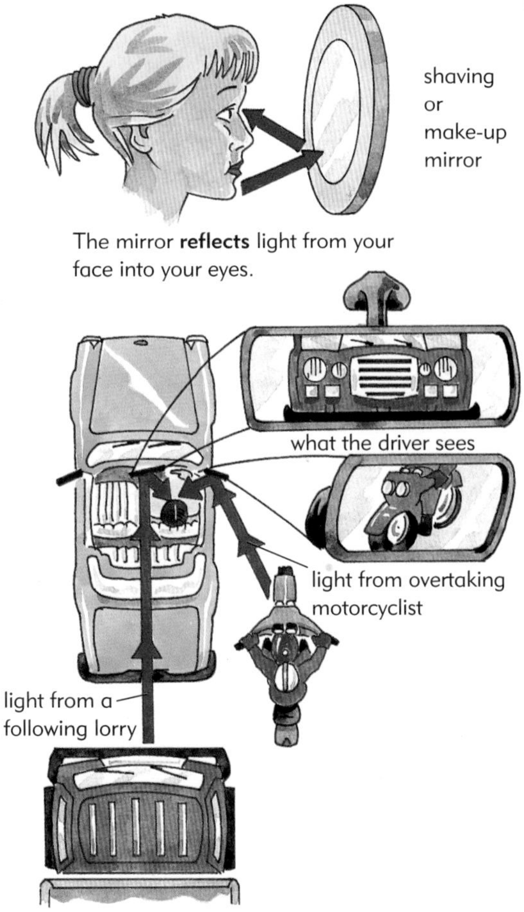

Finding out more about reflection

A mirror that is flat is called a **plane** mirror.
The diagrams show how a plane mirror reflects light.

Look at the angle with the mirror:

- of the beam of light that comes from the lamp
- of the beam of light after it is reflected.

4 Copy the following headings.
Then complete the table.

Angle of beam going towards mirror	Angle of beam reflected from mirror
15°	
60°	
80°	

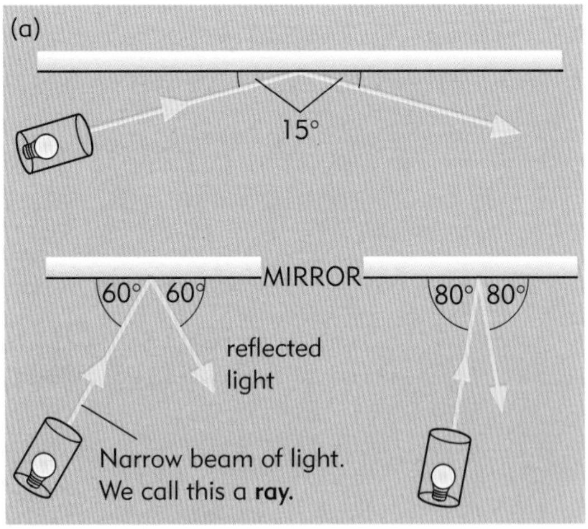

Light is reflected from a plane mirror at the same **angle** as it strikes the mirror.

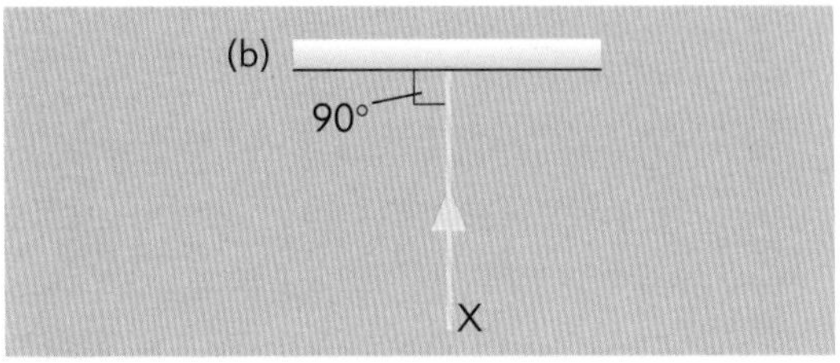

5 Ray X is going straight towards a mirror.
At what angle will it be reflected from the mirror?

Give a reason for your answer.

How to see round corners

It is sometimes useful to be able to see round a corner.

Look at the diagram. It shows how you can do this.

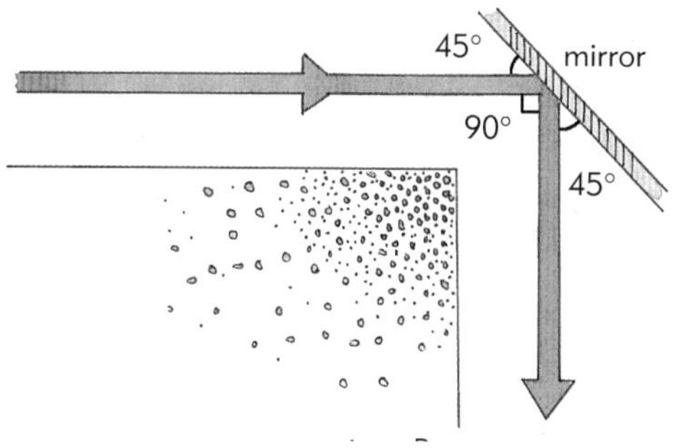

6 Copy and complete the following sentences.

To see round a corner you have to turn the light through an angle of __________ degrees.

This means that the light must strike the mirror at an angle of __________ degrees.

The diagram shows how this idea is used in a camera.

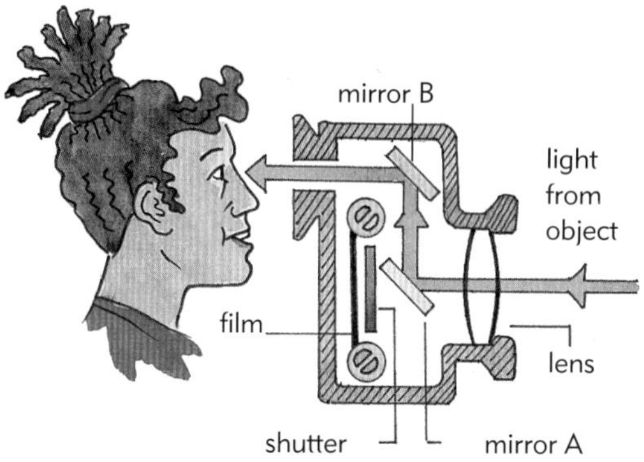

In this camera you look through the main lens. When you take a photograph, the shutter and mirror A move out of the way.

7 Write down the following sentences in the correct order. The first one has been done for you.

Light goes through the lens of the camera.

- The light is turned through an angle of 90° and reflected up to mirror B.
- The light strikes mirror A at an angle of 45°.
- The light is turned through an angle of 90° and reflected into your eye.
- The light strikes mirror B at an angle of 45°.

8 Copy the diagram of a periscope.

Then complete it to show how the person in the submarine can see the ship. Start with the light coming from the ship.

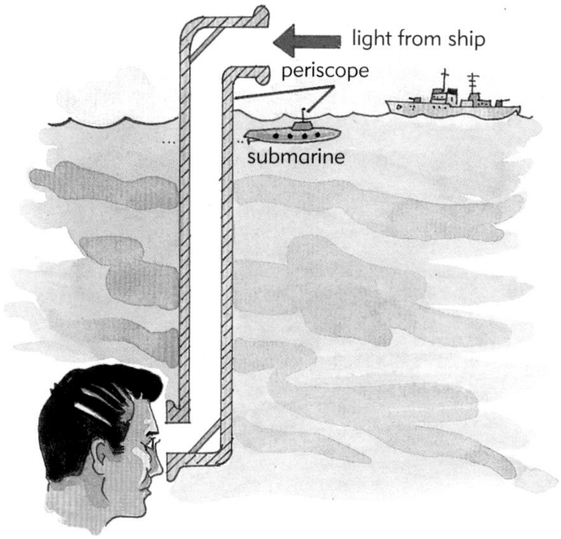

What you need to remember [Copy and complete using the **key words**]

Doing things with mirrors

A flat, shiny surface is called a ______________ mirror.
A narrow beam of light is called a ______________.
A mirror ______________ a ray of light at the same ______________ as it strikes the mirror.

[You should be able to show, on a diagram, how rays of light are reflected from a plane mirror.]

2

Bending light

A ray of light usually travels in a straight line. So when we see an aeroplane straight above us, we know that this is where the aeroplane really is.

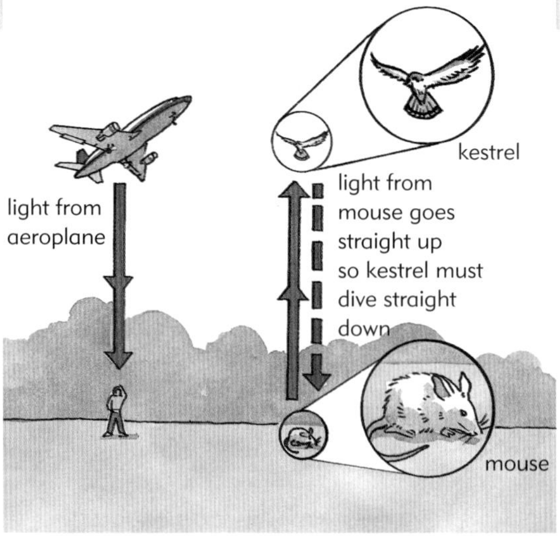

1 Look at the diagram of the kestrel. Why is it helpful for a kestrel that rays of light travel in straight lines?

But when a ray of light goes from water into air it can bend. Because the light changes **direction**, things under water are <u>not</u> where they seem to be.

2 Look at the diagram of the kingfisher.

(a) What will happen if the kingfisher dives towards where the fish seems to be?

(b) What causes this problem for the kingfisher?

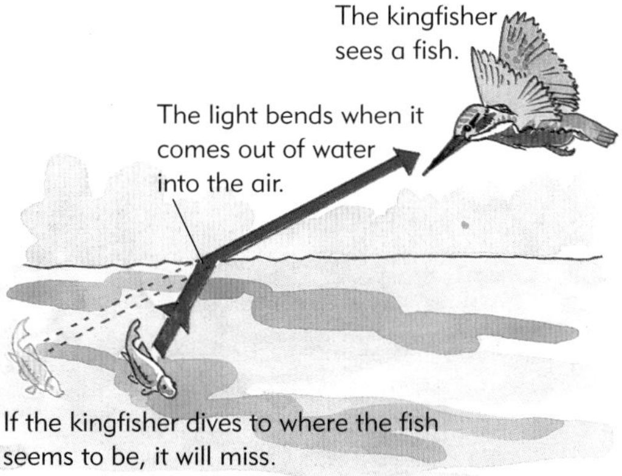

When a ray of light bends or changes direction in this way, we say that it is **refracted**.

Kingfishers allow for refraction, so they are good at catching fish.

Finding out more about refraction

Light can be refracted when it passes from one substance into another.

The diagrams show you more about the way light is refracted.

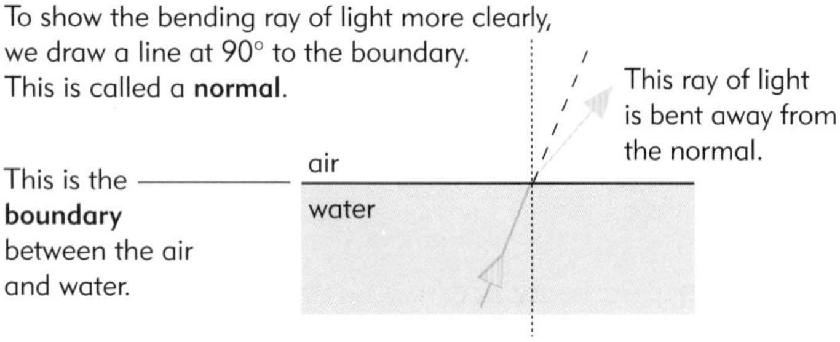

To show the bending ray of light more clearly, we draw a line at 90° to the boundary. This is called a **normal**.
This ray of light is bent away from the normal.
This is the **boundary** between the air and water.
air
water

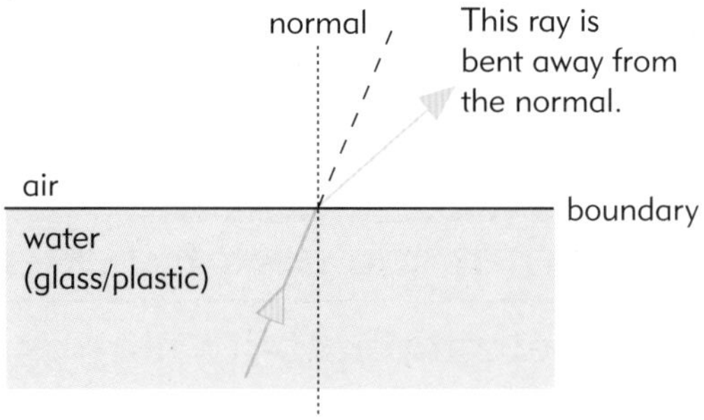

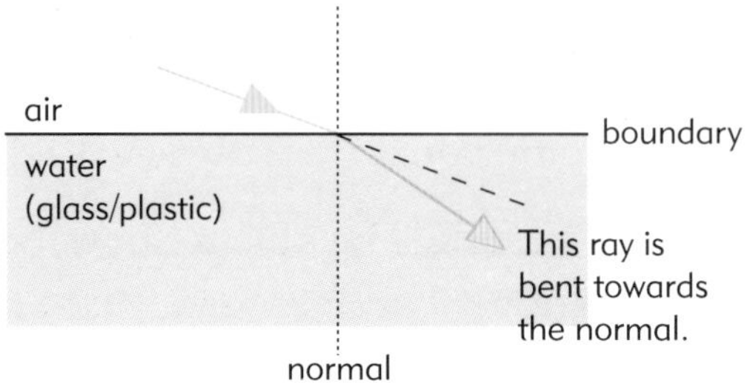

3 Copy the table. Then complete it.

Where the ray of light travels	What happens to the ray of light
from water into air	refracted ___________ the normal
from air into water	refracted ___________ the normal

Rays that aren't refracted

The diagrams show what happens to rays of light when they strike a boundary head-on at 90° (along a normal).

4 Copy and complete the following sentences.

A ray of light travelling along a normal strikes a boundary at __________ degrees.

When it crosses the boundary, the ray of light carries on travelling in the same __________.

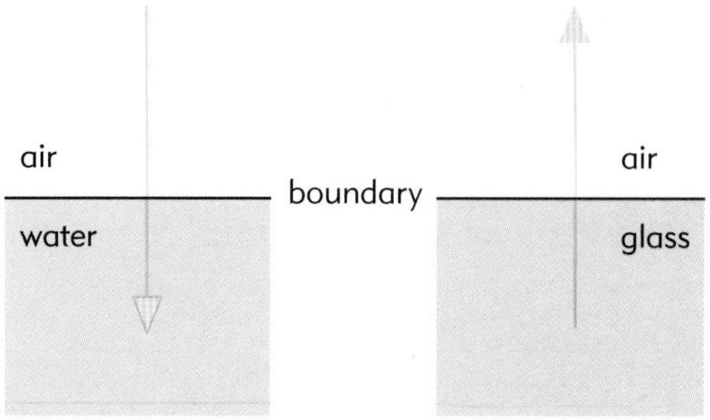

air
boundary
air
water
glass

These rays of light strike the boundary at 90°. They do not change direction.

Doing things with refraction

Refraction can cause problems, but it is also useful. To see clearly there must be a sharp image on the back of your eye.

To make this sharp image your eye must refract or bend the light.

5 Look at the diagram.
In which <u>three</u> places in your eye is light refracted?

Seeing a fish.

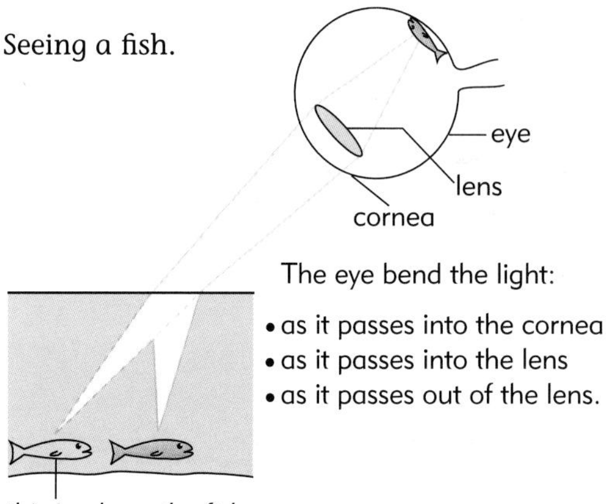

picture a fish on back of the eye, we call this an image
eye
lens
cornea
The eye bend the light:
• as it passes into the cornea
• as it passes into the lens
• as it passes out of the lens.
this is where the fish seems to be

What you need to remember [Copy and complete using the **key words**]

Bending light

Rays of light change ________________ when they pass from one transparent substance into another. We say they are ________________.
A normal is a line at 90° to the ________________ between two different substances.
A ray of light that is travelling along a ________________ does <u>not</u> change direction.

[You should be able to show, on a diagram, what happens to rays of light as they cross the boundary between two different substances.]

Bouncing and bending sounds

It isn't only light that can be reflected.
You can also reflect sounds.

1 Look at the diagram.

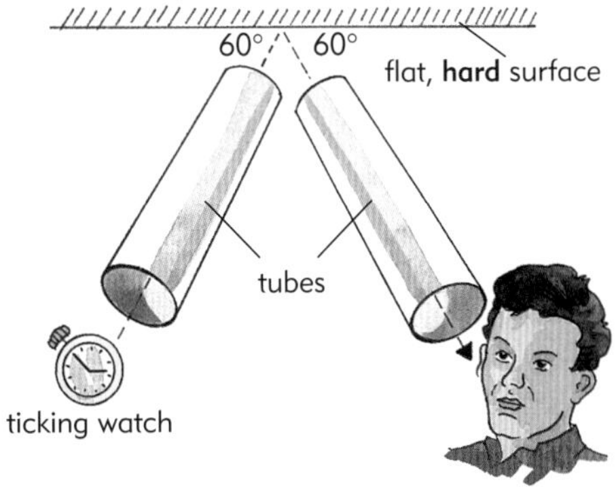

The ticks sound loudest when the tubes are at the same angle to the surface.

Copy and complete the following sentences.

Light reflects well from a __________, __________ surface.

Sound reflects well from a __________, __________ surface.

When a sound strikes a hard, flat surface at a certain angle, it reflects at the __________ angle.

REMEMBER

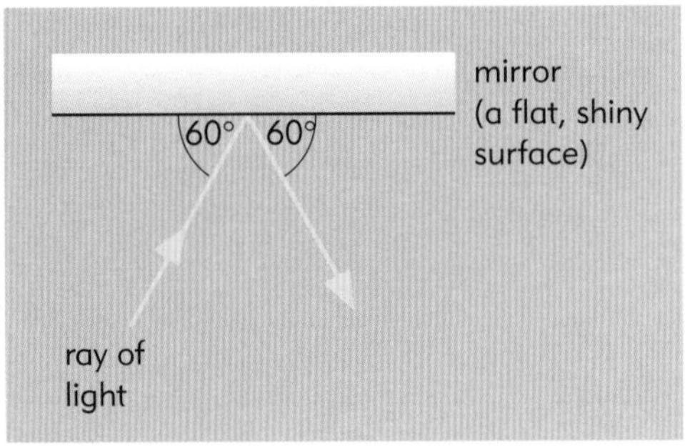

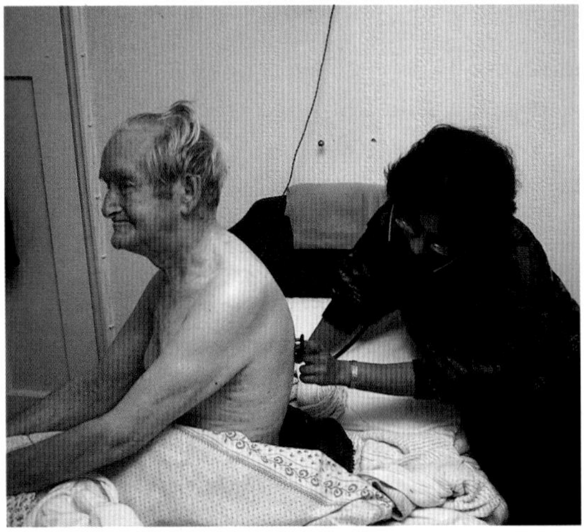

Doctors use stethoscopes to listen inside your body.

Listening to your heart beat

A doctor can use a stethoscope to listen to your heart beating.
The diagram shows how the stethoscope works.

2 Copy and complete the following sentence.

The sound is __________ over and over again from the __________ of the rubber tube.

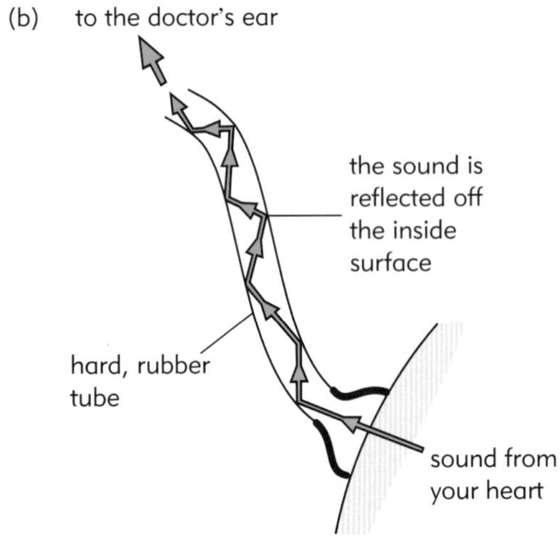

How do you get an echo?

The diagram shows how you can get an **echo** of your voice.

3 Explain as fully as you can, how you get an echo.

4 When you shout, you hear the echo one second later. How far away are you from the large, hard, flat surface?

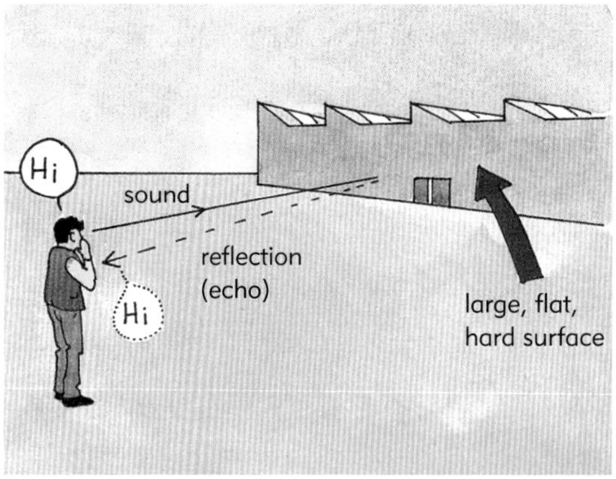

Sound takes about 1 second to travel 320 metres. So you can hear an echo a short time after you make a sound.

Bending sound

Sound can also be bent or **refracted**, just like light. This happens when sound travels across the **boundary** between two different substances.

5 Look at the diagrams.
Then copy and complete the following sentences.

Light is __________ as it passes into and out of the glass or plastic __________.

This brings the light to a __________ on the screen.

Sound is __________ as it passes into and out of the __________ __________ gas in the balloon.

This brings the sound to a __________ on the microphone.

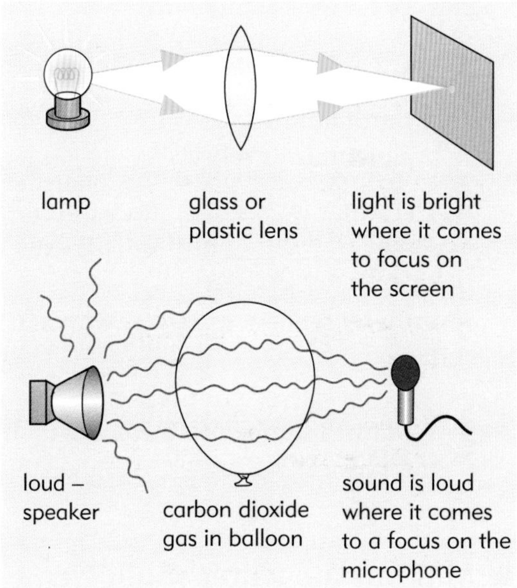

What you need to remember [Copy and complete using the **key words**]

Bouncing and bending sounds

Sounds are reflected from ________________ surfaces.
A sound that is reflected back to where it came from is called an ________________.
A sound can also be bent or ________________ when it crosses the ________________ between two different substances.

4 Why do people say that light and sound are waves?

REMEMBER

A normal is a line at 90° to a boundary.

You can see waves on lakes and on the sea. The wind makes these waves. But we can look at water waves more easily if we make them in a tank.
The diagram shows how you can do this.

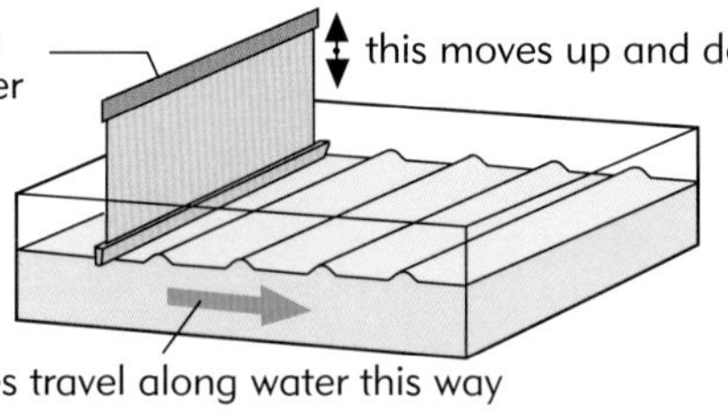

Reflecting water waves

The diagram shows what happens if you send water waves towards a **hard**, **flat** surface.

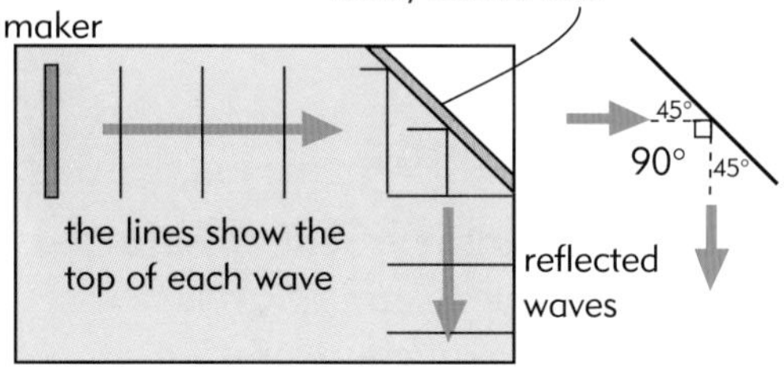

1 Copy and complete the following sentences.

A hard, flat surface __________ water waves just like a plane mirror reflects __________.

The water waves are reflected from the surface at the same __________ as they strike it.

Your friend sends some water waves at 90° to a hard, flat surface.

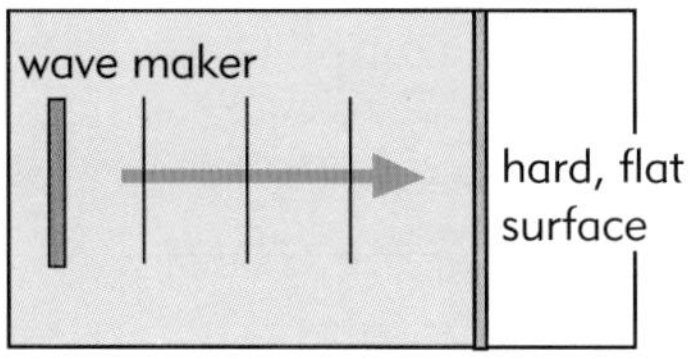

2 What will happen to these waves after they have hit the surface?

Making the water shallower

The diagrams show what happens to water waves when the water suddenly gets shallower.

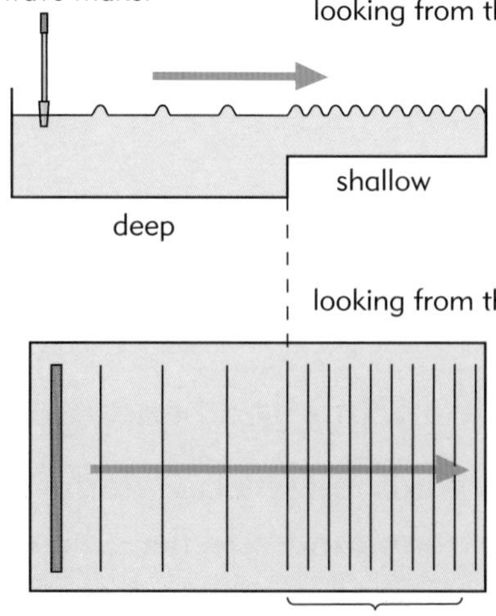

The waves get closer together here.
This is because they travel **slower**

3 (a) What happens to the <u>distance</u> between the water waves in the shallower water?

(b) Why does this happen?

4 What happens to the <u>direction</u> of these water waves when they move into the shallower water?

Refracting water waves

The diagram shows what happens if you send water waves into shallower water at an **angle**.

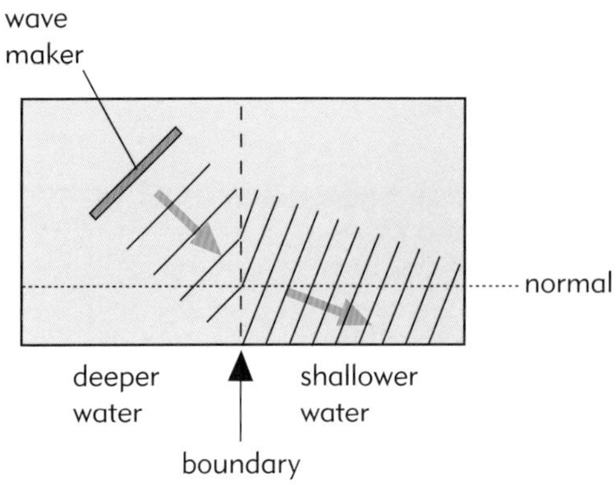

The waves change direction. They are **refracted**.

5 Copy and complete the following sentences.

As the water waves move into shallower water they don't just slow down. They also change __________.

The water waves are __________ towards the normal.

Light waves and sound waves

Water waves are reflected and refracted just like light and sound. So scientists think that light and sound are also waves.

Light and sound are refracted because they travel faster through some substances than through others. For example, light travels **slower** through glass or plastic than it does through air.

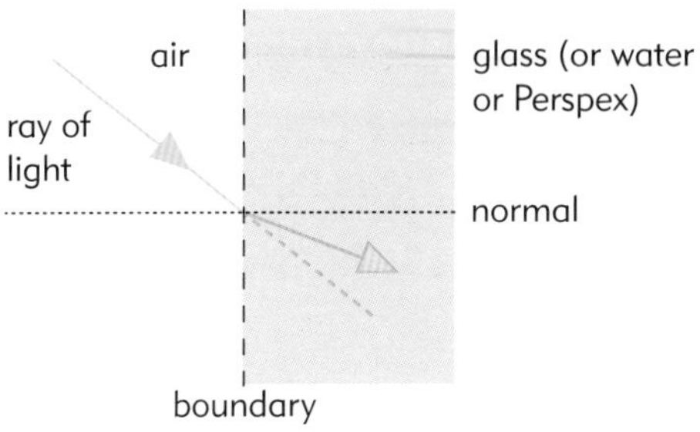

6 Copy and complete the following sentences.

When light passes from air into glass it travels __________.

So when light passes from air into glass it is __________ towards the normal.

7 Sound is refracted when it passes from air into carbon dioxide. Why does this happen?

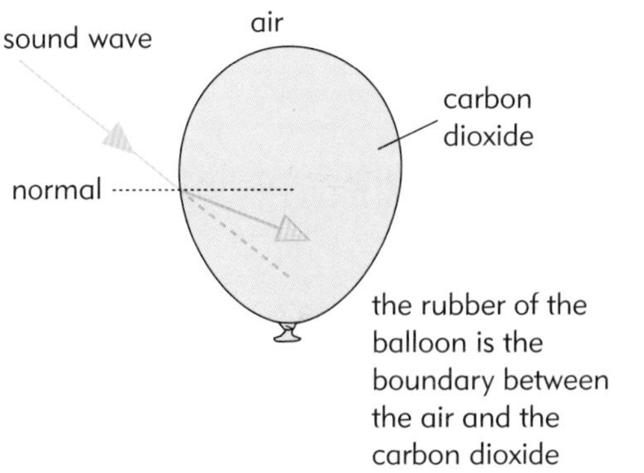

What you need to remember [Copy and complete using the **key words**]

Why do people say that light and sound are waves?

Water waves are reflected from a ______________, ______________ surface, just like light from a plane mirror.

Water waves are refracted towards the normal when they pass into shallower water at an ______________.

This happens because they travel ______________ in shallower water.

Light is also ______________ towards the normal when it travels from air into glass (or plastic or water).

This must be because it travels ______________ in glass (or plastic or water) than it does in air.

5

Looking at water waves: Part 1

Light and sound travel as waves.

We can't see light waves or sound waves.
But we can see water waves and waves travelling along a rope, so it is worth looking carefully at these waves.

This helps us to understand more about light waves and sound waves.

1 Look at the diagrams below. Then copy and complete the following sentences.

Waves can travel along the surface of __________ or along a __________.

The water or rope itself does not travel along.

Parts of the water or rope just move __________ and __________.

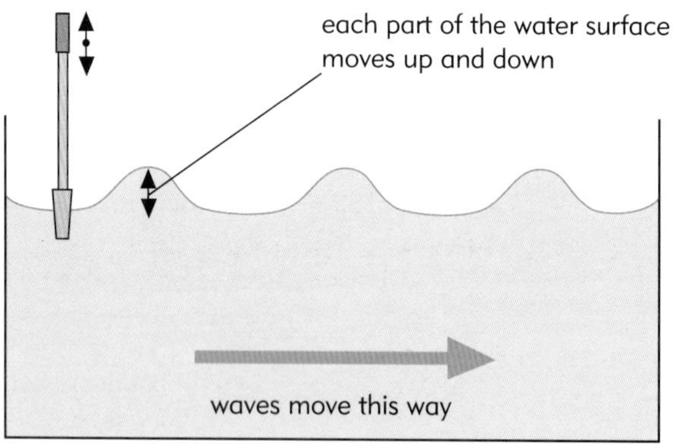

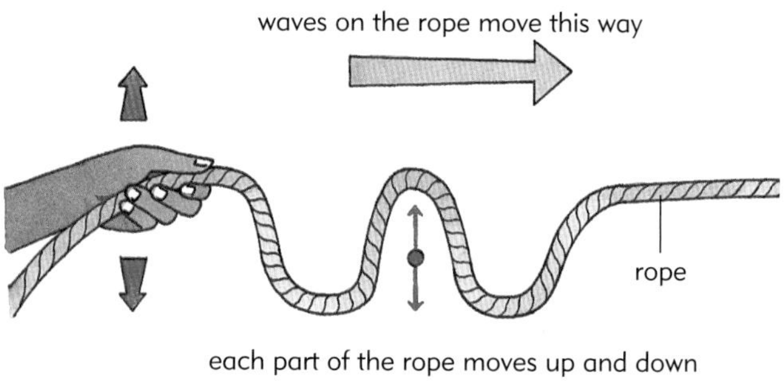

Describing waves

We say that the water and the rope are disturbed as waves travel through them. The disturbances can be different sizes and can be different distances apart.

2 Look at the diagram of a wave.

(a) What do we call the size of a disturbance?

(b) What do we call the distance between one disturbance and the next?

3 Copy and complete the following sentence.

The waves on the diagram have an amplitude of __________ cm and a wavelength of __________ cm.

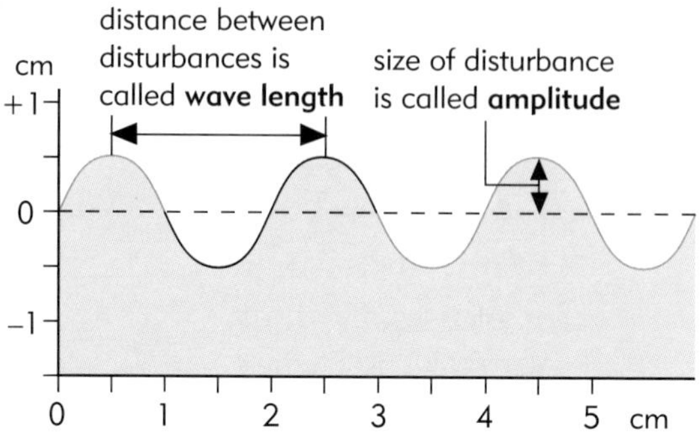

Differences between waves

The diagrams show three different sets of water waves: A, B and C.

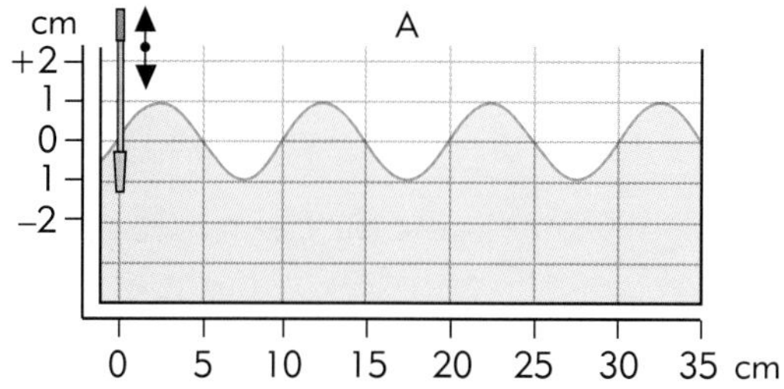

4 Look at the amplitudes and wavelengths of these waves.

Then copy and complete the table.

	Amplitude in cm	Wavelength in cm
A	1	10
B		
C		

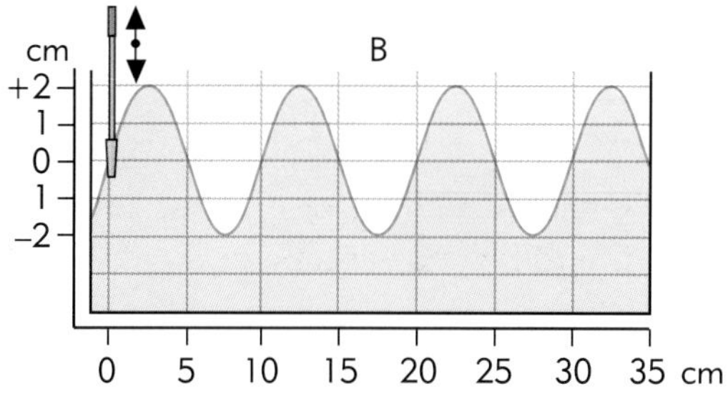

5 Copy and complete the following sentences.

Wave B has the same ___________ as wave A but it has a bigger ___________.

Wave C has the same ___________ as wave A but it has a shorter ___________.

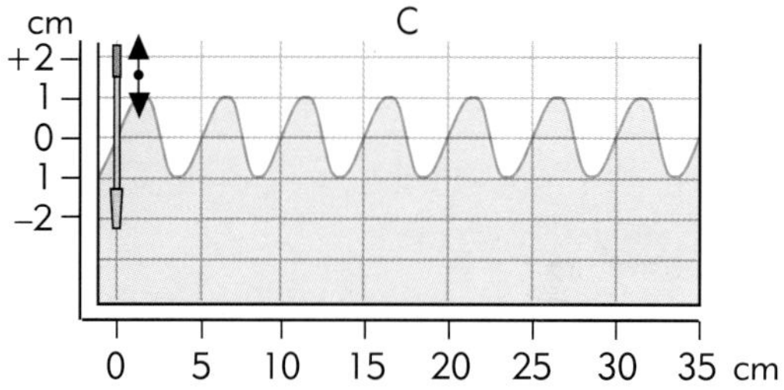

What you need to remember [Copy and complete using the **key words**]

Looking at water waves: Part 1

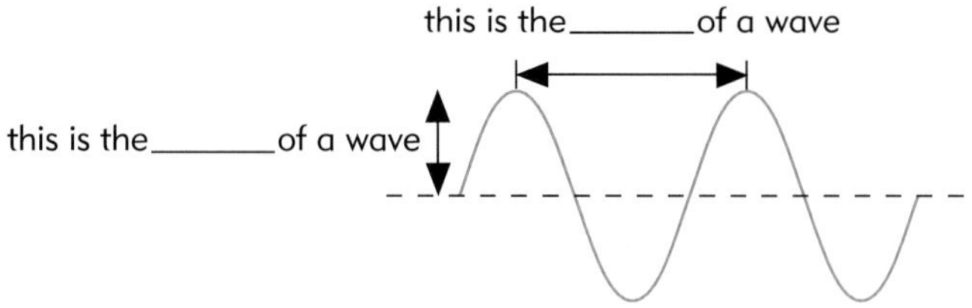

Looking at water waves: Part 2

You already know that water waves can have different wavelengths and different amplitudes. But there is another way in which waves can be different from each other.

REMEMBER

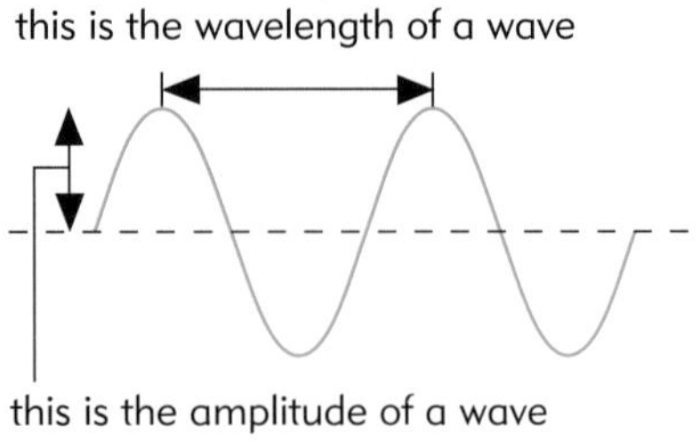

Another difference between waves

You can make a lot of waves each second or just a few waves each second.
If there are 10 waves each second, we say that the **frequency** is 10 **hertz** (Hz, for short).

The diagrams show what happens when you start to make water waves on calm water.

1 (a) How many complete waves are there after 1 second?

(b) How many complete waves are there after 2 seconds?

(c) How many complete waves are made during each second?

(d) What is the frequency of the water waves?

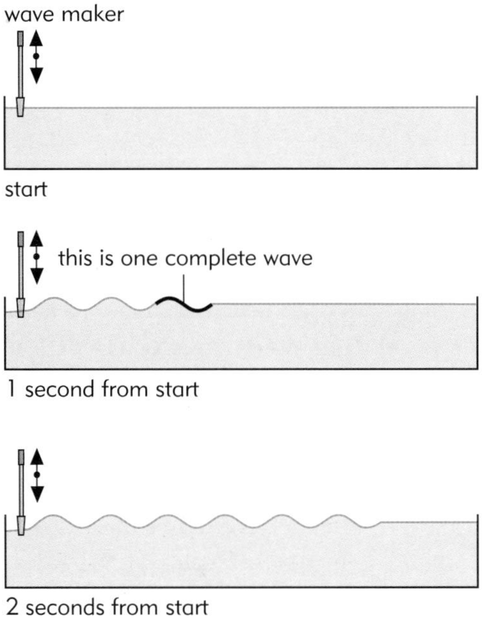

A connection between frequency and wavelength

The diagram shows what happens if you now make waves with double the frequency. The water is the same depth as before.

2 What happens to the wavelength when you double the frequency of the waves?

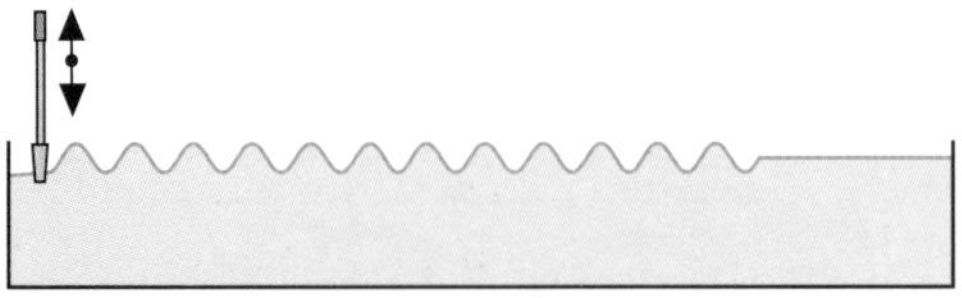

This is what you see after 2 seconds, if you make twice as many waves each second.

What's special about waves?

Waves transfer **energy** from one place to another.

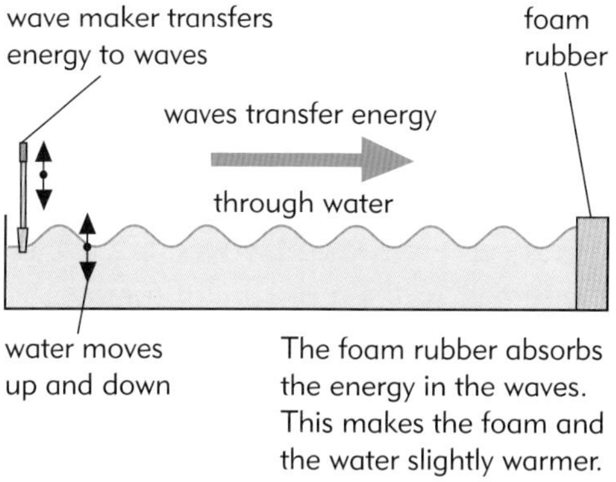

3 Look at the diagram. Then write down the following sentences in the correct order.

- The waves carry energy across the surface of the water.
- The foam rubber at the end of the tank absorbs the energy.
- Energy from the wave maker produces waves.

Waves transfer energy through the water from the wave maker to the foam rubber. But the water itself does not move from one end of the tank to the other.

4 Which way does the water move as the waves travel across it?

5 What happens to the energy carried by the waves when it is absorbed by the foam?

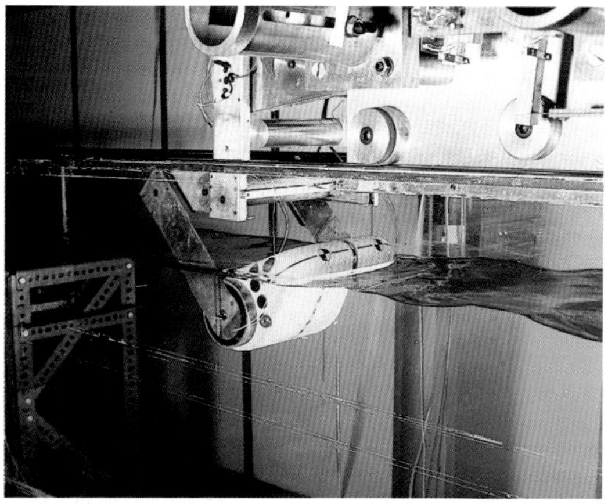

A scale model of the wave energy machine. The energy in the waves has been absorbed by the 'duck'. The duck bobs up and down and this movement energy is converted into electricity.

Using the energy from water waves

The diagrams show how we can use the energy from water waves.

6 (a) What useful form of energy do the 'ducks' produce from the energy carried by waves?

(b) You can tell by looking at the water that the 'ducks' have transferred most of the energy from the waves. Explain how you can tell.

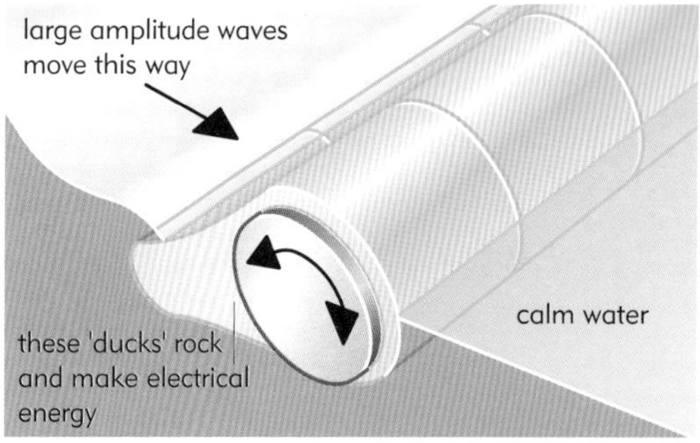

What you need to remember [Copy and complete using the **key words**]

Looking at water waves: Part 2

The number of waves each second is called the ________________, and it is measured in ________________ (Hz, for short).
Waves transfer ________________ from one place to another without any substance, such as water, being transferred.

Looking at sound waves

When things **vibrate** they make sound waves.
Sound waves are disturbances that travel through the air.
You can't see sound waves, but the diagram shows how you can make a picture of them.

1 Look at the diagram.
Then write down these sentences in the correct order to explain how you can make a picture of a sound.
The first sentence has been done for you.

A loudspeaker vibrates to make a sound.

- A microphone changes the sound waves into an electrical signal.
- The oscilloscope uses the electrical signal to make a picture.
- Sound waves travel through the air.
- The electrical signal is fed into an oscilloscope.

REMEMBER

Waves are disturbances.

The size of the disturbances is called their amplitude.

The number of disturbances each second is the frequency.

We measure frequency in hertz (Hz).

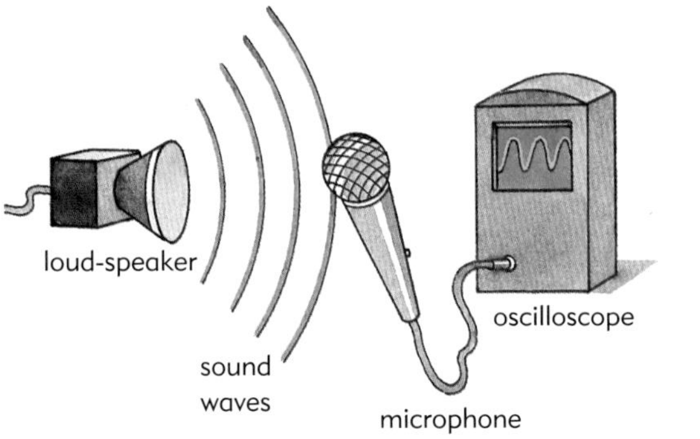
loud-speaker
sound
waves
oscilloscope
microphone
This changes the sound
waves into an electrical signal.

Sounds with different loudness

The diagrams show oscilloscope pictures of two sounds, A and B.
The two sounds are exactly the same note, so we say that they have the same pitch. But sound B is louder than sound A.

2 Look at the waves picture for sound A.

(a) How many complete waves are there on the oscilloscope picture?

(b) How long did it take for all these waves to hit the microphone?

(c) How many complete waves would there be in a whole second?

(d) What is the frequency of the sound waves? (Use the REMEMBER box to help you.)

3 Copy and complete the following sentences.

Sound B has a __________ amplitude than sound A.
This is because sound B is a __________ sound.

The loudness of a sound depends on the **amplitude** of the sound waves.

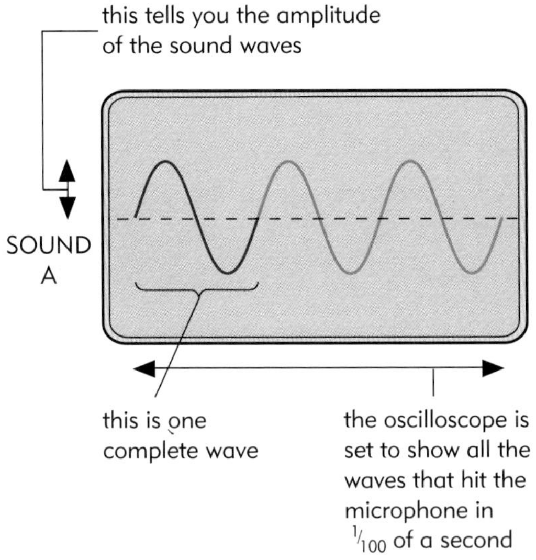
this tells you the amplitude
of the sound waves
SOUND
A
this is one
complete wave
the oscilloscope is
set to show all the
waves that hit the
microphone in
1/100 of a second

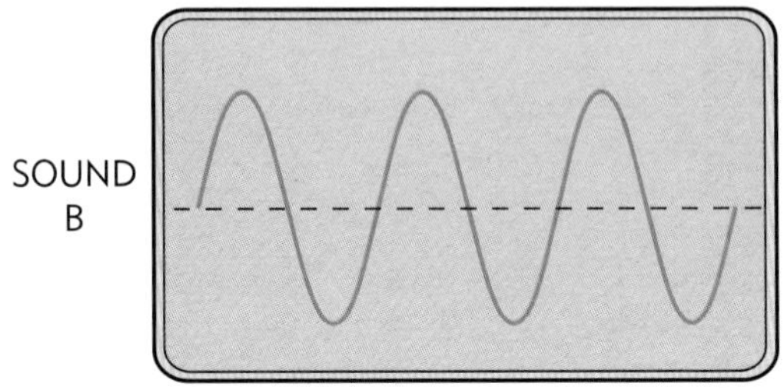
SOUND
B

Sound B is louder than sound A.

Sounds with different pitch

The diagram shows the oscilloscope picture of sound C.
Sound C is the same loudness as sound A, but sound C is a higher note than sound A.
We say that it has a higher pitch.

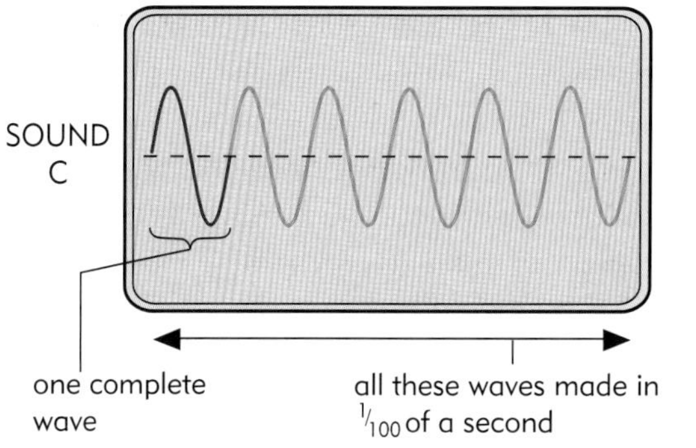

4 (a) How many complete waves are there on the oscilloscope picture of sound C?

(b) How long did it take for all these waves to be made?

(c) How many complete waves would there be in a whole second?

(d) What is the frequency of sound C?

5 Copy and complete the following sentences.

Sound C has a __________ frequency than sound A.
This is what gives it a higher __________.

The higher the **frequency** of a sound, the higher its pitch is.

Another difference between sounds

Sounds A, B and C are pure sounds. They have only one frequency.
Most sounds are mixtures of different frequencies, but they usually have one main frequency.
This frequency gives the sound its pitch.

Look at the pictures of sounds D, E and F.

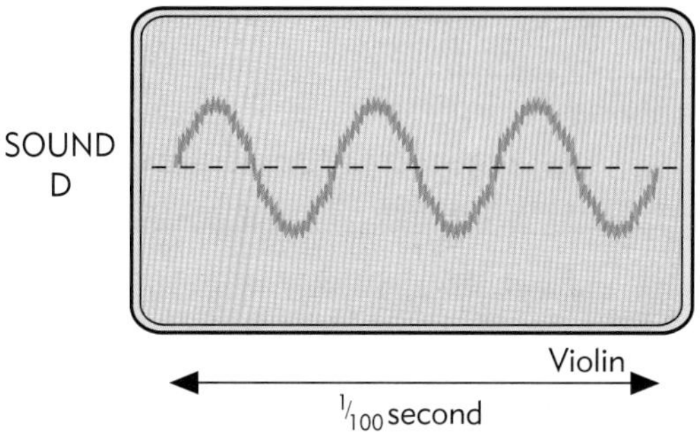

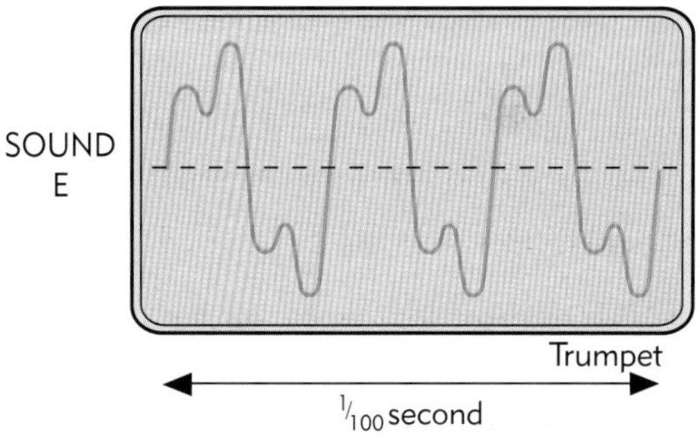

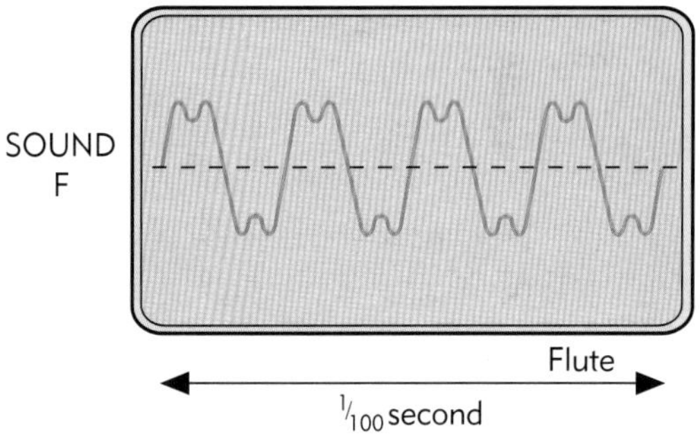

6 Which is the loudest sound?

7 (a) Which sound has the highest pitch?

(b) What is the frequency of this sound?

What you need to remember [Copy and complete using the **key words**]

Looking at sound waves

Sounds are made when things ________________.
Loud sounds have waves with a large ________________.
Sounds that have a high pitch have waves with a high ________________.

[You should be able to compare the amplitudes and frequencies of sounds from their oscilloscope pictures.]

8 'Sound' you can't hear

If the frequency of a 'sound' is too high or too low you can't hear it.

The diagram shows what frequencies of sound humans can hear. It shows what some other animals can hear as well.

1 Which animal can hear the highest frequency?

2 What range of frequencies can a child hear?

3 As you get older, the range of frequencies you can hear changes.

How does it change?

4 Farmers sometimes control their sheepdogs with a 'silent' whistle.

How can a dog whistle be silent?

Sound with a very high frequency that is too high for humans to hear is called **ultrasound**.

REMEMBER

The higher the frequency of a sound, the higher its pitch is.

Frequency is measured in waves per second or hertz (Hz).

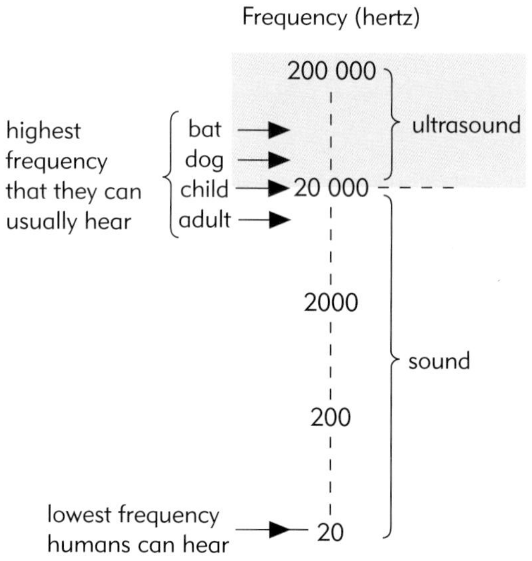

Making ultrasounds

The photograph shows how you can make sound of any frequency, including ultrasound.

5 Copy and complete the following sentences.

Inside a signal generator an __________ circuit can produce electrical vibrations of any frequency you choose.

These signals are sent to a __________ or a __________ and make it vibrate with the same __________.

These vibrations make waves of sound or ultrasound.

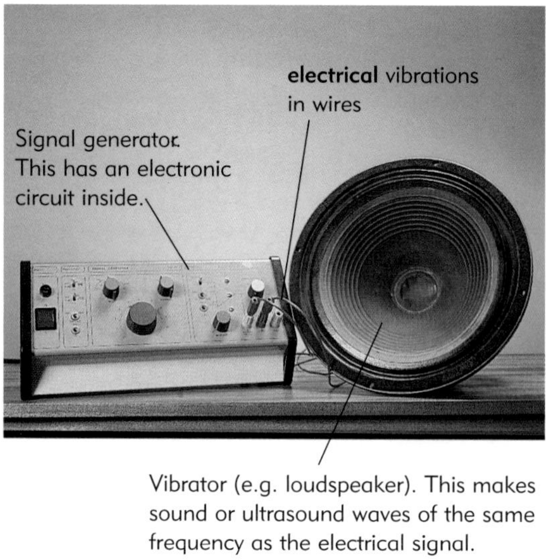

Cleaning things with ultrasound

You can use ultrasound to **clean** a delicate wind-up watch without having to take it apart.

The diagram shows how you can do this.

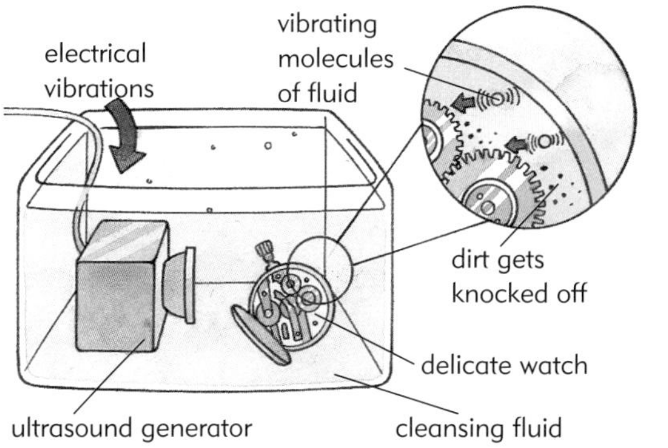

electrical vibrations
vibrating molecules of fluid
dirt gets knocked off
delicate watch
ultrasound generator
cleansing fluid

6 Copy and complete the following sentences.

An __________ generator makes the __________ of the cleaning fluid vibrate.

These then gently knock tiny bits of __________ off the delicate parts of the watch.

Ultrasound scans

Doctors use ultrasound to 'see' how a baby is developing inside its mother's womb. They make an ultrasound **scan**.

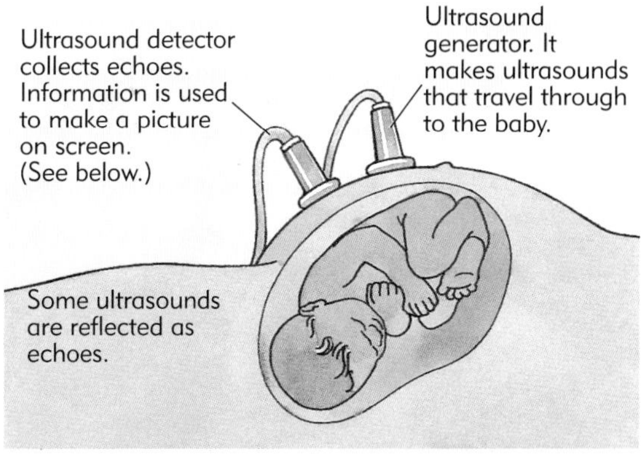

Ultrasound detector collects echoes. Information is used to make a picture on screen. (See below.)
Ultrasound generator. It makes ultrasounds that travel through to the baby.
Some ultrasounds are reflected as echoes.

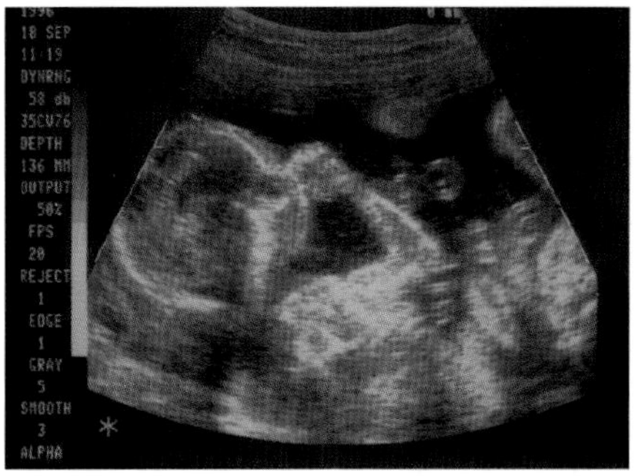

7 Look at the diagram.
Then write down the following sentences in the right order to explain how an ultrasound scan works. The first sentence has been done for you.

The doctor places an ultrasound generator on the mother's stomach.

- The echoes are collected by an ultrasound detector.
- Ultrasounds travel through the mother's and the baby's bodies.
- The signals from the detector are made into a picture on a screen.
- When the ultrasound crosses from one substance into another, some ultrasound is reflected as an echo.

8 Write down one other use of ultrasound scanning.

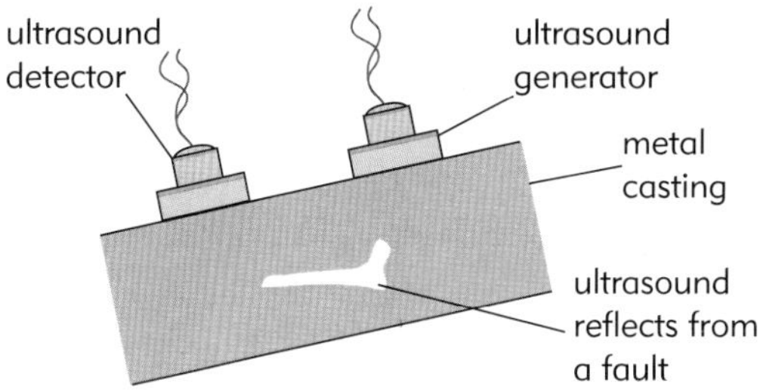

ultrasound detector
ultrasound generator
metal casting
ultrasound reflects from a fault

What you need to remember [Copy and complete using the **key words**]

'Sound' you can't hear

Sound with a frequency that is too high for humans to hear is called __________.
Sound, or ultrasound, of any frequency can be made from __________ vibrations produced by electronic circuits.
You can use ultrasound to __________ delicate mechanisms like wind-up watches.
Doctors can make an ultrasound __________ of a developing baby inside its mother's womb.

Why are there different colours of light?

Sunlight looks white but it is made up of many different **colours**.

We can see all these colours in a rainbow.

> **REMEMBER**
>
> Light is bent or refracted when it passes from air into glass, or glass into air.

Splitting light into the colours of the rainbow

The diagram shows how you can split up white light into all the colours of the rainbow. The pattern of colours is called a **spectrum**.

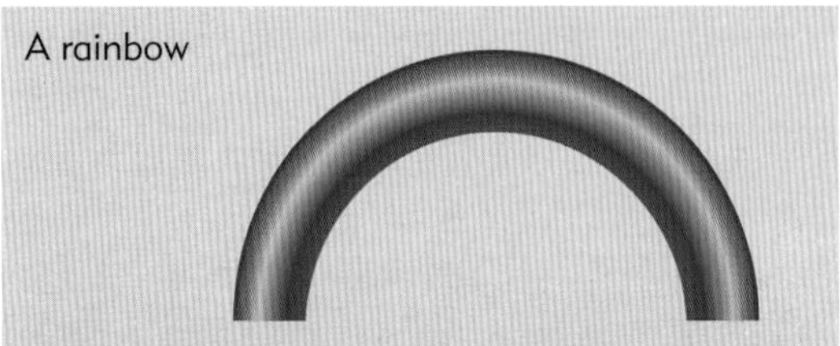

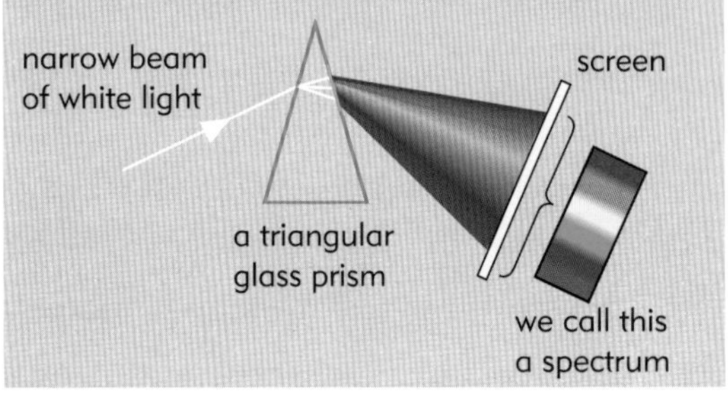

1 Copy and complete the following sentences.

We can split up white light into many different colours using a glass __________.

We then get what is called a __________.

Looking at the colours of the spectrum

Our eyes can pick out hundreds of different colours in a spectrum, but we usually group all these colours into a few broad bands.

These bands do not have sharp edges; each band of colour shades gradually into the next one.

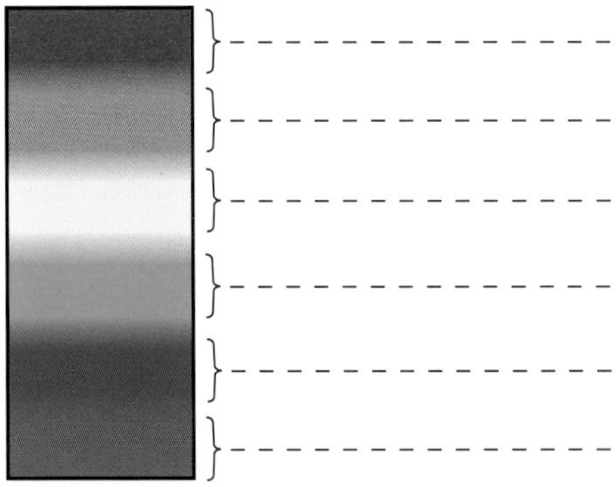

The bands of colour in the spectrum.

2 (a) Make a copy of the spectrum using coloured pens or pencils.

(b) Write the names of the following bands of colour on your diagram in the right order:

blue, green, orange, red, violet, yellow

Why a prism produces a spectrum

The diagram shows what a prism does to a narrow beam of red light.

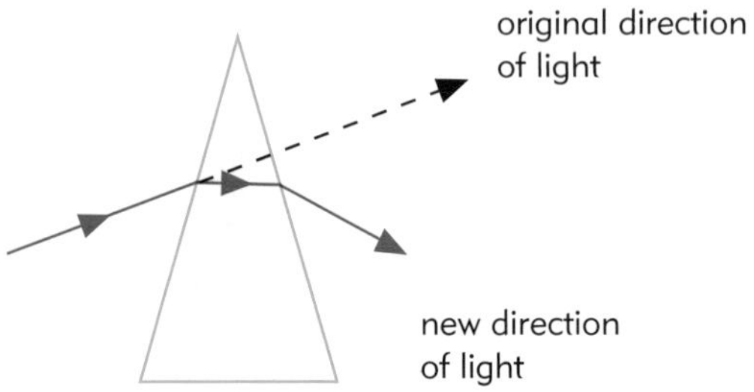

3 Copy and complete the following sentences. (Use the REMEMBER box to help you.)

The prism changes the __________ of the red light.

This happens because the light is __________ as it goes into and out of the glass.

The prism **refracts** different colours of light by different amounts.

So some colours of light change their **direction** more than other colours.

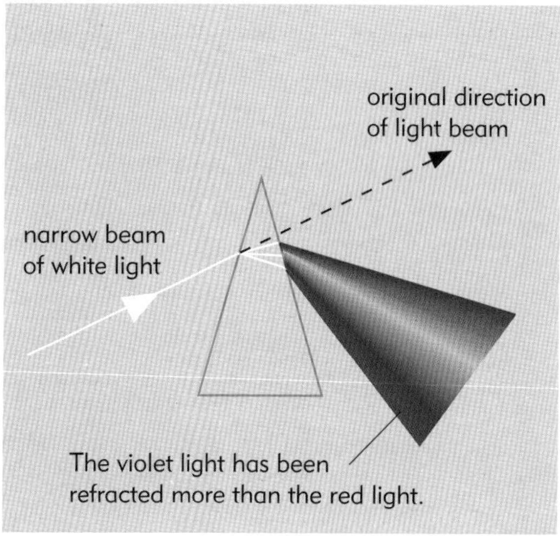

4 Copy and complete the following sentences.

The prism changes the direction of __________ light the most and the direction of __________ light the least.

This is because violet light is refracted __________ than red light.

Why are there different colours of light?

Light travels as waves. Different colours of light have different **wavelengths**.

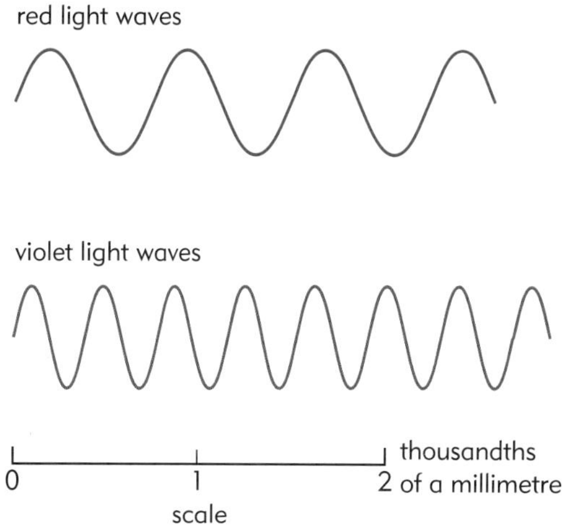

5 Look at the diagrams of red and violet light waves. Then copy and complete the following sentence.

Red waves have a __________ wavelength than violet waves.

The wavelengths of light waves are all very small.

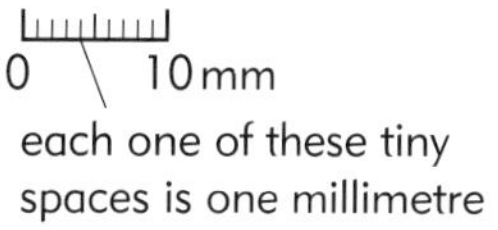

6 How many violet waves are there:

(a) in a thousandth of a millimetre?

(b) in a whole millimetre?

What you need to remember [Copy and complete using the **key words**]

Why are there different colours of light?

When rays of light pass through a prism their ______________ is changed.
You can use a prism to split up white light into all its ______________. The pattern of colours is called a ______________.
The prism splits up light because the prism ______________ different colours by different amounts.
Different colours of light have different ______________.

[You should be able to show, on a drawing, what happens when a ray of white light passes through a prism.]

Waves beyond the ends of the rainbow

White **light** is a mixture of many different colours. Different colours of light have different wavelengths.

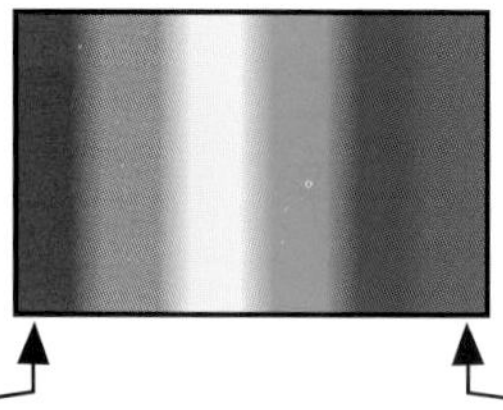
longest wavelength
shortest wavelength

1 (a) Look at the diagram. Then copy and complete the following sentences.

Red light has the __________ wavelength.

Violet light has the __________ wavelength.

(b) Make a copy of the diagram.

Make sure that the diagram is in the centre of your page with plenty of room at both sides. You will need to add things to it later on.

Are there other waves we can't see?

We know that there are 'sounds' that we can't hear. This is because their frequency is too high or too low. Our ears can only hear certain frequencies.

There is also 'light' that we can't see.

This is because its wavelength is too long or too short. Our eyes can only see certain wavelengths.

The diagram shows how we can tell that these waves are there, even though we can't see them.

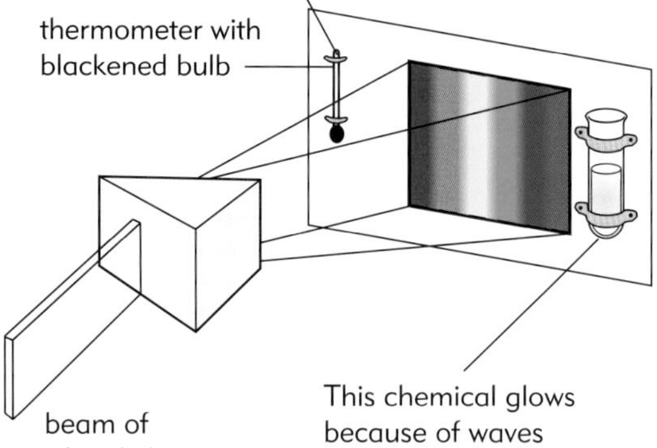
The thermometer gets hot because of waves outside the red end of the spectrum. We call them **infrared** waves.
thermometer with blackened bulb
beam of white light
This chemical glows because of waves outside the violet end of the spectrum. We call them **ultraviolet** waves.

2 (a) How do we know that there are waves outside the red end of the spectrum?

(b) What do we call these waves?

3 (a) How do we know there are waves outside the violet end of the spectrum?

(b) What do we call these waves?

Infrared and ultraviolet waves are also called infrared and ultraviolet radiation.

4 Add infrared and ultraviolet radiation to your diagram of the spectrum.

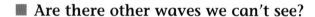

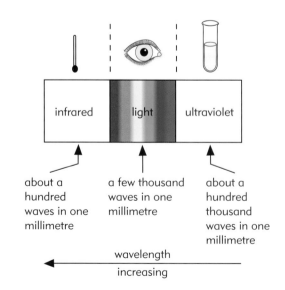

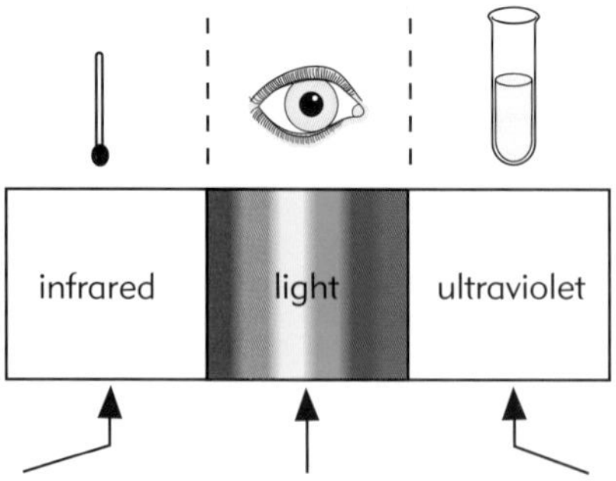
infrared
light
ultraviolet
about a hundred waves in one millimetre
a few thousand waves in one millimetre
about a hundred thousand waves in one millimetre
wavelength
increasing

Adding more waves to the spectrum

There are waves with longer wavelengths than infrared waves.

There are also waves with shorter wavelengths than ultraviolet waves.

All of these waves are parts of a bigger spectrum, which we call the **electromagnetic** spectrum.

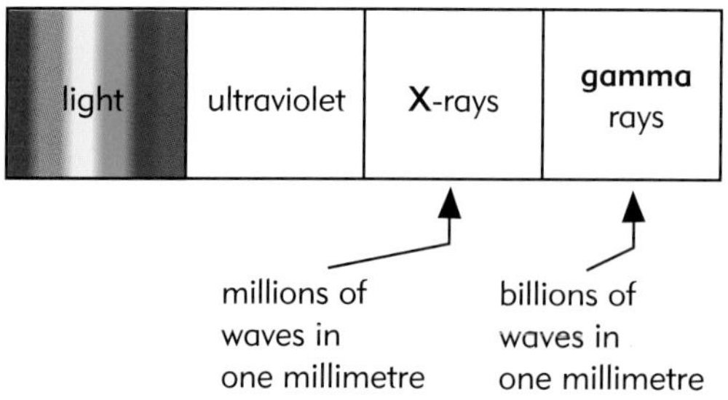

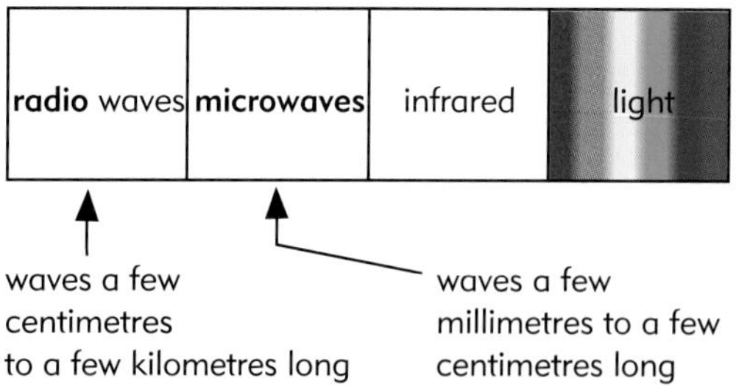

5 Add all these other types of waves to your diagram of the electromagnetic spectrum.

How fast do electromagnetic waves travel?

All the different kinds of electromagnetic waves travel at the same **speed** through space. So the waves with the shortest **wavelength** also have the highest **frequency**.

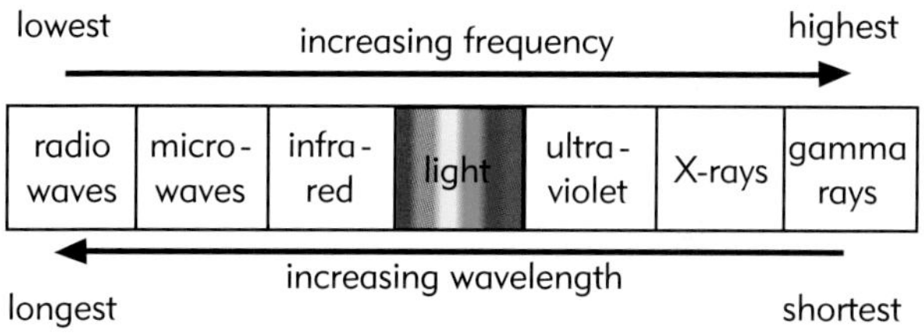

6 Add the information about wavelength and frequency to your diagram.

7 Copy and complete the following sentences.

Radio waves have the __________ wavelength and the __________ frequency.

Gamma rays have the __________ wavelength and the __________ frequency.

In space all electromagnetic waves travel at the same speed.

This speed is 300 million metres per second.

Electromagnetic waves are also called electromagnetic radiation.

What you need to remember [Copy and complete using the **key words**]

Waves beyond the ends of the rainbow

The table shows all the different kinds of waves in the ________________ spectrum.

__________ waves	__________- **waves**	__________ waves	__________	__________ waves	_____-rays	__________ rays

longest wavelength red violet shortest ________________

lowest ________________ highest frequency

All types of electromagnetic radiation travel through space at exactly the same ________________.

11 What happens when electromagnetic waves hit things?

REMEMBER

radio waves	micro-waves	infrared	light	ultra-violet	X-rays	gamma rays

All these types of electromagnetic waves or radiation travel at the same speed in space.

There are many different types of electromagnetic waves.

1 Write down the names of <u>seven</u> different types of electromagnetic waves.

2 Write down <u>one</u> thing that is the <u>same</u> about all the types of electromagnetic waves.

All electromagnetic waves can travel easily through space.

But electromagnetic waves often bump into matter in the form of solids, liquids or gases.

The diagrams show what can then happen.

3 What <u>three</u> things can happen when electromagnetic waves hit matter?

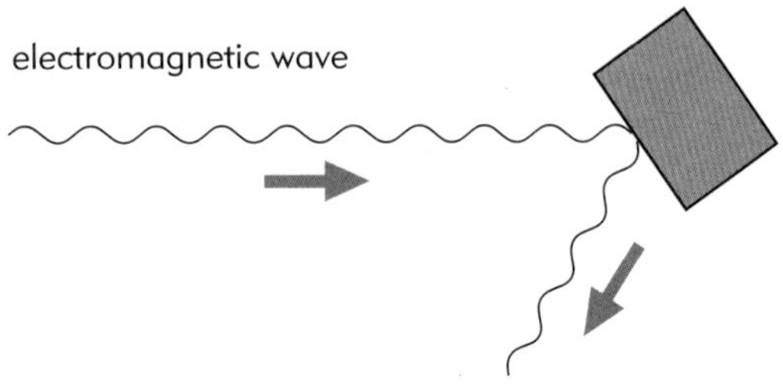

The waves can bounce off the matter. We say the matter reflects the waves.

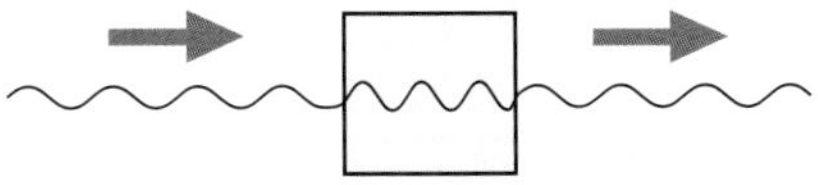

The waves can pass through the matter. We say the matter transmits the waves.

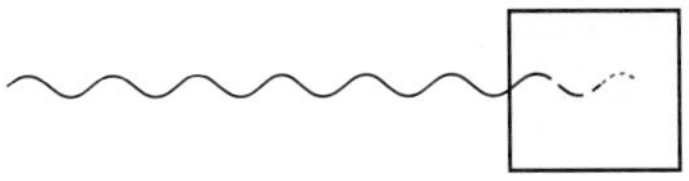

The matter can absorb the waves.

Absorbing electromagnetic radiation

Sometimes when radiation hits a solid, liquid or gas, some of the radiation is **transmitted** and some is **absorbed**.

This is what happens when light hits polythene. The diagram shows how you can find out how much light polythene lets through.

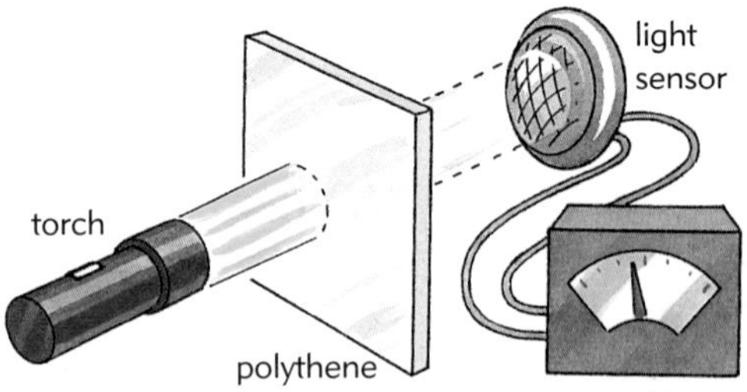

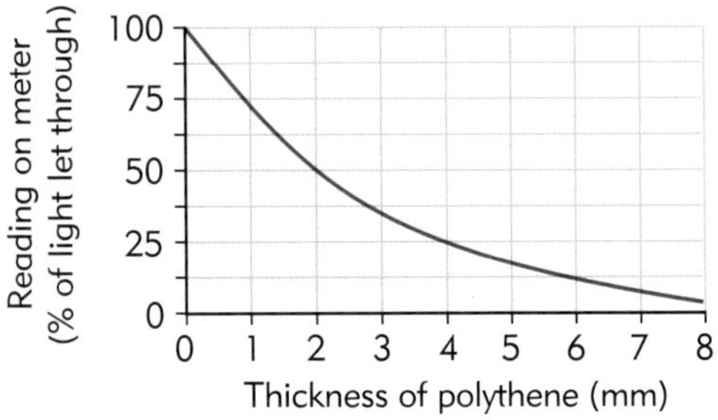

4 Look at the graph. Then copy and complete the following sentences.

The thicker the polythene is, the __________ light it lets through.

To absorb half of the light you need __________ mm of polythene.

A thickness of 4 mm of polythene lets through only __________ per cent of the light.

■ What happens when electromagnetic waves are absorbed?

Like all waves, electromagnetic waves carry **energy** from one place to another. We say that the waves transfer energy.

When waves are absorbed, this energy is transferred to the material that absorbs them. The diagram shows what happens then.

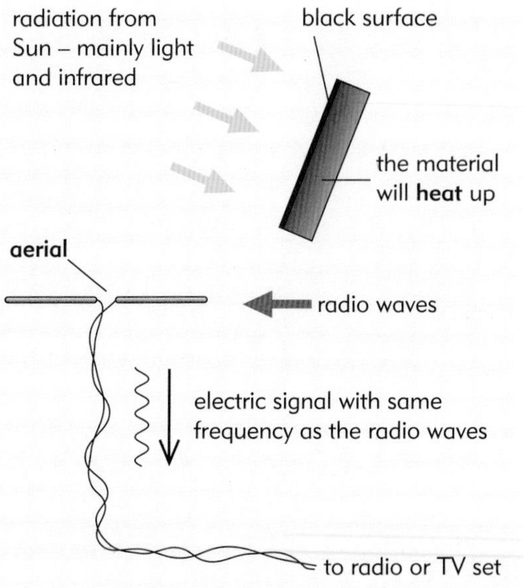

5 A black surface absorbs light and infrared radiation. What happens to the energy carried by this radiation?

6 Radio waves are absorbed by an aerial. What happens to the energy carried by these waves?

■ Surfaces that partly reflect

Light passes quite easily through transparent substances. But when light passes from one transparent substance to another, some light is always **reflected**.

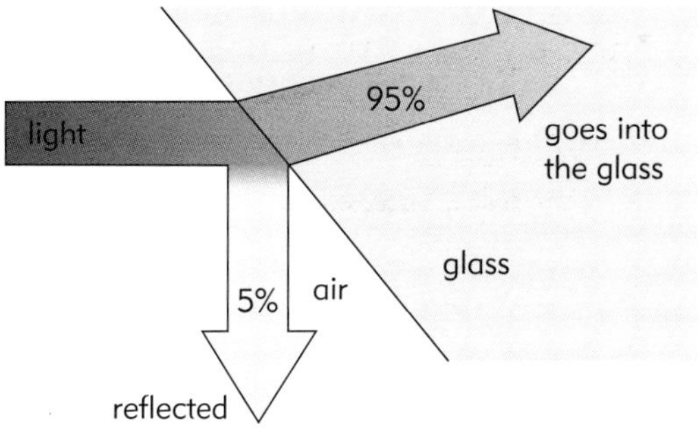

7 Look at the diagram. Then copy and complete the following sentences.

When light strikes the boundary between air and glass, about __________ per cent of the light passes into the glass.

But about __________ per cent of the light is __________ by the glass.

8 The piece of glass transmits only about 89 per cent of the light that falls on it. Explain, as fully as you can, what happens to the other 11 per cent.

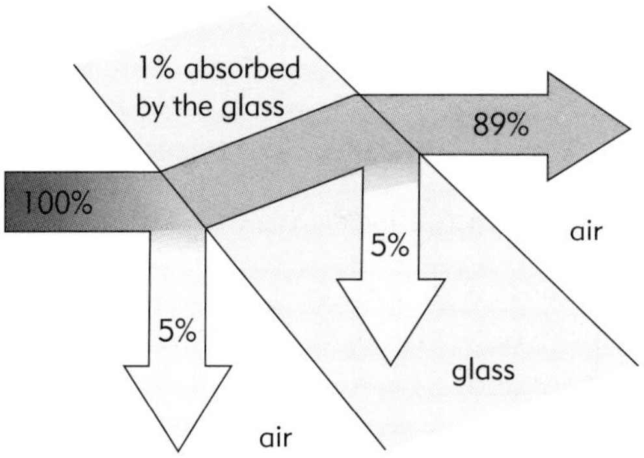

Different types of electromagnetic radiation are transmitted, reflected or absorbed by different materials.

What you need to remember [Copy and complete using the **key words**]

What happens when electromagnetic waves hit things?

When electromagnetic waves hit a solid, liquid or gas they may be ________________, ________________ or ________________ (or more than one of these).

Electromagnetic waves transfer ________________. When the waves are absorbed by matter, this energy may make the matter ________________ up.

When radio waves or microwaves are absorbed by an ________________, they produce an electric signal.

How a doctor can see inside your stomach

A doctor thinks a patient has an stomach ulcer, so she needs to look inside the patient's stomach. The diagram shows how she can do this.

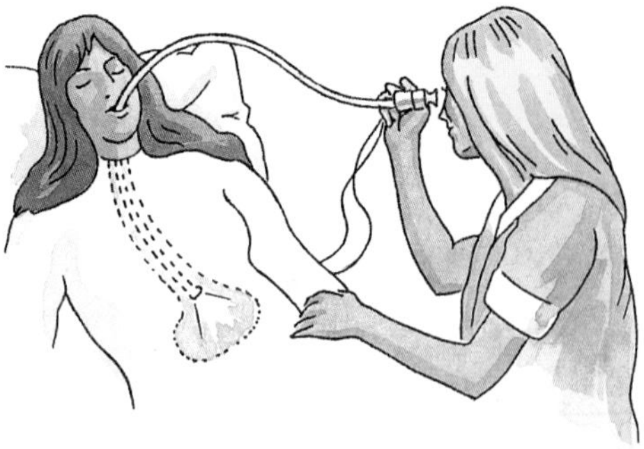

Using an endoscope ('endo' means 'inside', 'scope' means 'looking for').

1 What instrument does the doctor use?

2 Why does the instrument have this name?

The **endoscope** works by sending light waves down very thin fibres made from glass, called **optical** fibres.

How do optical fibres work?

Light waves travel through an optical fibre just like sound waves travel through a pipe.

You can even use an optical fibre to send light round corners.

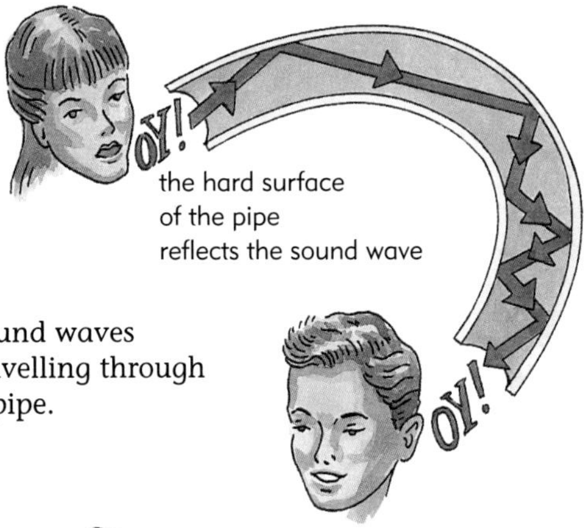

Sound waves travelling through a pipe.

3 Look at the diagrams. Then copy and complete the following sentences.

Sound waves are __________ over and over again from the __________ surface inside a pipe.

Light waves are __________ over and over again inside an optical __________.

4 (a) What are optical fibres made from?

(b) How thick is an optical fibre?

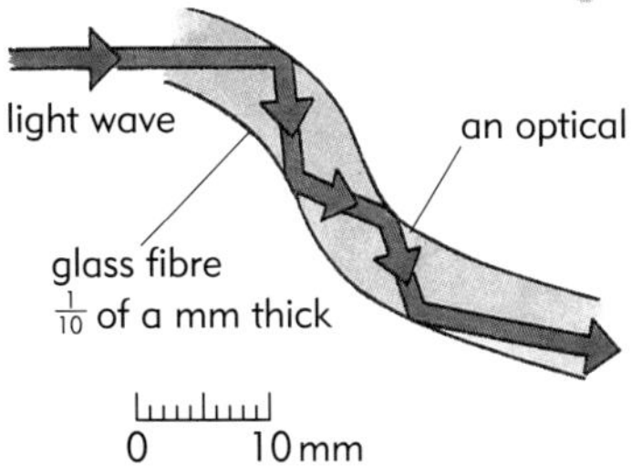

Light waves travelling through an optical fibre.

Why doesn't light get out of an optical fibre?

The diagrams show what happens to some beams of light when they meet the boundary between glass and air.

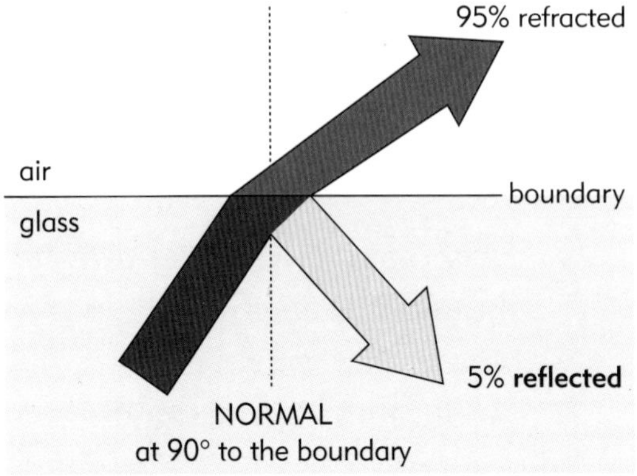

5 Copy and complete the following sentences.

__________ per cent of the light passes out of the glass and is refracted.

__________ per cent of the light is reflected back inside the glass.

The diagrams show what happens as a ray of light makes a bigger and bigger angle with a normal.

6 Copy and complete the following sentences.

A ray of light which is at an angle of __________° with a normal only just gets out of the glass.

If a ray of light is at a bigger angle than 42° with a normal, it is all __________ inside the glass.

This is called __________ internal reflection.

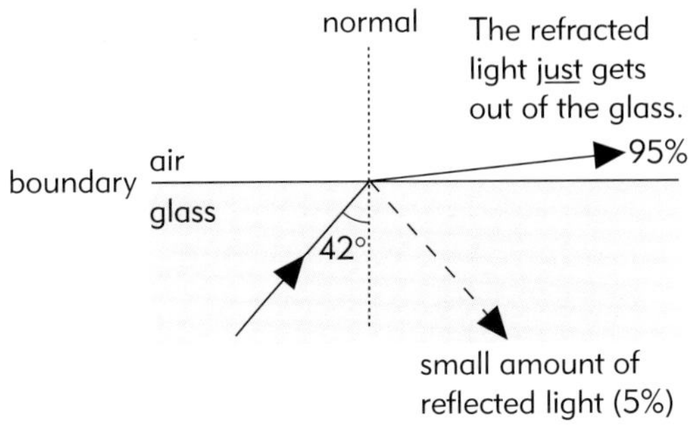

The angle at which you start to get total internal reflection is called the **critical angle**.

7 What is the critical angle for glass?

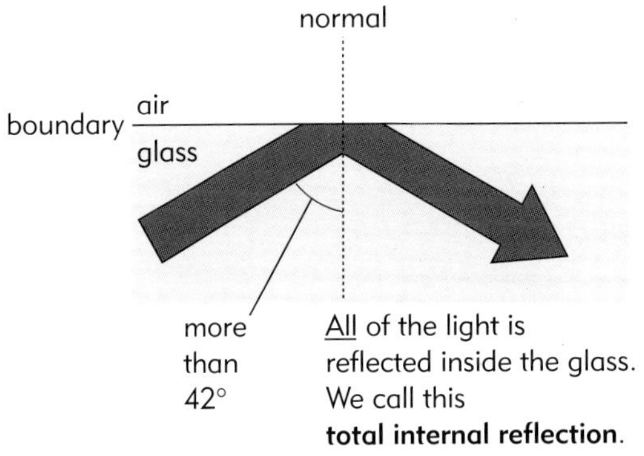

How an endoscope works

The diagram shows how an endoscope lets a doctor see the inside of your stomach.

8 Write down the following sentences in the right order. The first one has been done for you.

Light from a lamp travels down a bundle of optical fibres to your stomach.

- This light goes into the doctor's eye so she sees the inside of your stomach.
- Some light is reflected from the lining of your stomach.
- Light shines on to the inside of your stomach.
- The reflected light travels up a different bundle of optical fibres.

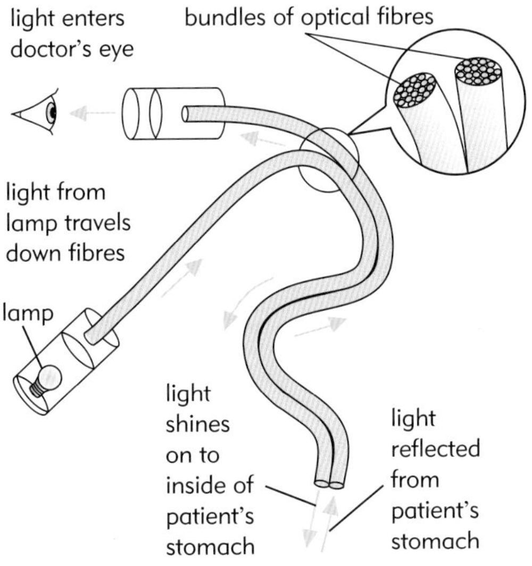

How the endoscope works.

What you need to remember [Copy and complete using the **key words**]

How a doctor can see inside your stomach

A doctor can see inside a patient's stomach using an ______________.
This works by sending light along ______________ fibres.
All of the light is ______________ over and over again from the inside of the fibre.
This is called ______________ ______________ **reflection**. This happens when the angle of the light to the normal is bigger than the ______________ **angle**.

Using radio waves

REMEMBER

increasing frequency →

radio waves	micro-waves	infrared	light	ultra-violet	X-rays	gamma rays

← increasing wavelength

When we use any kind of waves, we need to know what will reflect them, what will transmit them and what will absorb them.

Transmitting and absorbing radio waves

Radio waves are used to carry **radio** and **television** programmes. The diagrams show why they are suitable for this job.

1 What substances will radio waves pass through easily?

2 What happens when radio waves are absorbed by an aerial?

3 Why can't you send a radio message to or from a submarine?

(a)

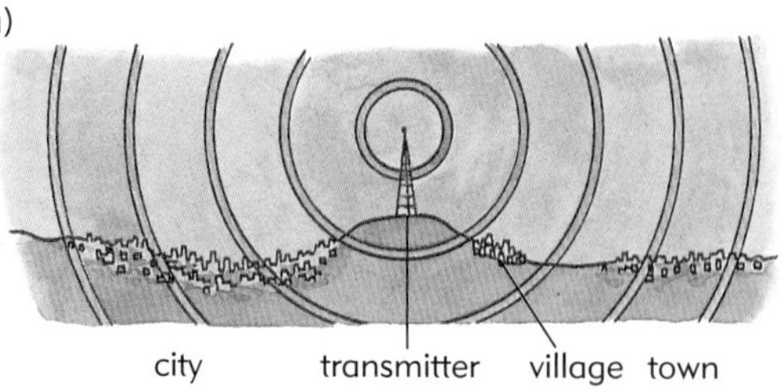

Radio waves can pass easily through **air**.

(b)

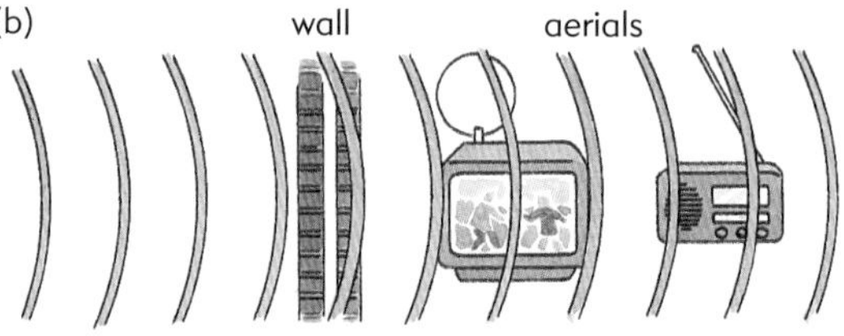

Radio waves can pass through **dry** non-metals.

Aerials transfer energy waves into electrical energy.

(c) Water absorbs radio waves.

Reflecting radio waves

The Earth's atmosphere has electrically charged layers. One of the electrically charged layers **reflects** radio waves with long wavelengths.

The diagram shows how we can use these reflections.

4 Why is it useful to be able to reflect long wavelength radio waves?

5 What is the wavelength of these radio waves?

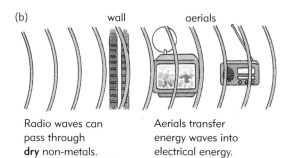

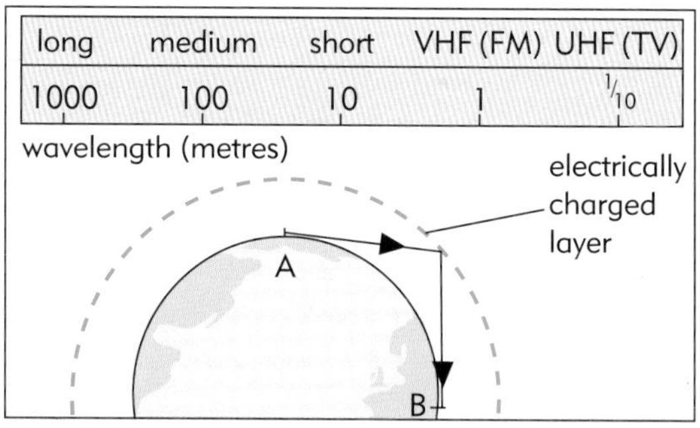

Sending radio waves round the **curved** surface of the Earth.

What you need to remember [Copy and complete using the **key words**]

Using radio waves

Radio waves can pass easily through __________ and through __________ non-metals.
This is what makes them useful for carrying __________ and __________ programmes.
A layer in the Earth's atmosphere __________ radio waves with long wavelengths.
We use this idea to send radio waves around the __________ surface of the Earth.

14 Using microwaves

To make good use of microwaves, we need to know what will reflect them, transmit them or absorb them.

REMEMBER

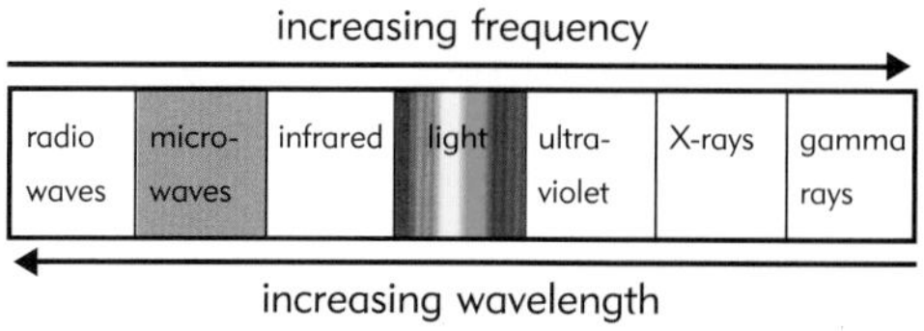

Microwave ovens

The diagram shows how a microwave oven works.

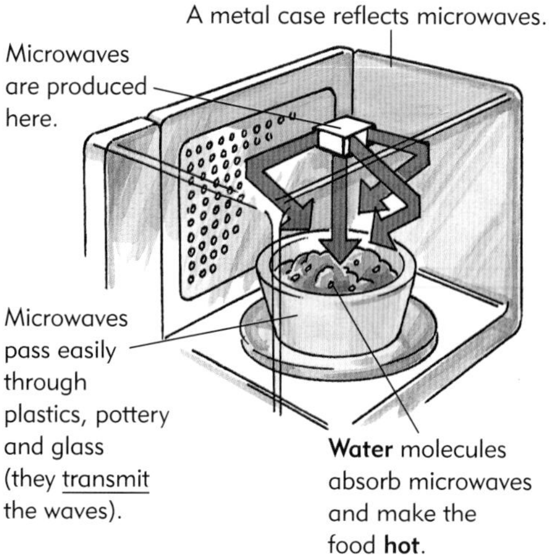

1 Copy and complete the following sentences.

The case of a microwave oven is made of __________ This __________ microwaves.

Food contains __________ molecules. These __________ microwaves and become hot.

The food is put into containers made of __________, __________ or __________. These materials allow microwaves to pass through them very easily. We say that they __________ the microwaves.

Satellite television

The diagram shows how television **satellites** use microwaves with certain wavelengths.

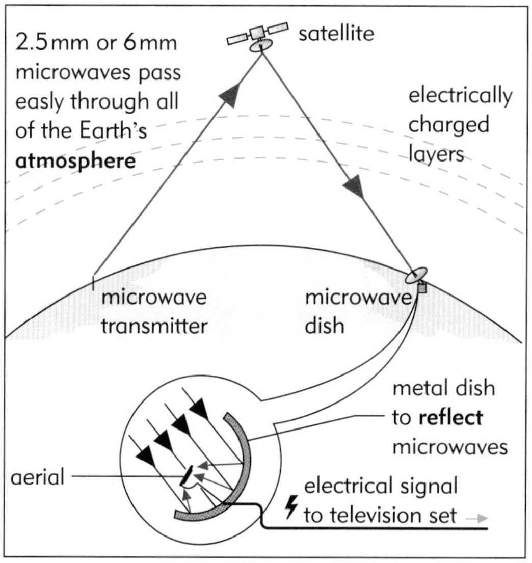

2 (a) What wavelengths of microwaves are used for satellite television?

(b) Why are these wavelengths used?

3 Copy and complete the following sentences.

We use a __________ dish to collect enough microwaves for a strong signal. This __________ the microwaves on to an aerial.

The aerial transfers energy from the microwaves as an __________ signal.

What you need to remember [Copy and complete using the **key words**]

Using microwaves

In microwave ovens, the microwaves are strongly absorbed by __________ molecules in food. The energy from the microwaves makes the food __________.
Metal things __________ microwaves, even if they are full of small holes.
Some microwaves can pass easily through the Earth's __________.
These microwaves are used to carry information to and from __________.

Using infrared radiation

Hot things send out **infrared** radiation, and when things
absorb infrared radiation they get hot.
So infrared rays are often called heat rays.

Infrared radiation can be used for cooking, for example
in toasters and grills.

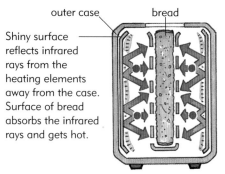

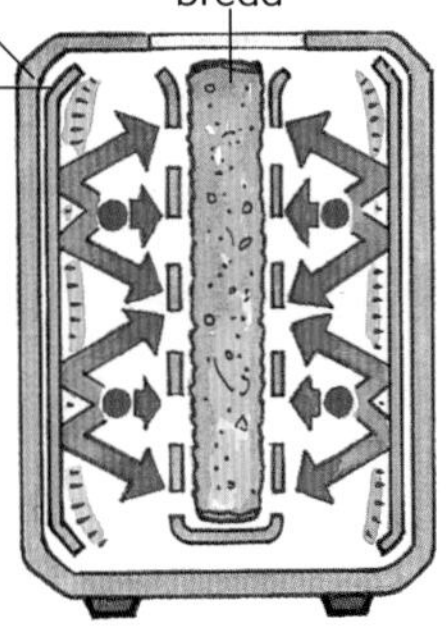

1 An electric toaster has a shiny surface between the
heating elements and the outer case.
Write down <u>two</u> reasons for this.

■ Infrared rays for lazy people

You can often change channels on a **television** set, or
switch on a **video** player, using a remote control. The
diagram shows how this works.

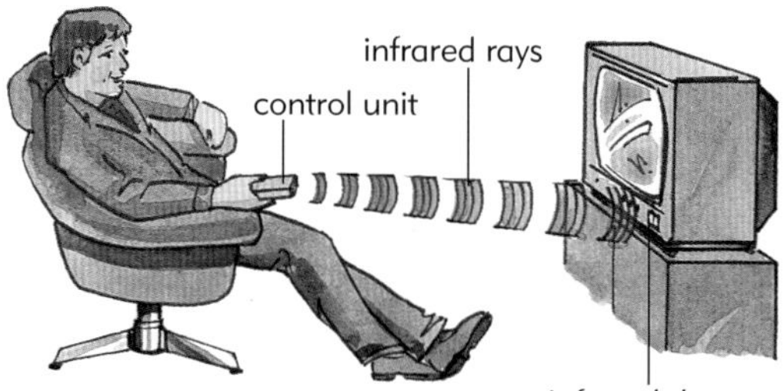

2 (a) How is your instruction carried to the television
set or video player?

(b) Why must you point the remote control at the
television set or video player?

■ Infrared telephone calls

Long-distance telephone messages used to be sent as
electrical signals through copper wires. They are now
mainly carried by infrared rays inside **optical** fibres.

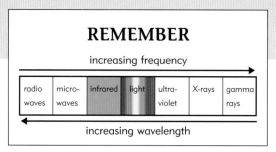

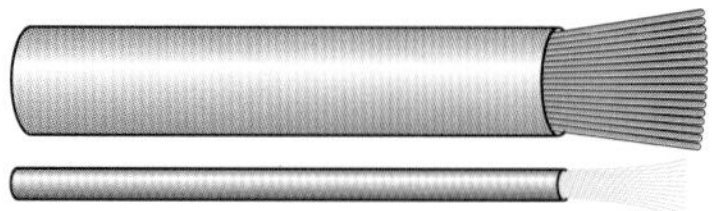

3 Write down <u>two</u> advantages of using the optical
fibres.

REMEMBER

increasing frequency →

radio waves	micro- waves	infrared	light	ultra- violet	X-rays	gamma rays

← increasing wavelength

How a toaster works.

Shiny surface reflects infrared rays from the heating elements away from the case. Surface of bread absorbs the infrared rays and gets hot.

outer case bread

infrared rays
control unit
infrared detector

(a) copper wires / optical fibres

The cable of optical fibres has a much **smaller**
diameter but it can still carry the same number of
telephone calls.

(b)
With copper wires the signal gets weak so you need to
boost the signal every 4 or 5 km. With optical fibres
there is less **weakening** of the signal.

What you need to remember [Copy and complete using the **key words**]

Using infrared radiation

Toasters and grills cook food using _____ radiation.

Foods become hot when they _____ this radiation.

Infrared rays are used to control a _____ set or a _____

player, and to send telephone messages along _____ fibres.

This is better than sending electrical signals along wires, because the cable has a

_____ diameter and there is less _____ of the signal.

16 Using ultraviolet radiation

The Sun sends out lots of **ultraviolet** radiation, some of which falls on the Earth.
Most of this is absorbed by the Earth's atmosphere but some of it gets through.

1 You get a lot of ultraviolet radiation if you go skiing in the mountains.
Write down <u>two</u> reasons for this.

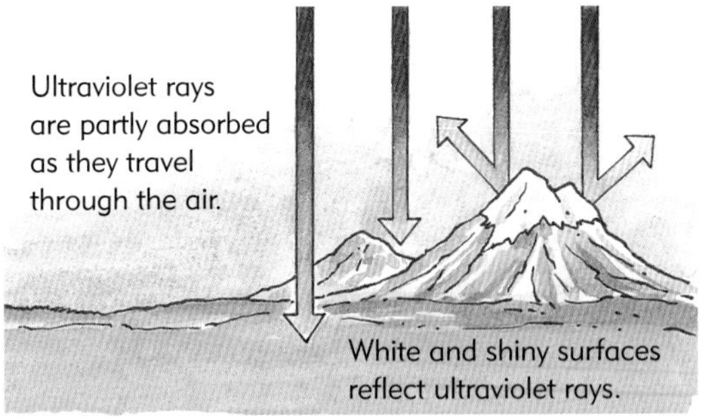

■ Ultraviolet radiation and your body

The diagrams show some of the effects ultraviolet rays can have on your body.

2 Write down:

(a) <u>two</u> reasons why people might want to let ultraviolet rays on to their skin

(b) <u>two</u> ways in which ultraviolet radiation can harm your body.

You can read more about the harmful effects of ultraviolet rays on page 126.

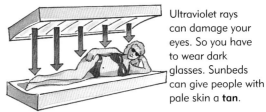

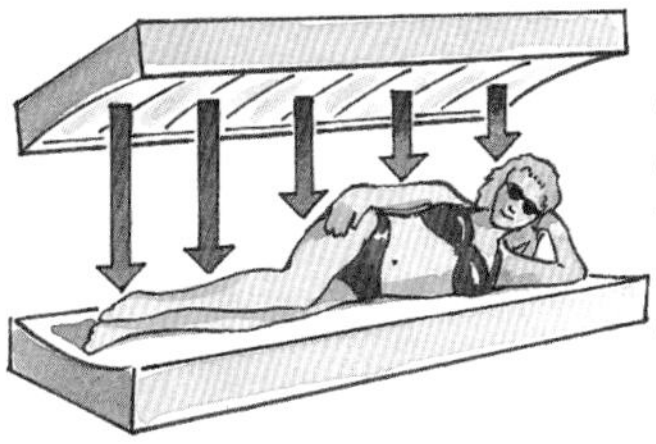

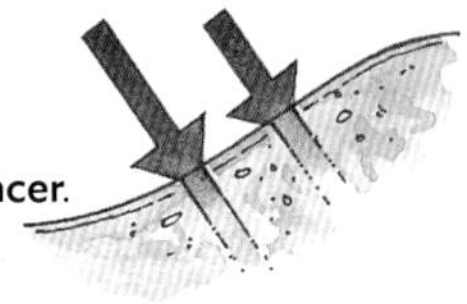

■ Changing ultraviolet radiation into light

Some substances can **absorb** the energy from ultraviolet radiation and use it to produce **light**. We say that these substances are **fluorescent**.

The diagrams show some uses for fluorescent substances.

3 Write down <u>two</u> uses for fluorescent substances.

REMEMBER

increasing frequency →

| radio waves | micro waves | infrared | light | ultra-violet | X-rays | gamma rays |

← increasing wavelength

Ultraviolet rays are partly absorbed as they travel through the air.

White and shiny surfaces reflect ultraviolet rays.

Ultraviolet rays can damage your eyes. So you have to wear dark glasses. Sunbeds can give people with pale skin a **tan**.

Ultraviolet rays absorbed by your skin are used to make vitamin D, but they can also cause skin **cancer**.

Using fluorescent substances.
You can put invisible marks on to valuable things.

a strip light

in light

in UV rays

JO BLOGGS
071 29643

energy sent out as light waves

UV waves absorbed by fluorescent substance

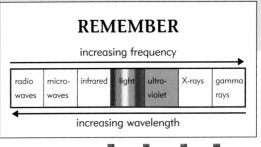

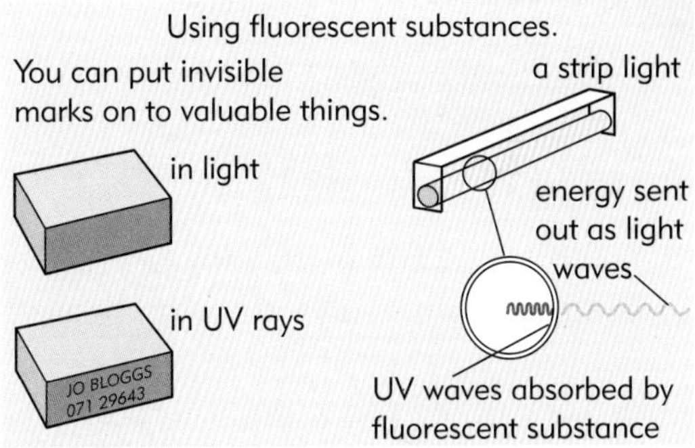

What you need to remember [Copy and complete using the **key words**]

Using ultraviolet radiation

Radiation from the Sun, or from a sunbed, can give pale skins a _____.
But it can also damage skin cells and cause skin _____.
These things happen because of _____ radiation.
Some substances _____ ultraviolet radiation and use the energy to produce _____. We say that these substances are _____.

[You should know some uses for fluorescent substances.]

Using X-rays

X-rays can pass easily through some substances but not through others.

To use X-rays safely and in a useful way, we need to know what substances they will, or won't, pass through.

REMEMBER

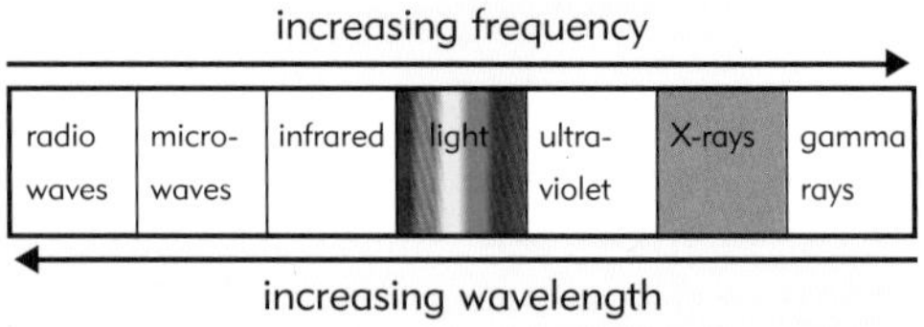

Taking an X-ray picture

The diagrams show how you can use X-rays to make a shadow **picture** of the **bones** inside a person's hand.

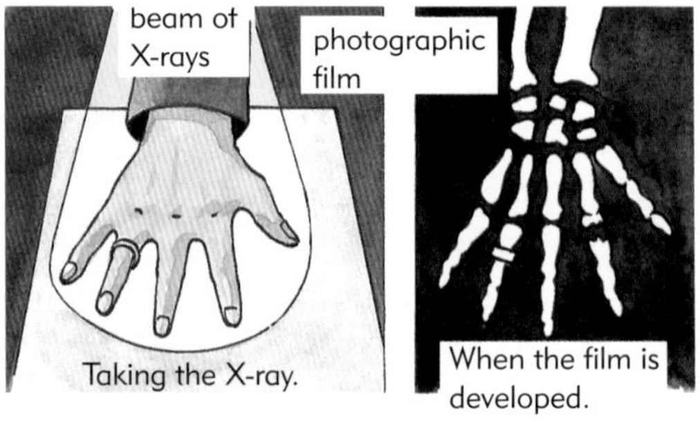

The X-rays do not pass through the areas that show up as white. You can't see the skin or flesh because X-rays pass through these areas easily, and turn the photographic film black.

1 Copy and complete the following sentences.

X-rays can pass easily through skin and flesh but not through __________ or __________.

Photographic __________ absorbs any X-rays that fall on it.

These parts of the film then go __________ when the film is developed.

2 The X-ray above shows a broken finger. Which finger is this?

3 Doctors can use X-rays to see whether your lungs are healthy. How do they know if there is diseased tissue in your lungs?

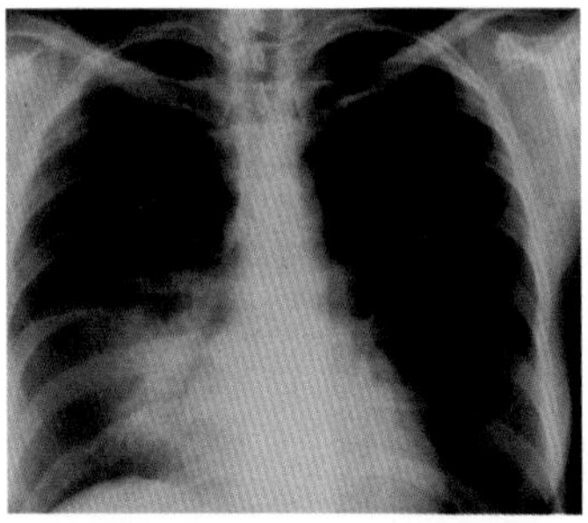

A chest X-ray. **Diseased** tissue absorbs X-rays more than healthy tissue.

Using X-rays safely

X-rays can damage the cells of your body. Because metals **absorb** X-rays, they can be used to **protect** you.

4 Look at the photograph. Then write down two other ways of reducing the risk of damaging the cells in people's bodies with X-rays.

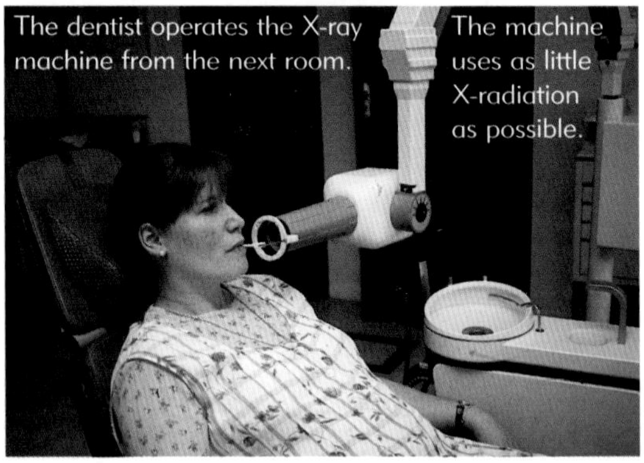

The dentist operates the X-ray machine from the next room.
The machine uses as little X-radiation as possible.

An X-ray at the dentist.

What you need to remember [Copy and complete using the **key words**]

Using X-rays

X-rays do not pass through the ______________ in your body.
X-rays pass through skin and flesh, but do not pass so easily through __________ tissue.
Doctors can use X-rays to make a shadow ______________ of the inside of your body.
Metals ______________ your body because they ______________ X-rays.

Using gamma (γ) radiation

REMEMBER

increasing frequency →

radio waves	micro-waves	infrared	light	ultra-violet	X-rays	gamma rays

← increasing wavelength

You can kill living **cells** by giving them a high dose of gamma radiation.

Smaller doses can damage cells. Damage to the cells of your body may cause cancer.

Killing bacteria with gamma rays

We sometimes want to kill harmful **bacteria**.
We can do this using gamma radiation.

1 Write down two uses of gamma rays to kill harmful bacteria.

2 Using gamma rays, you can kill the bacteria on things inside completely sealed packets.

(a) Why is this possible?

(b) Why is this very useful?

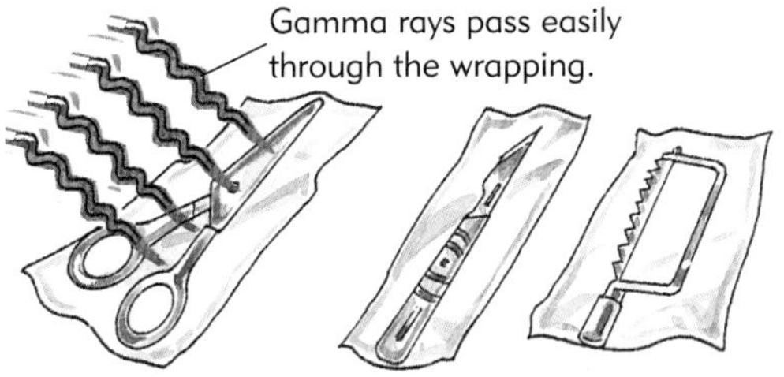

Gamma rays pass easily through the wrapping.

A surgeon's instruments must have no bacteria on them, so we sterilise them with gamma rays.

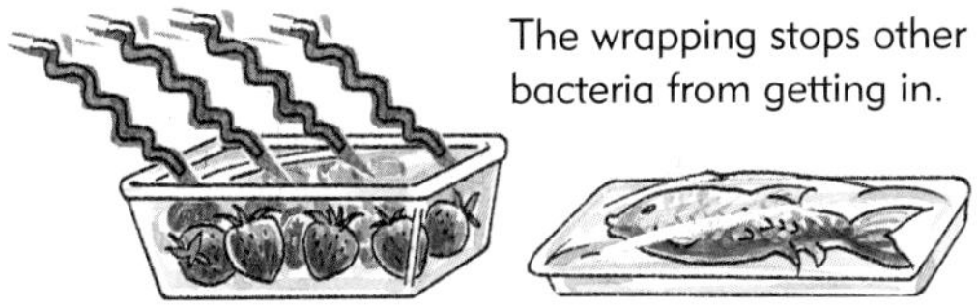

The wrapping stops other bacteria from getting in.

Bacteria make food go bad. If we kill the bacteria, the food stays fresh for longer.

Killing cancer cells with gamma radiation

Doctors can use gamma rays to kill **cancer** cells inside a person's body, but they must be careful not to damage healthy cells. The diagram shows how they can do this.

3 Copy and complete the following sentences.

The source of the gamma radiation __________ in a circle around the patient's body.

The cancer cells are at the __________ of this circle.

So the gamma rays hit the cancer cells __________ of the time.

But they only hit the healthy cells for __________ of the time.

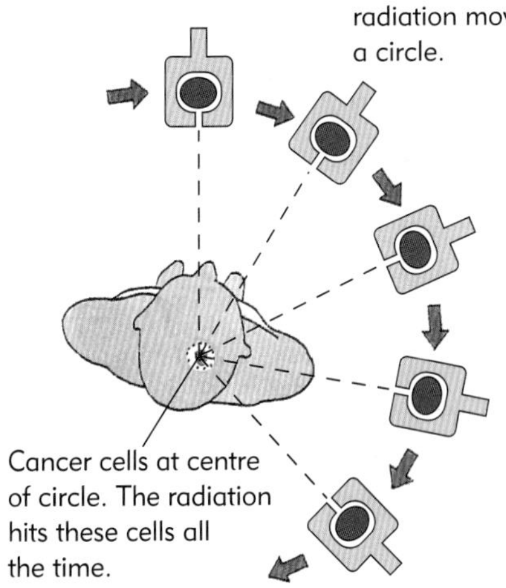

What you need to remember [Copy and complete using the **key words**]

Using gamma (γ) radiation

Gamma radiation can kill living __________________.
It is used to kill harmful __________________ or __________________ cells inside people's bodies.

Radiation that harms your body

When electromagnetic waves are absorbed they release energy. This energy can damage cells or even kill them. Different types of electromagnetic radiation damage cells in different ways.

REMEMBER

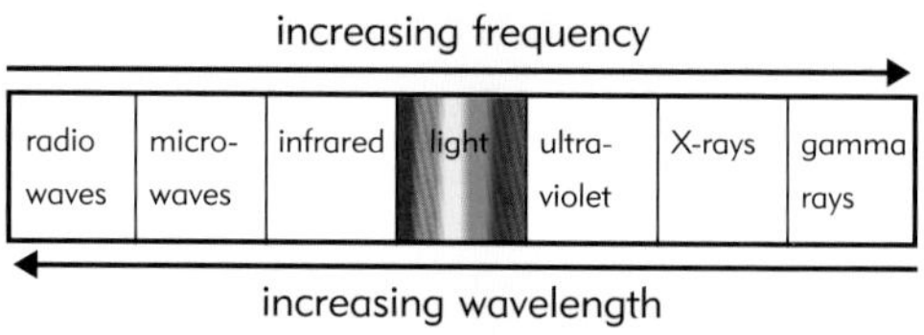

Radiation that 'cooks' cells

Your cells become **hot** if they absorb infrared radiation or microwaves.

This heat can damage or kill the cells.

1 Look at the diagrams.

(a) Why are microwaves more dangerous than infrared radiation?

(b) Why can't you accidentally damage your cells with the microwaves from a microwave oven?

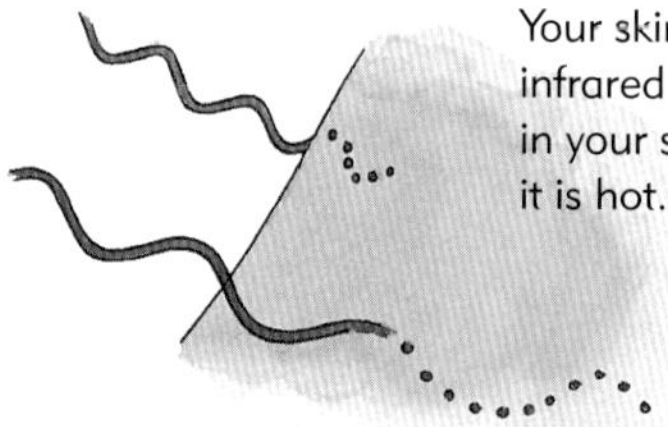

Your skin absorbs infrared waves. Sensors in your skin tell you it is hot.
Microwaves go deeper into your body. There are no temperature sensors there so you don't know the cells are getting hot.

There's nothing to stop you putting your hand under a grill...

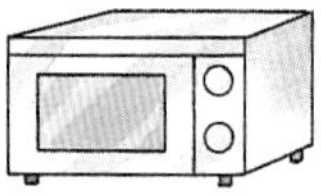

...but if you open the door of a microwave oven it switches off.

Radiation that causes skin cancer

Ultraviolet radiation from the Sun is mainly absorbed by your **skin**.

This can damage the molecules inside skin cells.

The cells can then start to multiply very quickly and also spread to other parts of the body. This is called **cancer** and may cause death.

2 What type of electromagnetic radiation usually causes skin cancer?

3 People with dark skins are less likely to get skin cancer. Why is this?

4 How can you protect yourself against skin cancer? Explain your answer.

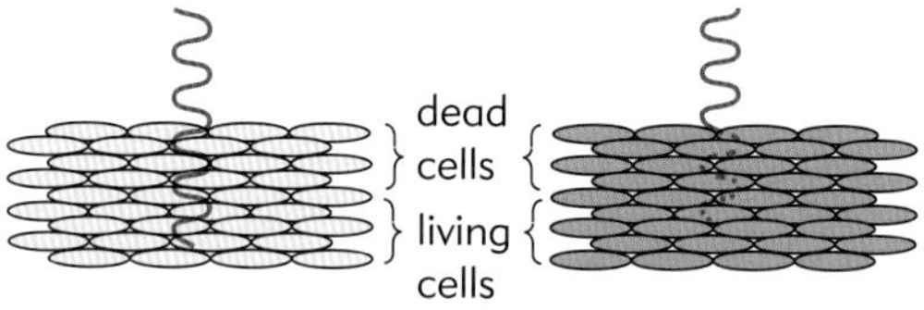

If you have pale skin, ultraviolet rays can get through to the living cells.

If you have dark skin, more ultraviolet rays are absorbed by the layers of dead cells.

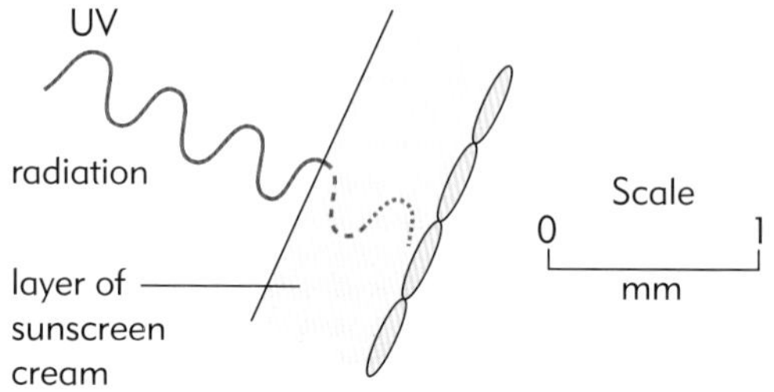

How to protect your skin against cancer. Sunscreen cream absorbs the ultraviolet rays.

Radiation that can cause cancer inside people's bodies

X-rays can pass fairly easily through the soft parts of your body.

Gamma radiation can pass quite easily through any part of your body.

Both types of radiation can cause cancer.

5 Look at the diagram.

(a) Why can X-rays and gamma rays cause cancer?

(b) Where in a person's body can these types of radiation cause cancer?

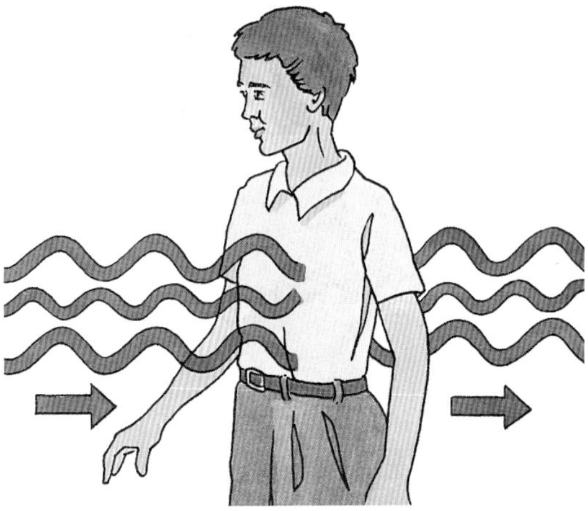

X-rays and gamma rays can pass through your body. But some are absorbed by your cells. This can cause cancer anywhere in your body.

Can any other sorts of radiation cause cancer?

Substances that give out gamma radiation are called **radioactive** substances. The diagram shows two other types of radiation which radioactive substances can give out.

6 What three types of radiation can radioactive substances give out?

All three types of radiation from radioactive substances can damage **molecules** in cells. So they can all cause cancer.

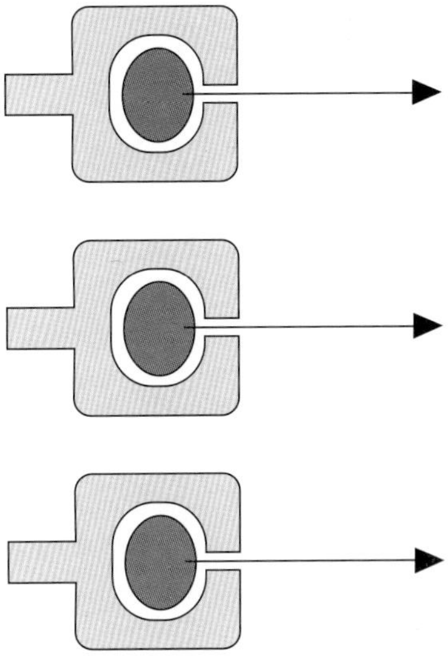

We say that radioactive sources emit radiation. A radioactive source can emit more than one type of radiation.

What you need to remember [Copy and complete using the **key words**]

Radiation that harms your body

Infrared radiation and microwaves can damage cells by making them ______________.
Ultraviolet radiation can damage the cells in your ______________ and may cause skin cancer.
Some types of radiation can pass through your body, for example ______________ and the radiation from ______________ substances.
If any of these types of radiation is absorbed, it can damage the ______________ in your cells and may cause ______________.

20

How much harmful radiation do you get?

X-rays and the radiation from radioactive substances can cause **cancer** anywhere in our bodies. So we should avoid these types of radiation if we can.

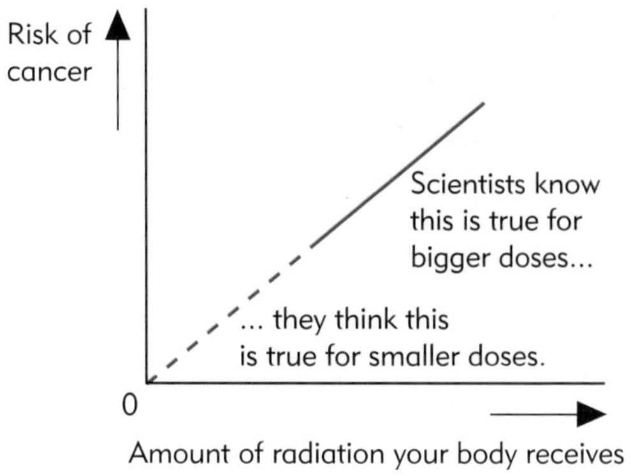
Risk of cancer
Scientists know this is true for bigger doses...
... they think this is true for smaller doses.
0
Amount of radiation your body receives

What amount of radiation is safe?

The amount of radiation your body gets is called your radiation dose. The graph shows how the risk of cancer depends on the size of your radiation dose.

1 Copy and complete the following sentences.

The bigger the dose of radiation your body gets, the __________ the risk of cancer.

The graph suggests that there is some risk of cancer even with a very __________ radiation dose.

Unfortunately, we're surrounded by harmful radiation. So we can't avoid it all.

Radiation that we can't avoid

We are bombarded with radiation from space, called **cosmic** radiation. There are also **radioactive** substances all around us and even inside the cells our bodies are made from. So our bodies receive radiation all the time, which we call **background** radiation.

2 The boxes on this page and the maps on the next page show the main sources of background radiation. Copy the table. Then fill in the figures for each source of the background radiation that your body gets.

How much background radiation my body gets each year	
Source of background radiation	Annual radiation dose (units)
cosmic rays	
buildings	
food and drink	
the ground	
the air	
TOTAL	

Cosmic rays

These come from the Sun and from space.

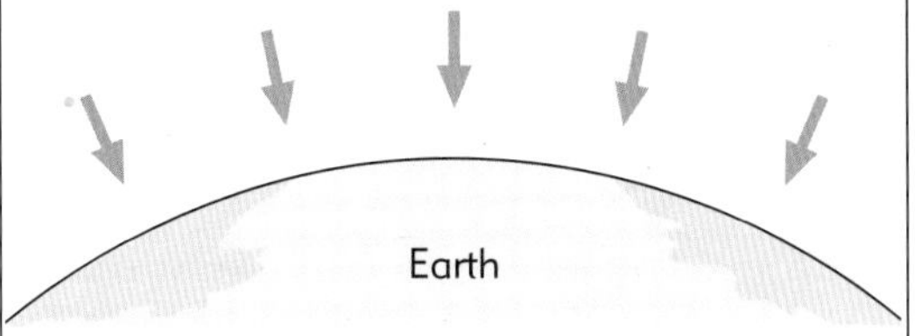
Earth

We all get 250 units of cosmic radiation each year.
You get 1 unit more for every 30 m you live above sea level.

Buildings

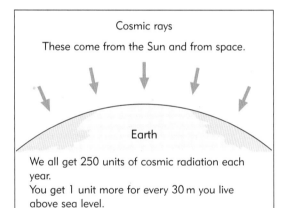

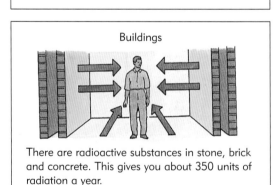

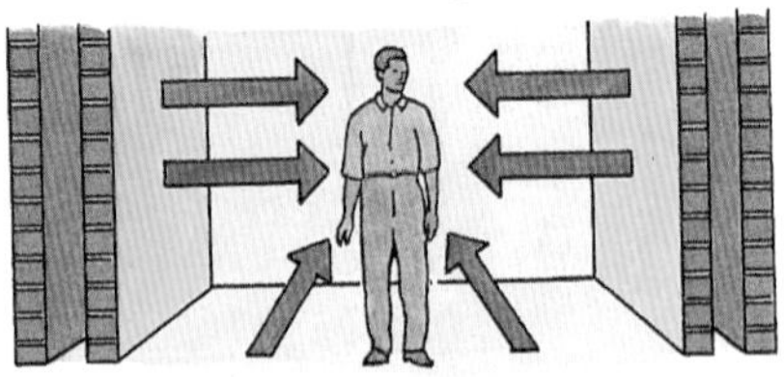

There are radioactive substances in stone, brick and concrete. This gives you about 350 units of radiation a year.

Food and drink

Radioactive substances dissolve. They get in plants, animals that eat the plants and into water. This gives you about 300 units of radiation each year.

Radiation from nuclear power stations

If you live within a mile of a nuclear power station, you should add an extra 5 units a year to your radiation dose.

This is much less than many people think.

Radiation that depends on what you do

The table shows the main sources of any extra radiation which people may receive.

Other sources of radiation	Dose
dental X-ray	20 units each time
chest/leg/arm X-ray	50 units each time
flying	4 units per hour

3 (a) Write down any of the sources that you think have affected you during the past year.

(b) Add your radiation dose from these sources to your total from background radiation.

Scientists think that the average annual radiation dose in Britain is reasonably safe.

4 (a) What is the average annual radiation dose in Britain?

(b) How does your own annual dose compare with the average?

5 Some people get a bigger radiation dose because of their job.

Write down <u>two</u> jobs that give people a bigger radiation dose.

Radiation from the ground

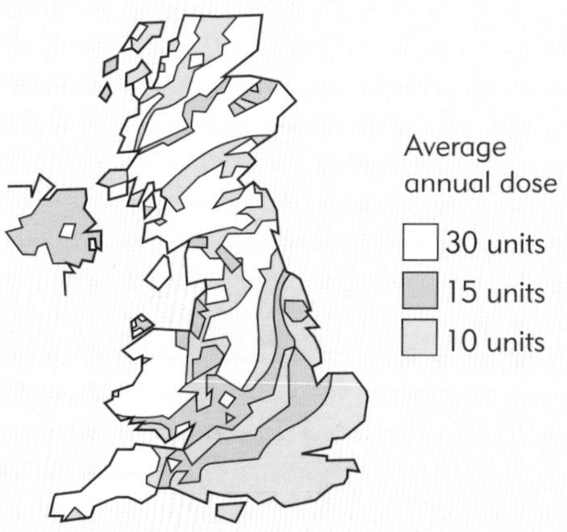

The soil and rocks beneath your feet contain radioactive substances. How much radiation you get depends on where you live.

Radiation from the air

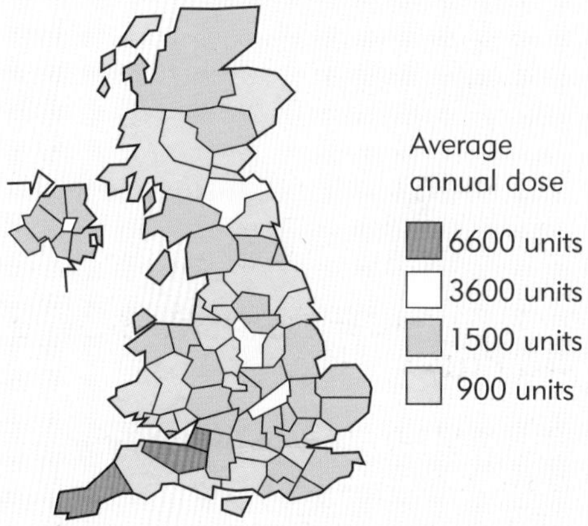

Radioactive radiation gas seeps into the air from the ground. The figures in some areas are <u>very</u> high (up to 100 000 units a year).

The average radiation dose in Britain is about 2500 units each year.

What you need to remember [Copy and complete using the **key words**]

How much harmful radiation do you get?

The bigger the dose of radiation you get, the greater the risk of ________________.
Our bodies receive radiation all the time from ________________ substances in the air, the ground, food, water and building materials.
Our bodies also receive ________________ radiation from space.
All this radiation is called ________________ radiation.

Investigating radioactive substances

Substances that give out alpha, beta or gamma radiation are called radioactive substances. We say that these substances **emit** radiation.

Radioactive substances emit radiation all the time. There is **nothing** you can do to stop this.

1 Look at the diagrams.
Then write down what happens to the amount of radiation a radioactive substance emits:

(a) when you heat it up or cool it down

(b) when you dissolve it

(c) when you break it up into small pieces.

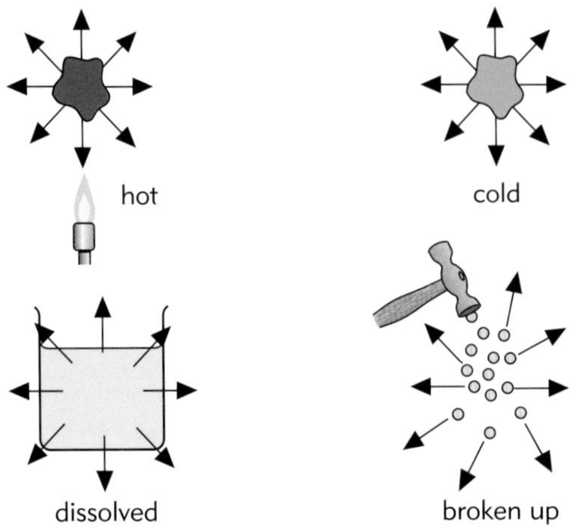

Nothing you can do to a radioactive substance changes how much radiation it emits.

You can't make a radioactive substance emit radiation faster or slower.

This makes it different from other kinds of radiation, which you can control.

2 (a) What can you do to a substance to make it emit light?

(b) How can you make a substance emit less infrared radiation?

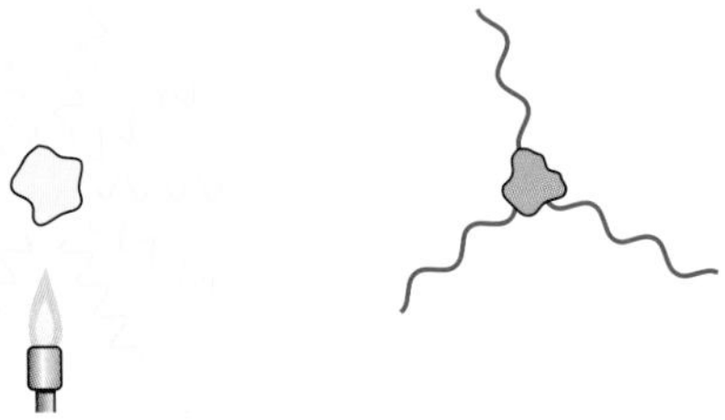

An object emits light if you make it hot enough.

A cold object emits less infrared radiation than a hotter object.

How do we know that radioactive substances emit radiation?

You can't see, hear or feel the radiation from radioactive substances, but you can tell that it is there. The diagrams show how you can do this.

3 Write down two ways of detecting the radiation from a radioactive substance.

4 Which would be the best way:

(a) of measuring how fast a radioactive source is emitting radiation?

(b) of telling how much radiation a person has been exposed to during a whole week?

5 Even when it isn't near a radioactive source, a Geiger counter gives a small reading. Why is this?

Detecting radiation.

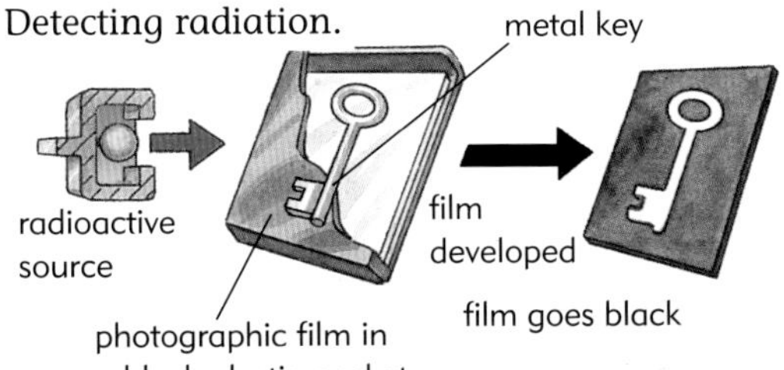

How black the film goes depends on how much radiation has fallen on it.

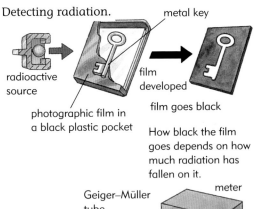

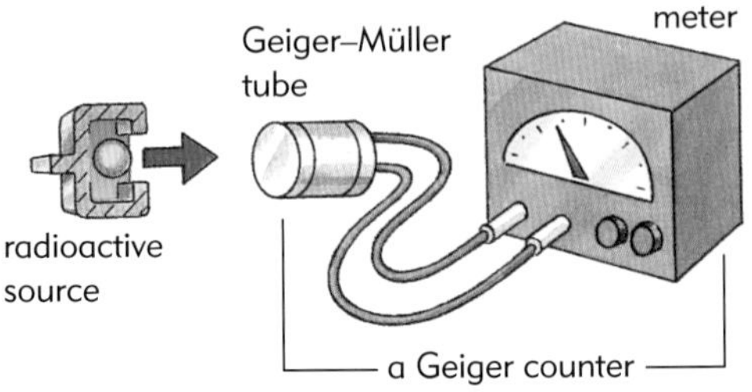

The faster the source emits radiation, the bigger the reading on the meter. You always get some reading because of background radiation.

How do we know that there are three types of radiation?

Radioactive substances emit three types of radiation.

6 What are the three types of radiation called?

We know radioactive sources emit three different types of radiation because they are absorbed by different materials.

7 Look at the diagrams. Then copy and complete the following sentences.

The radiation emitted by source A is absorbed by air or by paper.
Source A emits __________ radiation.

To absorb the radiation emitted by source B you need a sheet of __________ a few __________ thick.
Source B emits __________ radiation.

To stop most of the radiation from source C you need a thick sheet of __________.
Source C emits __________radiation.

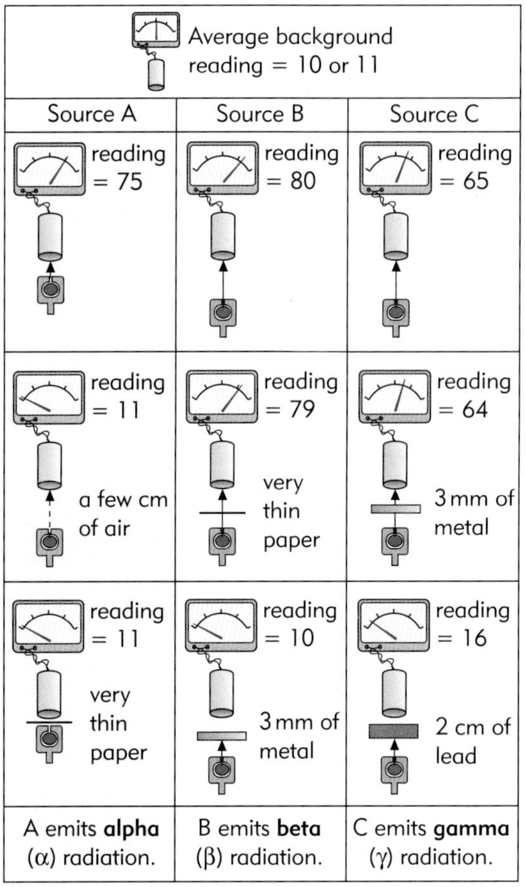

Average background reading = 10 or 11
Source A
Source B
Source C
reading = 75
reading = 80
reading = 65
reading = 11
a few cm of air
reading = 79
very thin paper
reading = 64
3 mm of metal
reading = 11
very thin paper
reading = 10
3 mm of metal
reading = 16
2 cm of lead
A emits **alpha** (α) radiation.
B emits **beta** (β) radiation.
C emits **gamma** (γ) radiation.

How does a Geiger counter work?

The diagram shows what happens inside a Geiger–Müller tube.

8 Copy and complete the following sentences.

Energy from radiation gives gas molecules an __________ charge.

Stronger radiation makes more __________ electrically charged.

So you get a __________ reading on the meter.

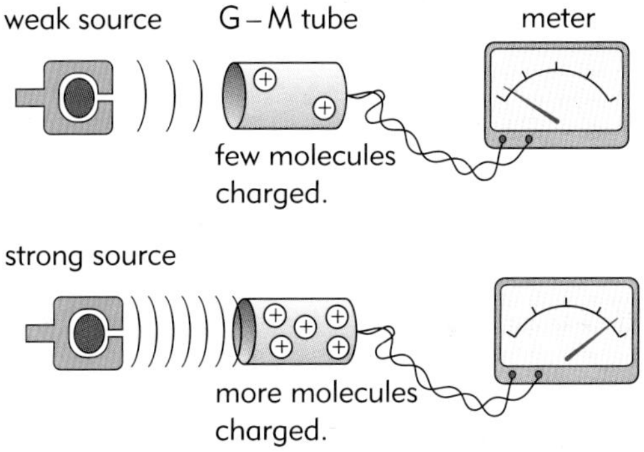

When radiation hits gas molecules in the G–M tube they become electrically **charged**.

What you need to remember [Copy and complete using the **key words**]

Investigating radioactive substances

Radioactive substances __________ radiation all the time.
You can do __________ to change this.
A few centimetres of air or a thin sheet of paper absorbs most __________ (α) radiation.
A metal sheet a few millimetres thick absorbs most __________ (β) radiation.
Even a thick sheet of lead only partly absorbs __________ (γ) radiation.
When radiation strikes atoms or molecules they become electrically __________.

22 Using radioactive substances safely

Radioactive substances are very useful. We use them to kill cancer cells or harmful bacteria. We also use them as fuels in nuclear power stations.

But the radiation from radioactive materials is very dangerous. So we must do everything we can to protect our bodies from this radiation.

REMEMBER

Radiation from radioactive substances can change healthy cells into cancer cells.

1 Why is the radiation from radioactive substances dangerous?

Shielding the radiation from radioactive sources

We need to stop the radiation from radioactive sources from reaching our bodies. To do this we must shield the radioactive sources with substances that **absorb** the radiation.

2 (a) What are small, not very strong radioactive sources used for?

(b) How are these radioactive sources shielded?

3 (a) Where would you find large and very powerful radioactive sources?

(b) How are these radioactive sources shielded?

Thick layers of metal and concrete are needed so that almost all of the gamma radiation is absorbed.

Shielding a small radioactive source (for killing bacteria or cancer cells).

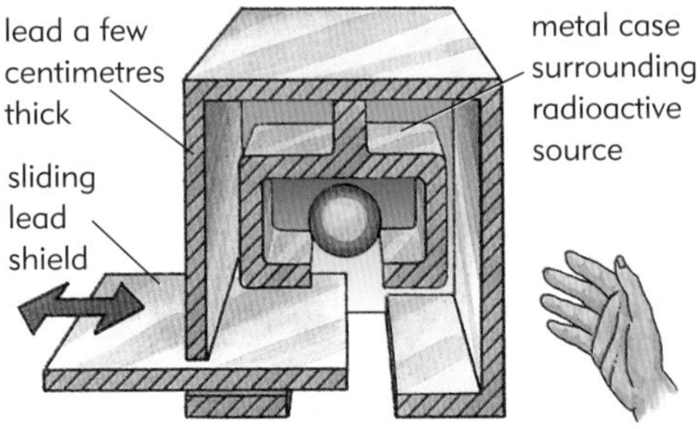

Shielding large, very powerful radioactive sources in nuclear power stations.

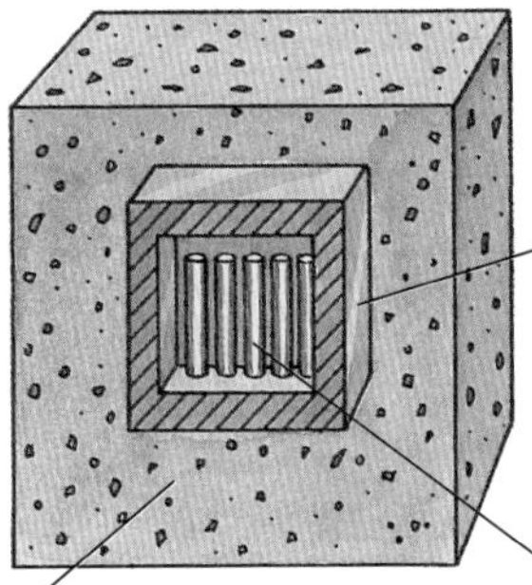

Keeping radioactive substances contained

Radioactive substances are especially dangerous if they get inside our bodies. The radiation that can damage cells is then emitted very near to the cells, or even inside them.

4 Radioactive substances from nuclear power stations sometimes escape into the environment.
Write down <u>three</u> ways in which this can happen.

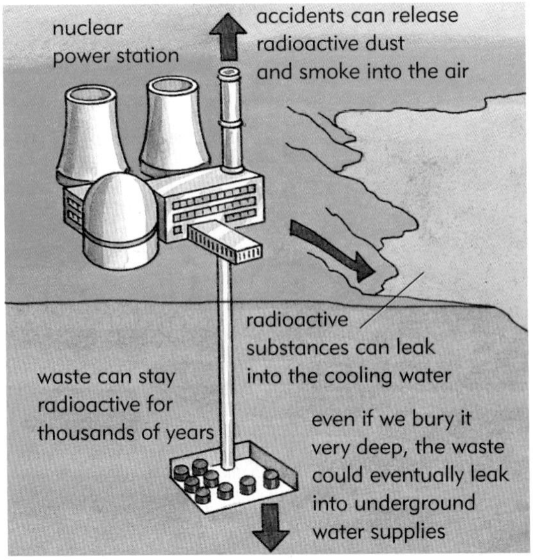

Checking radiation doses

People who work with radioactive materials often wear film badges. They can then check how much radiation their bodies have received each week.

5 Look at the diagrams.
What does the developed film tell you?

When the film is developed, it goes dark in the places where radiation has been absorbed. The film goes darkest where the most radiation has fallen.

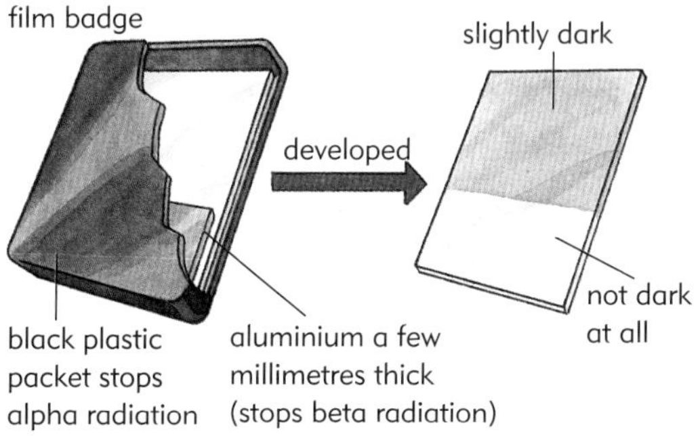

Another use for radioactive substances

Radioactive substances can help us to make things into thin sheets.

For example, aluminium cooking foil is very thin. So it only partly absorbs beta radiation.

The thicker the foil is, the more beta radiation it absorbs. We can use this idea to control the **thickness** of aluminium foil when we are making it. The diagrams show how we can do this.

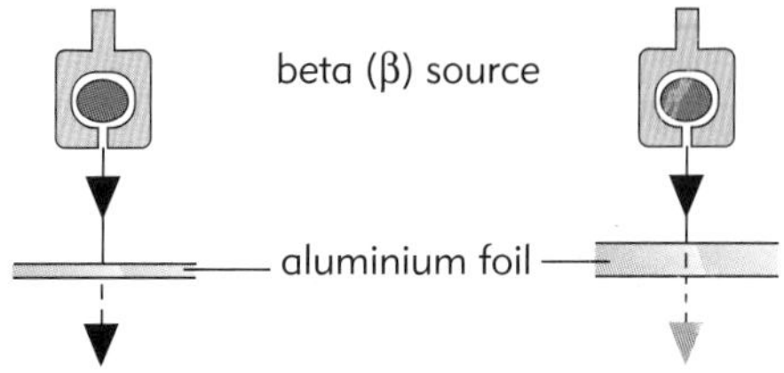

6 Write down the following sentences in the right order. The first one has been done for you.

A thin sheet of aluminium is sent between two rollers.

- A radioactive source sends beta radiation through the foil.
- Pressure on the rollers squeezes the aluminium sheet into thin foil.
- The aluminium foil is now made a little thicker.
- A signal from the control box reduces the pressure on the rollers.
- If the foil is too thin, too much beta radiation gets through to the control box.

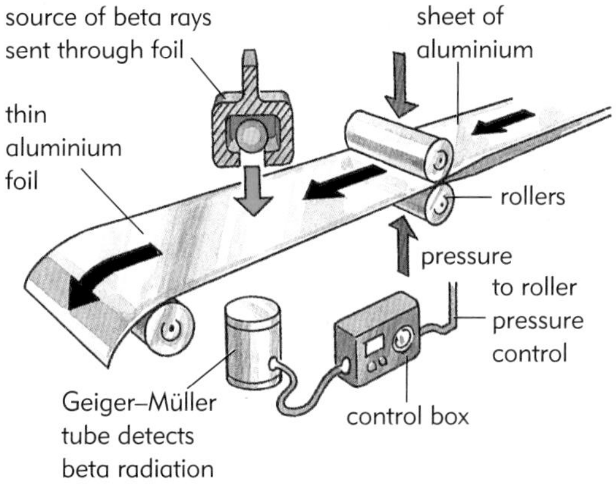

7 Look at the diagram.

Then explain why alpha radiation and gamma radiation are not suitable for controlling the thickness of aluminium foil.

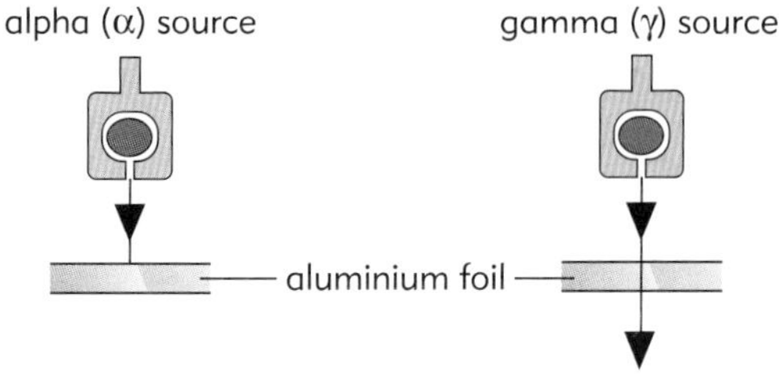

What you need to remember [Copy and complete using the **key words**]

Using radioactive substances safely

The thicker a material is, the more radiation it will ________________.
This idea is used in factories to control the ________________ of materials.

What are atoms made of?

Radioactive substances, like all other substances, are made from atoms. They emit radiation because of changes inside their atoms.

To understand these changes, you need to know how atoms themselves are made.

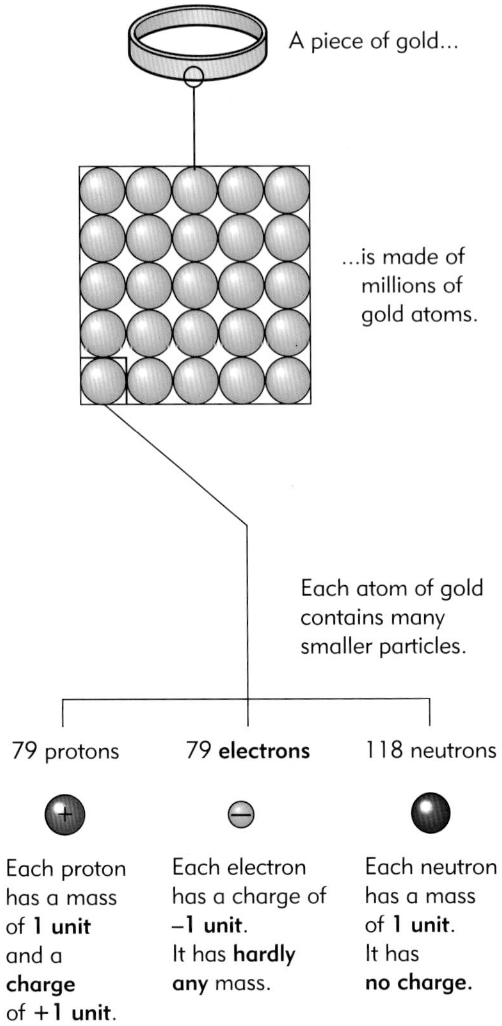
A piece of gold...
...is made of millions of gold atoms.
Each atom of gold contains many smaller particles.
79 protons
79 **electrons**
118 neutrons
Each proton has a mass of **1 unit** and a **charge** of **+1 unit.**
Each electron has a charge of **–1 unit.** It has **hardly any** mass.
Each neutron has a mass of **1 unit.** It has **no charge.**

What's inside an atom?

In some substances all the atoms are the same; these substances are called elements.

Gold is an element. The diagram shows what each atom of gold is made of.

1 Each gold atom contains three different kinds of particles.

(a) What are the three different kinds of particles called?

(b) Which of these particles have an electrical charge?

2 Copy and complete the following sentences.

A gold atom has no electrical charge.

This is because the positive (+) charges of the __________ are exactly balanced by the __________ (–) charges of the electrons.

Atoms have the **same** number of protons and electrons.

The Christmas pudding model of an atom

The particles inside atoms are very, very small.

You can't see them even with a very powerful microscope.

But scientists once thought that atoms were probably made like a Christmas pudding.

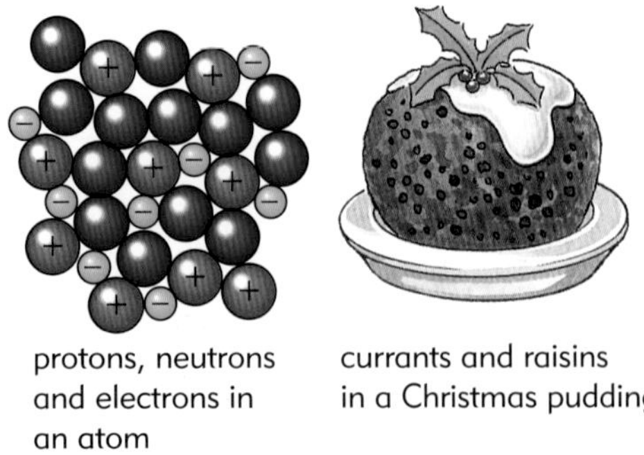
protons, neutrons and electrons in an atom
currants and raisins in a Christmas pudding

Christmas pudding model of an atom.

3 Look at the diagram. Then copy and complete the following sentences.

Scientists thought that protons, __________ and __________ filled up all the space in an atom just like currants and raisins in a __________ __________.

Testing the Christmas pudding model

When scientists tested their idea about atoms, they found out that they were wrong.

You can make gold into very thin sheets, just a few atoms thick. This is called gold leaf. Scientists tried firing some very fast particles at a sheet of gold leaf.

The diagrams showed what the scientists expected to happen and what actually happened.

4 (a) What did the scientists expect to happen?

(b) What actually happened?

This test meant that scientists had to change their mind about how atoms were made.

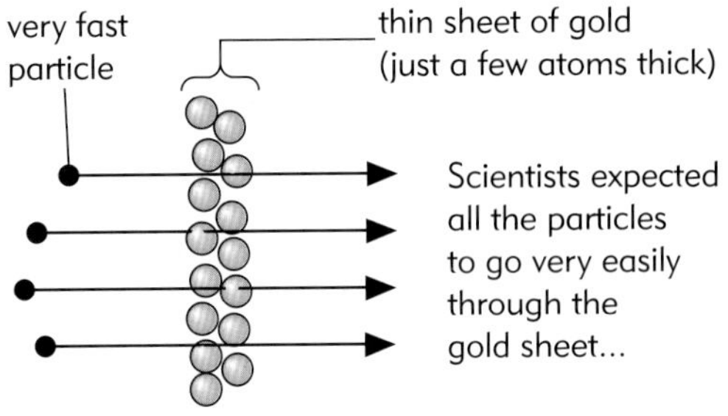

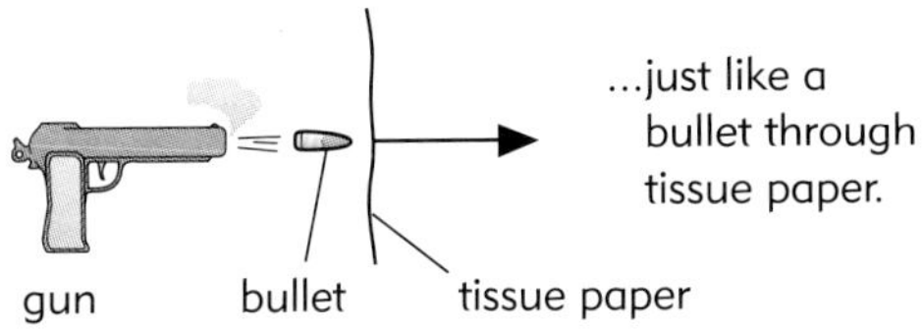

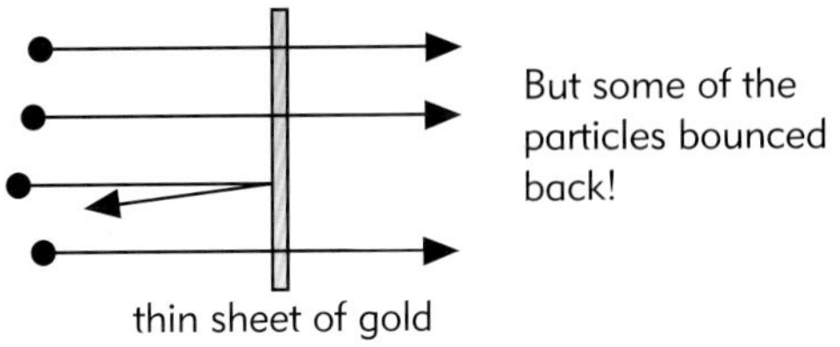

A new model of an atom

Scientists now think that atoms are mainly empty **space**. The protons and neutrons are in a very small **nucleus**. Electrons move about in the space around the nucleus.

5 Why did a few of the fast moving particles bounce back from the sheet of gold leaf?

New model of an atom.

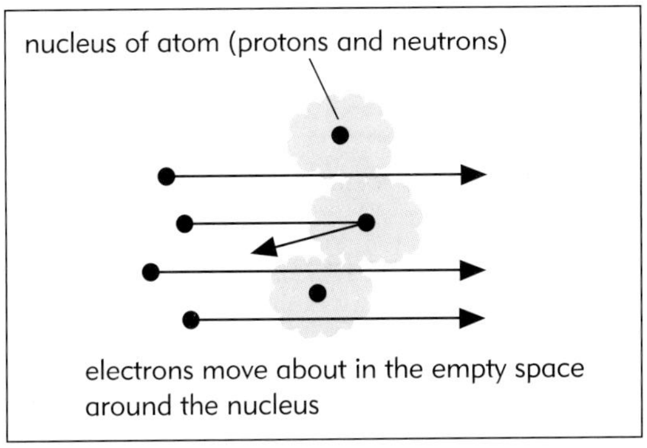

What you need to remember [Copy and complete using the **key words**]

What are atoms made of?

Atoms have a small ________________ made of protons and neutrons.
Particles called ________________ move around in the empty ________________ around the nucleus.

Particle	Mass	Charge
proton	________________	________________
neutron	________________	**no charge**
electron	**hardly any**	________________

Each atom of the same element has the ________________ number of protons and electrons. So it has no overall electrical ________________.

[You need to know why scientists changed their minds about the Christmas pudding model of an atom.]

24 Why are some atoms radioactive?

REMEMBER

Atoms have a small nucleus made of protons and neutrons.

Electrons move about in the empty space around the nucleus.

In most atoms the nucleus doesn't change, so the numbers of protons and neutrons stay the same. We say that these atoms have a stable nucleus.

But some atoms have an unstable nucleus. Sooner or later, an unstable nucleus will emit radiation. The nucleus changes when it does this, and we say that the nucleus **decays**.

Stable and unstable carbon atoms

The diagrams show two carbon atoms.

One carbon atom has a stable nucleus, the other carbon atom has an unstable nucleus.

Nucleus of a stable carbon atom. Nucleus of an unstable carbon atom.

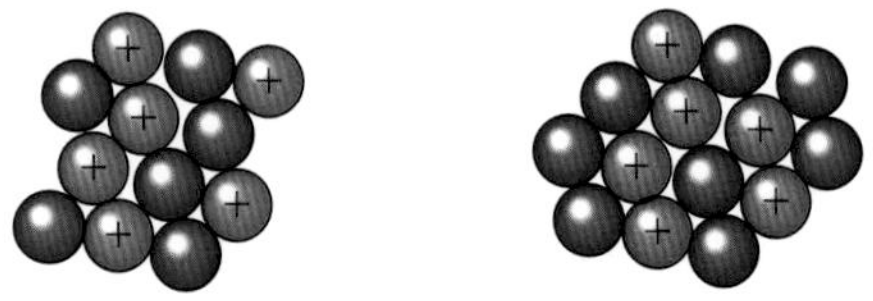

Both atoms have six electrons in the space around the nucleus.

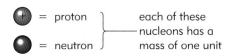

= proton
= neutron
each of these nucleons has a mass of one unit

1 Copy the table. Then complete it.

	Number of protons	Number of neutrons	Number of nucleons
stable carbon atom	6	6	12
unstable carbon atom			

2 (a) What is the <u>same</u> about both carbon atoms?

(b) What is <u>different</u> about the two carbon atoms?

All atoms of the same element have the same number of **protons**.

Atoms of the same element can have different numbers of **neutrons**.

Atoms of the same element with different numbers of neutrons are called **isotopes**.

We can show a stable carbon atom like this.

this is the mass or nucleon number → 12

this is the proton number → 6

$^{12}_{6}C$

← this stands for carbon

We call this a carbon-12 atom.

We can show an unstable carbon atom like this.

$^{14}_{6}C$

We call this a carbon-14 atom.

What happens when an unstable nucleus splits up?

When an unstable atom decays:

- it changes into an atom of a different **element** with a different number of **protons** in its nucleus
- it emits **radiation**.

The diagram shows what happens to the nucleus of a carbon-14 atom when it decays.

3 Copy and complete the following sentence.

When a carbon-14 atom decays:

- it emits __________ radiation
- its nucleus turns into the nucleus of a __________ atom.

4 (a) What is the <u>same</u> about a carbon-14 nucleus and a nitrogen-14 nucleus?

(b) How is a nitrogen-14 nucleus <u>different</u> from a carbon-14 nucleus?

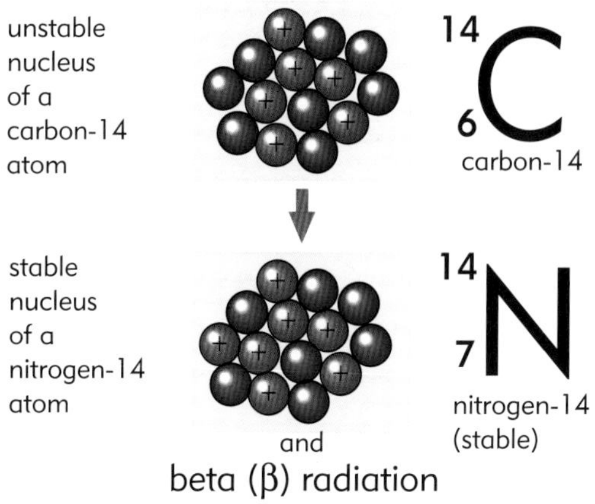

Using radioactive substances to tell dates

Wood always contains a small amount of radioactive carbon. As the radioactive atoms decay, the carbon in the wood emits **less** radiation.

Archaeologists use this idea to **date** things.

5 Look at the graph.

Some archaeologists find a piece of wood in an ancient tomb.

The carbon in the wood is only 60 per cent as radioactive as the carbon in some new wood.

How old is the piece of wood from the tomb?

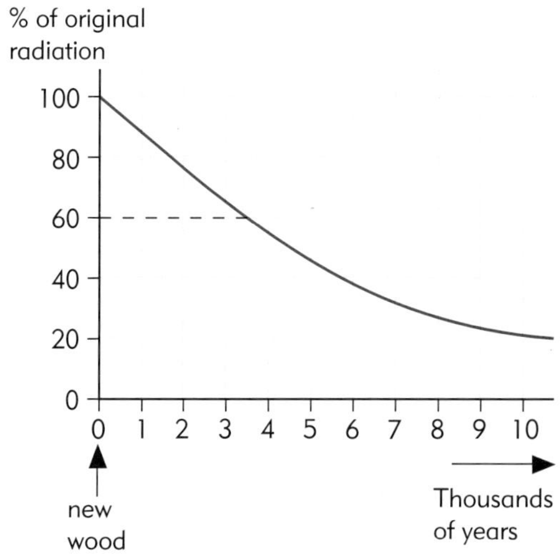

What you need to remember [Copy and complete using the **key words**]

Why are some atoms radioactive?

Atoms of the same element always have the same number of __________.
But they can have a different number of __________.
Atoms of the same element with different numbers of neutrons are called __________.
Sooner or later, an atom with an unstable nucleus will change; we say that it __________.
It changes into an atom of a different __________ with a different number of __________. It also emits __________.
As its atoms decay, a radioactive substance emits __________ radiation.
We can use this idea to __________ things.

What makes things stand still?

Tug of war

You might think that things stay still because no forces are acting on them. A tug of war shows that this isn't so. When both teams pull with equal force in opposite directions, the forces cancel out. When the forces are **balanced**, the rope does not move. The rope is **stationary**.

1 Copy and complete the following sentence.

If something is stationary, the forces on it must be __________.

2 Look at the picture of a dumb-bell being held still.

(a) What force is acting downwards on the dumb-bell?

(b) What force is acting upwards on the dumb-bell?

(c) Copy and complete the following sentence.

The dumb-bell stays still because the force acting upwards __________ the force acting downwards.

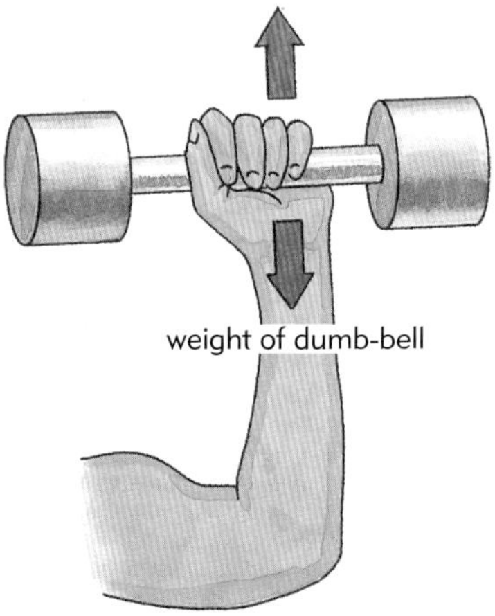

Why you don't fall through the floor

Your weight is always pushing **downwards** against the floor. The floor holds you up, so it must be pushing **upwards** on you. The two forces are **equal** in size but act in **opposite** directions. So the forces balance and you stay where you are.

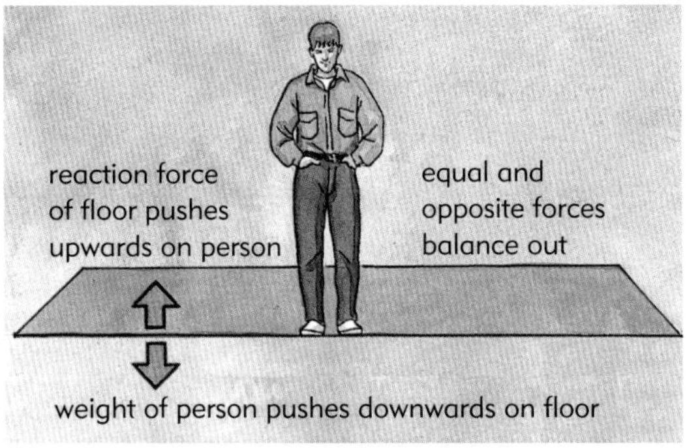

People don't fall through floors.

3 Look at the picture of a book on a table. Explain as fully as you can, why the book doesn't fall through the table.

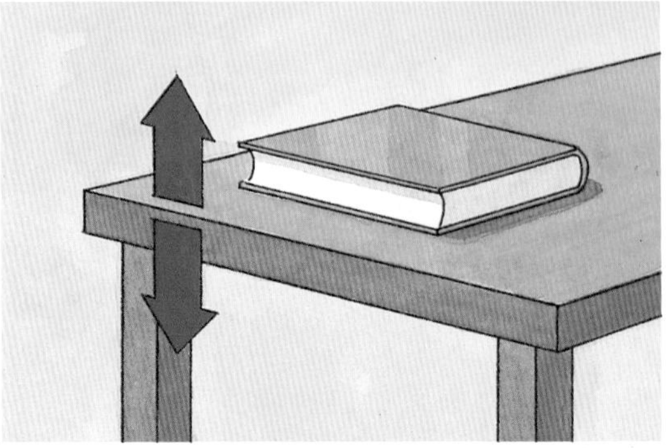

Books don't fall through tables.

How can a helicopter hover?

When people are lifted from a boat, the helicopter has to keep very still. This is difficult because the weight of the helicopter is always pulling it downwards.

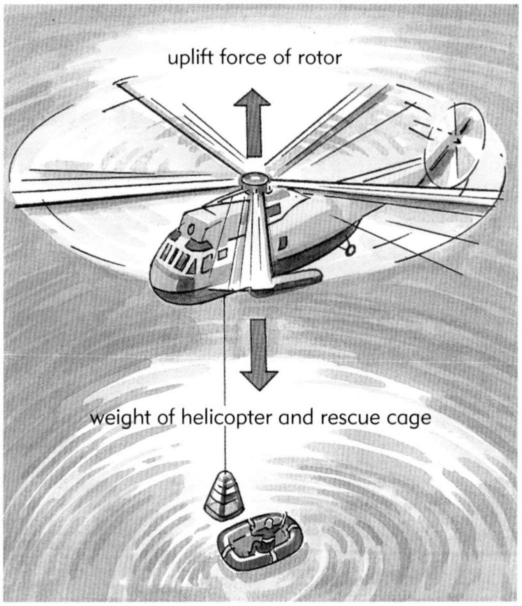

4 (a) What force is acting upwards on the helicopter?

(b) Explain how the helicopter can keep still.

5 What would happen to the helicopter if

(a) the uplift was greater than the weight?

(b) the weight was greater than the uplift?

Using forces to keep still

6 Look at the pictures of stationary objects.
For each one:

(a) copy the picture

(b) mark on the forces that are acting on the object

(c) label the forces that you have marked on the picture

(d) explain why the object keeps still.

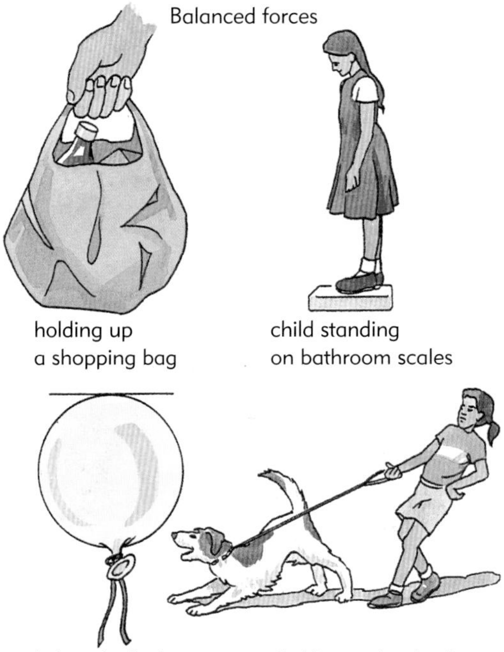

What you need to remember [Copy and complete using the **key words**]

What makes things stand still?

When an object rests on a surface its weight pushes ________________.
The surface pushes ________________ on the object.
The two forces are ________________ in size but they act in ________________ directions, so the forces are ________________.
When balanced forces act on a stationary object it will remain ________________.

Why do objects slow down?

If a fish stops pushing itself forwards it will slow down and stop. The same thing happens with a car – if the engine stops, the car slows down. This happens because of the force of **friction** when things move through air or water.

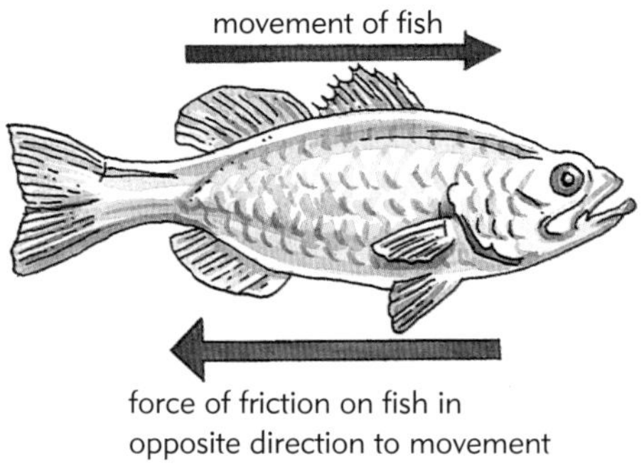

1 Copy and complete the following sentences.

When a fish moves through __________, a force of friction acts in the opposite __________. This force __________ the fish down.
When a car moves along, a force of friction acts in the __________ direction. This __________ the car down.

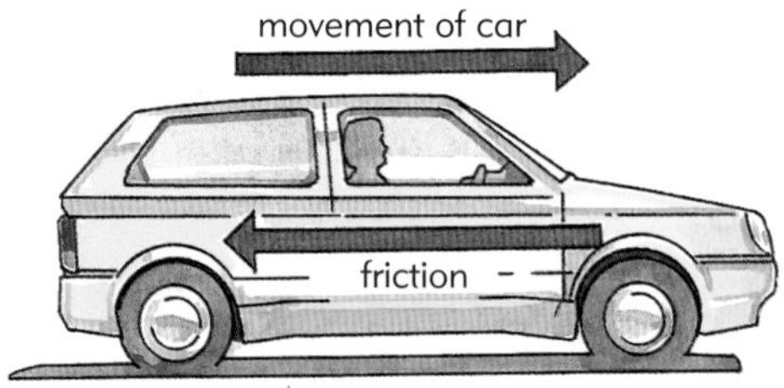

The force of friction slows down the fish and the car.

Forces all around us

Whenever an object moves through air or water, there will be a force of friction acting on it in the **opposite** direction. This force makes the object **slow** down.

2 (a) Copy the diagrams. In each one, mark the direction of movement and the direction of the force of friction.

(b) Why do all the objects slow down?

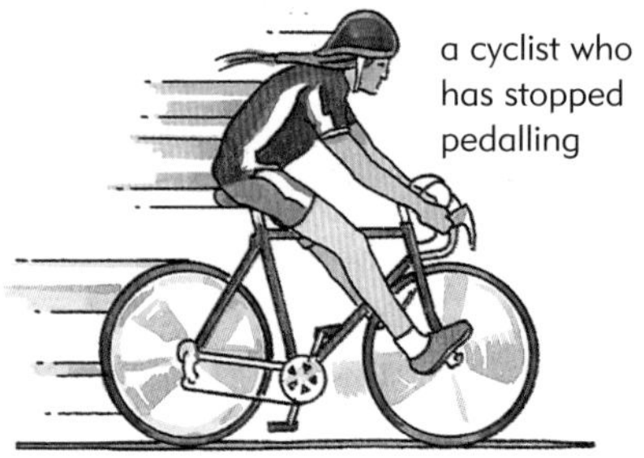

Balanced forces

When a fish is moving, a force of friction acts against it. To move at a **steady** speed its swimming force must **balance** the friction force.

3 (a) What happens if the friction force is greater than the swimming force of the fish?

(b) What must the fish do to speed up?

4 A car is moving along a level road at a steady speed. How big is the driving force of the car compared to the friction force?

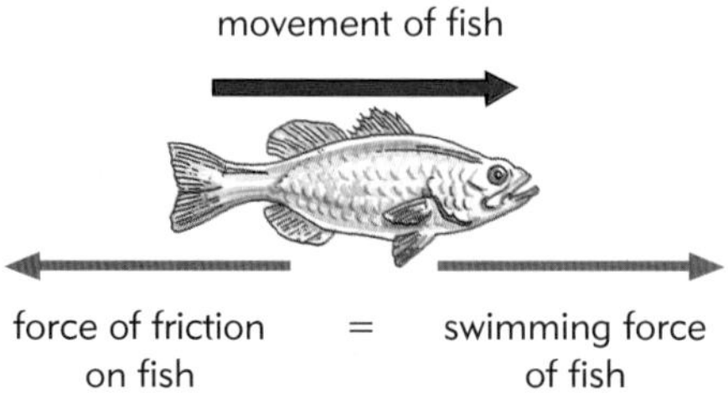

Forces balance so the fish moves at a steady speed.

Saving fuel

The friction force of the air is called air resistance. If there is a lot of air resistance, a greater force is required to move a car forwards. This means more fuel is used by the engine. Car designers try to produce streamlined shapes that make the air flow smoothly around the car.

5 Copy and complete the following sentences.

A car is shaped so that the air flows smoothly __________ the car instead of against it.
We say that the car has a __________ shape. This is to reduce the air __________.

Getting in shape for victory

Chris Boardman won a gold medal for cycling in the 1992 Olympics. His bicycle was designed to reduce friction with the air. He could then reach a higher speed using the same pedalling force.

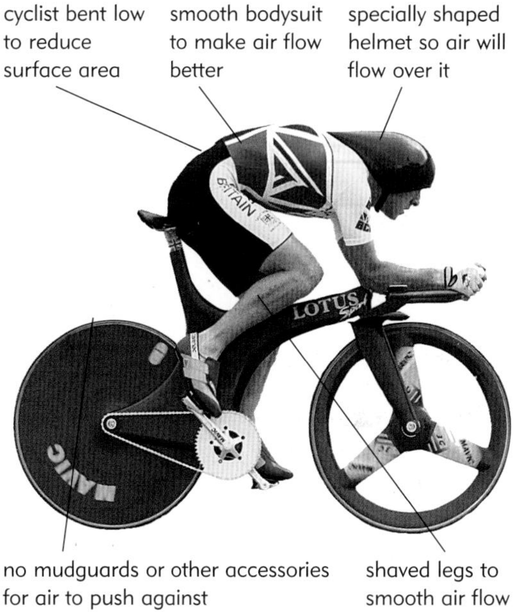

6 Look at the picture. Write down five ways in which friction was reduced.

Making the most of air resistance

Air resistance is also called drag. It can be very useful if you actually want to slow down. The space shuttles use this idea. As the shuttle lands it opens a parachute to help the braking. The parachute provides a bigger surface for more air to push against.

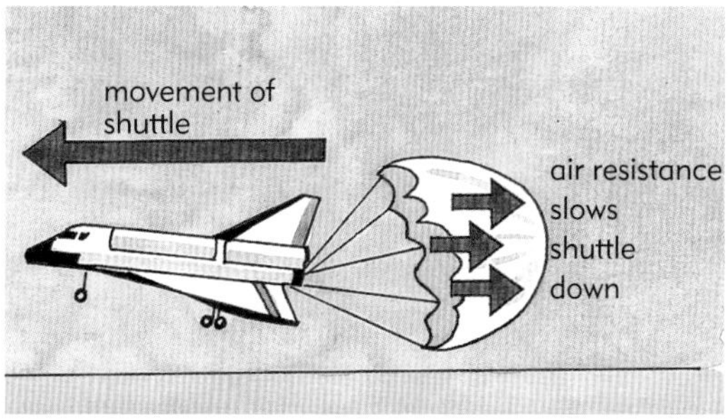

7 Why do you think the shuttle needs a large parachute?

What you need to remember [Copy and complete using the **key words**]

Why do objects slow down?

When an object moves through air or water or along the ground, a force of __________ acts.
The direction of this force of friction is always __________ to the direction in which the object is moving. This makes the object __________ down.
To keep an object moving at a steady speed, you need a driving force to __________ the force of friction.
If balanced forces act on a moving object it will keep moving with a __________ speed.

Taking the rough with the smooth

You don't just get friction when things move through air or water. **Friction** also acts when solid surfaces slide across each other. This is because parts of the two surfaces catch on each other. When a surface is moving one way, the friction force acts on it in the **opposite** direction.

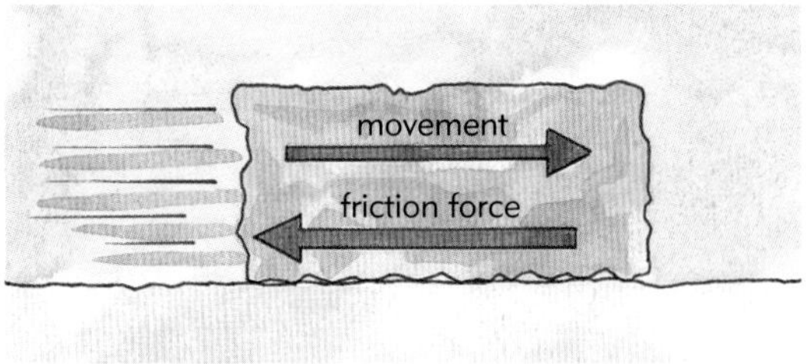

1 Copy the diagram and use it to explain why there is friction between the brick and the ground.

There is less friction between smooth surfaces.

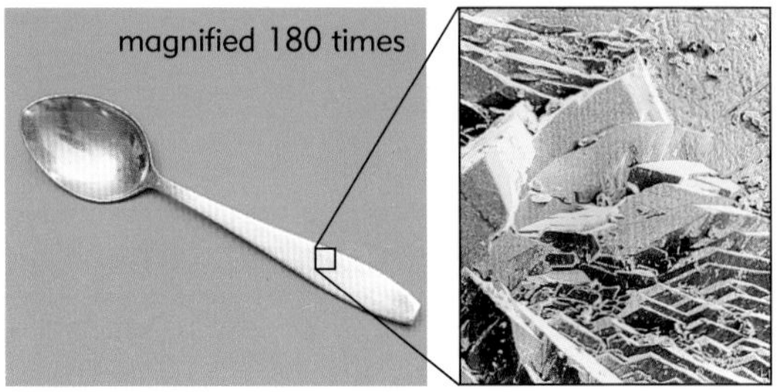

A polished surface looks smooth … … but it's really quite bumpy.

2 Look at the pictures. Why is there still some friction between objects with polished surfaces?

3 (a) What stops you from slipping every time you take a step forwards?

(b) Why is it difficult to walk on an icy pavement?

There's no friction without heat

Rub your hands together quickly for a few seconds and they will feel warm. Friction causes surfaces to **heat** up.

Look at the pictures and answer the following questions.

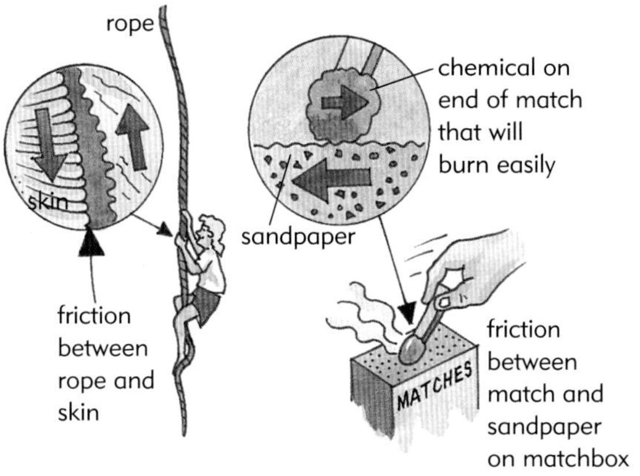

4 Why should you never slide down a rope?

5 Why does a match light when you strike it?

Putting friction to good use

Friction against a moving surface makes it slow down. This is how **brakes** for bicycles and cars work. A car needs a big force to stop it, so a lot of heat is produced. Car brake pads are made from a special material that can stand the heat. Look at the diagrams and answer the following questions.

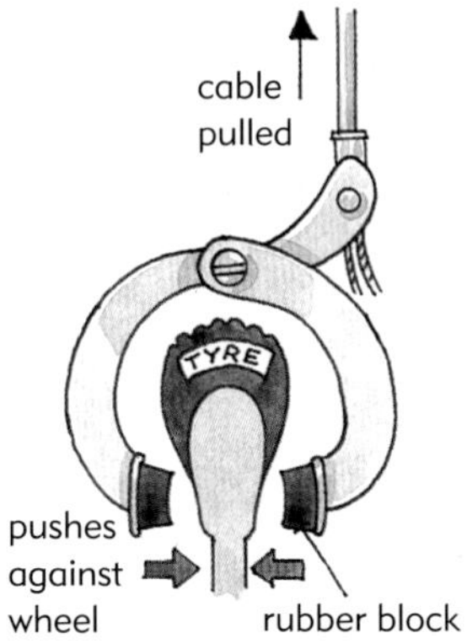

Bicycle brakes.

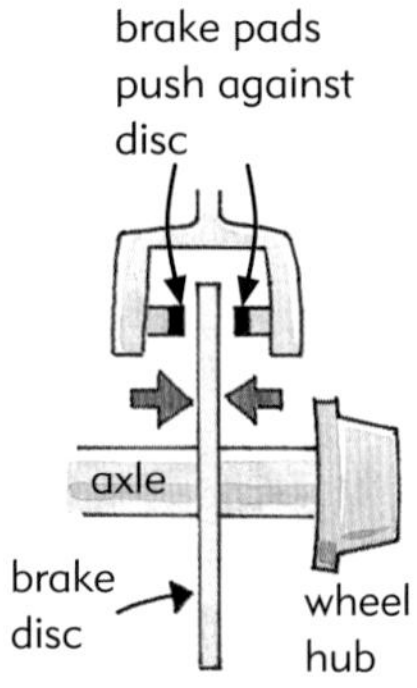

Disc brakes in a car.

6 Copy and complete the following sentences.

When the cyclist pulls the brake lever, __________ blocks press against the wheel. The force of friction then __________ the bike down.

When the driver pushes the brake pedal, brake __________ press against the brake disc attached to the wheel axle. The force of __________ then slows the car down.

What are you wearing out today?

Friction causes objects to **wear** away. Tiny pieces break off the surface when it rubs against another surface. This can happen quickly or slowly depending on the materials.

7 Why does blackboard chalk wear away faster than stone steps?

8 Why do brake blocks have to be replaced quite often?

9 Friction forces make clothes wear away.

(a) Which parts wear away first in shoes? Give a reason for your answer.

(b) Why do elbows in jumpers wear away first?

10 A pencil eraser loses tiny pieces of rubber each time you use it. Why does this happen?

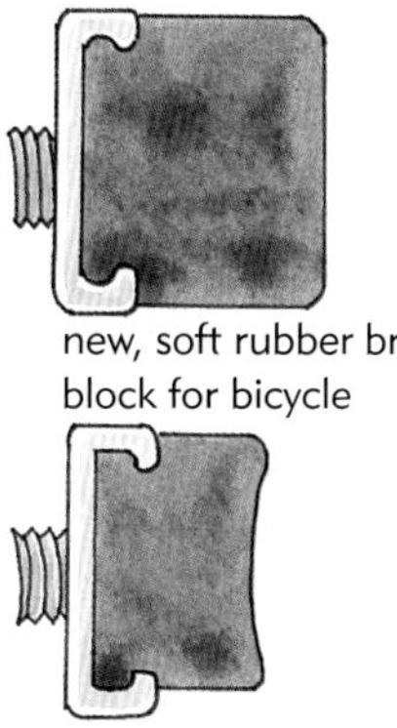
new, soft rubber brake block for bicycle
a few months later

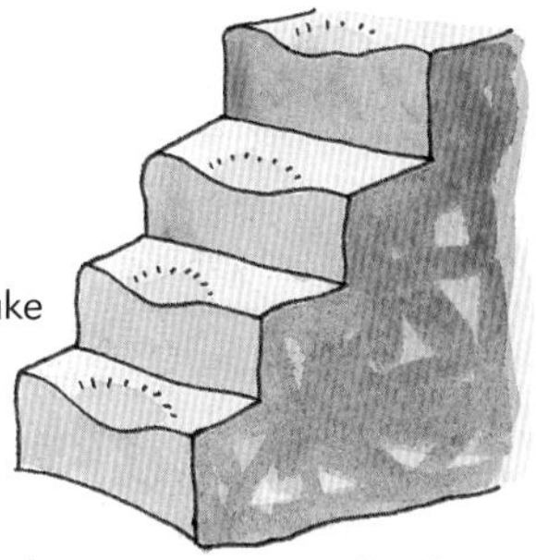
friction wears away hard stone steps in a few centuries

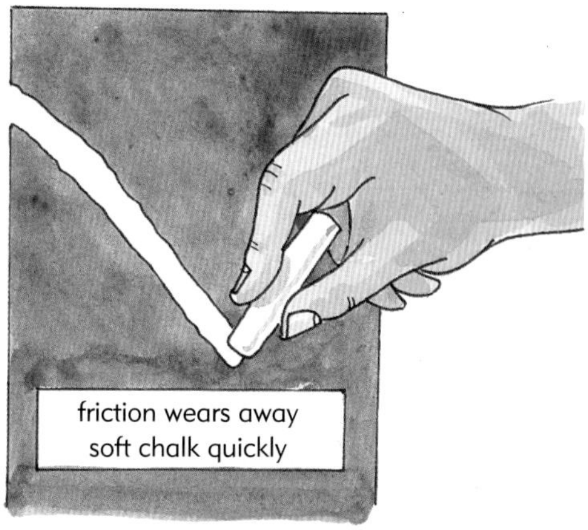
friction wears away soft chalk quickly

Rock and rollers

Large stone blocks produce a lot of friction if they are dragged along the ground. This makes moving them very slow work, and causes wear to the block and to the ground. Rollers between these two surfaces reduce the friction.

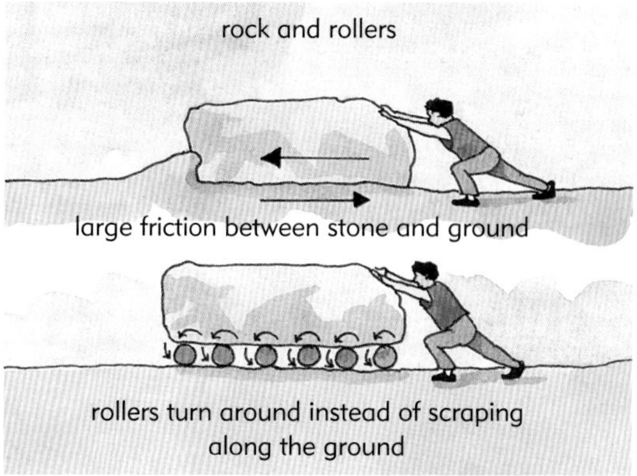
rock and rollers
large friction between stone and ground
rollers turn around instead of scraping along the ground

What you need to remember [Copy and complete using the **key words**]

Taking the rough with the smooth

When solid surfaces slide across each other, a force of ______________ acts.
The direction of this force is always ______________ to the direction in which the object or surface is moving.
Friction causes objects to ___________ up. It also makes surfaces ___________ away.
The friction between solid surfaces is used in ______________ to slow down and stop moving vehicles.

Stop that car!

You can't stop instantly

If someone steps out in front of a car, it takes time for the driver to react. This is called **reaction** time. The distance the car travels during the reaction time is called the thinking distance.

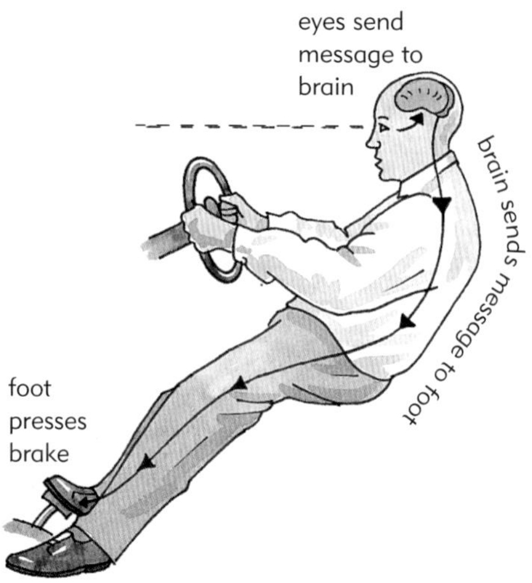
eyes send message to brain
brain sends message to foot
foot presses brake

Making a quick stop.

1 Look at the diagram. Why does it take time to react?

2 Look at the table.

(a) What is the thinking distance when travelling at 30 miles per hour?

(b) What happens to the thinking distance if the speed is doubled?

When the driver presses the brake pedal, it takes **time** for the brakes to slow the car down. During this time the car travels a **distance** called the braking distance.

Stopping distances on dry roads.

Speed in miles per hour	Thinking distance in metres	Braking distance in metres	Stopping distance in metres
20	6	6	12
30	9	14	23
40	12	24	36
50	15	38	53
60	18	55	73
70	21	75	96

30 miles per hour is 48 kilometres per hour

3 Look at the table.

(a) What is the braking distance for a speed of 30 miles per hour?

(b) What happens to the braking distance if the speed is increased?

(c) Copy and complete.

stopping distance = thinking distance + ________ distance

4 After drinking alcohol people may feel perfectly normal but actually their reactions are much slower.

Why is it a bad idea for people to drive after drinking alcohol?

Why do tyres have tread?

You need good tyres to stop quickly. Tyres can grip the road only if they are touching it. They lose their grip when the road is **wet**. The tread on a tyre is designed to push away the water. In dry conditions the tread doesn't help. In dry weather, racing cars use tyres with no tread.

5 Why do racing drivers stop to change their tyres when it starts raining?

Getting a grip ... but don't overdo it

There is friction between tyres and the road, which makes the tyres grip the road. When you brake there is friction between the brakes and the wheels, which slows the wheels down.

6 Look at the diagram.

(a) What job does friction do when the car is driving along?

(b) What are the <u>two</u> jobs done by friction when the car brakes?

(c) Which friction force is larger when the car brakes?

(d) What is happening when the car skids?

(e) Which friction force is larger when the car skids?

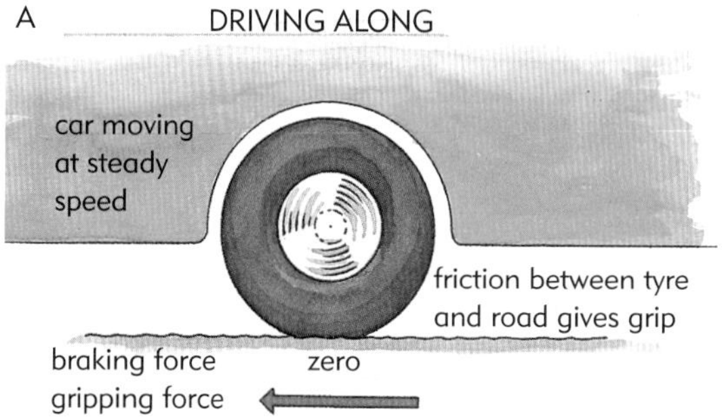

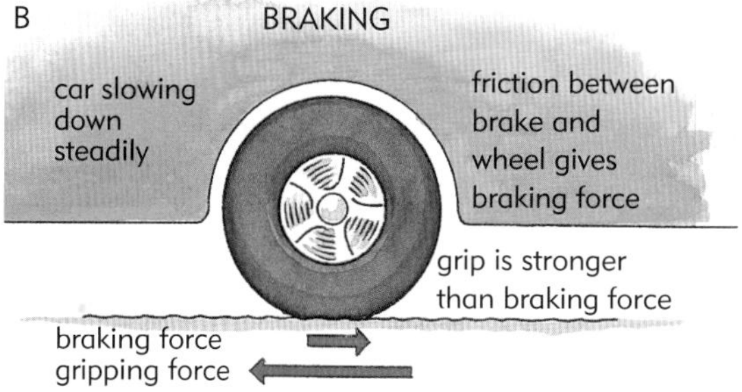

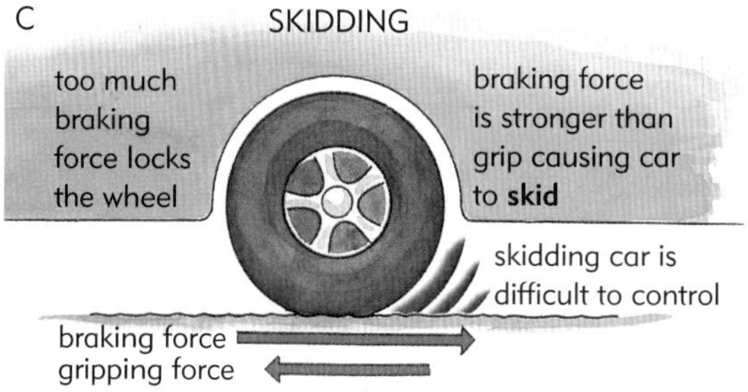

How to reduce skidding

There is less chance of skidding when there is a lot of **friction** between the tyres and the road. That is why there are often very rough road surfaces at crossings and junctions. An **icy** road has very little friction. It is very difficult to stop a car quickly without skidding on an icy road.

7 Explain the following as fully as you can.

(a) Why is it safer to have a rough road surface before a pedestrian crossing?

(b) Why must a driver brake very carefully when there is ice on the roads?

What you need to remember [Copy and complete using the **key words**]

Stop that car!

The greater the speed of a vehicle, the longer the ______________ it takes to stop and the greater the ______________ it travels.
If the braking force is too large the vehicle may ______________.
Stopping distance is affected by the ______________ time of the driver. It also depends on the ______________ between the road and the tyres.
There is less friction when the road is ______________ or ______________.

Travelling at speed

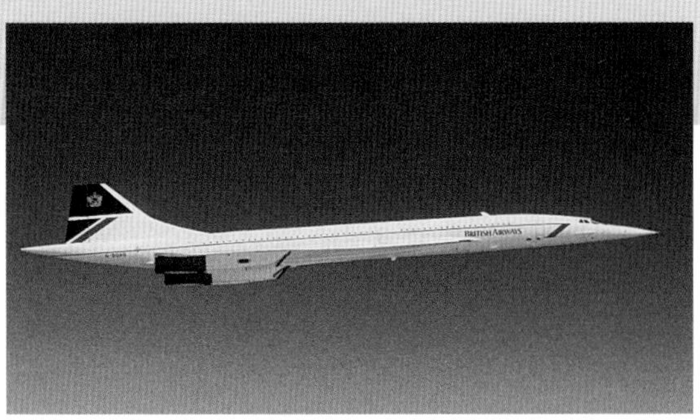

Faster than the speed of sound

Concorde was built for **speed**. It can travel a very long **distance** in a very short **time**. In fact, it has so much speed that you can travel faster than sound travels through the air!

1 Copy and complete the following sentence.

At top speed you cover the longest __________ in the shortest __________.

How to calculate speed

You can work out speed like this:

$$\text{speed (metres per second)} = \frac{\text{distance travelled (metres)}}{\text{time taken (seconds)}}$$

[On your calculator: distance ÷ time]

Example: On a motorway, a car travels 300 **metres** in 10 **seconds**.

distance travelled = 300 metres (m)
time taken = 10 seconds (s)
speed = ?

so speed = $\frac{300}{10}$ = 30 **metres per second** (m/s)

2 Look at the examples in the picture and work out the missing item for each one.

time taken = distance ÷ speed
distance = speed × time

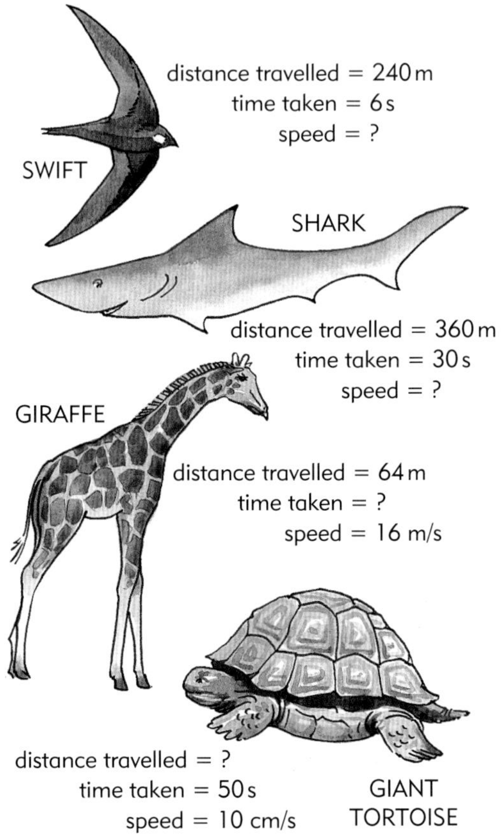

Showing movement on a graph

This graph shows distance travelled against time taken, so it is called a **distance–time** graph. You can read from the graph the distance travelled in a period of time. For example, it takes 4 seconds to travel 20 metres.

3 What speed is this?

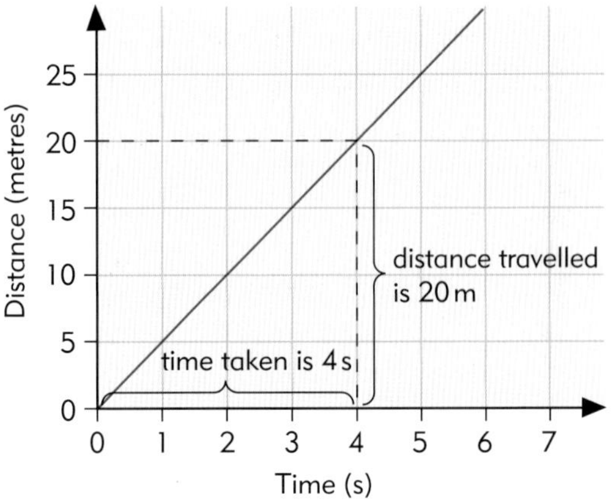

A distance-time graph.

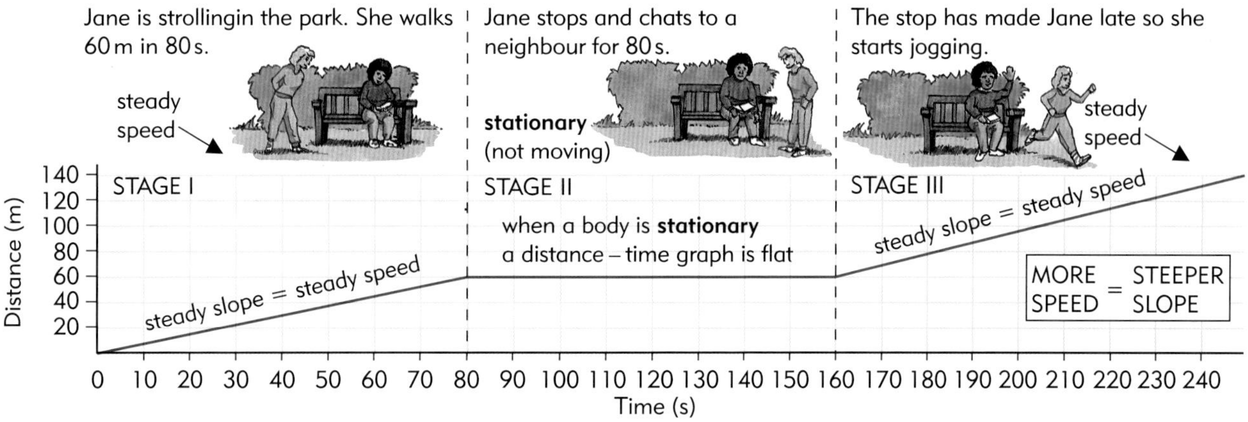

Jane's journey

This example shows how a journey can be described on a distance–time graph. Look at it carefully and use it to answer the questions.

4 Look at stage I of the journey, where Jane is walking.

(a) How many metres does Jane walk?

(b) How long does it take Jane to walk this distance?

(c) What is her speed for this part of her journey?

The **slope** of the graph tells you about the speed.

5 (a) What is Jane's speed when she chats (stage II)?

(b) Describe the shape of the graph for this stage.

(c) Write down a rule for telling when something is stationary on a distance–time graph.

6 (a) Which part of the graph is steeper, (I) or (III)?

(b) Which stage of the journey is faster, (I) or (III)?

(c) What is the connection between speed and slope on a distance–time graph?

What you need to remember [Copy and complete using the **key words**]

Travelling at speed

We calculate speed like this: speed = $\frac{\text{\_\_\_\_\_\_\_\_\_\_ travelled}}{\text{\_\_\_\_\_\_\_\_\_\_ taken}}$

The units of speed are ________________ **per** ________________. The distance travelled is measured in ________________. The time taken is measured in ________________.
You can show speed on a ________________–________________ graph.

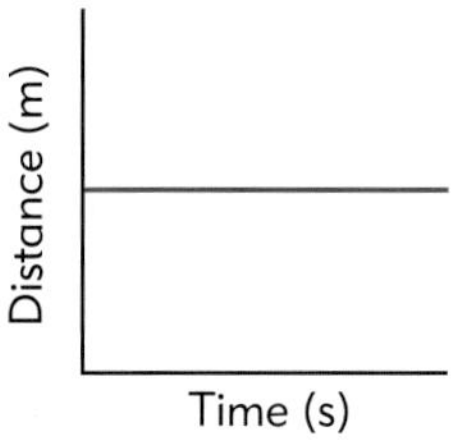

This graph shows the distance moved by an object that is ________________.

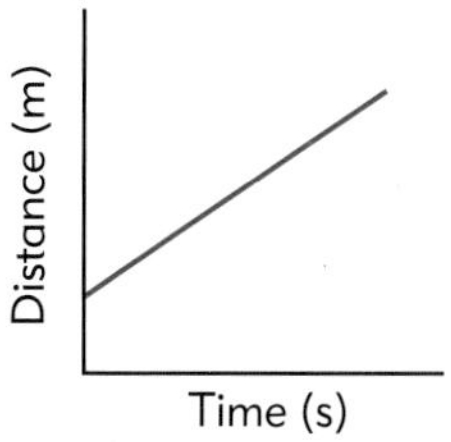

This graph shows the distance moved by an object that is moving with a steady ________________.

If an object has more speed, the graph has a steeper ________________.

Springs and things

Forces don't just speed things up or slow them down. They can also change the **shape** of things.

When you pull a spring it stretches. When you let go, the spring quickly goes back to its original shape. Anything which does this is called **elastic**.

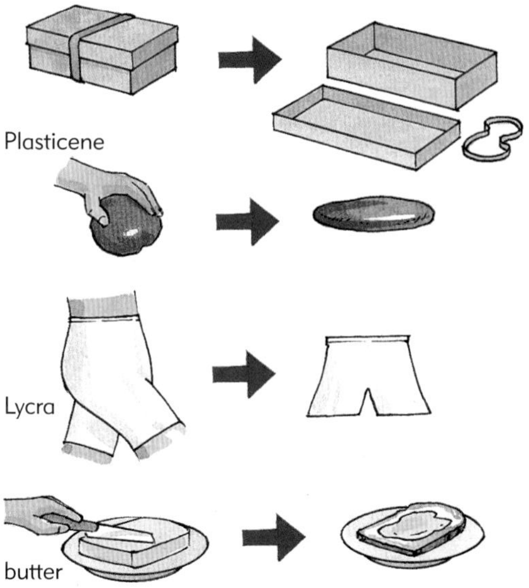

1 Look at the four materials in the picture. Say which are elastic and which are not elastic. Give reasons for your answers.

A toy with a lot of potential

Look at the diagram. You launch the ball by giving it a lot of kinetic energy. This energy comes from the spring. When you do **work** to stretch the spring, energy stores up in it. This stored energy is called **elastic potential** energy. When you let go, this energy is released.

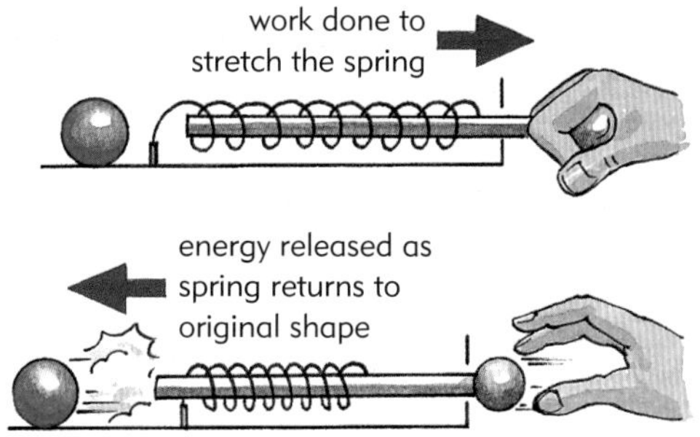

2 Copy and complete the following sentences.

While a spring is being __________, it stores up __________ __________ energy inside. When the spring is released, this energy is transferred to the __________.

The ball moves, so we say that it has kinetic energy.

The restaurant mystery

Stephan works in a self-service restaurant. Customers take trays from a tray holder. One of Stephan's jobs is to clean the trays and put them back into the holder. He notices that the top tray is <u>always</u> level with the top of the holder. He can't understand why.

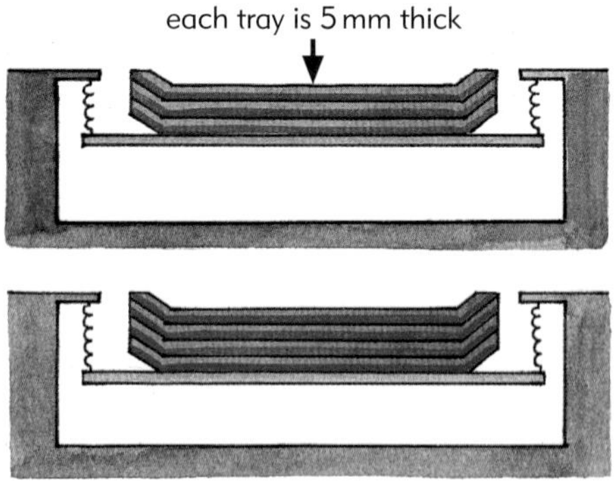

the weight of 1 tray stretches the springs by 5 mm

3 Look at the diagram. Then explain why there is always a tray level with the top of the holder.

Experimenting with springs

Stephan takes one of the springs to investigate how it stretches. He uses 1 newton (1 N) weights to stretch it. Each time he adds another weight he measures how far the spring stretches. This is called the **extension**. The graph on the next page shows Stephan's results.

4 (a) What is the extension of the spring with a force of 1 N?

(b) What happens to the extension as the force is increased?

5 What extension would you expect with a force of 10 N?

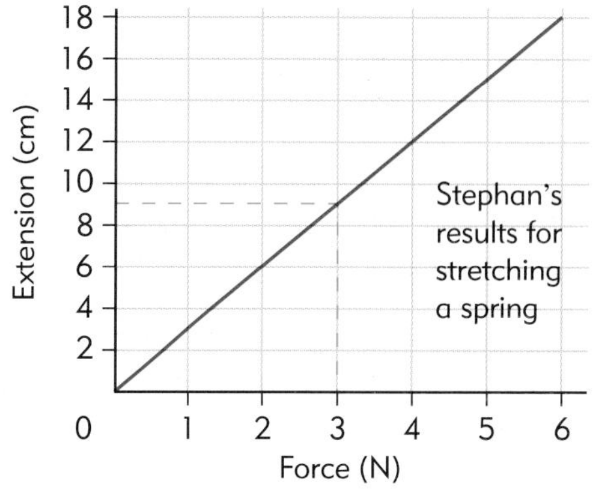

The graph shows that a **force** of 3 N produces an extension of 9 cm.

A stretch too far

A spring can stand only so much stretching. The graph shows what happens when Stephan's spring is stretched too far.

6 (a) How far does the spring actually extend with a force of 10 N?

(b) Was this bigger or smaller than you expected?

7 How does the extension change with force when the spring is stretched too far?

8 What happens when the overstretched spring is released?

When a spring is **overstretched** we say it has been stretched beyond its elastic limit.

9 What force will stretch Stephan's spring beyond its elastic limit?

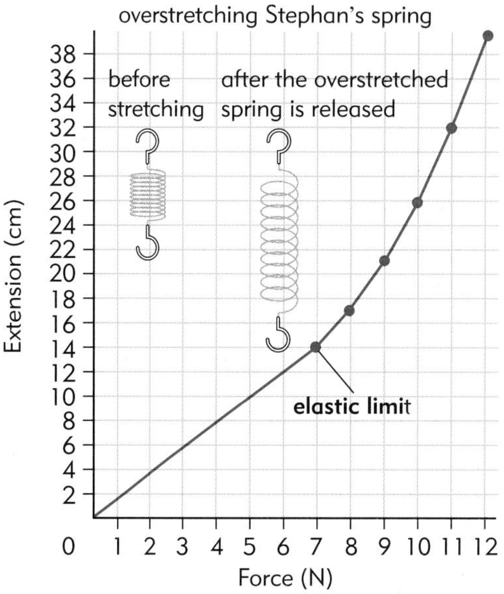

What you need to remember [Copy and complete using the **key words**]

Springs and things

When a spring is stretched and then released, it returns to its original ________________. Materials that do this are called ________________.

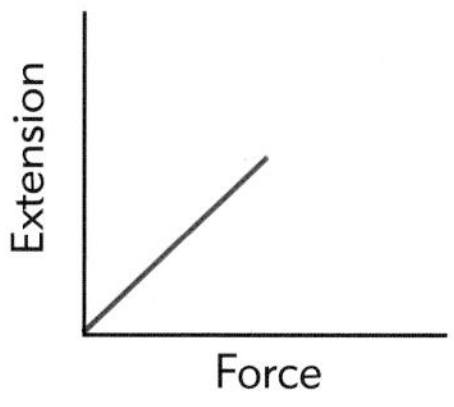

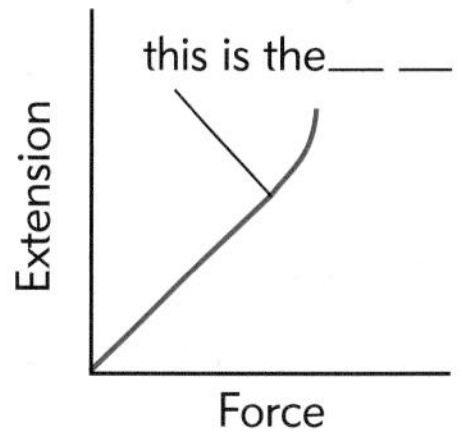

This graph shows that equal amounts of ________________ produce equal amounts of ________________ in a spring.

This is the graph for a spring which has been ________________. It does not go back to its original shape.

To stretch a spring you have to do ________________ on it.
The spring then stores energy called ________________ ________________ energy.

7 Bridges and bungee cords

Bridging the gap

The world's longest bridges hang from metal cables. It is important to know exactly how much the cables might stretch, or else a bridge could collapse. Thicker cables stretch less than thin ones.

1 Look at the diagram of the bridge cables. What do you notice about the cables?

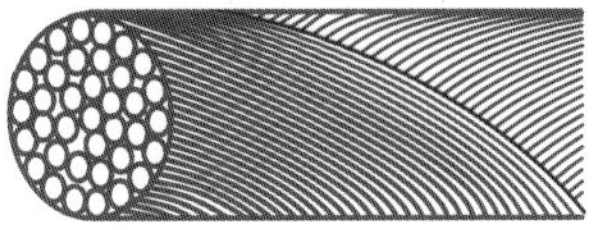

Each cable is made of many thinner cables.

Using a lot of thin cables has the same effect as using a thicker one.

How metal wires stretch

If a wire is stretched by a small force, it will return to its original length when the force is removed. Materials that do this are called **elastic**. Metal wires are not elastic if too much force is applied. They stay stretched when the force is removed.

Stretching a metal wire.

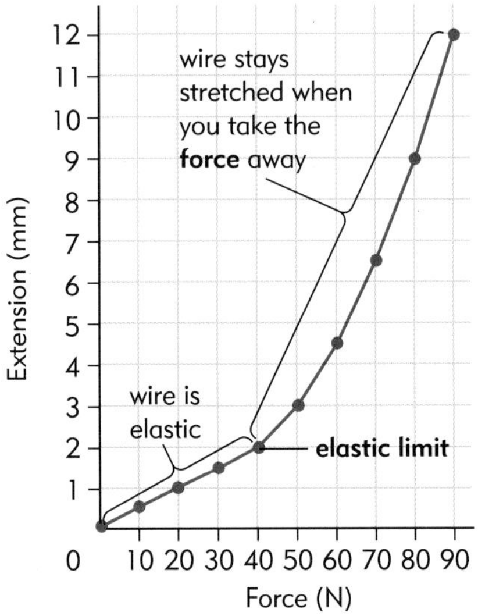

2 Look at the graph for the stretching of a wire. Copy and complete the following sentences.

To begin with, each extra 10 N of force stretches the wire another __________ mm.

When you get past the elastic limit, each extra 10 N of force stretches the wire __________ than it did before.

3 The wire is stretched with a force of 90 N. Then the force is removed. What will have happened to the wire? Give a reason for your answer.

Through thick and thin

The thickness of a wire affects how it stretches. Look at the graph comparing two wires.

Stretching wires of the same length but different thicknesses.

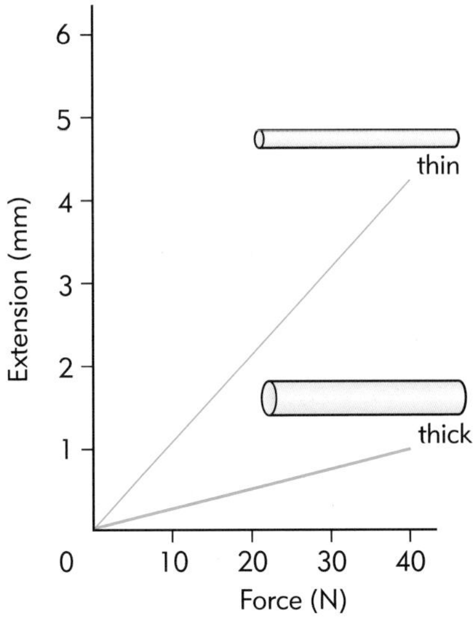

4 (a) How much does each wire stretch with a force of 40 N?

(b) Which stretches more easily, thick or thin wire?

5 How does the slope of the graph tell you which stretches more easily?

Why bungees bounce

Rubber is also elastic but it stretches a lot more than a metal wire. You can survive a bungee jump because of the way the rubber stretches. It slows you down gradually so your legs don't break. The pictures show what happens during the jump.

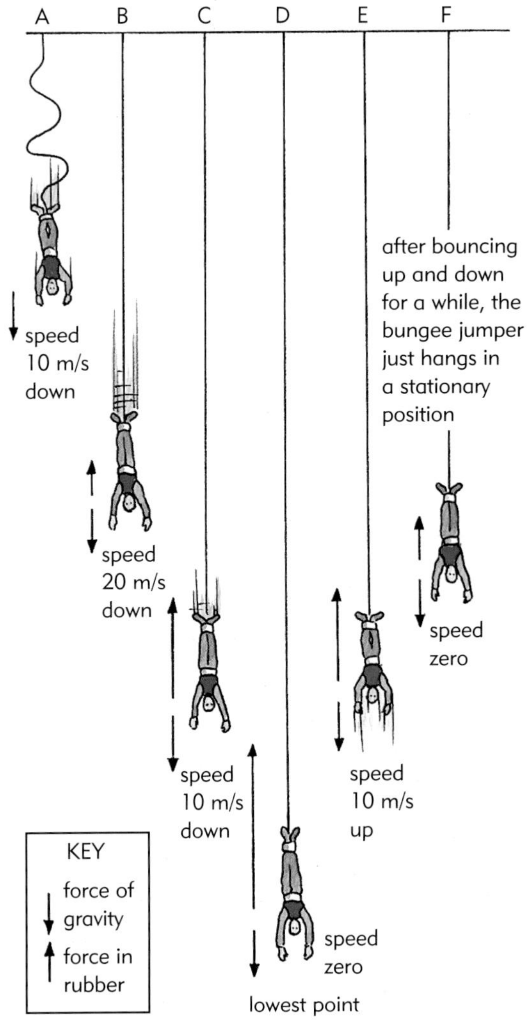

Bungee jumps and energy changes

The faster an object moves, the more kinetic energy it has. The more a bungee cord is stretched, the more **energy** it stores. This is called **elastic potential** energy.

6 (a) What happens to the bungee jumper's kinetic energy during the first half of the fall?

(b) How much kinetic energy does the bungee jumper have at the lowest point?

7 To make the bungee jumper move back up again, energy must be transferred. Where is this energy transferred from?

What you need to remember [Copy and complete using the **key words**]

Bridges and bungee cords

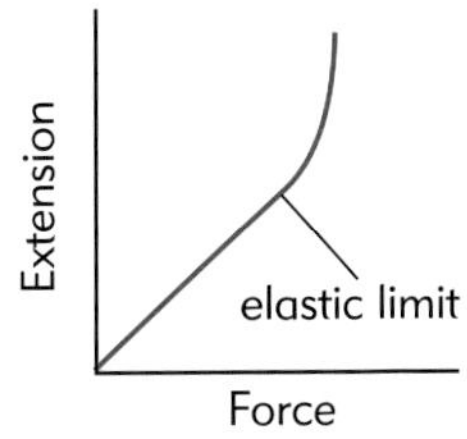

You can stretch a wire using a ________________. Unless the force is too big, the wire goes back to its original length when you remove the force. We say the wire is

________________.

If you stretch a wire further than its ________________ ________________, it stays stretched.

To stretch anything you have to do work and transfer ________________. This energy is stored in the stretched material.

It is called ________________ ________________ energy.

Bursting balloons and protecting brains

Forces can damage things. Big forces usually do more damage than small ones. But the area on which a force acts also matters. A force that acts on a small area does more damage than the same force acting on a large area. This is because the force produces a bigger **pressure**.

a small force acting on a balloon just dents it

BANG

the same force acting on a smaller area bursts the balloon

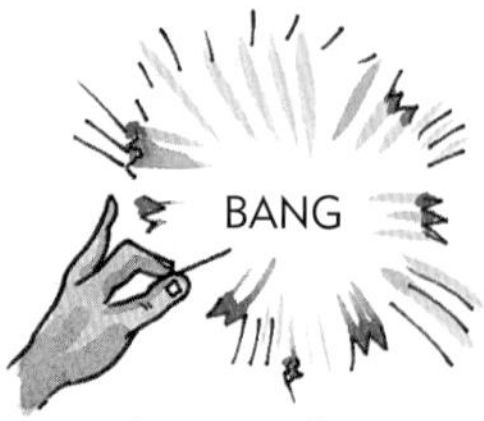

1 Look at the pictures. Use the idea of pressure to explain the following:

 (a) Why it is easier to burst a balloon with a pin than with your finger?

 (b) How does a safety helmet protect a cyclist's skull?

a hard fall can fracture your skull

the same force spread over a bigger area does less damage

tight-fitting helmet

Look at the items in the picture.

The end of the chisel handle has a large area. This reduces the pressure on the mallet and stops it being damaged. The sharp end of the chisel has a small area. This increases the pressure on the wood and cuts it better.

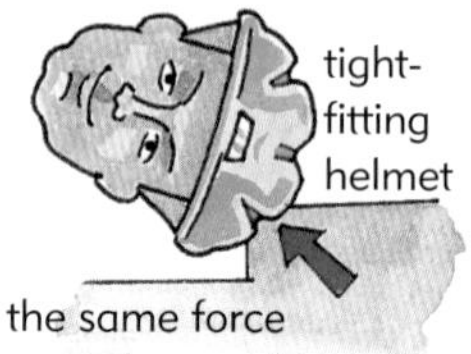

> The weight of anything is the <u>force</u> of gravity that acts on it.

2 Explain the parts of the drawing pin and the kitchen knife in the same way.

3 Explain why:

 (a) heavy suitcases are more comfortable to carry when they have thick handles

 (b) hospital patients with severely damaged skin are put on beds that mould themselves to the shape of the person.

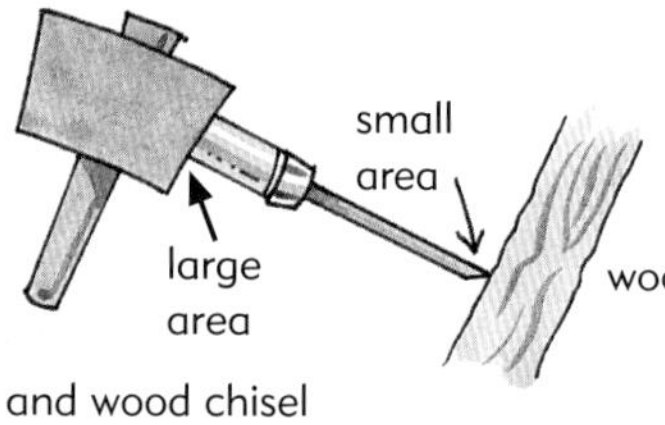

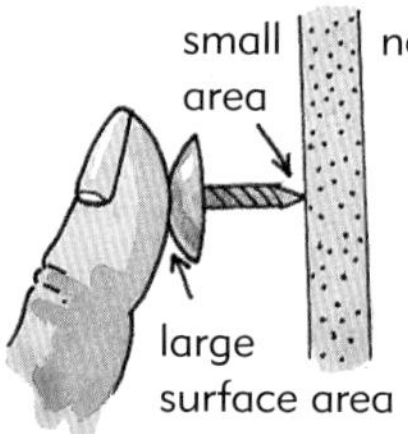

small area

large area

wood

mallet and wood chisel

small area

notice board

large surface area

drawing pin

edge has very small area

handle has large area

kitchen knife

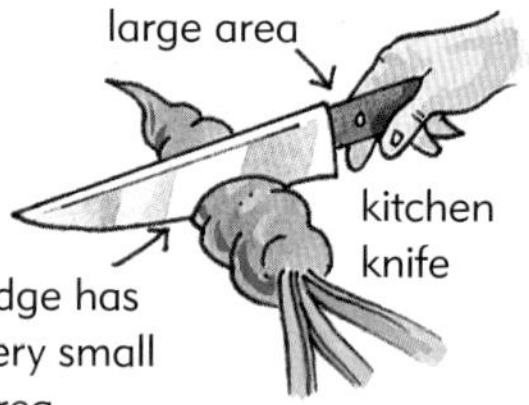

■ Calculating pressure

The amount of pressure depends on the **force** that is applied and the **area** that the force is spread over. We can work it out like this:

$$\text{pressure} = \frac{\text{force}}{\text{area}} \qquad \left(\begin{array}{l} \text{On your calculator:} \\ \text{pressure} = \text{force} \div \text{area} \end{array} \right)$$

Force is measured in newtons (N) and area is measured in square metres (m^2).
So pressure is measured in **newtons per square metre** (N/m^2). These units are also called **pascals** (Pa).

A pressure of 1 Pa is very small. It is roughly the pressure of a small piece of newspaper, folded double and placed flat on your hand. This means that pressure measurements are often large numbers, so you can use other units of pressure to keep the numbers smaller.

4 Look at the examples shown in the pictures and work out the missing information for each one. The first one has been done for you.

How much pressure in...

a book resting on a table
Weight = 10 N (= force)
Base area = $0.2\,m^2$
Pressure = force ÷ area
= 10 ÷ 0.2
= $50\,N/m^2$

mattress resting on its base
Weight = 250 N
Area = $2\,m^2$
Pressure = ? N/m^2 (or Pa)

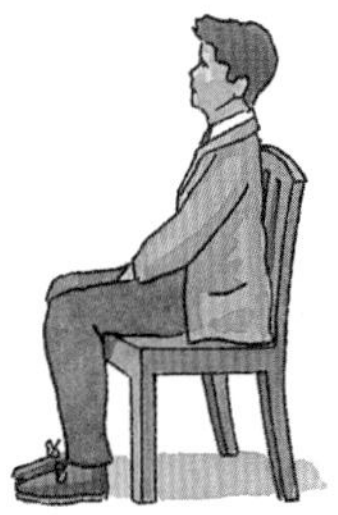

normal sitting
Weight = 600 N
Total area of chair touching floor = $20\,cm^2$
Pressure = ? N/cm^2

rocking back
Weight = 600 N
Total area of chair touching floor = $2\,cm^2$
Pressure = ? N/cm^2

The same weight can cause different pressures

A stone block for a monument is shown in the diagram. The pressure on the ground is different depending on which way up the block is.

5 Copy the table and then complete it.

Face on ground	Force (weight) in N	Area of face in m^2	Pressure (force ÷ area) in N/m^2
A	120 000	2 × 1 = 2	60 000
B			
C			

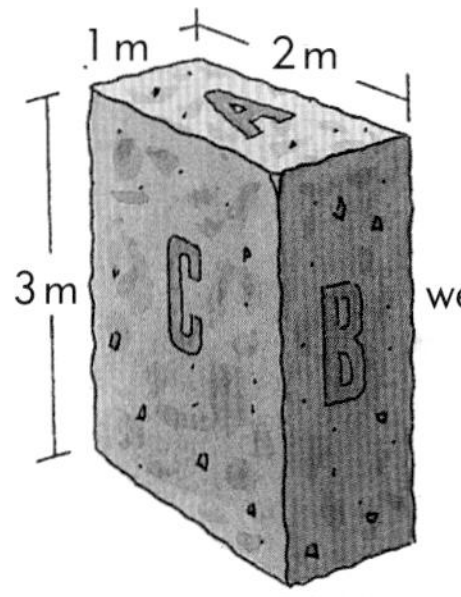

stone block

What you need to remember [Copy and complete using the **key words**]

Bursting balloons and protecting brains

If you spread a force out over a large area you get a smaller ________________.
To get a large pressure you need a large ________________ acting on a small ________________.

pressure = $\dfrac{\_\_\_\_\_\_\_\_\_\_}{\_\_\_\_\_\_\_\_\_\_}$

Pressure is measured in ________________ **per** ________________ ________________(N/m^2).
These units are also called ________________ (Pa).

Deep sea divers – standing the pressure

Many people dive for fun, but divers also do very important jobs. For example in the North Sea, divers inspect oil rigs and repair them to make them safe.

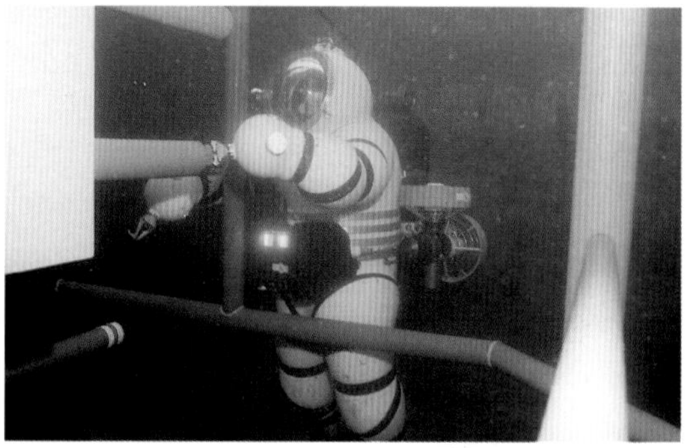

Why diving can be dangerous

Diving can be dangerous because the **weight** of the water above a diver can produce a very big **pressure**. How big the pressure is depends on how deep the diver goes. The water pressure increases as you dive deeper below the surface.

1 Copy and complete the table.

Diver	Depth in metres	Pressure in thousands of pascals
Linda		
Suresh		

2 What would the pressure be on a diver 100 metres below the surface?

The deeper you go, the more water presses down on you.

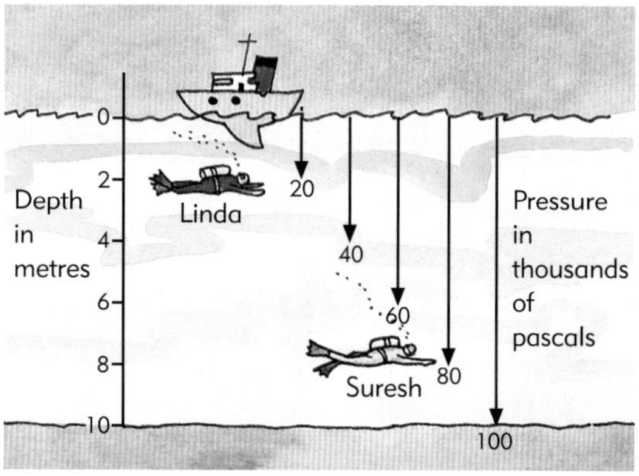

Why you can't shelter from water pressure

An experiment with a plastic bottle shows you that water presses sideways as well as downwards. In fact, water pressure at any particular depth is exactly the same in all **directions**.

Being at a high pressure for too long can be dangerous. When you come up from diving, bubbles of gas can form in your blood. This is painful and can kill you.

3 A diver stays down longer than she should. She thinks she is safe from the water pressure because she is inside a cave. Explain why she is wrong.

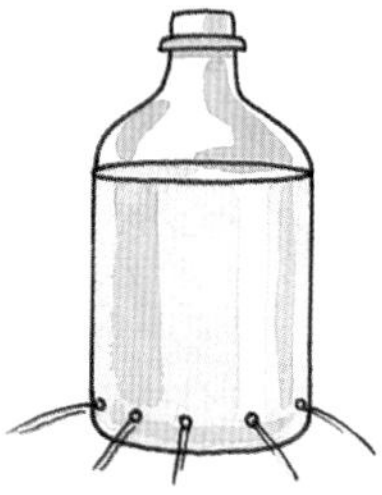

The sideways pressure pushes water out of the holes.

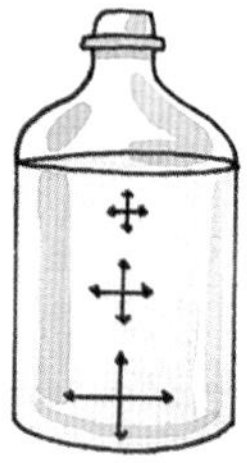

Water presses equally in all directions.

You can't hide from water pressure.

Why is there air pressure?

It isn't just under water that there is a pressure. As you go deeper in to any **fluid** the pressure increases. All liquids are fluids. Gases, including air, are also fluids. We live at the bottom of a deep layer of air called the atmosphere. The pressure of this air is called **atmospheric** pressure.

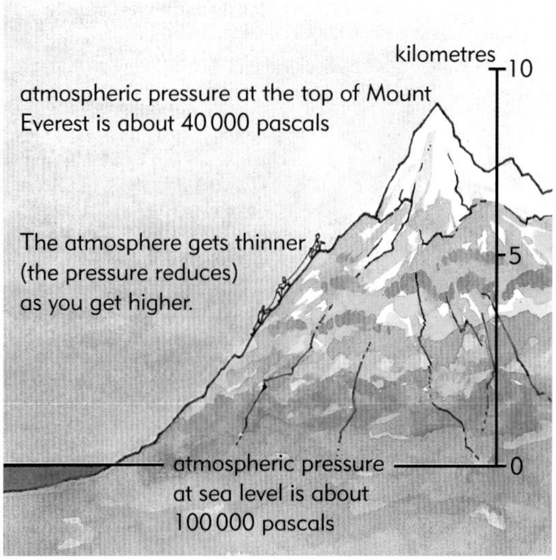

kilometres
10
5
0
atmospheric pressure at the top of Mount Everest is about 40 000 pascals
The atmosphere gets thinner (the pressure reduces) as you get higher.
atmospheric pressure at sea level is about 100 000 pascals

4 Some mountaineers travel from the coast of India to the top of Mount Everest.

(a) What happens to the pressure of the air around them?

(b) Explain why this happens.

5 Copy and complete the following sentence.

The pressure of the atmosphere at sea level is the same as the pressure of water about __________ metres deep.

A useful unit of pressure

We sometimes compare large pressures with the pressure of the atmosphere.
Read the article about Deep Flight.

6 How big is the pressure at the bottom of the Marianas Trench?

7 (a) Why can't an ordinary submarine go there?

(b) What <u>two</u> things enable Deep Flight to stand the pressure?

Deep Flight

The Marianas Trench in the Pacific Ocean is 11 km deep. It is the deepest place on Earth. The pressure at the bottom is more than 1000 times greater than atmospheric pressure. This is enough to crush any large submarine. The Deep Flight submarine is an American project designed to take a single passenger to the bottom. The rounded shape of Deep Flight helps it to stand the huge pressure. It is also made of specially strong materials.

What you need to remember [Copy and complete using the **key words**]

Deep sea divers – standing the pressure

The pressure in water is caused by the ________________ of the water pressing down.
The deeper you go under water, the bigger the ________________ is.
Water pressure acts equally in all ________________.
Gases and liquids are all types of ________________.
The pressure of the air around us is called ________________ pressure.

Using liquids to push harder

We can use liquids to help us operate all kinds of machines.

The vehicle that lifts and drops the earth uses a hydraulic system.

How do car brakes work?

It's easy to stop a car with your foot. All you have to do is press the brake pedal. This puts brake fluid (a liquid) under **pressure**. This pressure then operates the brakes.

We can use liquids to send large forces to where they are needed, in what is called a **hydraulic** system. The car uses a hydraulic braking system.

1 Look at the diagrams then write down the sentences in the right order. The first sentence has been done for you.

The driver presses the brake pedal.

- A force acts on the master piston.
- The slave pistons push against the wheel disc.
- The master piston presses on the brake fluid.
- This slows the car down.
- The brake fluid presses on the slave pistons.

2 The pressure in brake fluid acts equally in all directions. This makes it easy for the hydraulic system to do <u>three</u> important things. Write down these three things.

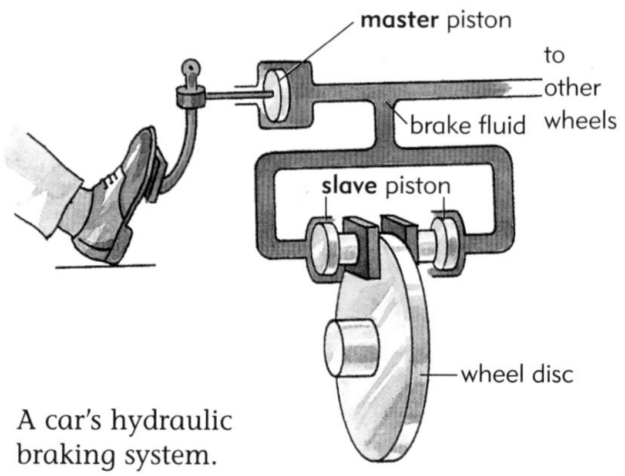

A car's hydraulic braking system.

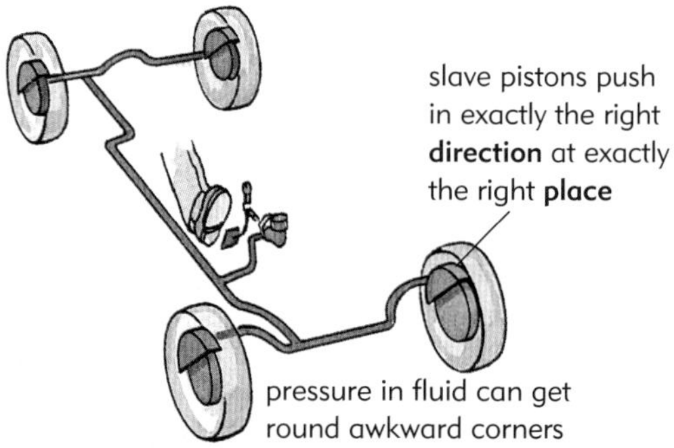

slave pistons push in exactly the right **direction** at exactly the right **place**
pressure in fluid can get round awkward corners

Lifting a car using a jack

To change a car wheel you must lift one corner of the car off the ground.

3 What do you use to help you do this?

You only need to apply a small force to the jack. The jack changes this to a bigger force and lifts the car. We say that the jack is a force **multiplier**.

Using a jack to lift a car.

How does a hydraulic jack work?

To lift a heavy vehicle, you can use a hydraulic jack.

REMEMBER

force = pressure × area

4 Look at the diagram then copy and complete the following sentences.

At the master piston a __________ force acts on a __________ area. All the brake fluid is then at the __________ pressure.

The slave piston has a __________ area so it pushes the car up with a __________ force.

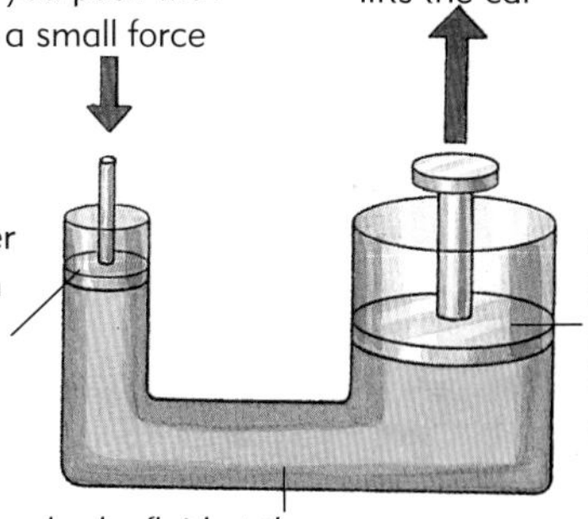

you push with a small force
a large force lifts the car
master piston has a small area
slave piston has a large area
brake fluid at the same pressure

You never get anything for nothing

The jack changes a small force into a much bigger one. This makes it easier to lift the car. But you still have to do just as much work. The diagram shows why.

5 Copy and complete the following sentences.

Using a jack, you can lift a car with a small __________.

But you have to move this force through a __________ distance, so you still have to do as much __________.

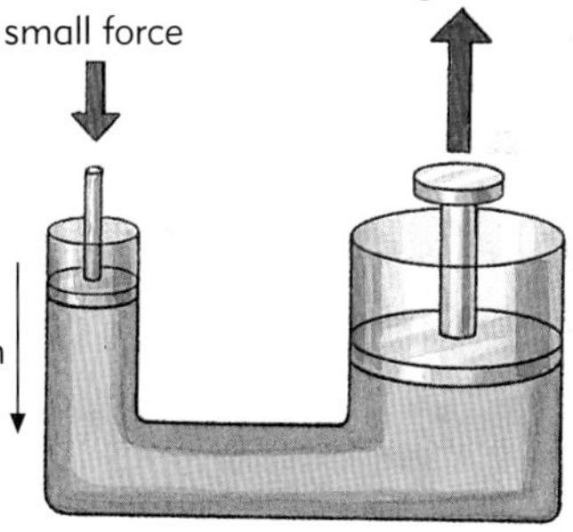

small force
large force
you have to push a long way
but car is lifted only a small distance

What you need to remember [Copy and complete using the **key words**]

Using liquids to push harder

We can use liquids to send forces to where they are needed. This is called a ______________ system.

A force is applied to the liquid using a ______________ piston. This puts the liquid under ______________.

This pressure exerts a force on a ______________ piston.

Pressure in a liquid acts equally in all directions. This makes it easy to send forces to the right ______________ and make them act in the right ______________.

A hydraulic system can also make forces bigger; it can be used as a force ______________.

The light of day, the dark of night

We get days and years because of the way the Earth moves.

Why does it go dark at night?

The Sun shines non-stop, sending its light out into space in all directions.

The light that hits the Earth makes it **daytime** on one side. On the other side, facing away from the Sun, there is no light. It is dark there so it is **night**.

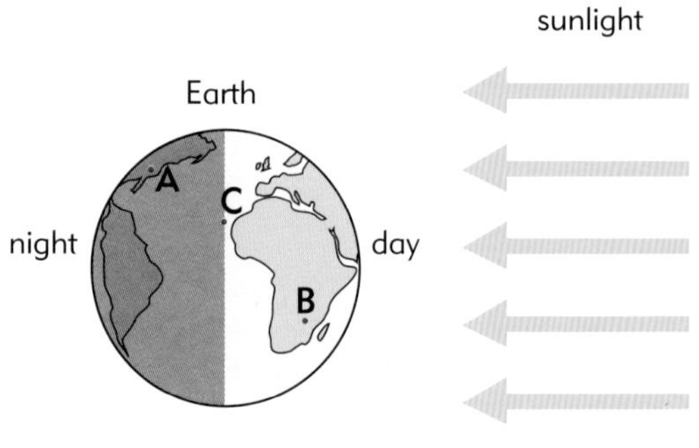

1 (a) Is it night or day at the places marked A and B on the diagram?

(b) What is happening at place C?

The spinning Earth

Places move from the dark side into the light because the Earth spins. It turns around once every 24 hours. So every **24** hours we have a period of dark then light (night then day).

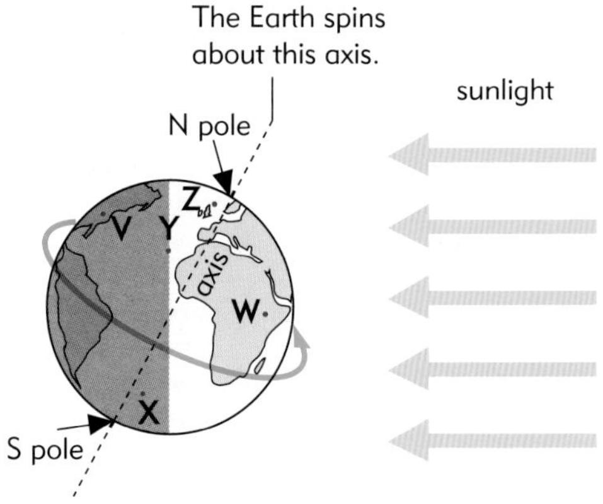

2 (a) Which places are in daylight in this picture? (Write the letters which mark the places.)

(b) Which places are in night?

(c) Which place is going from night into day (dawn)?

3 The Earth spins about a line called an axis. What do we call the ends of this axis?

The leaning Earth

The Earth's **axis** is tilted over. The dark/light dividing line does not go from pole to pole. This makes different parts of the Earth have days and nights of different lengths.

The Earth in June.

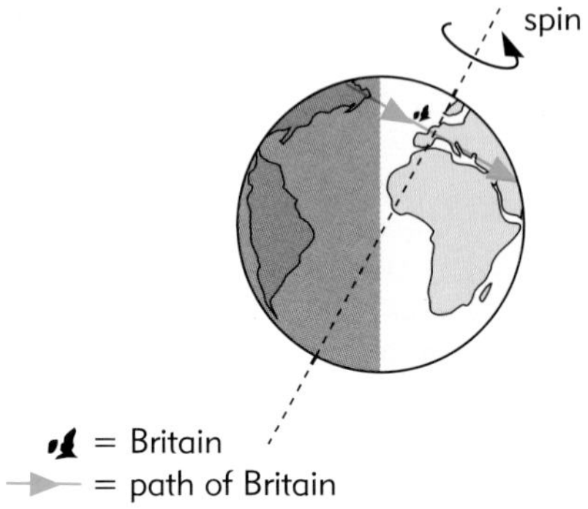

4 The diagram shows the path of Britain in June as the Earth spins. Will Britain have 8, 12 or 16 hours of daylight? Explain your answer.

What is a year?

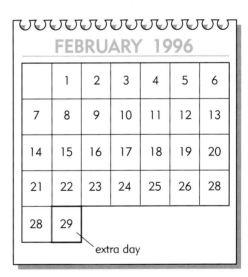

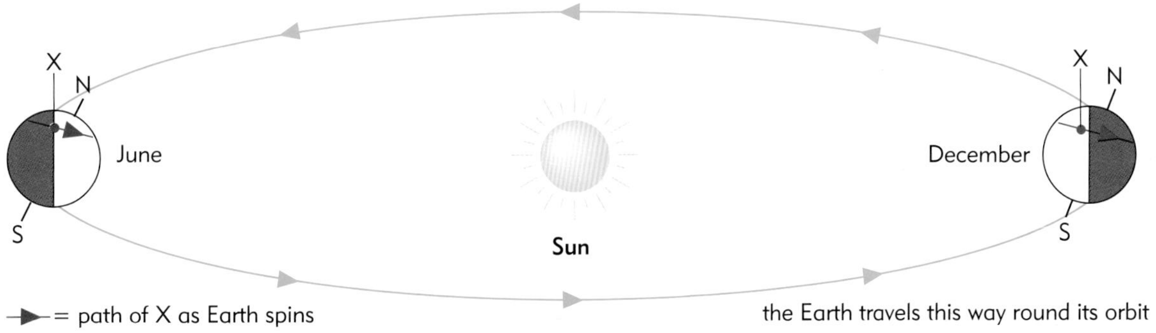

The Earth moves around the Sun in a path that is almost a circle. This is called the Earth's **orbit**. The Earth completes one journey around the Sun in **$365\frac{1}{4}$** days. This is one **year.**

5 Copy and complete the following sentences.

In June, place X will have __________ days and short nights. In December, place X will have __________ days and __________ nights.

Why do we have leap years?

We have only whole days in the calendar for each year. So for three calendar years running there are only 365 days. Then we have a leap year with 366 days.

6 What date is the extra day in a leap year?

7 Why do we have to have a leap year every four years?

FEBRUARY 1996

	1	2	3	4	5	6
7	8	9	10	11	12	13
14	15	16	17	18	19	20
21	22	23	24	25	26	28
28	29					

extra day

What you need to remember [Copy and complete using the **key words**]

The light of day, the dark of night

The Earth spins on its ________________ once every ________________ hours.
The Sun shines on one half of the Earth, where it is ________________.
The other side of the Earth is in shadow, where it is ________________.
The Earth goes around the ________________ once in ________________ days. This is called one ________________.
The path around the Sun is called an ________________.

12 Distant suns

What is a star?

Our Sun is an ordinary **star**. It is a huge ball of very hot, glowing gas. In the centre of the Sun, hydrogen is turned into helium in nuclear reactions that give off vast amounts of energy. This energy is radiated from the Sun as light and heat.

1 What is the temperature of the Sun

(a) in the centre?

(b) at the surface?

2 Why is it dangerous to look straight at the Sun?

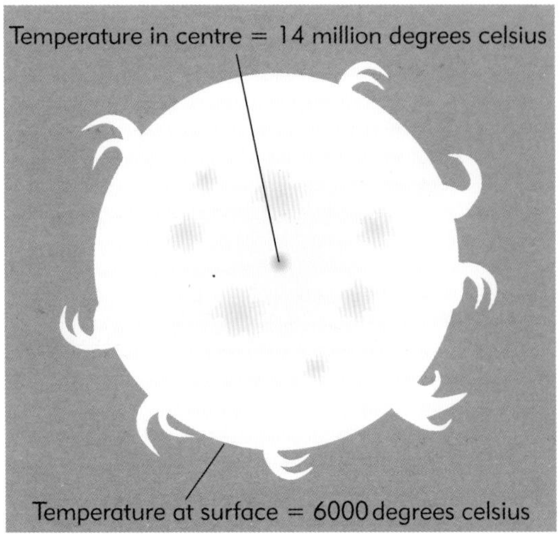

The Sun produces so much light that looking at it is dangerous. It is so bright it can damage the sensitive parts of your eye.

Why do other stars look so faint?

The stars that you can see in the night sky are made from hot **gas**, like the Sun. They all look faint, but some are actually much bigger and brighter than the Sun. They only look so faint because they are so **far** away.

3 The star Sirius is actually 26 times brighter than the Sun. Explain why it looks so much fainter.

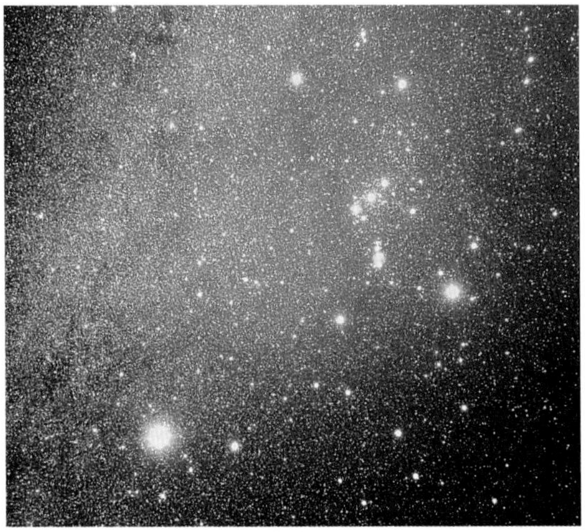

Sirius is the bright star at the bottom left.

Could we travel to the stars?

Concorde can fly at 2500 kilometres per hour. This is about 1 kilometre every 1.5 seconds! You might think this is very fast, but a spaceship travelling at this speed would take 2 million years to reach the nearest star (other than the Sun). Even in a very fast spaceship the journey would take thousands of years.

4 A speed of 2500 kilometres per hour is about 22 million kilometres per year.

(a) How long would it take a spaceship travelling at this speed to reach our nearest star, the Sun? (The Sun is 15 million kilometres away.)

(b) How far away is the nearest star, other than the Sun?

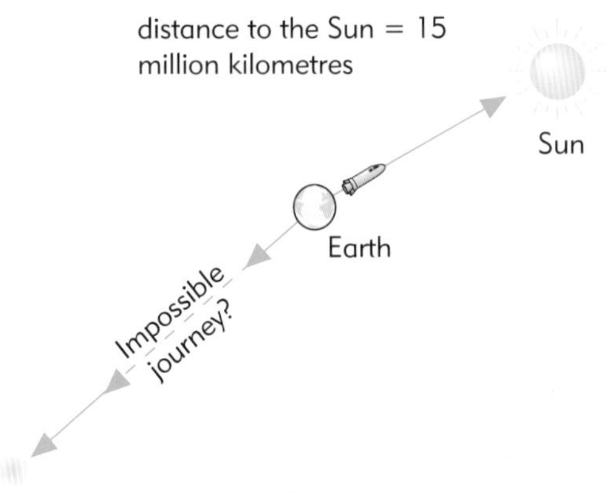

Patterns in the sky

The stars in the night sky make patterns called **constellations**. These patterns do not **change** from year to year. A famous example is Orion the Hunter, which you can see in the evening sky in mid-winter. People imagine the stars joined up to make shapes.

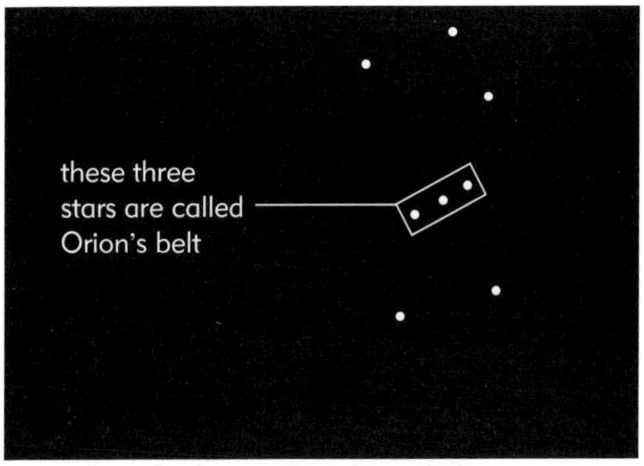
these three stars are called Orion's belt

Orion

5 Copy the constellations below and then draw pictures to show how they got their names.

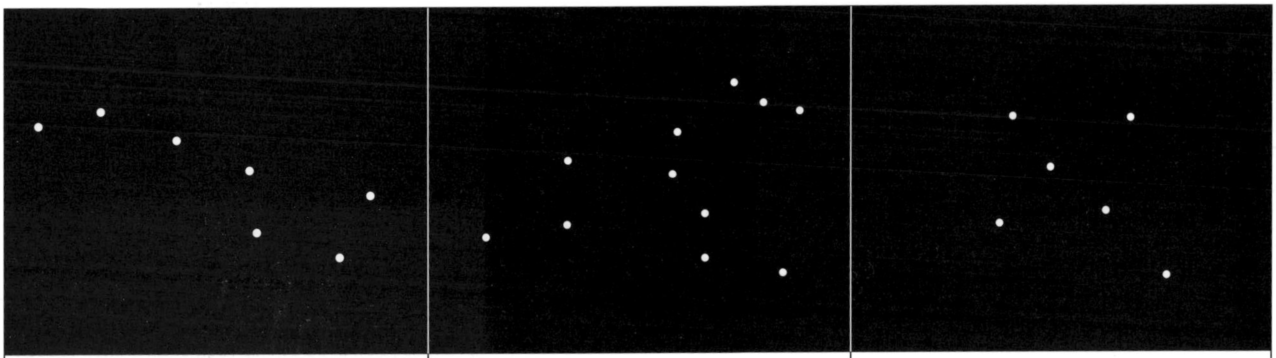

The Plough	Leo the Lion	Cygnus the Swan

Shifting patterns

The Earth spins, so we do not always look out at the same constellations. The patterns seem to spin around us each night because the Earth is turning.

6 Look at the diagram. Does the sky seem to be turning clockwise or anticlockwise?

7 Which star do the other stars seem to be turning around?

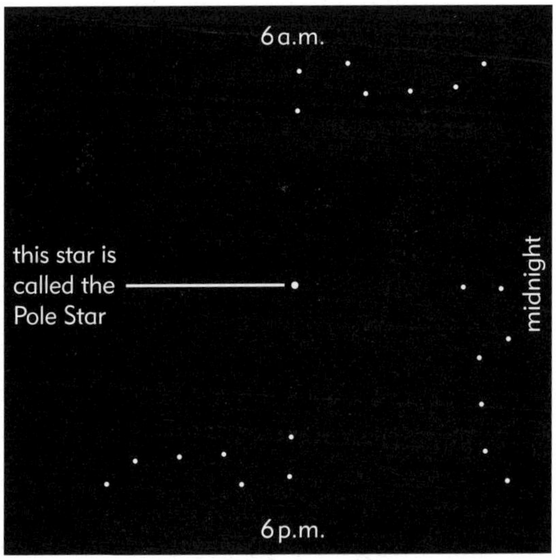
6 a.m.
this star is called the Pole Star
midnight
6 p.m.

What you need to remember [Copy and complete using the **key words**]

Distant suns

The Sun is a ________________. Stars are made of very hot, glowing ________________.
Stars other than the Sun do not look so bright because they are very ____________ away.
We give the stars in the sky patterns called ________________.
These patterns do not ________________ from year to year.

Why do planets look like stars?

What is a planet?

Planets are much smaller than the stars. They go around the **Sun** in almost circular paths called **orbits**.

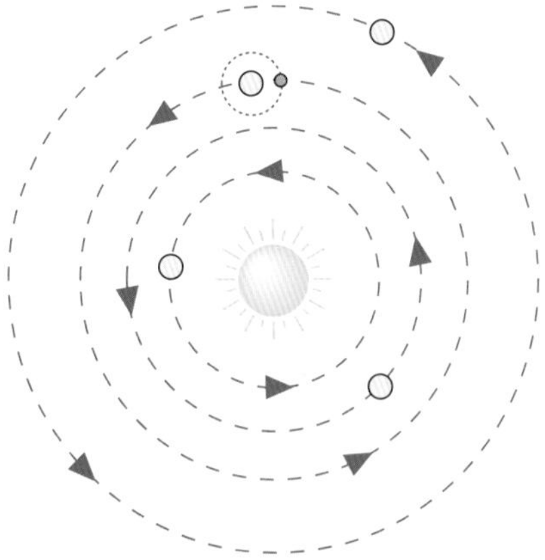

1 Copy the diagram. Then put the names of the first four planets beside them. You can use the table below to find the right order.

Planet	Diameter (compared to Earth)	Distance from Sun (compared to Earth's)
Mercury	0.38	0.39
Venus	0.95	0.72
Earth	1	1
Mars	0.5	1.5
Jupiter	11.2	5.2
Saturn	9.4	9.5
Uranus	4.0	19.2
Neptune	3.8	30.1
Pluto	0.2	39.4

2 (a) Which planet is furthest away from the Sun?

(b) How many times further away is it than the Earth?

3 (a) Which is the biggest planet?

(b) How many times bigger is this planet's diameter than the Earth's?

Jupiter and Venus in the evening sky.

How can you see a planet in the night sky?

Planets look like very bright stars in the night sky, but they do not shine with their own **light**. They only **reflect** light from the Sun back to us. This diagram shows how sunlight hits Jupiter and reflects back to us on Earth. This makes Jupiter look bright against the darkness of the sky. It also looks brighter than the much more distant stars behind it.

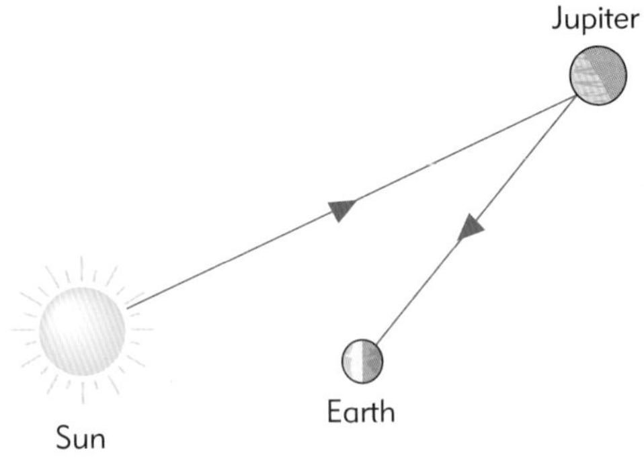

You can see Venus from place X on the Earth in the early morning.

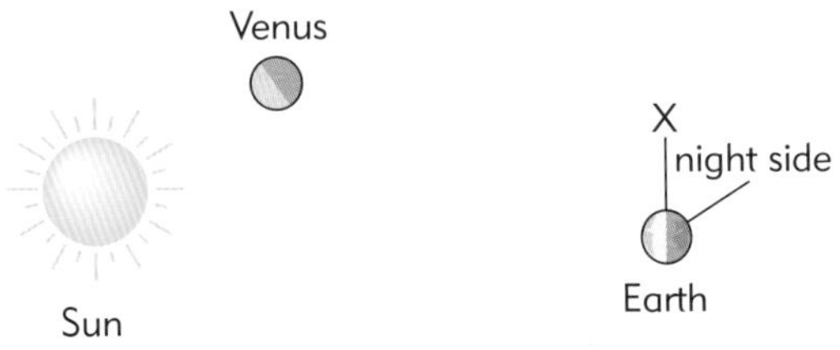

4 Copy the diagram and draw arrows to show how sunlight is reflected off Venus so that we can see it.

A morning star or an evening star?

People often call Venus the 'Evening Star'. This is wrong because it is not a star at all. But we often see it in the early evening sky after sunset, and it does look like a very bright star.

Venus is nearer to the Sun than Earth, so it always appears close to the Sun in the sky.

A few months later, when it has gone round its orbit, Venus appears in the early morning sky. People then call it the 'Morning Star'.

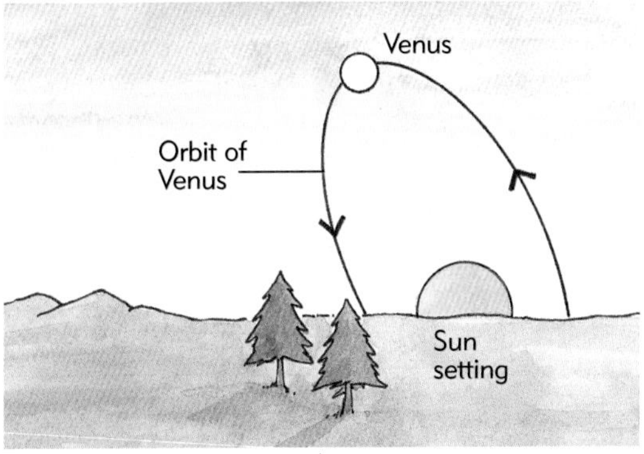

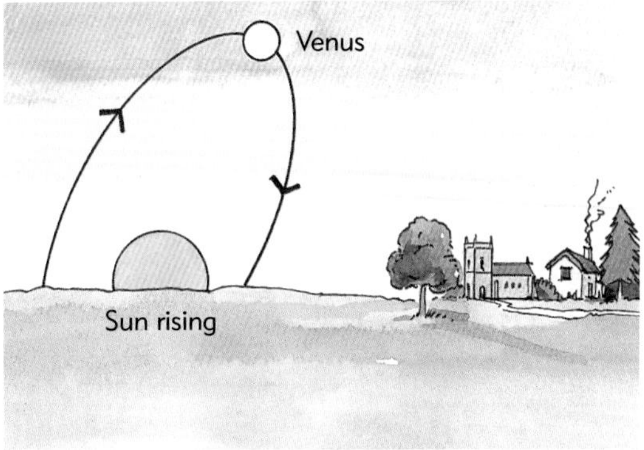

5 People sometimes call Venus the 'Evening Star'.

(a) Why do they call it this?

(b) Why is this name wrong?

6 Copy the diagrams below. Then complete them to show how the sunlight is reflected for the Morning Star and the Evening Star.

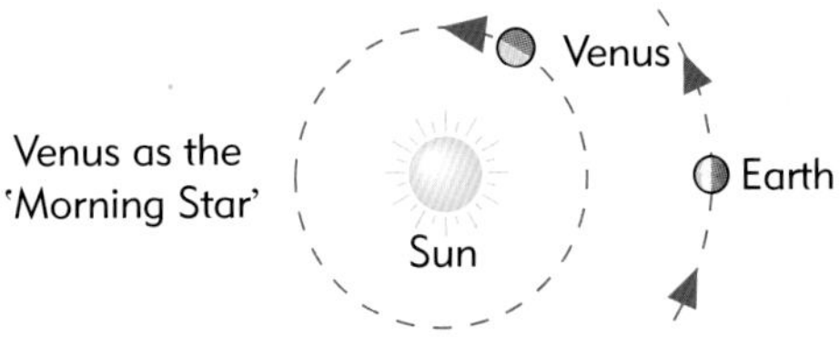

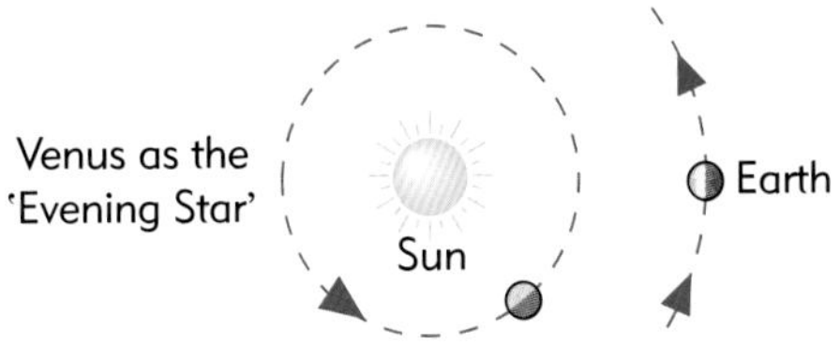

Planets are wanderers in the sky

Planets do not keep fixed positions amongst the background patterns of the stars. They slowly wander about past these **constellations**. This is because the planets are much nearer than the stars. Also the planets, including the Earth, are all moving in their orbits about the Sun.

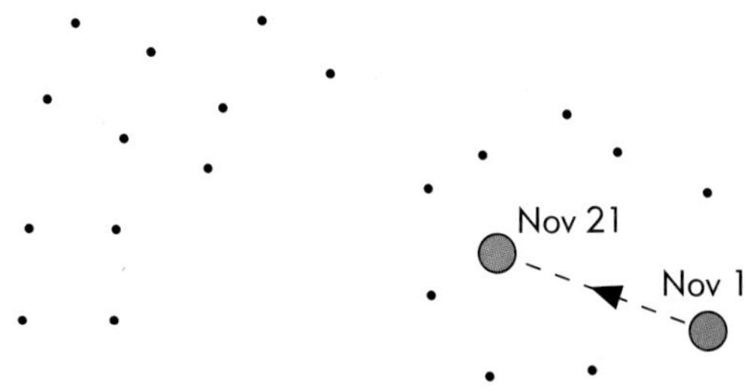

The planets appear to move slowly through the constellations.

7 Copy the diagram. Show where you think the planet might be in another 20 days.

What you need to remember [Copy and complete using the **key words**]

Why do planets look like stars?

Planets do not give out their own ________________. They look bright because they ________________ light from the Sun.

Planets travel around the ________________ in almost circular ________________.

This makes the planets appear to move slowly against the background of the ________________.

Why do the planets orbit the Sun?

What is gravity?

To understand why the planets move in orbits we need to understand a bit more about gravity.

The force of gravity

Any two objects pull each other together with a force called **gravity**. Two milk bottles on a doorstep **attract** each other. We do not notice the force because it is a million times smaller than the tiniest brush of a feather. The force is only big enough to feel if one of the objects is very big, like the Earth or one of the other **planets.**

1 Try holding up two books or two pencils. Why can't you feel them pulling each other together?

The Earth's gravity

The **Earth** has a million, million, million, million times more mass than books or bottles so we can feel the pull of its gravity.

2 What happens to the pull of Earth's gravity if you get further from the Earth?

Forces of gravity in the solar system

Every planet in the solar system pulls on every other planet. But the distances between them are so large that for most of them the force is felt only faintly. The Sun attracts all the planets too. Look at the forces acting on the planet Mercury.

3 Copy and complete the following sentences.

At Mercury the force of the Sun's gravity is _________ than the force of Venus' gravity. This is because the Sun has a lot more _________ than Venus.

Why the planets orbit the Sun

The **Sun** has an enormous pull of gravity on everything in the solar system. Its pull acts even across the great distances to the outer planets. This is because the Sun

REMEMBER

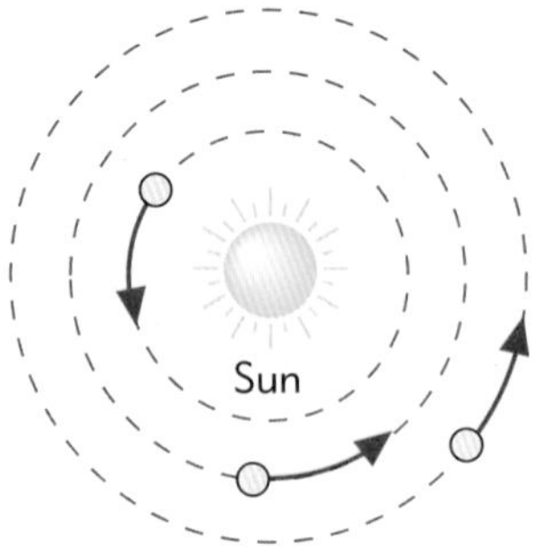

Planets move in orbits around the Sun.

The forces between the milk bottles are very tiny.

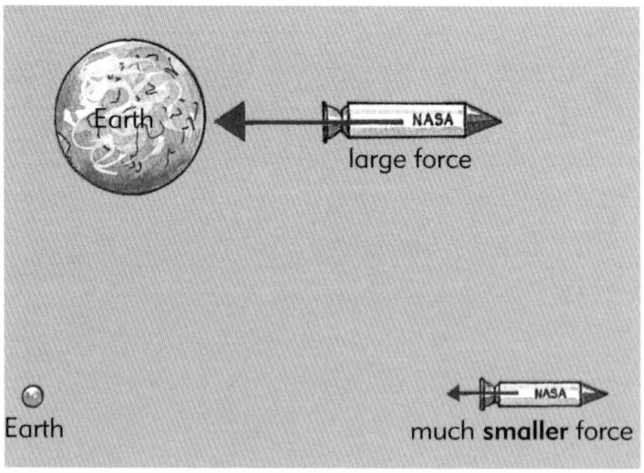

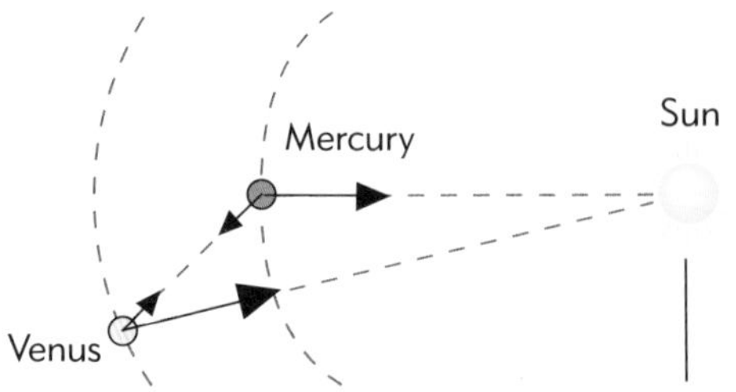

The Sun has much more mass than Mercury or Venus.

has a very large mass: a thousand times bigger than Jupiter's mass and 330 000 times bigger than Earth's.

Each planet would fall straight towards the Sun if it was not moving sideways at high **speed**. The Earth travels at 30 km/s along its orbit. This is exactly the right speed to keep it moving in a circle. We call this an orbit.

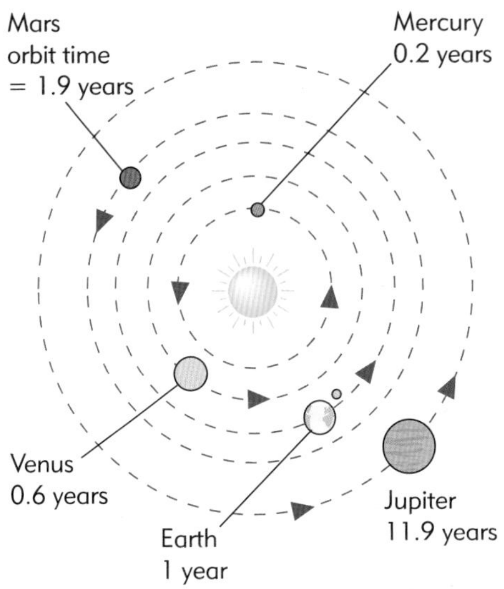

4 Copy the diagram and mark with an arrow the force of the Sun's gravity on each planet.

The orbits of the planets are not quite circular

All the planets except Pluto have orbits that are almost (but not quite) **circular** with the Sun at the centre. The circles are very slightly squashed, so they are called ellipses. Pluto's orbit is very **elliptical**.

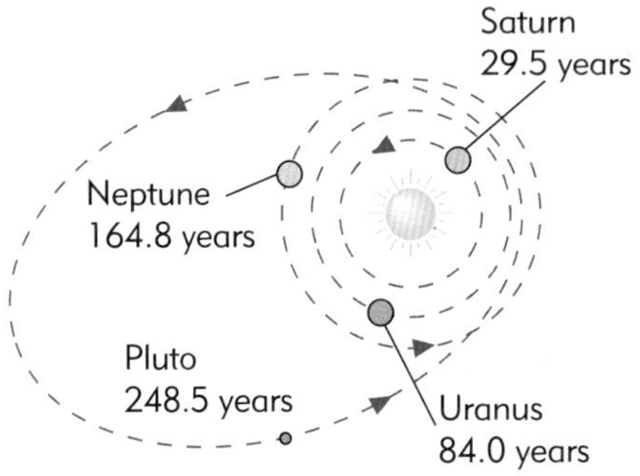

5 Explain why Pluto is not always the most distant planet from the Sun.

The outer planets orbit much more slowly than the inner ones and also have further to go to get around their orbit once.

6 Copy the table headings. Then list the planets in order, starting with the shortest orbit time.

Planet	Orbit time in Earth years

7 Copy and complete the following sentence.

The larger the orbit, the __________ a planet takes to get round once.

What you need to remember [Copy and complete using the **key words**]

Why do the planets orbit the Sun?

All objects ______________ each other with a force called ______________. This is very small for small masses but is big for very large objects such as the ______________ or the ______________ and the other ______________.
Distance also affects gravity. The greater the distance, the ______________ the force of gravity.
The orbits of the planets are nearly ______________ except for Pluto's orbit, which is very ______________.
Planets stay in their orbits because of the balance between their ______________ and the force of the Sun's gravity.

Satellites

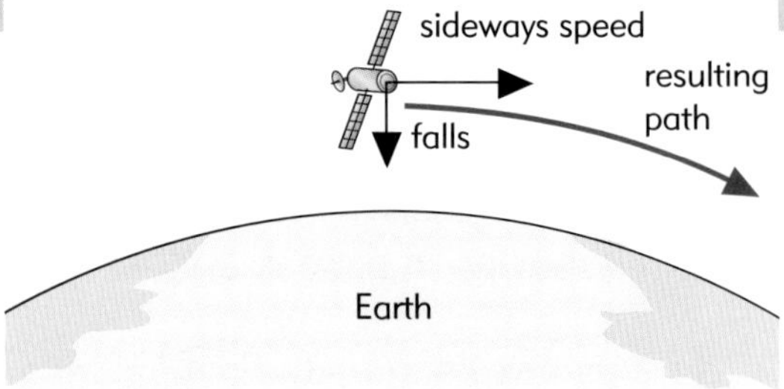

The Moon orbits the Earth. It is sometimes called the satellite of the Earth.

The first artificial satellite was sent into orbit around the Earth in 1957. Since then many satellites have been put into Earth orbit. We use these satellites to do many different jobs.

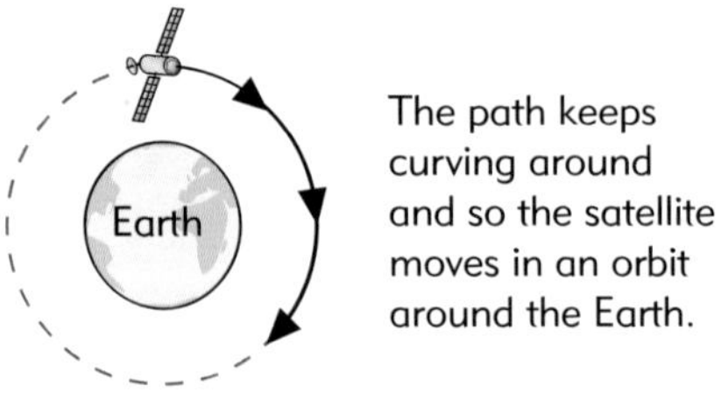

Earth
The path keeps curving around and so the satellite moves in an orbit around the Earth.

What makes satellites go round the Earth?

The force of **gravity** pulls a satellite down towards Earth. But when satellites are put up into space they are given a sideways **speed** so that as they fall they also move sideways. This makes them move in a curve. If a satellite has just the right speed for its height, it will move in an orbit around the Earth.

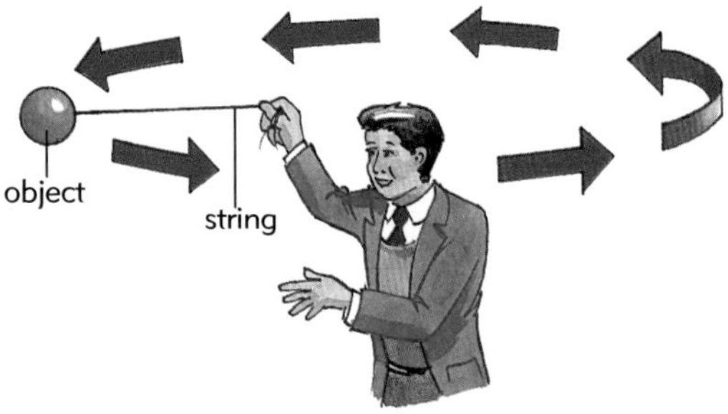

Making things move in a circle

You can tie a small object to a piece of string and whirl it around your head. The object travels in a circle, just like a satellite. You can feel a force in the string. This force pulls the object towards the centre of the circle.

1 (a) What two things keep the object moving in a circle around your head?

(b) What do you think would happen if you cut the string?

2 What provides the inwards force needed to keep a satellite moving in a circle?

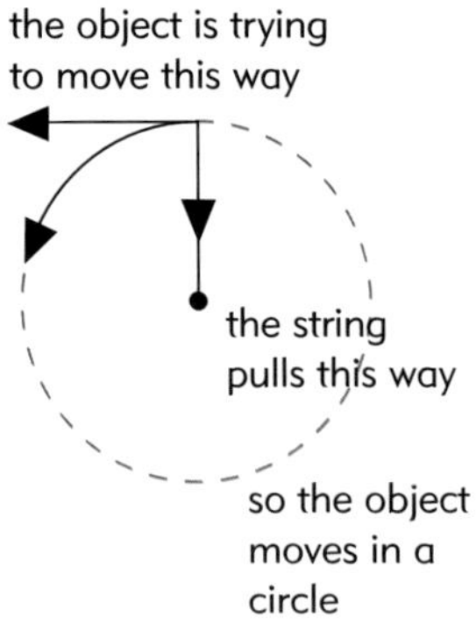

Are orbits always a circle?

Most satellites orbit the Earth in a path that is very close to a circle. Some are put into **orbits** that are slightly squashed circles called **ellipses**.

3 Copy the diagram. Then draw on it two arrows to show the force of gravity on the satellite in both the places marked.

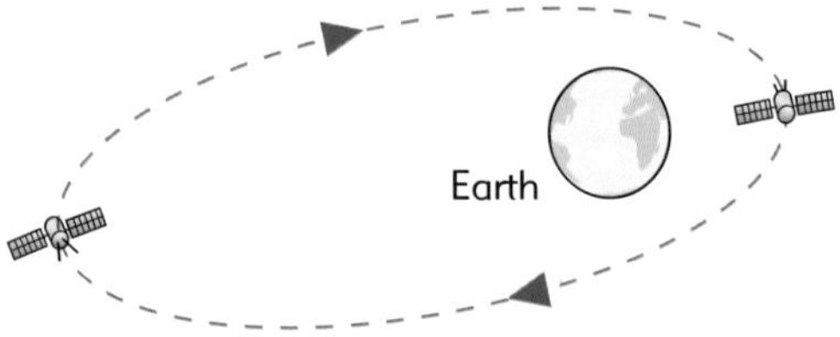

An elliptical orbit.

What can you see looking down from a satellite?

Some satellites carry cameras and infrared sensors. They can take pictures of cloud patterns, which are used to predict the **weather**. They can also be used for **spying**, taking pictures of airfields and harbours.

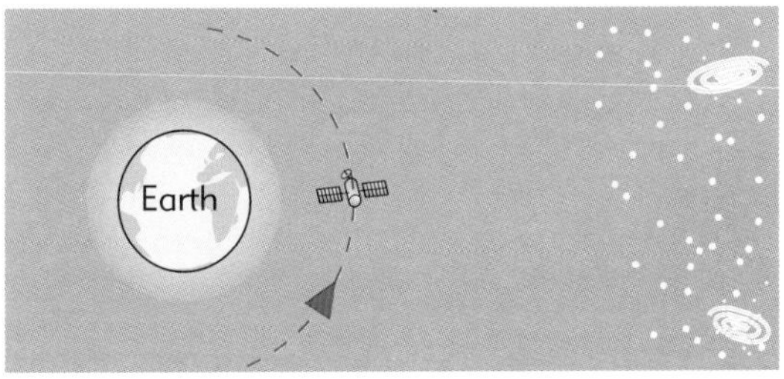

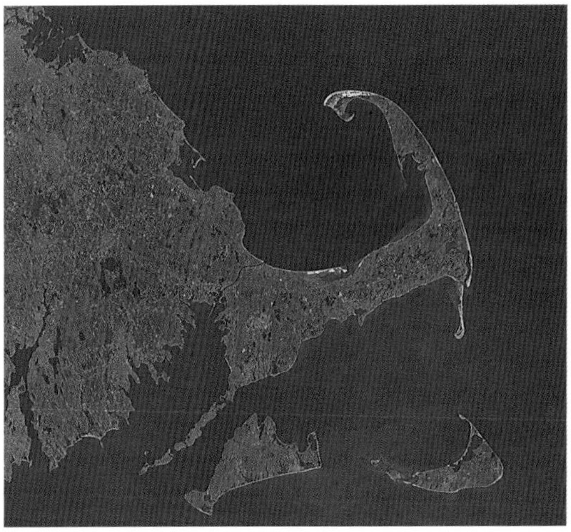

Cape Cod, in the United States, as seen from a satellite.

What can you see looking up from a satellite?

Satellites orbit above the **atmosphere**, so they get a very clear view of the stars and the rest of the Universe.

> With a telescope on a satellite
> - you can see fainter stars
> - you can see more distant galaxies
> - you can see more detail on the planets.

4 Write down one reason why you can see the Universe better from a satellite than from the ground.

5 Write down three things an astronomer could see better from a satellite than from Earth.

What else can we use satellites for?

If a satellite is at exactly the right height and speed, it will stay above the same place on the surface of the Earth. Satellites like this are used to send **telephone** messages and **television** programmes around the world.

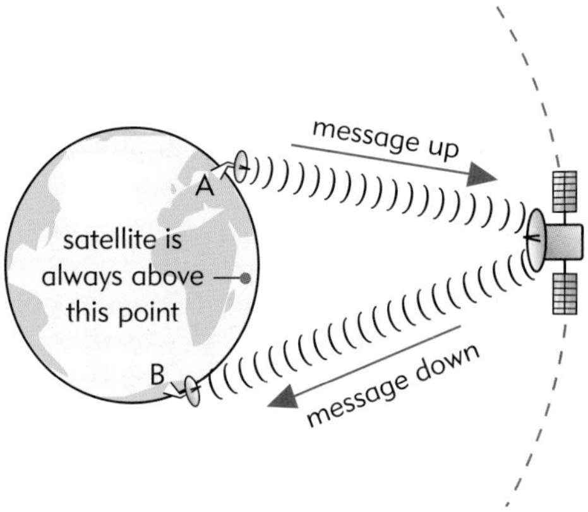

6 How is a message sent from A to B on the Earth?

What you need to remember [Copy and complete using the **key words**]

Satellites

Satellites are kept in their paths because they have a high sideways ________ and are pulled inwards by the force of ________. These paths are called ________ and can be circles or ________.

Satellites can be used to:
- take pictures of the Earth, for example to predict the ________ or for ________;
- take pictures of the Universe without the Earth's ________ getting in the way;
- send ________ messages and ________ programmes around the world.

The Universe

Our Sun is just one of many **billions** (thousands of millions) of stars in a galaxy. Our galaxy is just one of billions of galaxies in the **Universe**.

Some galaxies are beautiful spirals, like our galaxy. Others are round or cigar-shaped.

1 Look at the photograph. How many galaxies can you see?

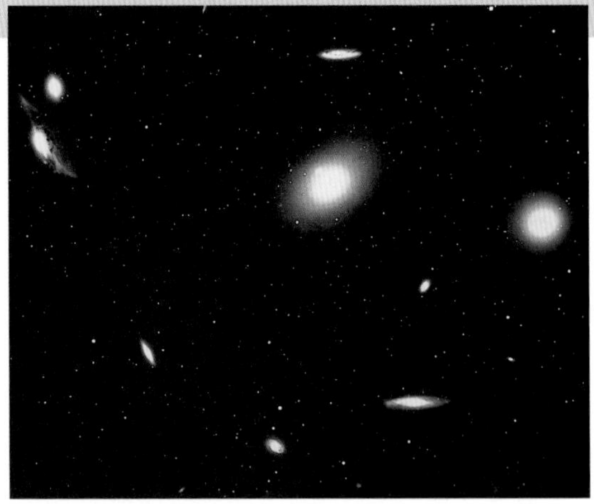

This shows part of the Virgo Cluster. It takes light about 40 million years to reach us from these galaxies.

How big is the Universe?

Stars in a galaxy are often millions of times further apart than the planets in the solar system.

Galaxies are often millions of times further apart than the stars inside a galaxy.

Astronomers often tell us how far away things are by saying how long it takes the light from them to reach us.

2 What is the name of our galaxy?

3 Where in our galaxy is the solar system?

4 Copy and complete the table:

Object	How long it takes light from the object to reach us
Sun	
nearest other star	
Virgo Cluster	

5 Light travels at 300 000 kilometres per second. Work out how far away the Sun is from the Earth.

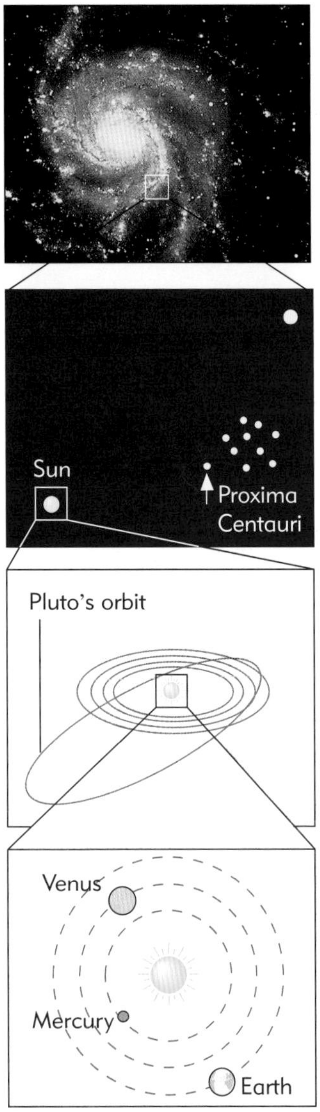

Our Sun is in a galaxy called the Milky Way, about two-thirds of the way out from the centre. It takes light about 100 000 years to cross the Milky Way.

It takes four years for light to travel to the Sun from the next nearest star.

It takes light about 10 hours to cross the solar system.

It takes light 500 seconds to travel from the Sun to the Earth.

How are stars made?

Galaxies don't just contain billions of stars. There is also a lot of **gas** and **dust** between the stars. The diagrams show how this gas and dust can form new stars.

There are clouds of dust and gas in galaxies.

The force of **gravity** between the bits of dust and the particles of the gas pulls them together. This takes a very long time because the force of gravity on such small objects is very tiny.

If enough material gets pulled together it gets very hot and starts to shine. A new star is born. The star can make the gas around it glow.

6 Copy and complete the following sentences.

New stars form from the __________ and __________ in galaxies.

This is all pulled together by the __________ of gravity.

7 Look at the photograph of the Orion Nebula. Find places where there is dark dust, places where there are hot, new stars, and places where the starlight is making the gas in the cloud glow pink.

How long do stars last?

Stars like the Sun do not burn for ever. They are so hot in the centre that **hydrogen** gas is turned into **helium** gas by a nuclear reaction called fusion. Vast amounts of heat and light are produced in this reaction. This is what makes stars shine brightly. Our Sun has been doing this for about 5 billion years, and it is only about halfway through its life.

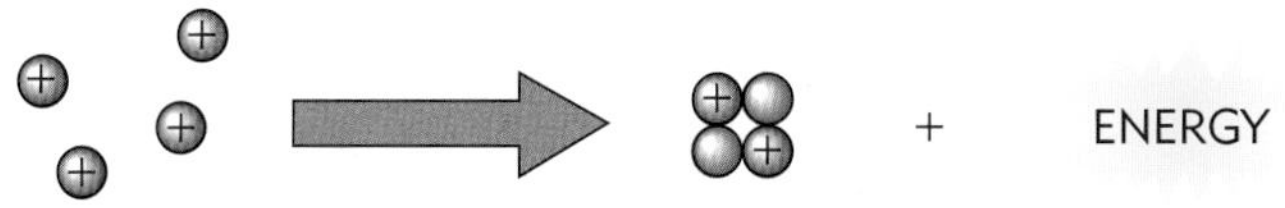

8 Why can't the Sun keep shining for ever?

9 For how much longer do scientists think the Sun will continue to shine?

The Orion Nebula, where stars are forming.

What you need to remember [Copy and complete using the **key words**]

The Universe

There are __________ of stars in a galaxy and billions of galaxies in the __________.
Galaxies also contain __________ and __________. The gas and dust clouds are pulled together under the force of __________ to form stars. Stars shine because of the nuclear fusion of __________ gas into __________ gas.

Models of the Universe

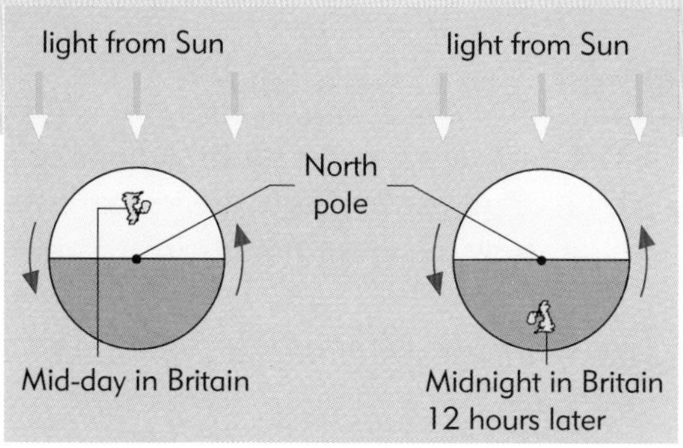
light from Sun
light from Sun
North pole
Mid-day in Britain
Midnight in Britain
12 hours later

Today we believe:

- that the Earth spins on its own axis;
- that the Earth moves in an orbit around the Sun, just like all the other planet do;
- that the Moon moves in an orbit around the Earth.

1 How long does it take:

(a) for the Earth to make one complete spin on its axis?

(b) for the Earth to make one complete orbit round the Sun?

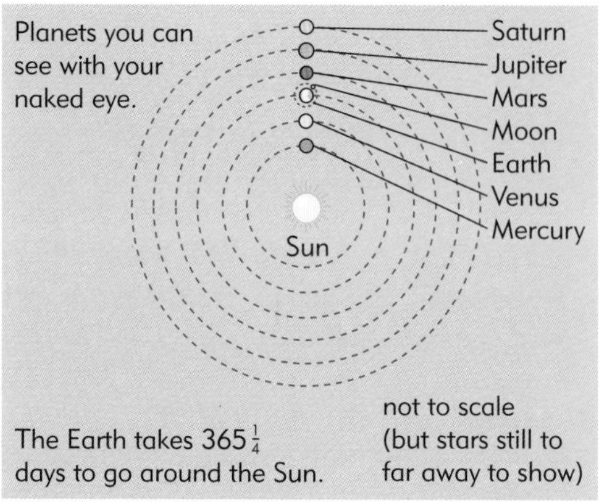
Planets you can see with your naked eye.
Saturn
Jupiter
Mars
Moon
Earth
Venus
Mercury
Sun
The Earth takes $365\frac{1}{4}$ days to go around the Sun.
not to scale (but stars still to far away to show)

Another model of the Universe

Astronomers used to think that the Sun, the Moon, the stars and the planets all moved round the Earth.

The diagrams below show why they thought this.

2 Why was it sensible to think:

(a) that the Sun went round the Earth?

(b) that the stars went round the Earth?

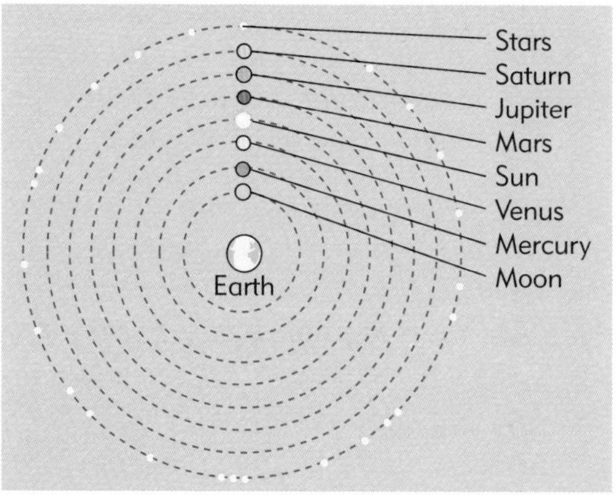
Stars
Saturn
Jupiter
Mars
Sun
Venus
Mercury
Moon
Earth

An older model of the Universe.

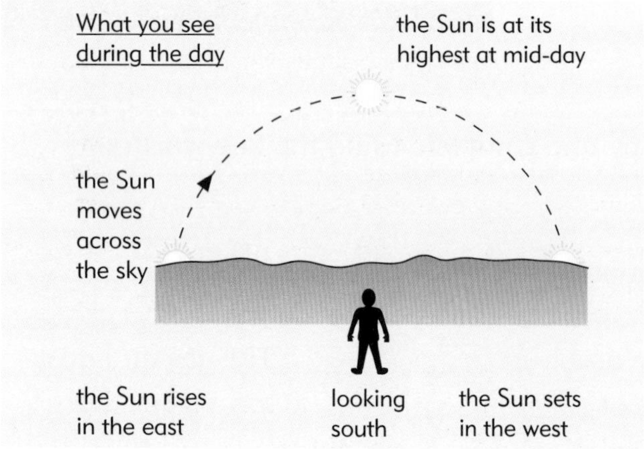
What you see during the day
the Sun is at its highest at mid-day
the Sun moves across the sky
the Sun rises in the east
looking south
the Sun sets in the west

What you see during the night
Each star appears to move around the Pole Star.

What you feel
The Earth doesn't feel like it's spinning or moving very fast around the Sun.

Problems with planets

The planets seem to move around the Earth every 24 hours, like the stars. But they also move slowly past the other stars.

Usually they move in the same direction past the other stars. But sometimes they move in the opposite direction for a few days or weeks.

3 Imagine that you are an astronomer who thinks that the planets move around the Earth.

How could you explain the 'backwards' movement of the planets?

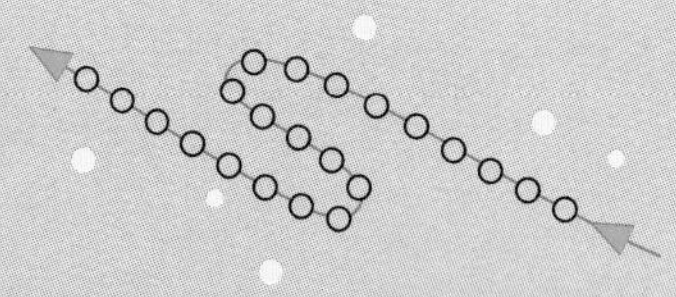

How a planet moves past the stars.
If the planets move around the Earth they must **either** slow down then speed up again every so often

or move in strange orbits like this

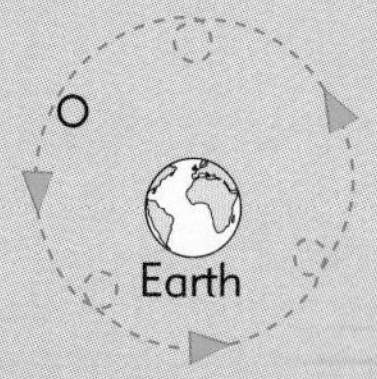

Solving the problems

About 400 years ago, Nicolai Copernicus worked out what we would see if the Earth and the planets all moved round the Sun, each at a certain distance and with a certain speed. He showed that planets would sometimes seem to move backwards.

At first, most other astronomers didn't agree with Copernicus.

But eventually they accepted his new model of the Universe.

4 Look at the photograph and the diagram. Write down two things that helped other astronomers to accept the new model.

In 1609, Galileo Galilei looked at Jupiter through a telescope, which he had just invented. He saw 'moons' which seemed to be going round Jupiter. (This photo is not to scale. The moons are really much smaller than Jupiter.)

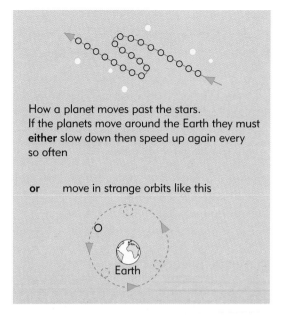

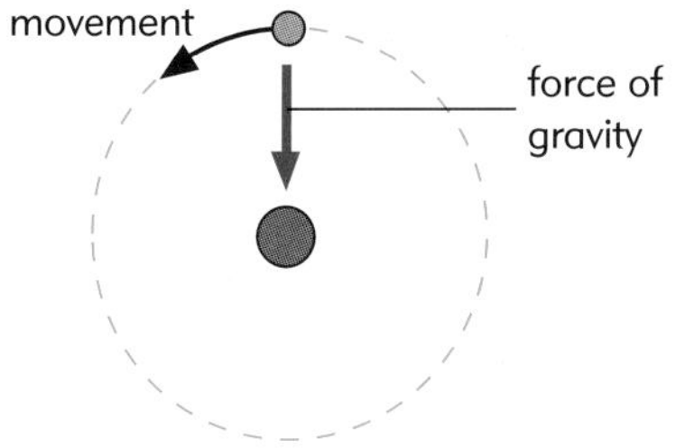

Later in the 17th century, Isaac Newton showed that the force of gravity could keep a smaller body in orbit around a larger one.

What you need to remember

Models of the Universe

You should be able to:

- describe the model of the Universe that had the Earth at the centre;
- explain why it was replaced by the present model.

Lose weight – become an astronaut

Now that Malcolm is older, he isn't so active and he has started to put on weight. Malcolm wants to lose weight. He reads in a magazine that people weigh less on Mars. He wishes he could go there.

Though Malcolm would weigh less on Mars, his body is still exactly the same. There is just as much of him. He still has exactly the same **mass**.

What is mass?

Mass tells you how much there is of something. A 10 kg bag of potatoes contains twice as much potato as a 5 kg bag, so it has twice the mass. We measure the mass of things in **kilograms** (kg).

1 Malcolm says his weight is 90 kg. This is wrong. What should he say?

What is weight?

When you drop something it falls downwards. That is because the force of gravity pulls it. The size of this force on an object is called **weight**. Objects with more mass have more weight. That is because there is more mass for the force of gravity to act on. We measure forces in **newtons**.

2 (a) What is the force that causes weight?

(b) In which direction does this force act?

3 Copy and complete the following sentence.

Weight is a __________ so we should measure it in __________.

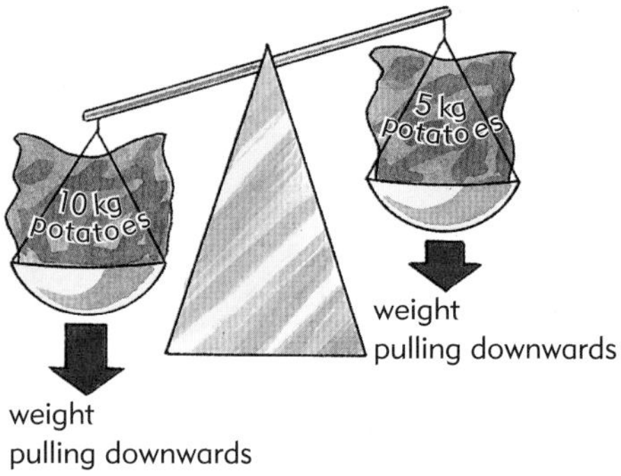

More mass means more weight.

What's the difference?

If two objects are in the same place, the one with more mass also has more weight. But mass and weight aren't the same thing. You will have the same mass wherever you are because you have the same amount of body. Your weight might not always be the same.

4 Look at the picture of astronauts. How much do the astronauts weigh? Explain your answer.

In space the force of gravity can be very, very small ...

... so astronauts have hardly any weight.

5 Copy and complete the following sentences.

The ________ of an object stays the same, unless you take some of it away. The ________ of an object can change if the force of ________ is different.

Working out weight

Weight depends on how much mass an object has. It also depends on the force of gravity. The diagrams show the weights of two objects on Earth.

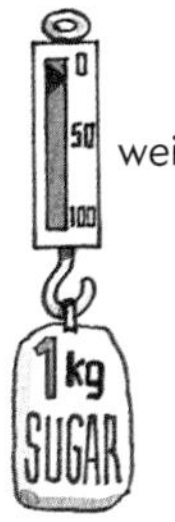

weight = 10 N

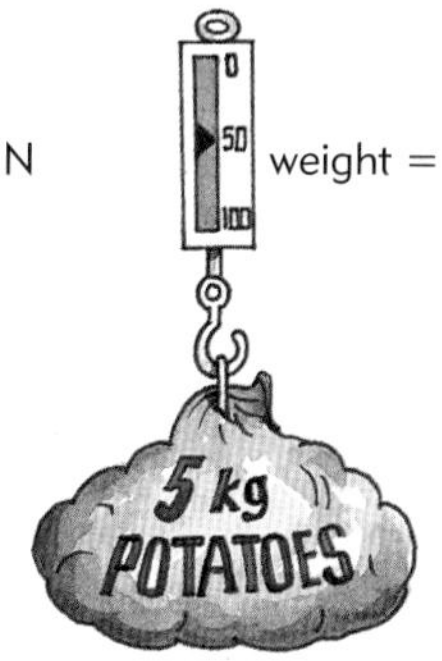

weight = 50 N

6 Copy and complete the following sentence.

On Earth, each 1 kilogram of mass has a weight of about __________ newtons.

We say that Earth's force of gravity per kilogram is **10 newtons per kilogram** (10 N/kg). We can work out the weight of an object as follows:

$$\underset{\textbf{(newtons)}}{\text{weight}} = \underset{\text{(kilograms)}}{\textbf{mass}} \times \underset{\text{(newtons per kilogram)}}{\text{force of gravity per kilogram}}$$

7 Look at the examples in the pictures and work out the missing numbers.

mass = 6 kg
weight = ?

mass = 60 kg
weight = ?

mass = 0.5 kg
weight = ?

mass = ? kg
weight = 12 000 N

Malcolm goes planet hopping

Malcolm has a mass of 90 kg. On Earth the force of gravity per kilogram is **10** N/kg. Therefore, his weight is 90 × 10 = 900 N.

8 Copy the table. Complete the table to show how Malcolm's weight would change in different parts of the solar system.

	Malcolm's mass (kg)	Force of gravity (N/kg)	Malcolm's weight (N)
Earth	90	10	900
Moon	90	1.6	
Mars		4	
Jupiter		23	

What you need to remember [Copy and complete using the **key words**]

Lose weight – become an astronaut

An object always has the same ______________. We measure this in ______________.
The ______________ of an object is the force of gravity that acts on it. We measure this in ______________.
On Earth the force of gravity per kilogram is about ______________ N/kg.
We can work out weights like this:

weight	=	______________	×	force of gravity per kilogram
(______________)		(kilograms)		(______________ **per** ______________)

Acceleration helps to win races

Quick off the mark

When you accelerate, you increase your speed. Racing drivers want a very large **acceleration**. This means they want to go from a slow speed to a fast speed in a very short **time**.

At the start of a race this car can accelerate up to 50 metres per second in just 5 seconds. (50 m/s is more than 100 miles per hour.)

1 Copy and complete the following sentence.

A big __________ means you reach the top speed in a short __________.

How to calculate acceleration

The racing car in the photograph takes 5 seconds to reach a speed of 50 metres per second. So every second its speed increases by 10 metres per second. This is its acceleration. You can work out acceleration like this:

$$\text{acceleration} = \frac{\text{change in velocity}}{\text{time taken}}$$

(On your calculator: change in velocity ÷ time)

So for the racing car,

$$\text{acceleration} = \frac{50\,\text{m/s}}{5\,\text{s}} = 10\,\text{m/s}^2$$

Don't worry about the word 'velocity' here. For the moment, think of it as another word for speed. The **change** in velocity is measured in metres per second (m/s). The time taken is measured in seconds (s). So the units of acceleration are metres per second, per second. We call these **metres per second squared** (m/s^2).

2 Look at the examples in the picture and work out the missing items in each one.

Rocket being launched

change in velocity = 600 m/s
time taken = 20 seconds
acceleration = ?

Cheetah hunting

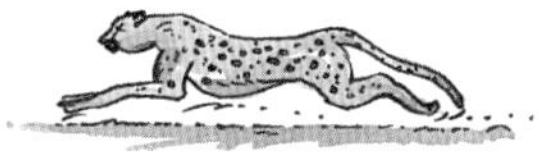

velocity at start = 0
new velocity = 20 m/s
time taken = 2 seconds
change in velocity = ?
acceleration = ?

Horse overtaking another

velocity at start = 15 m/s
new velocity = 23 m/s
time taken = 4 seconds
change in velocity = ?
acceleration = ?

Motorbike breaking

velocity at start = 20 m/s
new velocity = 0
time taken = 10 seconds
change in velocity = –20 m/s
acceleration = ?

Showing acceleration on a graph

The slope of a **velocity–time** graph tells you how the speed or velocity is changing.

Look at the velocity–time graph for a cyclist.

3 How does the graph show a steady speed?

4 What is the cyclist's speed

(a) to begin with? (b) after she accelerates?

5 How does the graph show an acceleration?

6 How does the graph show that the cyclist slows down quicker than she speeds up?

A **steeper** slope on a velocity–time graph means a bigger acceleration (or deceleration).

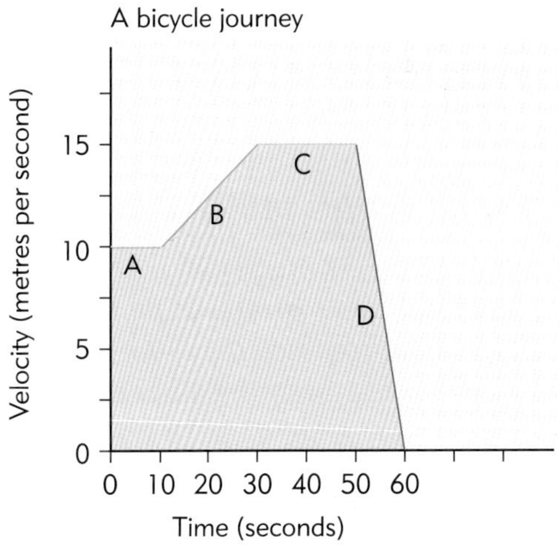

First the cyclist is at a **steady** speed (A) then she slowly **accelerates** to a higher speed (B). She travels at this higher speed for a while (C) then she quickly slows down (decelerates) and stops (D).

Why do we need another word for speed?

The diagram shows a ball being thrown into the air. When the ball comes back down it is moving at the same speed as you threw it up. But it is moving in the opposite direction. We say it has a different **velocity**.

7 (a) How much has the velocity of the ball changed?

(b) What is its acceleration?

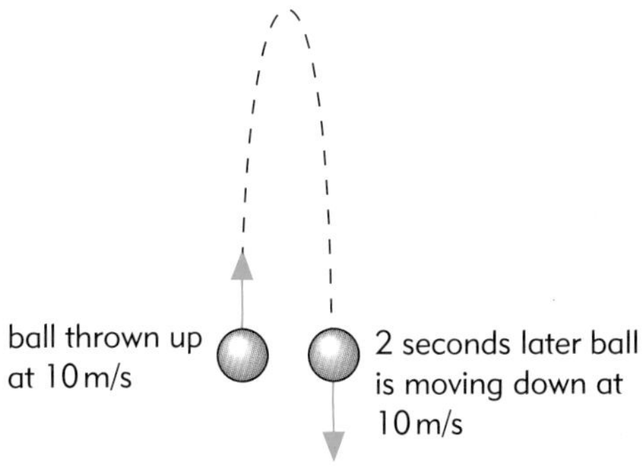

The speed of the ball has not changed. The velocity of the ball has changed by 20 m/s.

What you need to remember [Copy and complete using the **key words**]

Acceleration helps to win races

The speed of an object in a particular direction is called its ________________.

The rate at which the velocity of an object changes is called its ________________.

The units of acceleration are ____________ **per** ____________ ____________ (m/s^2).

Acceleration can be calculated like this:

$$\text{acceleration} = \frac{\text{\_\_\_\_\_\_\_\_ in velocity}}{\text{\_\_\_\_\_\_\_\_ taken}}$$

Acceleration can be shown on a ____________ – ____________ graph.

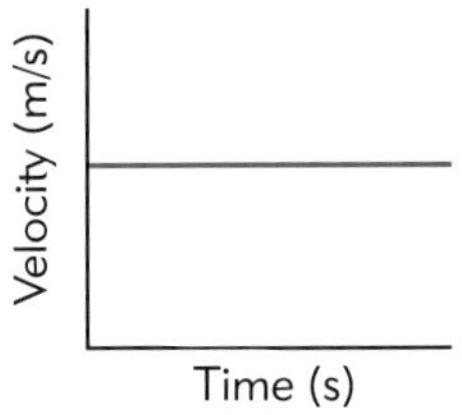

This graph shows the velocity of an object that is moving with a ____________ velocity.

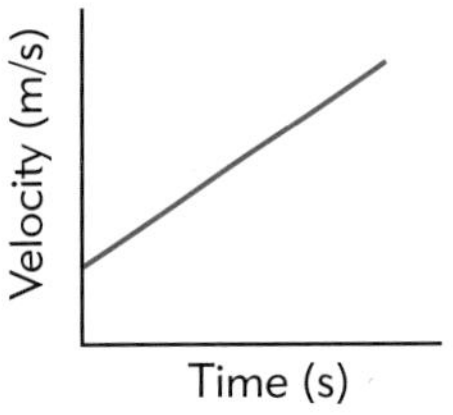

This graph shows the velocity of an object as it ____________.

If an object has a bigger acceleration, the graph has a ____________ slope.

20 Sport and transport – a lot of pushing and pulling

Pushing and pulling to win

Sumo wrestlers push against each other. When both wrestlers push with the same force nothing happens. The forces balance and cancel each other out. To win, one wrestler must push the other off the mat. He must push harder. The forces must be **unbalanced**.

1 Copy and complete the following sentence.

If one wrestler pushes harder than the other there is an __________ force, which __________ the other wrestler off the mat.

2 Look at the diagram of a tug-of-war. Which team will win? Give a reason.

In fact, any stationary object will start to **move** when an unbalanced force acts on it. The movement is always in the direction of the unbalanced force.

> **REMEMBER**
>
> A 10 kg bag of potatoes has more mass than a 5 kg bag.
>
> Acceleration is how fast something speeds up or slows down.

SUMO

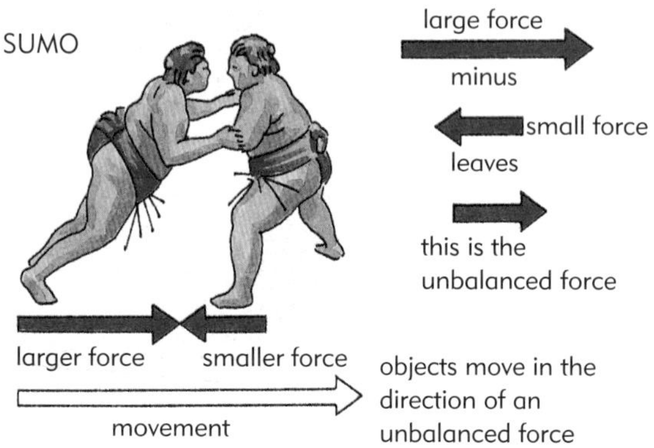

TUG-OF-WAR

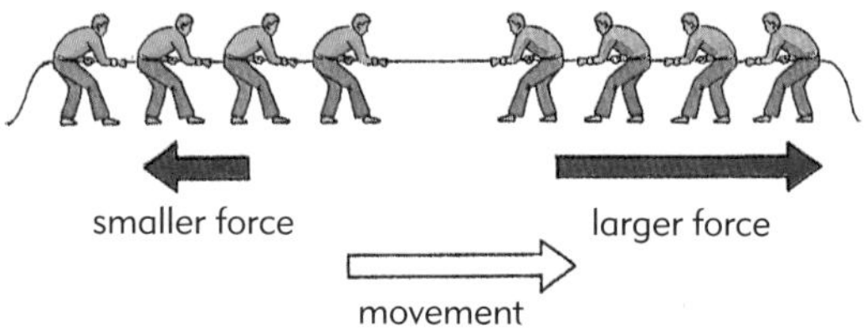

Speeding up a bobsleigh

A **force** is needed to **speed** up a bobsleigh. The bigger the force, the faster the bobsleigh speeds up. A bigger force produces a bigger **acceleration**.

3 Look at the picture of the bobsleigh.

How does the team start the sleigh? Explain as fully as you can why it is started in this way.

Slowing down a bicycle

Slowing something down also needs a force. A bicycle has front brakes and rear brakes. You could **slow** down a bicycle by just using the rear brake.

4 (a) What difference does it make if you use both brakes?

(b) What difference does it make if you squeeze the brakes harder?

(c) Copy and complete the following sentence.

A bigger force makes an object slow down __________.

■ Accelerating trucks and trains

The bigger the mass of an object, the harder it is to make it speed up or slow down. Look at the picture of three lorries. The lorries have identical engines so each lorry produces the same force.

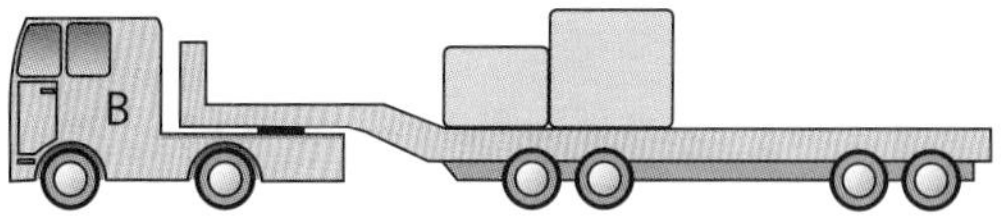

5 (a) Which lorry has the smallest mass?

(b) Which lorry speeds up the fastest?

(c) Which lorry speeds up most slowly?

(d) Copy and complete the following sentence.

The lorry with the biggest mass needs the _________ time to reach the same speed.

6 (a) If all the lorries are moving at the same speed, which one can slow down in the shortest time?

(b) Copy and complete the following sentences.

The lorry with the biggest mass takes the ___________ time to slow down.

7 Work out the accelerations of the three lorries.

> REMEMBER
>
> $$\text{acceleration} = \frac{\text{change in speed (metres per second)}}{\text{time taken (seconds)}}$$
>
> The answer is in metres per second squared.

Look at the picture of four trains. Each engine [] is identical and produces the same force.

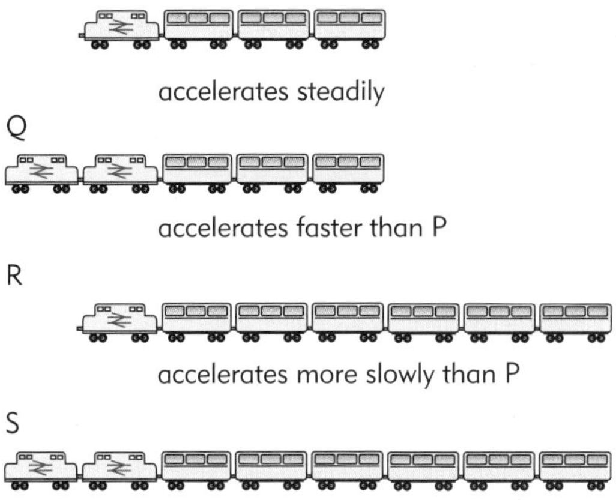

8 (a) Why does train Q accelerate faster than train P?

(b) Why does R accelerate more slowly than P?

(c) Why does S have the same acceleration as P?

What you need to remember [Copy and complete using the **key words**]

Sport and transport – a lot of pushing and pulling

Sometimes the forces acting on an object do not cancel each other out.
We say they are __________________.
A stationary object will start to ______________ in the direction of the unbalanced force.
An unbalanced force makes a moving object _____________ up or _____________ down.
We say that an unbalanced force produces an __________________.
The bigger the mass of an object, the more _________________ is needed to accelerate it.

Experiments in space

Space scientists need to send a spaceship to just the right place. So they need to know just how much acceleration the rockets will produce. A spaceship is also a good place to measure the accelerations produced by different forces.

1 Why is a spaceship a good place to do experiments on force and acceleration?

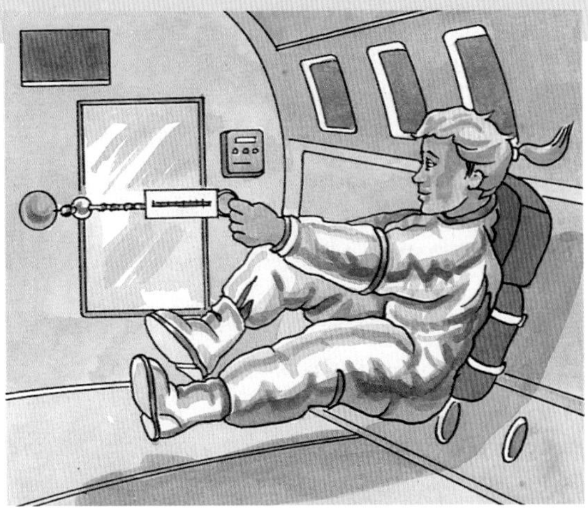

In space, friction and gravity don't mess up our experiments with forces.

How force affects acceleration

The diagrams show some experiments in a spaceship. The same 1 kg mass is accelerated using different forces.

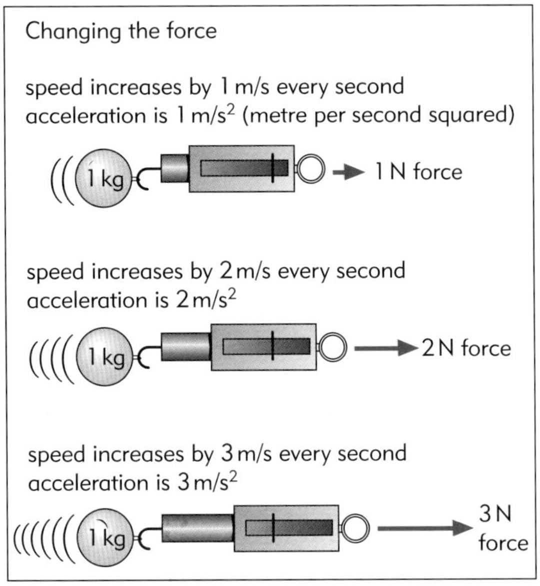

Changing the force
speed increases by 1 m/s every second
acceleration is 1 m/s² (metre per second squared)
1 kg
1 N force
speed increases by 2 m/s every second
acceleration is 2 m/s²
1 kg
2 N force
speed increases by 3 m/s every second
acceleration is 3 m/s²
1 kg
3 N force

2 (a) How much acceleration does a 1N force give to the 1kg mass?

(b) How much acceleration does a 2 N force give?

(c) Copy and complete the following sentence.

When the force on an object is doubled, its acceleration is __________.

How mass affects acceleration

A 1 N force is then used to accelerate different masses.

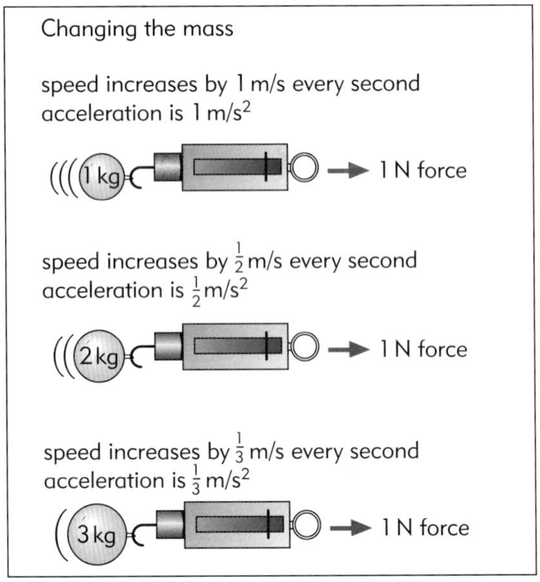

Changing the mass
speed increases by 1 m/s every second
acceleration is 1 m/s²
1 kg
1 N force
speed increases by ½ m/s every second
acceleration is ½ m/s²
2 kg
1 N force
speed increases by ⅓ m/s every second
acceleration is ⅓ m/s²
3 kg
1 N force

3 (a) How much acceleration do you get when the mass is twice as big?

(b) How much acceleration do you get when the mass is three times as big?

(c) Copy and complete the following sentence.

If the force stays the same, an object with twice as much mass is given half as much __________.

A **force** of 1 N acting on a **mass** of 1 kg produces an **acceleration** of 1 m/s^2.

4 (a) Copy and complete the table using the results of all the experiments shown in the six experiment diagrams.

Force (N)	Mass (kg)	Acceleration (m/s^2)	Mass × Acceleration
1	1	1	1

(b) What do you notice about the first and last columns in the table?

The force is always the same as the mass times the acceleration.

force	=	mass	×	acceleration
(newtons)		(kilograms)		**(metres per second squared)**

5 Look at the examples in the picture. Use the formula to work out the missing items. The first one is done for you.

FORCE (f) = MASS (m) x ACCELERATION (a)
ACCELERATION = FORCE ÷ MASS
MASS = FORCE ÷ ACCELERATION

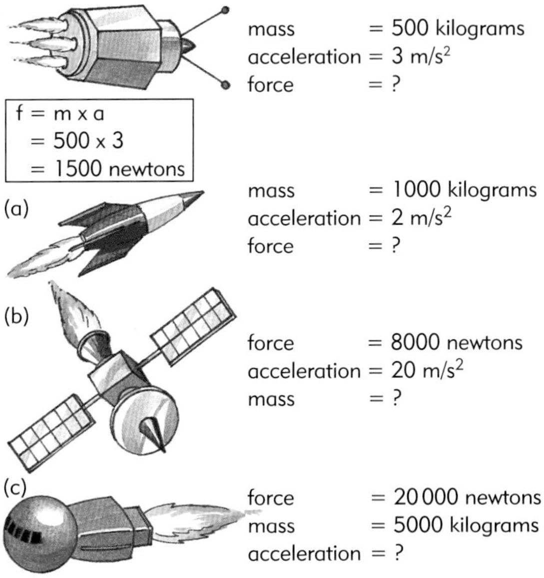

mass = 500 kilograms
acceleration = 3 m/s²
force = ?
f = m x a
= 500 x 3
= 1500 newtons
(a)
mass = 1000 kilograms
acceleration = 2 m/s²
force = ?
(b)
force = 8000 newtons
acceleration = 20 m/s²
mass = ?
(c)
force = 20 000 newtons
mass = 5000 kilograms
acceleration = ?

Meanwhile, back on Earth ...

All objects on Earth are pulled by **gravity**. This makes them fall with the same **acceleration** unless friction from the air interferes. Try dropping a paper clip and a boot together, from the same height. They should hit the floor together even though the boot has a lot more **mass**.

6 Look at the diagram then copy and complete the following sentences.

The boot has more __________ than the paper clip. But this means that more __________ force acts on it.

There is the same amount of force for each unit of mass. So the boot and the paper clip have the same __________.

7 The gravitational force on 1 kilogram is 10 newtons. What acceleration does this produce?

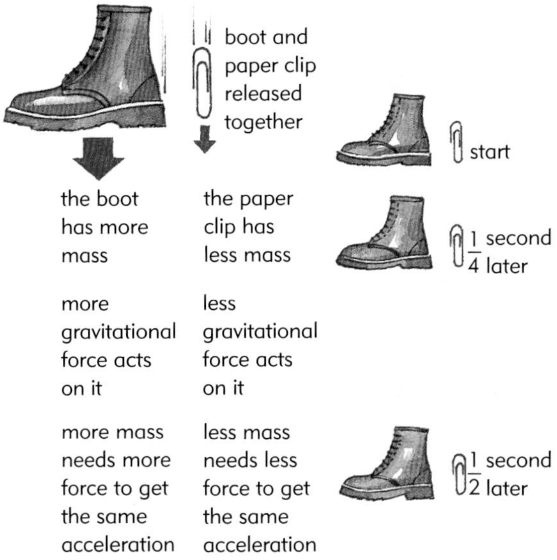

boot and paper clip released together
start
1/4 second later
1/2 second later
the boot has more mass
the paper clip has less mass
more gravitational force acts on it
less gravitational force acts on it
more mass needs more force to get the same acceleration
less mass needs less force to get the same acceleration

What you need to remember [Copy and complete using the **key words**]

Experiments in space

One newton is the ______________ required to give a ______________ of one kilogram an ______________ of one metre per second squared.
The force you need to produce an acceleration can be worked out like this:

force	=	__________	×	acceleration
(__________)		(kilograms)		(__________ **per second** __________)

On Earth, the force of ______________ pulls things down with a force of 10 newtons for every kilogram. This gives them an ______________ of 10 metres per second squared.

22 Speed limits

A sky-diver jumps out of an aeroplane. The graph below shows what happens to her speed as she falls.

1 Copy and complete the following sentences.

As the sky-diver falls she __________.

This happens quickly at first and then more and more __________.

Eventually she stops accelerating and falls at a __________ speed.

When the sky-diver stops accelerating we say that she has reached her **terminal velocity**.

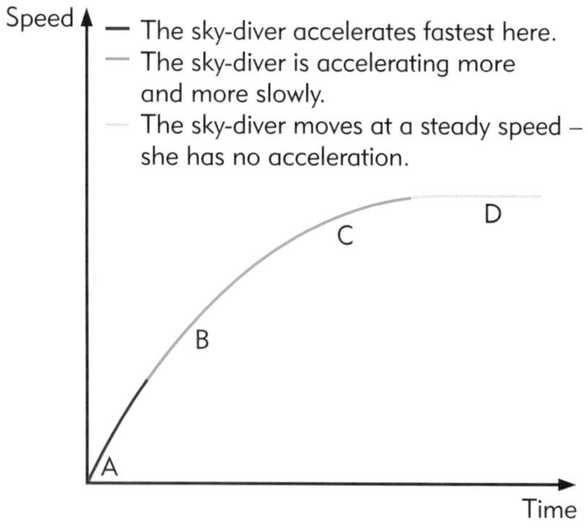
Speed
The sky-diver accelerates fastest here.
The sky-diver is accelerating more and more slowly.
The sky-diver moves at a steady speed – she has no acceleration.
A
B
C
D
Time

Why does the sky-diver stop accelerating?

The sky-diver accelerates when there is an unbalanced force acting on her.

The diagram shows the forces acting on the sky-diver at points A, B, C and D on the graph.

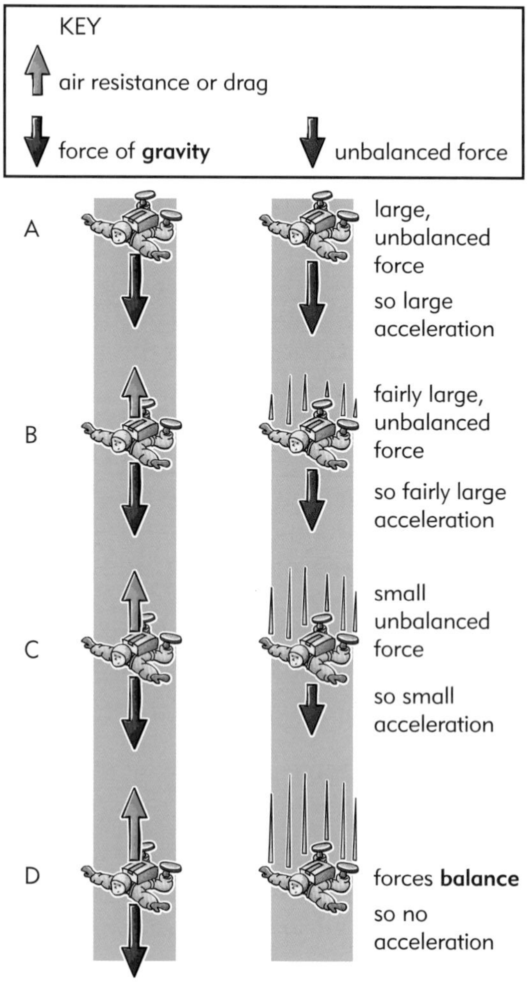
KEY
air resistance or drag
force of **gravity**
unbalanced force
A
large, unbalanced force
so large acceleration
B
fairly large, unbalanced force
so fairly large acceleration
C
small unbalanced force
so small acceleration
D
forces **balance**
so no acceleration

2 Copy and complete the following sentences.

The sky-diver accelerates because of the downwards force of __________.

As she falls faster and faster, there is a bigger and bigger upwards force because of air __________.

This upwards force eventually __________ the force of gravity.

Making a safe landing

Well before she reaches the ground, the sky-diver opens her parachute.

3 Explain why opening her parachute gives her a much smaller terminal velocity.

Large area gives more air resistance. So this balances gravity at a much lower speed.

Cruising along the motorway

The diagrams show two cars moving at a steady speed along a flat stretch of motorway.

4 Copy and complete the following sentence.

To keep a car moving at a steady speed, the driving force from the engine must exactly __________ the frictional forces.

5 You need a much bigger driving force to keep a car going at 70 miles per hour than at 50 miles per hour. Explain why.

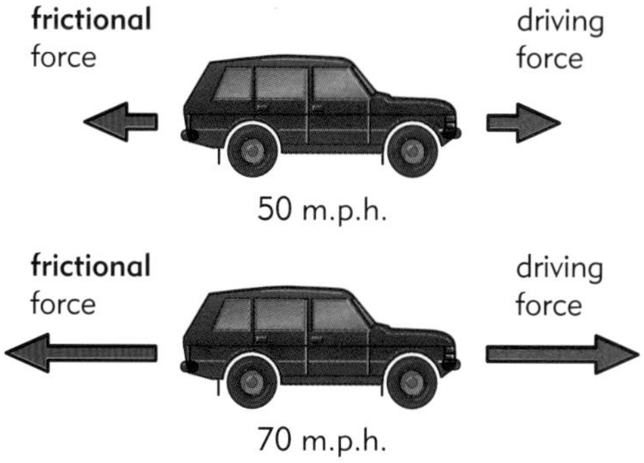

frictional force
driving force
50 m.p.h.
frictional force
driving force
70 m.p.h.

Falling through liquids

There is a lot more friction when things fall through liquids than when they fall through air. So things falling through liquids have a much smaller terminal velocity.

6 Look at the pictures.

What do they tell you about the terminal velocity of the two marbles?

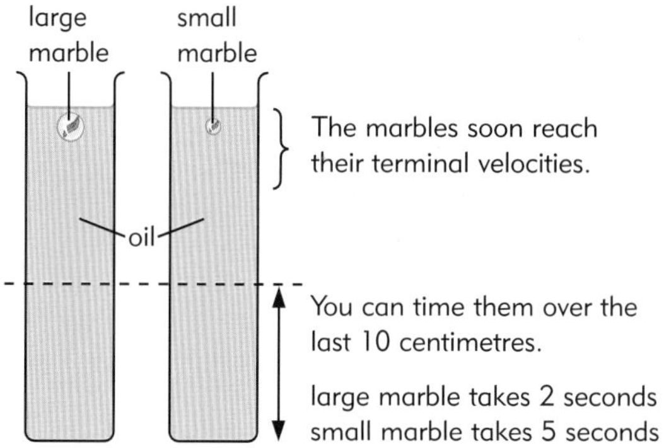

large marble
small marble
The marbles soon reach their terminal velocities.
oil
You can time them over the last 10 centimetres.
large marble takes 2 seconds
small marble takes 5 seconds

What you need to remember [Copy and complete using the **key words**]

Speed limits

When an object falls through a gas or a liquid:

- it accelerates at first due to the force of __________;
- frictional forces increase until they __________ the force of gravity;
- the object then falls at a steady speed called the __________ __________.

When a vehicle travels at a steady speed, the driving force exactly balances the __________ forces.

23 All in a day's work

Trolleys won't push themselves

You move a shopping trolley by applying a force to it. When you push the trolley you transfer **energy** to it. We say that you are doing **work**. Work, like energy, is measured in joules.

1 Copy and complete the following sentences.

To make an object move, you must transfer __________ to it. You can do this by applying a __________ to the object. The energy you transfer like this is called __________.

Who does the most work?

Three shoppers are pushing trolleys to their cars.

2 (a) Who does more work, Ravi or Mandy? Explain why.

(b) Who does more work, Mandy or Jeroen? Explain why.

The amount of work done depends on how much force is used and what distance is moved. In fact, we can calculate it like this:

work done	=	force	×	distance moved
(joules)		(newtons)		**(metres)**

3 Look at the pictures and work out the missing numbers. The first one is done for you.

WORK DONE = FORCE x DISTANCE
DISTANCE = WORK DONE ÷ FORCE
FORCE = WORK DONE ÷ DISTANCE

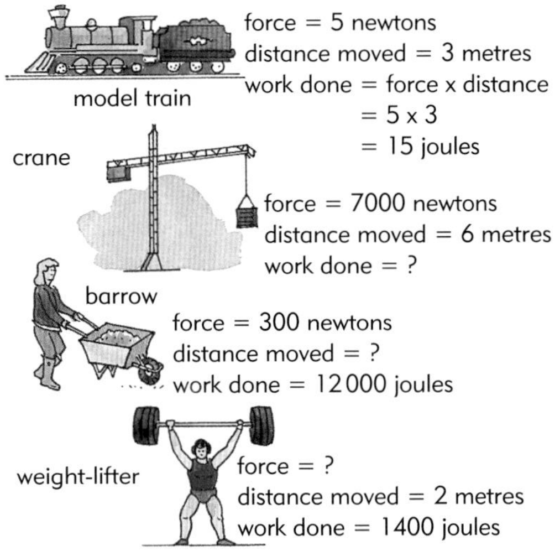

Energy on the move

To make a trolley move you must transfer energy to it. The trolley then has what we call **kinetic** energy (movement energy). Objects with a lot of kinetic energy are more difficult to stop. Look at the picture of runaway trolleys and answer the following questions.

4 (a) Which trolley is easier to stop, P or Q?

(b) Which trolley is easier to stop, R or S?

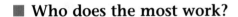

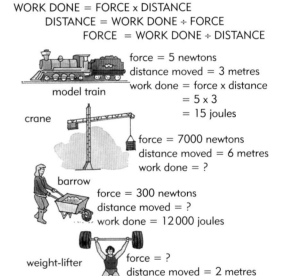

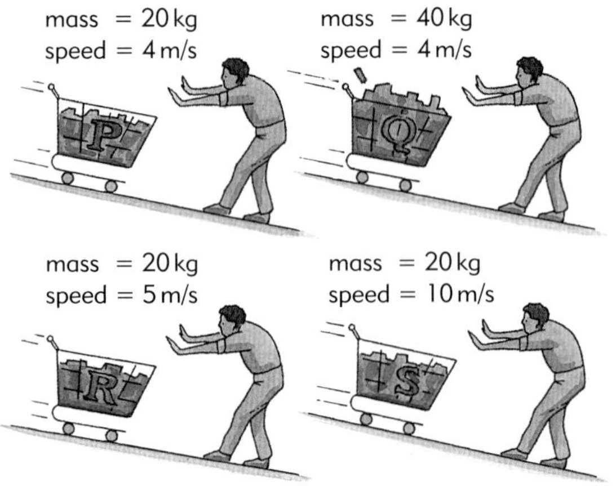

Runaway trolleys. Trolleys with a big **mass** and a big **speed** have a lot of kinetic energy.

5 Copy and complete the following sentences.

An object has more kinetic energy when it has __________ mass.

An object has more kinetic energy when it has __________ speed.

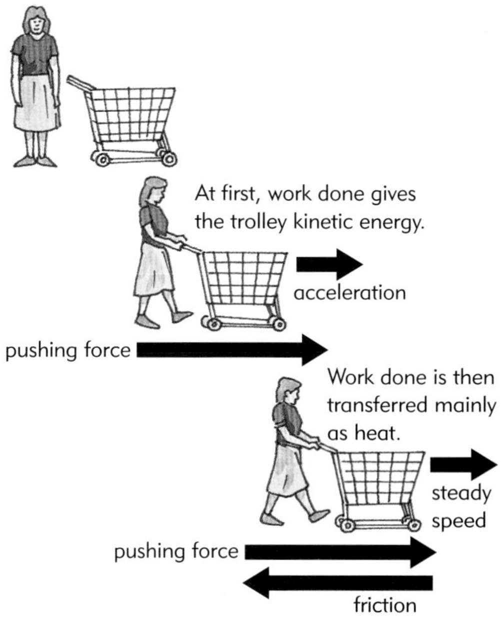
At first, work done gives the trolley kinetic energy.
acceleration
pushing force
Work done is then transferred mainly as heat.
steady speed
pushing force
friction

Friction is a waste of work

When you first push a shopping trolley it starts to move. But you then have to keep on pushing to keep it moving at the same speed. You are then doing work against the force of friction. All the work you do ends up as **heat**.

6 Copy and complete the following sentences.

When you start a trolley moving, work done is transferred as __________ energy.

When you keep a trolley moving, work done is transferred as __________ energy.

Working your way up the stairs

When you walk up stairs you are doing work. You are lifting your own weight so you are working against gravity. The distance you move your weight is the height of the stairs.

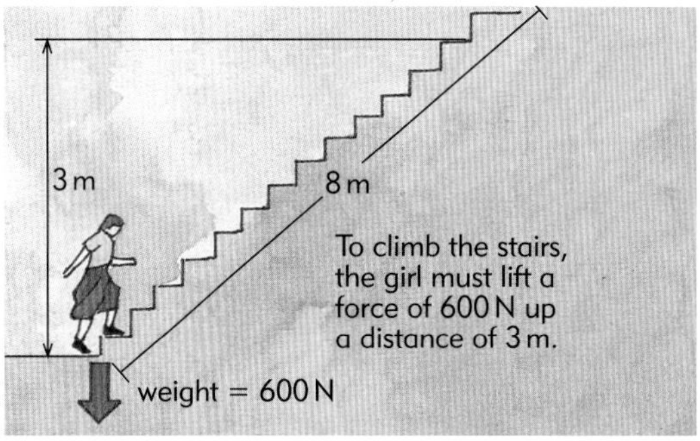
3 m
8 m
To climb the stairs, the girl must lift a force of 600 N up a distance of 3 m.
weight = 600 N

Climbing stairs.

7 How much work must the person in the diagram do against gravity to climb the stairs?

What you need to remember [Copy and complete using the **key words**]

All in a day's work

When a force moves an object, __________ is transferred and __________ is done.
You can calculate the amount of work done like this:

work done (__________) = __________ (newtons) × distance moved (__________)

The energy an object has because of its movement is called __________ energy.
An object has more kinetic energy if it has a bigger __________ or a greater __________.
Work done against friction is mainly transferred as __________.

Handling data

In tests and examinations, you will be asked to interpret scientific data. This data may be presented in several different ways.

Pie charts

Generating electricity in the UK

You need some other energy source to generate electricity.

The pie chart shows the energy sources used in the United Kingdom in 1995.

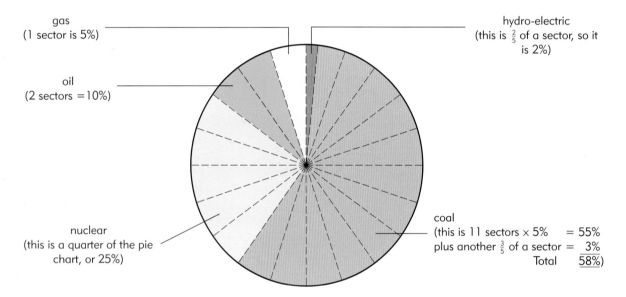

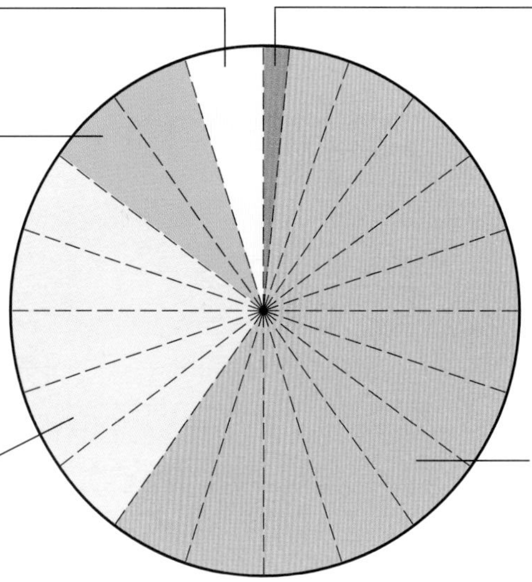

You may be asked to compare the amounts of electricity generated from nuclear fuel and from gas.

You could say that more is generated from nuclear fuel.

A better answer is to say that there is a lot more electricity generated from nuclear fuel.

An even better answer is that there is five times as much electricity generated from nuclear fuel than from gas.

You may be asked to complete a pie chart.

Remember:

- to draw thin, straight lines through the centre of the circle
- to mark off each 1% in some of the sectors if you need to, like this

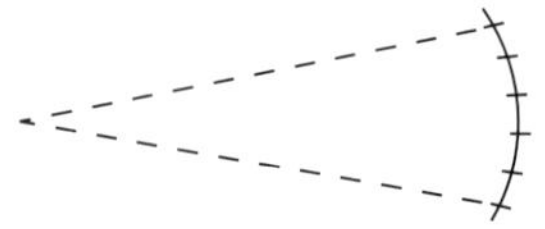

- to add labels, or use a key like this

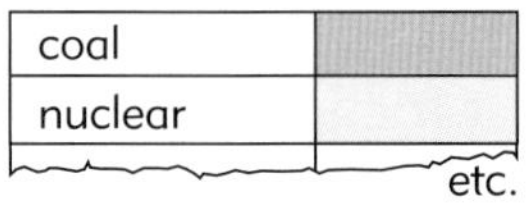

Bar charts

How well do metals conduct electricity?

The bar chart shows how much wires made from different metals resist an electric current flowing through them. The wires are all the same thickness.

The metal with the lowest resistance is the best conductor.

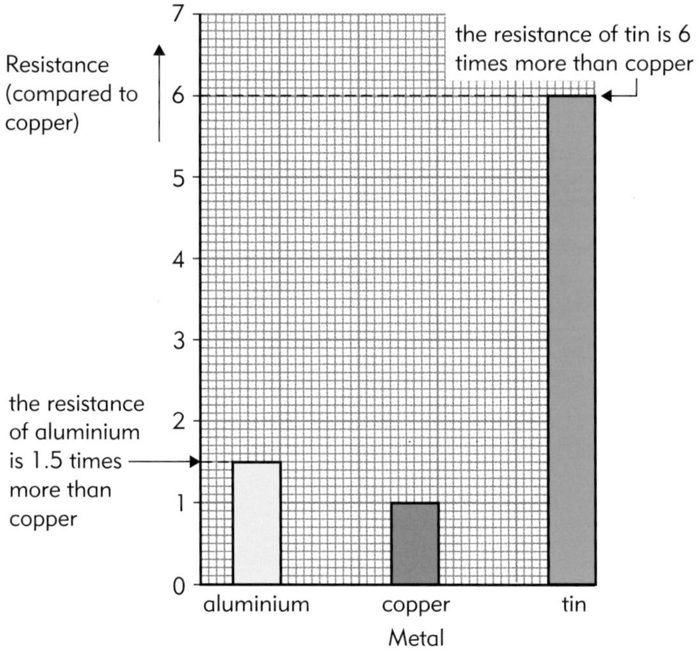

You may be asked to put the metals in order, starting with the best conductor, like this:

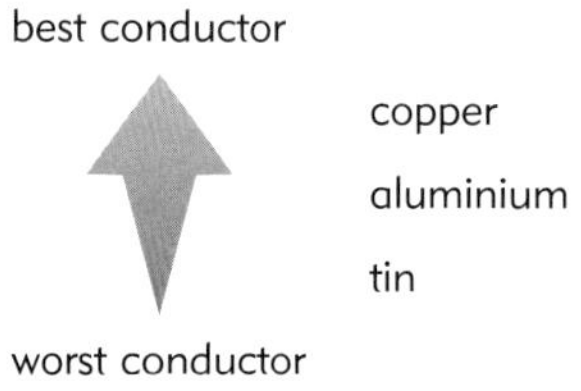

You may be asked to draw bars on a bar chart.

Remember:

- to look carefully at the scale
- to draw the bars the same thickness and equally spaced out
- to draw the top of each bar with a thin, straight line
- to label each bar, or colour the bars and draw a key like this

aluminium	
copper	
tin	

Sankey diagrams

What happens to the energy from petrol?

The diagram shows what happens to each 100 J of energy from petrol when it is burnt in a car engine.

Remember, all the energy must be transferred in some form:

$70\,J + 25\,J + 5\,J = 100\,J$

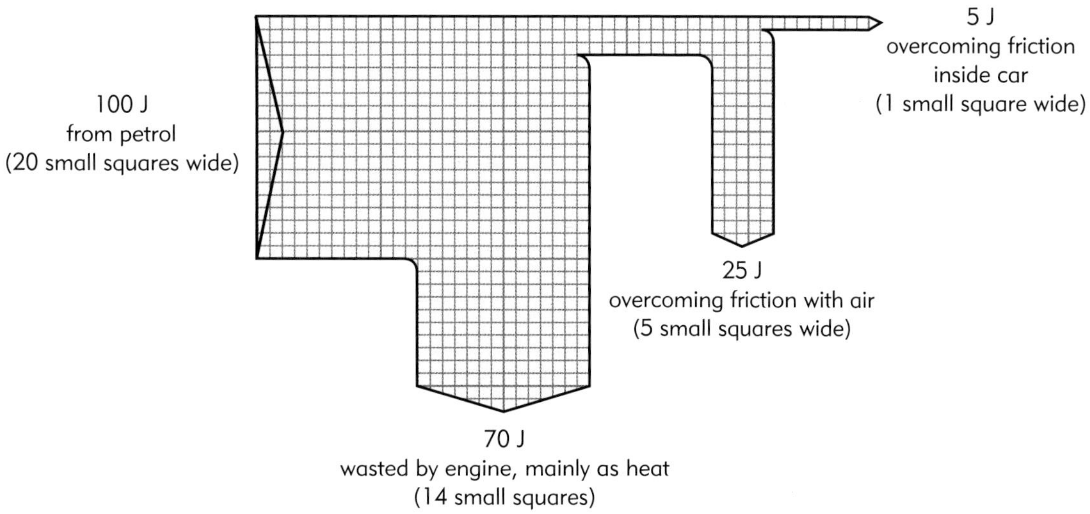

Line graphs

Keeping soup hot

The graph shows how well two different flasks keep soup hot.

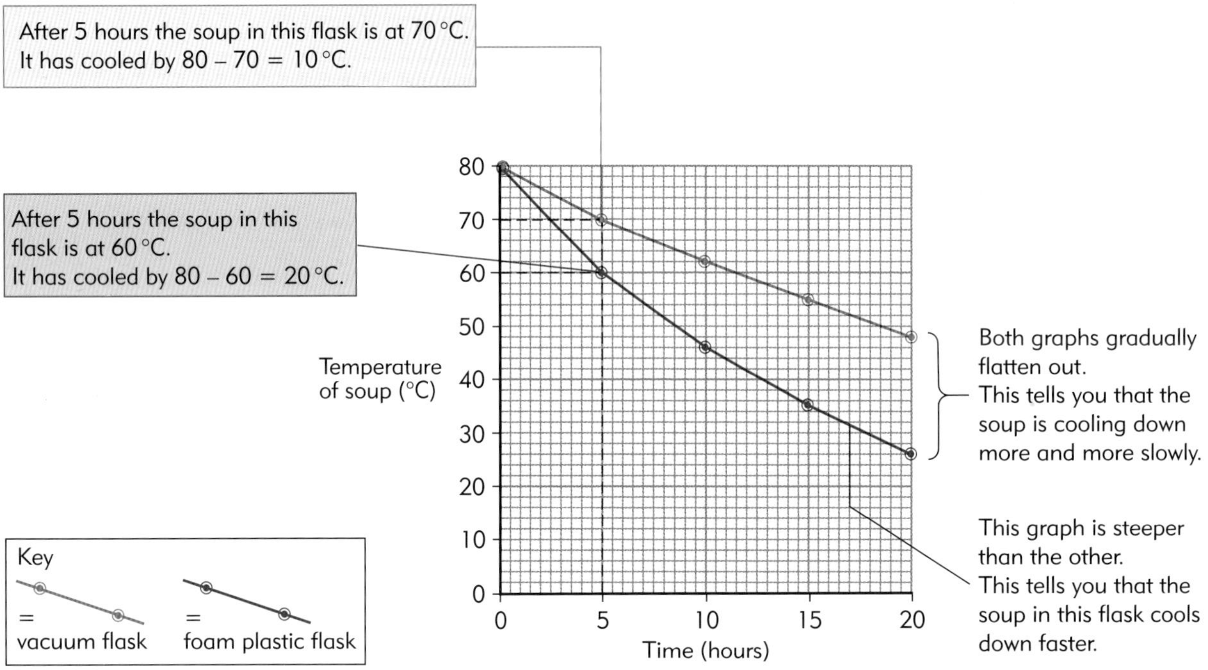

You may be asked to plot a line graph from a table of results like this:

Time (hours)	0	5	10	15	20
Temperature (°C)	80	70	62	55	49

Remember

- to look carefully at the scales
- to label both of the axes
- to mark the points carefully like this 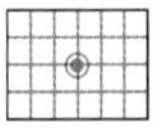 or 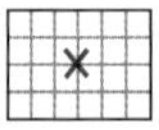
- to draw a line through the points using a sharp pencil
  - draw any straight parts of the graph using a ruler
  - draw any curved parts of the graph without bumps

Revising for tests and examinations

Stage 1

See if you know which words go into the **What you need to remember** boxes for the pages you are revising.

Try to do this without looking at the text or diagrams on the pages. Then, if there is anything that you can't do, read the text and look at the diagrams to find the answer.

Remember

- the key words are printed like this

  frictional **gravity** **balance**
  terminal velocity

- you can check your answers at the back of the book (pages 188–199).

But you don't just have to remember the scientific ideas. You also need to be able to use these ideas. You may be asked to do this in a situation you haven't met before.

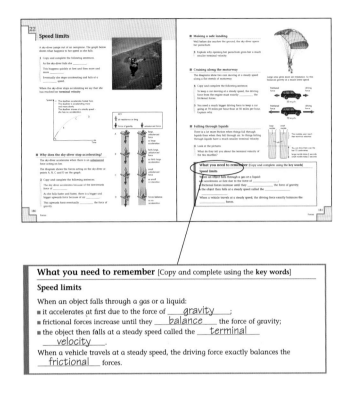

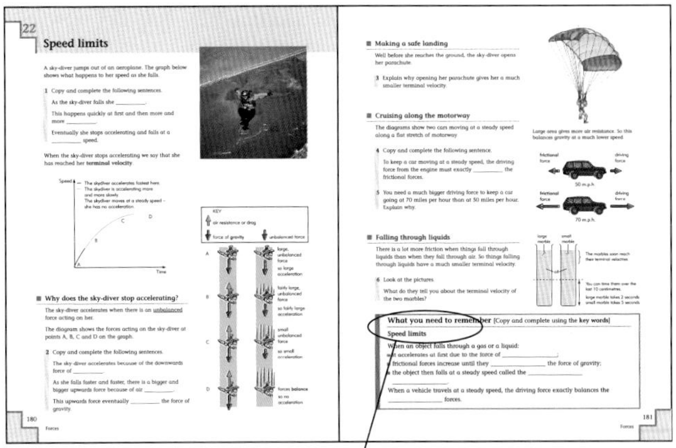

What you need to remember [Copy and complete using the **key words**]

Speed limits

When an object falls through a gas or a liquid:
- it accelerates at first due to the force of gravity ;
- frictional forces increase until they balance the force of gravity;
- the object then falls at a steady speed called the terminal velocity .

When a vehicle travels at a steady speed, the driving force exactly balances the frictional forces.

Example of a question

The force of gravity on the Moon is a lot less than on Earth. There is no atmosphere on the Moon. An astronaut drops a table-tennis ball over a cliff on the moon.

Write down two differences in the way the table tennis ball falls compared to dropping it over a cliff on the Earth. Give reasons for your answers.

Answer

1 The table tennis ball falls more slowly (or with a smaller acceleration) because there is a smaller force of gravity.

2 The table tennis ball never reaches a terminal velocity because there is no friction with air (there is no air resistance).

Stage 2

See if you can use the ideas you have revised. There are lots of questions in the text which ask you to do this. Your teacher should be able to give you some extra questions. Some of these may have been used in examinations in previous years.

Energy

1 Controlling heat transfer in solids

Heat moves from hot places, where the **temperature** is high, to colder places.
This movement of energy is called heat **transfer**.
Heat is transferred through solids by **conduction**.
All **metals** are good conductors of heat.
We surround things with **insulation** to stop heat getting into or out of them.

2 How liquids and gases transfer heat

Liquids and **gases** can both flow.
When part of a liquid or gas is hotter than the rest, it **rises**.
When part of a liquid or gas is cooler than the rest, it **falls**.
Transferring heat in this way is called **convection**.
This movement of a liquid or gas is called a **convection current**.

3 How can heat energy travel through space?

Heat rays can travel through empty **space**.
Another name for empty space is a **vacuum**.
Heat radiation is also called **infrared** radiation.
A **black** surface is good at absorbing infrared radiation.
This means that it **reflects** very little radiation.
A **white** or **shiny** surface is good at reflecting infrared radiation.
This means that it is not a good **absorber** of radiation.
The hotter something is, the **more** energy it radiates.

4 Conduction, convection and radiation – putting it all together

Materials that are used for **insulation** often contain air.
This air is trapped so it can't move about.
A gas, such as air, is a very poor **conductor**.

5 Losing heat from buildings – and how to stop it

Heat energy can be lost from buildings by conduction through the **ceilings**, **floors**, **walls** and **window glass**.
It is also lost by convection because of **draughts**.
Homes lose less heat if they have **fewer** outside walls.
You can save heat energy by **insulating** the loft, fitting **draught** excluders, putting in cavity wall **insulation** and **double glazing** windows.

7 Making use of electricity

We use a lot of electrical **energy** in our homes and in industry.
Electricity can easily be **transferred** as other sorts of energy such as **light**, **sound**, **heat** and **kinetic** (or movement) energy.

8 How much electricity do you use?

Power is measured in **watts** (W).
The name for 1000 watts is a **kilowatt** (kW).

How much electrical energy is transferred depends on:

- how **long** an appliance is switched on for
- how **fast** the appliance transfers energy (its **power**).

The energy used in an electrical appliance is worked out by multiplying the **power** (in kW) by the **time** (in hours):

energy transferred (**kilowatt–hours**) = power (kilowatts) × time (hours)

A kilowatt–hour of electrical energy is called a **Unit**.

9 Paying for electricity

An electrical Unit is a **kilowatt–hour** (kWh).
You can work out the cost of electrical energy used by using this equation:

total cost for electricity used = **number of Units used** × **cost per Unit**

10 Energy to make electricity

To generate electricity we always need some other energy **source**.
Electricity is a **secondary** source of energy.
It is generated from fuels like **coal**, **oil**, **gas** and **nuclear** fuel.
These fuels cannot be **replaced** once they have been burned. We say they are non-renewable.
Sources of energy like wood, sunlight, wind, waves, running water and the tides are called **renewable** energy sources.

11 Using fuels to generate electricity

Coal, oil and gas are called **fossil fuels**.
Examples of nuclear fuels are **uranium** and **plutonium**.
All these fuels are non-renewable – once they are used up, they are gone **forever**.
All non-renewable fuels transfer energy as **heat**.
For coal and oil power stations, this energy is used to boil water. This produces **steam**, which is used to turn a **turbine**. This drives a shaft connected to a **generator**, which produces **electricity**.

13 Generating electricity with water

Renewable energy resources are constantly being **replaced**.
Energy from these sources is free but it is expensive to **capture**.
Water trapped behind dams and barrages can be used to turn a **turbine**, which then turns a **generator**.
You can generate electricity when you need it from a **hydro-electric** power station. Reservoirs for these power stations flood **land**.
You can generate electricity only at certain times each day using a **tidal** power station. Barrages for these power stations flood **estuaries**, which are the habitats for wading birds.

14 Generating electricity with wind

We can capture the **kinetic energy** of the wind using a **turbine**.
This then drives a **generator**, which produces electricity.
Wind generators need to be on hills and coasts where there is plenty of **wind**.
You need **hundreds** of wind generators to produce as much electricity as a **coal-fired** power station.
Large groups of wind generators are called wind **farms**.
These can spoil countryside that people like to **visit**.
Also, wind generators do not produce electricity all the **time**.

15 Generating electricity from the Sun and the Earth

Energy from the Sun can be transferred as electricity using **solar cells**.
Each Unit of electricity from a solar cell is very **expensive**.
But solar cells will work for many years and are useful in **remote** places on Earth and on **satellites**.
They are also useful in things that need very little electricity, such as **calculators**.
Geothermal energy is produced by the reactions of **radioactive** elements (like **uranium**) in the Earth's rocks.
The **heat** released can be used to change water into **steam**, which can then be used to generate electricity.

17 Lifting things with electricity

The force that pulls things down is called **gravity**.
When you lift something up to a **height** above the ground it stores energy.
This stored energy is called **gravitational potential** energy.
To lift things up using electrical energy, you can use a **motor**.
If a motor works faster it has more **power**.
Power is measured in **watts** (W) or in **kilowatts** (kW).
1 kW = 1000 W

18 Measuring power and energy

Energy is measured in **joules** (J). Power is measured in **watts** (W).

One watt is one **joule** of energy transferred every **second**.

$$\underset{\text{(watts)}}{\textbf{power}} = \frac{\text{energy transferred (joules)}}{\text{time taken (seconds)}}$$

$$\underset{\text{(joules)}}{\textbf{energy transferred}} = \underset{\text{(watts)}}{\text{power}} \times \underset{\text{(seconds)}}{\text{time}}$$

19 Energy where you want it

We try to use energy in the most **efficient** way.
This means that more of the energy we use is **usefully** transferred.
Any energy that is not transferred usefully is **wasted**.

20 Energy of the sort you want

Wasting energy reduces **efficiency**.
Energy is most often wasted as **heat** energy.
In machines, moving parts rub together and waste energy because of **friction**.
An engine with 100 per cent efficiency transfers all its energy as **useful work**.

21 What happens to all the wasted energy?

Some of the energy you put into a device will be transferred in a **useful** way but some of it will be **wasted**.
The useful energy plus the wasted energy always adds up **exactly** to the energy you put in.
All the energy eventually ends up as **heat**, which makes everything a bit **warmer**.
But this energy **spreads out**, which makes it more difficult to transfer in a useful way.

Electricity

1 Are you a conductor or an insulator?

The European mains electricity supply is about **230** volts.
This is big enough to **kill** people.
Electrical appliances are usually connected to the mains using **cables** and three-pin **plugs**.
These are made from the materials shown on the diagrams, so that they work well and are **safe**.

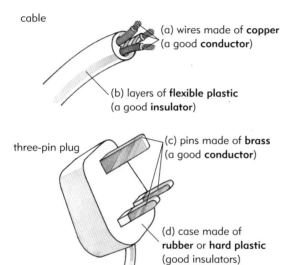

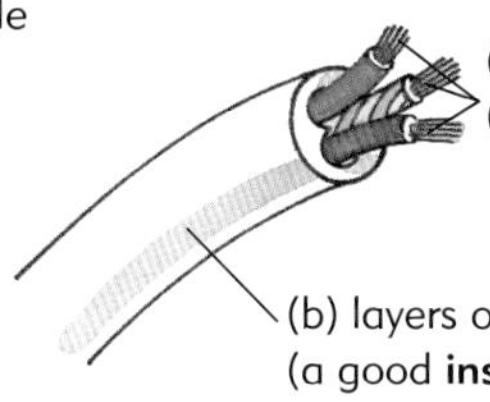

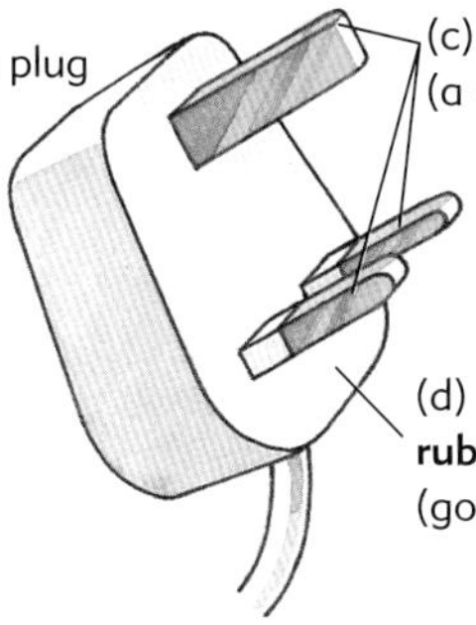

2 Wiring a three-pin plug

The current to an electrical appliance is supplied through the **live** and **neutral** pins.
The earth pin is there for **safety**.
Appliances with **metal** cases are usually earthed.
To prevent strain where the copper wires are connected to the terminals, we use a **cable grip**.

4 Why do plugs have fuses?

A three-pin plug won't work unless it is fitted with a **fuse**.
If the current becomes too big, the fuse becomes **hot** and then **melts**.
This **cuts off** the current. Fuses make circuits much **safer**.
You should always replace a fuse with the type recommended by the makers of the **appliance**. This will normally be the **same** type as the fuse you are replacing.
Dangerous currents can also be switched off using **circuit breakers**.

5 V/a.c./d.c./Hz What do they all mean?

An electric current through a wire is, in fact, a flow of **electrons**.
The current from a battery always flows in the same **direction**.
It is called a **direct** current, or **d.c.** for short.
A current that constantly changes direction is called an **alternating** current, or **a.c.** for short.
Mains electricity is an a.c. supply. In Europe, it has a frequency of 50 **cycles** per second, or 50 **hertz** (Hz for short).
The mains supply in Europe is about 230 **volts**, or 230 **V** for short.

6 Why is mains electricity a.c? Why is it 230 volts?

You can change the voltage of an a.c. supply using a **transformer**.
Electricity from power stations reaches us through the **National Grid**.
Electricity is sent through the Grid at a very high **voltage**.
This is produced using a **step-up** transformer and means that less **energy** is wasted.
Before it reaches homes and factories, the voltage is reduced using a **step-down** transformer. This makes the electricity **safer** to use.

7 Doing things with magnets

A force pulls together a magnet and anything made from **iron** or **steel**.
We say they **attract** each other.
If a magnet is **free** to **move**, it will come to rest pointing north and south.
The part of the magnet that points north is called the **north-seeking pole**.

8 What do magnets do to each other?

Two magnets may attract each other.
If one of them is then turned round they will **repel**.
Two poles that repel each other must be the same; they are **like** poles.
Two poles that attract each other must be different; they are **unlike** poles.
The area around a magnet that affects other magnets and pieces of iron or steel is called a **magnetic field**.

9 Using magnets to lift things

When an electric **current** flows through a coil of wire it acts like a bar **magnet**.
It has a **north-seeking pole** at one end and a **south-seeking pole** at the other end.
This type of magnet is called an **electromagnet**.
Electromagnets are useful because you can **switch** them off.
More turns, an iron core and a bigger current are three ways of making an electromagnet **stronger**.

10 How do loudspeakers work?

To reverse the poles of an electromagnet, you need to **reverse** the direction of the current that flows through it. This idea is used to make the cone of a loudspeaker **vibrate** and produce a sound.
An **alternating** current is fed into the coil of the loudspeaker. This produces a sound with the same **frequency** as the a.c.

11 How do electric motors work?

An electric **motor** uses electricity to produce movement.
The forces between a permanent **magnet** and an **electromagnet** are used to produce this movement.
The electromagnet is called an **armature**.
The armature of a motor keeps on turning because the current is **reversing** over and over again.

12 How to make a magnet move a copper wire

A **magnetic** field will only move a copper wire if an electric **current** flows through the wire.
To make the wire move the opposite way you can:
- **reverse** the direction of the current
- reverse the **poles** of the permanent magnet.

The size of the force acting on a wire can be increased:
- by increasing the size of the **current** through the wire
- by increasing the strength of the magnetic **field**.

13 Electricity that can make your hair stand on end

When you rub two **different** materials together they become **charged** with electricity. This is called **static** electricity.
There are two types of charge, called **positive** (+) and **negative** (–).
Charges of the same type **repel** each other.
Charges of different types **attract** each other.

We say:
like charges repel; **unlike** charges attract.

14 Why rubbing things together produces electricity

When two different materials are rubbed together, **electrons** are rubbed off one material and on to the other.
Each electron carries a small, **negative** electrical charge.
The material that gains electrons becomes **negatively** charged.
The material that loses electrons becomes **positively** charged.
These two charges are exactly **equal** in size.

16 Danger from sparks

A charged conductor can be discharged by connecting it to the **earth** with a **conductor**.

17 How to produce an electric current.

You can produce an electric current by moving a **magnet** into a coil of wire. We say that the current has been **induced**.
If you move the magnet <u>out</u> of the coil or move the <u>opposite end</u> of the magnet into the coil, you get a current in the **opposite** direction.
To induce a bigger current you can:
- use a **stronger** magnet;
- move the magnet **faster**;
- have more **turns** on the coil of wire.

In a generator, a magnet **spins** inside a coil of wire. This induces a current if the coil is connected to a complete **circuit**. Otherwise it induces a **voltage** but not a current.

18 How many batteries do I need?

To make an electric current flow through a bulb there must be a **voltage** (also called a **potential difference**) across it.
We measure voltage in units called **volts (V** for short) using a **voltmeter**.
This meter is connected **in parallel** with the bulb.
To get a bigger voltage, you can connect more than one cell **in series**.
This is called a **battery**.
To find the total voltage of a battery, you should **add** the voltages of the **cells**.

19 Making a current flow

We measure electric currents in units called **amperes** (A for short) using an **ammeter**.
To measure the current through a bulb, you must connect the ammeter **in series** with it.
A bulb **resists** a current flowing through it.
The bigger the resistance of a bulb, the bigger the **voltage** you need to send a particular current through it.

20 Connecting several things to the same supply

When bulbs (or other components) are connected in parallel:

- the full **voltage** of the supply is connected across each component;
- the current through each component depends upon its **resistance**;
- the total current from the supply is the **sum** of the currents through the separate components.

21 Different ways of connecting things in circuits

When bulbs (or other components) are connected in series:

- the total resistance is the **sum** of the separate resistances;
- exactly the **same** current flows through each component;
- the supply voltage is the **sum** of the voltages across each component.

22 Electric circuits and energy transfer

An electric current is a flow of negatively charged **electrons**.
When a current passes through a resistance, electrical energy is transferred as **heat**.
How fast an electrical appliance transfers energy is given by

power (in **watts**)	=	**potential difference** (in volts)	×	**current** (in amperes)

23 How does current change with voltage?

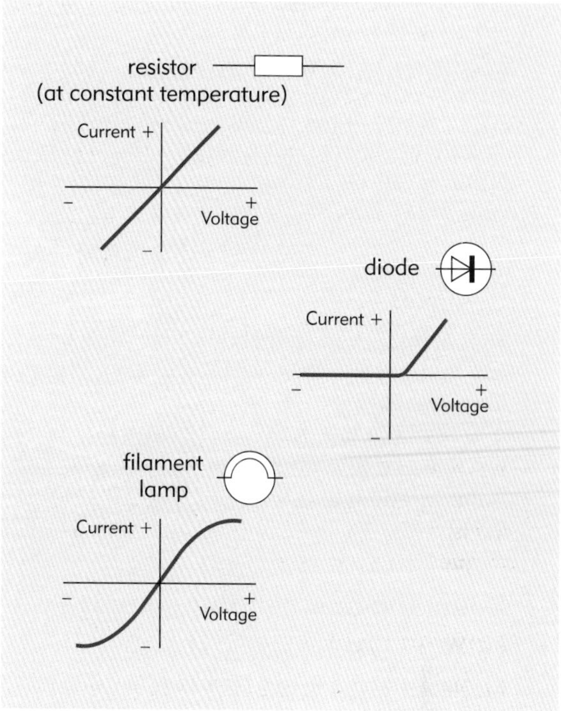

24 Using electricity to split things up

Some substances are made of electrically charged particles called **ions**.
These ions can move about if the substance is **melted** or **dissolved**.
Negatively charged ions move to the **positive** electrode.
Positively charged ions move to the **negative** electrode.
The substance gets split up into **simpler** substances.
This is called **electrolysis**.

Waves and radiation

1 Doing things with mirrors

A flat, shiny surface is called a **plane** mirror.
A narrow beam of light is called a **ray**.
A mirror **reflects** a ray of light at the same **angle** as it strikes the mirror.

2 Bending light

Rays of light change **direction** when they pass from one transparent substance into another. We say they are **refracted**.
A normal is a line at 90° to the **boundary** between two different substances.
A ray of light that is travelling along a **normal** does not change direction.

3 Bouncing and bending sounds

Sounds are reflected from **hard** surfaces.
A sound that is reflected back to where it came from is called an **echo**.
A sound can also be bent or **refracted** when it crosses the **boundary** between two different substances.

4 Why do people say that light and sound are waves?

Water waves are reflected from a **hard**, **flat** surface, just like light from a plane mirror.
Water waves are refracted towards the normal when they pass into shallower water at an **angle**.
This happens because they travel **slower** in shallower water.
Light is also **refracted** towards the normal when it travels from air into glass (or plastic or water).
This must be because it travels **slower** in glass (or plastic or water) than it does in air.

5 Looking at water waves: Part 1

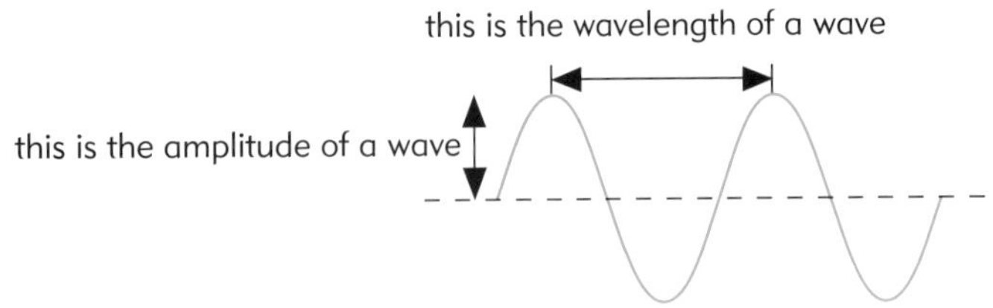
this is the wavelength of a wave
this is the amplitude of a wave

6 Looking at water waves: Part 2

The number of waves each second is called the **frequency**, and it is measured in **hertz** (Hz, for short).
Waves transfer **energy** from one place to another without any substance such as water, being transferred.

7 Looking at sound waves

Sounds are made when things **vibrate**.
Loud sounds have waves with a large **amplitude**.
Sounds that have a high pitch have waves with a high **frequency**.

8 'Sound' you can't hear

Sound with a frequency that is too high for humans to hear is called **ultrasound**.
Sound, or ultrasound, of any frequency can be made from **electrical** vibrations produced by electronic circuits.
You can use ultrasound to **clean** delicate mechanisms like wind-up watches.
Doctors can make an ultrasound **scan** of a developing baby inside its mother's womb.

9 Why are there different colours of light?

When rays of light pass through a prism their **direction** is changed.
You can use a prism to split up white light into all its **colours**. The pattern of colours is called a **spectrum**.
The prism splits up light because the prism **refracts** different colours by different amounts.
Different colours of light have different **wavelengths**.

10 Waves beyond the ends of the rainbow

The table shows all the different kinds of waves in the **electromagnetic** spectrum.

radio waves	micro-waves	infrared waves	light	ultraviolet waves	X-rays	gamma rays

longest wavelength — red — violet — shortest **wavelength**
lowest **frequency** — highest frequency

All types of electromagnetic radiation travel through space at exactly the same **speed**.

11 What happens when electromagnetic waves hit things?

When electromagnetic waves hit a solid, liquid or gas they may be **reflected**, **absorbed** or **transmitted** (or more than one of these).
Electromagnetic waves transfer **energy**. When the waves are absorbed by matter, this energy may make the matter **heat** up.
When radio waves or microwaves are absorbed by an **aerial**, they produce an electric signal.

12 How a doctor can see inside your stomach

A doctor can see inside a patient's stomach using an **endoscope**.
This works by sending light along **optical** fibres.
All of the light is **reflected** over and over again from the inside of the fibre.
This is called **total internal reflection**. This happens when the angle of the light to the normal is bigger than the **critical angle**.

13 Using radio waves

Radio waves can pass easily through **air** and through **dry** non-metals.
This is what makes them useful for carrying **radio** and **television** programmes.
A layer in the Earth's atmosphere **reflects** radio waves with long wavelengths.
We can use this idea to send radio waves around the **curved** surface of the Earth.

14 Using microwaves

In microwave ovens, the microwaves are strongly absorbed by **water** molecules in food. The energy from the microwaves makes the food **hot**.
Metal things **reflect** microwaves, even if they are full of small holes.
Some microwaves can pass easily through the Earth's **atmosphere**.
These microwaves are used to carry information to and from **satellites**.

15 Using infrared radiation

Toasters and grills cook food using **infrared** radiation.
Foods become hot when they **absorb** this radiation.
Infrared rays are used to control a **television** set or a **video** player, and to send telephone messages along **optical** fibres.
This is better than sending electrical signals along wires, because the cable has a **smaller** diameter and there is less **weakening** of the signal.

16 Using ultraviolet radiation

Radiation from the Sun, or from a sunbed, can give pale skins a **tan**.
But it can also damage skin cells and cause skin **cancer**.
These things happen because of **ultraviolet** radiation.
Some substances **absorb** ultraviolet radiation and use the energy to produce **light**. We say that these substances are **fluorescent**.

17 Using X-rays

X-rays do not pass through the **bones** in your body.
X-rays pass through skin and flesh, but do not pass so easily through **diseased** cells.
Doctors can use X-rays to make a shadow **picture** of the inside of your body.
Metals **protect** your body because they **absorb** X-rays.

18 Using gamma (γ) radiation

Gamma radiation can kill living **cells**.
It is used to kill harmful **bacteria** or **cancer** cells inside people's bodies.

19 Radiation that harms your body

Infrared radiation and microwaves can damage cells by making them **hot**.
Ultraviolet radiation can damage the cells in your **skin** and may cause skin cancer.
Some types of radiation can pass through your body, for example **X-rays** and the radiation from **radioactive** substances.
If any of these types of radiation is absorbed, it can damage the **molecules** in your cells and may cause **cancer**.

20 How much harmful radiation do you get?

The bigger the dose of radiation you get, the greater the risk of **cancer**.
Our bodies receive radiation all the time from **radioactive** substances in the air, the ground, food, water and building materials.
Our bodies also receive **cosmic** radiation from space.
All this radiation is called **background** radiation.

21 Investigating radioactive substances

Radioactive substances **emit** radiation all the time.
You can do **nothing** to change this.
A few centimetres of air or a thin sheet of paper absorbs most **alpha** (α) radiation.
A metal sheet a few millimetres thick absorbs most **beta** (β) radiation.
Even a thick sheet of lead only partly absorbs **gamma** (γ) radiation.
When radiation strikes atoms or molecules they become electrically **charged**.

22 Using radioactive substances safely

The thicker a material is, the more radiation it will **absorb**.
This idea is used in factories to control the **thickness** of materials.

23 What are atoms made of?

Atoms have a small **nucleus** made of protons and neutrons.

Particles called **electrons** move around in the empty **space** around the nucleus.

Particle	Mass	Charge
proton	**1 unit**	**+ 1 unit**
neutron	**1 unit**	**no charge**
electron	**hardly any**	**– 1 unit**

Each atom of the same element has the **same** number of protons and electrons. So it has no overall electrical **charge**.

24 Why are some atoms radioactive?

Atoms of the same element always have the same number of **protons**.
But they can have a different number of **neutrons**.
Atoms of the same element with different numbers of neutrons are called **isotopes**.
Sooner or later, an atom with an unstable nucleus will change; we say that it **decays**.
It changes into an atom of a different **element** with a different number of **protons**. It also emits **radiation**.
As its atoms decay, a radioactive substance emits **less** radiation.
We can use this idea to **date** things.

Forces

1 What makes things stand still?

When an object rests on a surface its weight pushes **downwards**.
The surface pushes **upwards** on the object.
The two forces are **equal** in size but they act in **opposite** directions, so the forces are **balanced**.
When balanced forces act on a stationary object it will remain **stationary**.

2 Why do objects slow down?

When an object moves through air or water or along the ground, a force of **friction** acts.
The direction of this force of friction is always **opposite** to the direction in which the object is moving. This makes the object **slow** down.
To keep an object moving at a steady speed, you need a driving force to **balance** the force of friction.
If balanced forces act on a moving object it will keep moving with a **steady** speed.

3 Taking the rough with the smooth

When solid surfaces slide across each other, a force of **friction** acts.
The direction of this force is always **opposite** to the direction in which the object or surface is moving.
Friction causes objects to **heat** up. It also makes surfaces **wear away**.
The friction between solid surfaces is used in **brakes** to slow down and stop moving vehicles.

4 Stop that car!

The greater the speed of a vehicle, the longer the **time** it takes to stop and the greater the **distance** it travels.
If the braking force is too large the vehicle may **skid**.
Stopping distance is affected by the **reaction** time of the driver. It also depends on the **friction** between the road and the tyres. There is less friction when the road is **wet** or **icy**.

5 Travelling at speed

We calculate speed like this:

$$\text{speed} = \frac{\textbf{distance}\text{ travelled}}{\textbf{time}\text{ taken}}$$

The units of speed are **metres per second**. The distance travelled is measured in **metres**. The time taken is measured in **seconds**.

You can show speed on a **distance–time** graph.

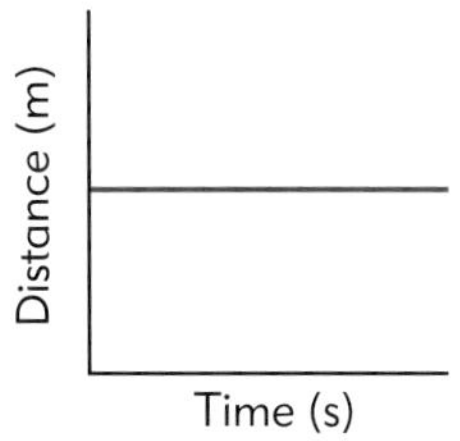

This graph shows the distance moved by an object that is **stationary**.

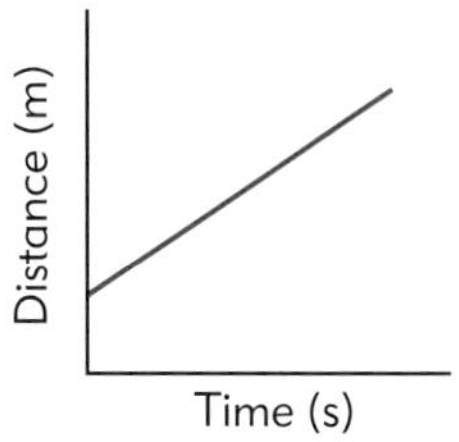

This graph shows the distance moved by an object that is moving with a steady **speed**.

If an object has more speed, the graph has a steeper **slope**.

6 Springs and things

When a spring is stretched and then released, it returns to its original **shape**.
Materials that do this are called **elastic**.

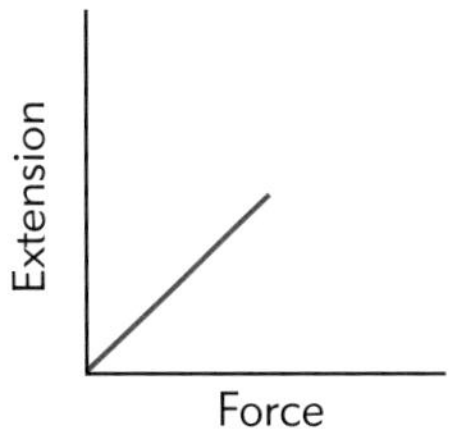

This graph shows that equal amounts of **force** produce equal amounts of **extension** in a spring.

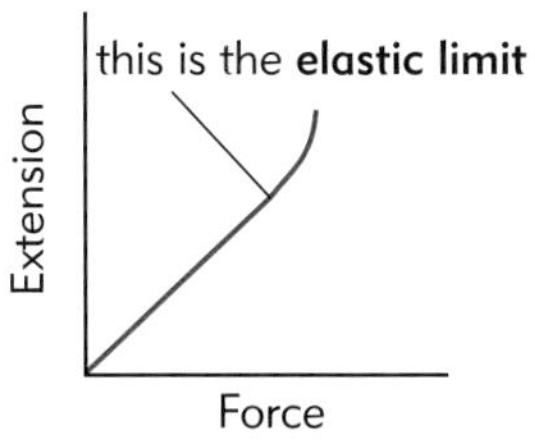

This is the graph for a spring which has been **overstretched**. It does not go back to its original shape.

To stretch a spring you have to do **work** on it. The spring then stores energy called **elastic potential** energy.

7 Bridges and bungee cords

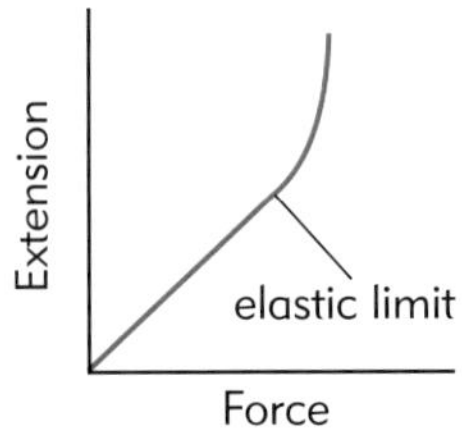

You can stretch a wire using a **force**. Unless the force is too big, the wire goes back to its original length when you remove the force. We say the wire is **elastic**.
If you stretch a wire further than its **elastic limit**, it stays stretched.
To stretch anything you have to do work and transfer **energy**. This energy is stored in the stretched material. It is called **elastic potential** energy.

8 Bursting balloons and protecting brains

If you spread a force out over a large area you get a smaller **pressure**.
To get a large pressure you need a large **force** acting on a small **area**.

$$\text{pressure} = \frac{\textbf{force}}{\textbf{area}}$$

Pressure is measured in **newtons per square metre** (N/m^2).
These units are also called **pascals** (Pa).

9 Deep sea divers – standing the pressure

The pressure in water is caused by the **weigh**t of the water pressing down.
The deeper you go under water, the bigger the **pressure** is.
Water pressure acts equally in all **directions**.
Gases and liquids are all types of **fluid**.
The pressure of the air around us is called **atmospheric** pressure.

10 Using liquids to push harder

We can use liquids to send forces to where they are needed. This is called a **hydraulic** system.
A force is applied to the liquid using a **master** piston. This puts the liquid under **pressure**.
This pressure exerts a force on a **slave** piston.
Pressure in a liquid acts equally in all directions. This makes it easy to send forces to the right **place** and make them act in the right **direction**.
A hydraulic system can also make forces bigger; it can be used as a force **multiplier**.

11 The light of day, the dark of night

The Earth spins on its **axis** once every **24** hours.
The Sun shines on one half of the Earth, where it is **daytime**.
The other side of the Earth is in shadow, where it is **night**.
The Earth goes around the **Sun** once in **365**$\frac{1}{4}$ days.
This is called one **year**.
The path around the Sun is called an **orbit**.

12 Distant suns

The Sun is a **star**. Stars are made of very hot, glowing **gas**.
Stars other than the Sun do not look so bright because they are very **far** away.
We give the stars in the sky patterns called **constellations**.
These patterns do not **change** from year to year.

13 Why do planets look like stars?

Planets do not give out their own **light**. They look bright because they **reflect** light from the Sun.
Planets travel around the **Sun** in almost circular **orbits**. This makes the planets appear to move slowly against the background of the **constellations**.

14 Why do the planets orbit the Sun?

All objects **attract** each other with a force called **gravity**. This is very small for small masses but is big for very large objects such as the **Sun** or the **Earth** and the other **planets**.
Distance also affects gravity. The greater the distance, the **smaller** the force of gravity.
The orbits of the planets are nearly **circular** except for Pluto's orbit, which is very **elliptical**.
Planets stay in their orbits because of the balance between their **speed** and the force of the Sun's gravity.

15 Satellites

Satellites are kept in their paths beacuse they have a high sideways **speed** and are pulled inwards by the force of **gravity**. These paths are called **orbits** and can be circles or **ellipses**.
Satellites can be used to:

- take pictures of the Earth, for example to predict the **weather** or for **spying**;
- take pictures of the stars and galaxies without the Earth's **atmosphere** getting in the way;
- send **telephone** messages and **television** programmes around the world.

16 The Universe

There are **billions** of stars in a galaxy and billions of galaxies in the **Universe**.
Galaxies also contain **dust** and **gas**. When the gas and dust clouds are pulled together under the force of **gravity**, stars may form in them. Stars shine because of the nuclear fusion of **hydrogen** gas into **helium** gas.

18 Lose weight – become an astronaut

An object always has the same **mass**. We measure this in **kilograms**.
The **weight** of an object is the force of gravity that acts on it. We measure this in **newtons**. On Earth the force of the gravity per kilogram is about **10** N/kg.
We can work out weights like this:

weight	=	**mass**	×	force of gravity per kilogram
(**newtons**)		(kilograms)		(**newtons per kilogram**)

19 Acceleration helps to win races

The speed of an object in a particular direction is called its **velocity**.
The rate at which the velocity of an object changes is called its **acceleration**.
The units of acceleration are **metres per second squared** (m/s^2). Acceleration can be calculated like this:

$$\text{acceleration} = \frac{\textbf{change}\text{ in velocity}}{\textbf{time}\text{ taken}}$$

Acceleration can be shown on a **velocity–time** graph.

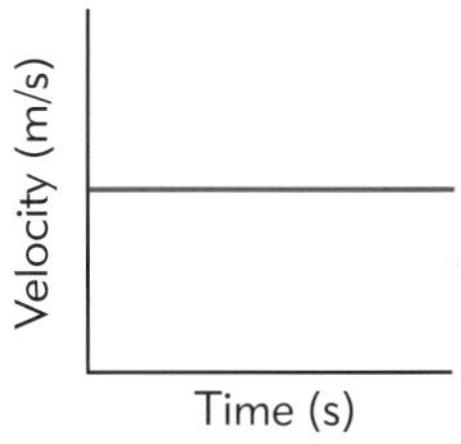

This graph shows the velocity of an object that is moving with a **steady** velocity.

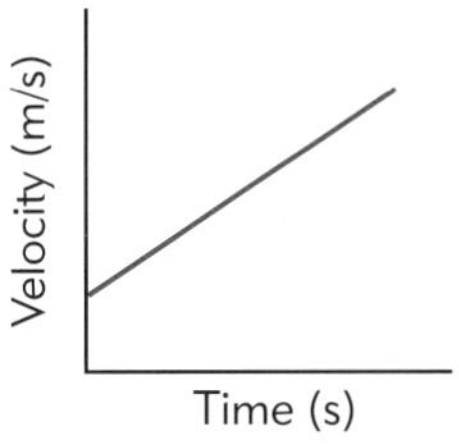

This graph shows the velocity of an object as it **accelerates**.

If an object has a bigger acceleration, the graph has a **steeper** slope.

20 Sport and transport – a lot of pushing and pulling

Sometimes the forces acting on an object do not cancel each other out.
We say they are **unbalanced**.
A stationary object will start to **move** in the direction of the unbalanced force.
An unbalanced force makes a moving object **speed** up or **slow** down. We say that an unbalanced force produces an **acceleration**.
The bigger the mass of an object, the more **force** is needed to accelerate it.

21 Experiments in space

One newton is the **force** required to give a **mass** of one kilogram an **acceleration** of one metre per second squared.
The force you need to produce an acceleration can be worked out like this:

force	=	**mass**	×	acceleration
(**newtons**)		(kilograms)		(**metres per second squared**)

On Earth, the force of **gravity** pulls things down with a force of 10 newtons for every kilogram. This gives them an **acceleration** of 10 metres per second squared.

22 Speed limits

When an object falls through a gas or a liquid:

- it accelerates at first due to the force of **gravity**;
- frictional forces increase until they **balance** the force of gravity;
- the object then falls at a steady speed called the **terminal velocity**.

When a vehicle travels at a steady speed, the driving force exactly balances the **friction** forces.

23 All in a day's work

When a force moves an object, **energy** is transferred and **work** is done.
You can calculate the amount of work done like this:

work done	=	**force**	×	distance moved
(**joules**)		(newtons)		(**metres**)

The energy an object has because of its movement is called **kinetic** energy.
An object has more kinetic energy if it has a bigger **mass** or a greater **speed**.
Work done against friction is mainly transferred as **heat**.

Glossary/index

The words 'energy' and 'transfer' are used on a very large number of pages.
The words 'electricity' and 'force' are also used a lot. These words are <u>not</u> included in this Glossary/index.

A

A: short for *amperes*

absorber: a surface that soaks up the energy from the *waves* (or *radiation*) that strike it **11, 116–117, 123, 132–133**

a.c.: short for *alternating current*

acid rain: rain that is more acid than usual because of dissolved *sulphur dioxide* or *nitrogen oxides* **28**

air resistance: the force of *friction* on an object that moves through air **141, 180–181**

alpha (α) radiation: one of the three types of *radiation* that *radioactive* substances can give out *(emit)* **127, 131**

alternating current: a.c. for short; an electric current that constantly changes direction **56–58**

ammeter: this is used to measure electric currents **85–87**

amperes: A for short; the size of an electric current is measured in units called amperes **85–87**

amplitude: the size of the disturbances that make up *waves* **104, 108**

armature: the part that turns round in an *electric motor* **68**

artificial satellite: a *satellite* that humans have put into *orbit* **166–167**

atoms: all substances are made of atoms; atoms have a *nucleus* that is made of *protons* and *neutrons* and is surrounded by *electrons* **134–137**

attract, attraction: the force that pulls magnetised or electrically charged objects together **60–63, 73**

axis: the Earth spins on its axis every 24 hours **158**

B

background radiation: the *radiation* from *radioactive* sources that is around us all the time **128**

battery: several electrical *cells* joined together **82–83**

beta (β) radiation: one of the three types of *radiation* that *radioactive* substances can give out *(emit)* **127, 131**

billion: 1 000 000 000 or one thousand million **168**

C

carbon dioxide: a gas produced when *fuels* burn; carbon dioxide in the atmosphere helps keep the Earth warm (*greenhouse effect*); too much carbon dioxide in the atmosphere makes the Earth warmer (*global warming*) **28**

cell: this uses chemicals to produce an electric current; connecting cells together makes a *battery* **82–83**

CHP: combined heat and power; a CHP power station makes use of heat that would normally be wasted, to heat buildings **29**

circuit breaker: this protects an electric circuit by switching off a current if it is too big; it is then re-set **65**

compass: a *magnet* that is free to move so that its ends (*poles*) point to the north and south **60–63**

conduction: **1** electrical conduction – the flow of an electric current through a substance **48–49**
2 thermal conduction – the transfer of heat (thermal energy) through a substance from hotter parts to colder parts **6, 12–13**

conductors: substances that *conduct* heat or electricity **6, 12–13, 48–49**

constellations: patterns of stars in the sky **161, 163**

convection: the transfer of heat (thermal energy) by the movement of a liquid or a gas **8–9, 12–13**

cooling towers: these are used in fuel-powered power stations to change steam back into water after it has passed through the *turbines* **26–27**

copper: a *metal* that is a very good *conductor* of heat and electricity **6, 48–51**

cosmic radiation: harmful *radiation* that comes from space **129**

critical angle: the angle at which you start to get *total internal reflection* **118–119**

cycle: one complete *wave* of an *alternating current*; the number of cycles per second is the *frequency* **57**

D

d.c.: short for *direct current*

diodes: these let a current pass through them in only one direction **93**

direct current: d.c. for short; an electric current that always flows in the same direction **56**

drag: another word for **air resistance**

E

earthed: something is earthed when it is connected to the ground with an electrical *conductor* **49–52, 78–79**

echo: an echo occurs when sound or *ultrasound* is *reflected* straight back to where it came from **101, 111**

efficiency: a measure of how much energy is usefully transferred as the form of energy you want **42–47**

elastic substance: something is elastic if it goes back to its original shape when you take away a force that was changing its shape **148–151**

elastic limit: if you change the shape of something beyond the elastic limit, it does not go back to its original shape **149–150**

elastic potential energy: the energy that is stored in an object such as a spring when a force changes its shape **148, 151**

electric motor: this transfers electrical energy as *kinetic* (movement) *energy* **68–69, 71**

electrodes: these are put into a melted or dissolved substance and connected to a *battery* or power supply so that *electrolysis* can happen **95**

electrolysis: the process of splitting up a melted or dissolved substance by passing an electric current through it **94–95**

electromagnet: a *magnet* that is only magnetised when an electric current is flowing through its coil **64–69**

electromagnetic radiation: *radio waves, microwaves, infrared* radiation, light, *ultraviolet* radiation, *X-rays* and *gamma* radiation are all types of electromagnetic radiation **114–117, 120–127**

electromagnetic spectrum: the different types of *electromagnetic radiation* arranged in order of their *wavelengths* or *frequencies* **114–117**

electrons: tiny particles with a *negative* charge (–1); they move when you give a solid a charge of static electricity, or when a current flows through a solid **56, 73–75, 95**

ellipse: the squashed circle shape of the *orbits* of the *planets* around the Sun **165–166**

emit, emission: we say that *radioactive* substances emit *radiation* **130**

endoscope: this is used by a doctor to see inside a patient's body **118–119**

extension: the change in the length of a spring or a wire when it is stretched by a force **148–150**

F

fluids: substances that can flow; liquids and gases are fluids **154**

fluorescent substances: substances that absorb *ultraviolet* radiation and transfer the energy as light **123**

fossil fuels: *fuels* that formed in the Earth over millions of years from the remains of dead plants and animals, for example coal, oil and natural gas **26–29**

frequency: the number of complete *waves* or vibrations in a second; frequency is measured in units called *hertz* or *cycles* per second **57, 106, 115**

friction: a force which acts on an object that is moving; the force acts in the opposite direction to the direction in which the object is moving **140–145**

fuels: substances that release energy when they are burned; nuclear fuels release energy when their *atoms* are split in a nuclear reactor **24**

fuses: these protect an electrical circuit by melting if the current is too big; they then have to be replaced **54–55**

G

galaxies: groups of *billions* of stars **168–169**

gamma (γ) **radiation:** very short *wavelength electromagnetic radiation*; one of the three types of *radiation* that *radioactive* substances can give out (emit) **125, 127, 131**

Geiger counter: this is used to measure the *radiation* from *radioactive* substances; a Geiger–Müller tube detects the *radiation* **130–131**

generator: this transfers *kinetic* (movement) *energy* as electricity **26, 30–31, 80–81**

geothermal energy: heat (thermal energy) from inside the Earth **35**

global warming: the strengthened *greenhouse effect*

gravitational potential energy: the energy that is transferred to an object by lifting it against the force of *gravity* **30, 38–39**

gravity: the force between objects because of their *mass* **38, 164–167, 169, 172–173, 179–181**

greenhouse effect: this describes the way in which the Earth is kept warm by gases such as *carbon dioxide* in the atmosphere; burning *fossil fuels* produces more *carbon dioxide*, so the greenhouse effect is strengthened – we call this *global warming* **28**

H

hertz: Hz for short; *frequency* is measured in units called hertz **57**

hydraulic systems: systems that use *pressure* in a liquid to send forces to where they are needed **156–157**

hydroelectricity: electricity generated using water collected behind a dam (which stores energy as *gravitational potential energy*) **25, 30**

Hz: short for *hertz*

I

induce, induction: the production of a *voltage* by moving a coil in a *magnetic field*, or by moving a *magnet* in a coil **80–81**

infrared: *radiation* that transfers heat (thermal energy) from hot objects; a form of *electromagnetic radiation* **10–11, 114, 122**

insulator: 1 electrical insulator – a substance that does not let electricity pass through it very easily **48–49**
2 thermal insulator – a substance that does not *conduct* heat (thermal energy) very well **6–7, 12–15**

ions: electrically charged particles in some melted or dissolved substances; ions move towards the *electrodes* during *electrolysis* **95**

J

J: short for *joules*

joules: J for short; energy or *work* is measured in units called joules **40, 182**

K

kilowatt-hours: kW h for short; 1 *Unit* of electricity; 1 kilowatt-hour is the energy transferred in 1 hour by a power of 1 *kilowatt* **21–23**

kilowatts: kW for short; 1 kilowatt is 1000 *watts* **20**

kinetic energy: this is the energy an object has because it is moving **38–39**

kW: short for *kilowatt*

kW h: short for *kilowatt-hour*

L

loudspeakers these devices transfer electrical energy as sound **66–67**

M

magnetic field: the area around a *magnet* where it has an effect; lines of magnetic force show the shape of the magnetic field **63**

magnets: these *attract* iron and steel and can *attract* or *repel* other magnets **60–63**

mains electricity: the electricity that is supplied to our homes **48–59**

mass: the amount of matter in an object; mass is measured in units called kilograms (kg) **172–173**

metals: substances that are good *conductors* of heat and electricity **6, 48–49**

microwaves: *electromagnetic radiation* with a *wavelength* between the wavelengths of *radio waves* and *infrared* radiation; they are used for cooking and to send signals to and from *artificial satellites* **121, 126**

N

N: short for *newtons*

National Grid: the network of cables that carry electricity from power stations to where it is used **59**

negative charge: the charge on an object that has gained *electrons* **73–75**

negative terminal: the side of a *cell* or power supply that *electrons* move away from **56**

neutrons: particles that may be found in the *nucleus* of an *atom*; a neutron has a *mass* of 1 unit but no electrical charge **134–137**

newtons: N for short; forces are measured in units called newtons **152, 172, 178–179**

nitrogen oxides: gases produced when *fossil fuels* burn; they are one of the causes of *acid rain* **28**

non-renewables: energy sources that gradually get used up and will eventually run out **24, 27**

normal: a line drawn at right angles to the boundary between two different substances **98–99, 103**

nuclear fuels: *radioactive* substances such as *uranium* and *plutonium*, which are used in nuclear power stations **26–27**

nucleus: the central part of an *atom*; the nucleus may contain *protons* and *neutrons* **134–137**

O

orbit: the path of a *planet* around the Sun or a *satellite* around a *planet*; it can be a circle or an *ellipse* **159**

P

Pa: short for *pascals*

parallel circuit: parts of a circuit are connected in parallel if an electric current can flow through each part <u>separately</u> **82, 86–88**

pascals: Pa for short; *pressure* is measured in units called pascals – 1 pascal is the same as 1 *newton* per square metre **152**

permanent magnets: *magnets* that stay magnetised all the time **64–71**

photocopiers: these use *static electrical* charges to make copies of printed pages **76–77**

pitch: we hear sound with a high *frequency* as a note with a high pitch **109**

plane mirror: this is a flat mirror; light is *reflected* from the mirror at the same angle as it strikes the mirror **96–97**

planets: very large objects, such as the Earth, which move in *orbits* around the Sun **162–165, 171**

plutonium: a *fuel* used in nuclear power stations **26**

poles: **1** the parts of a *magnet* that *attract* or *repel* **60–63**
2 the parts of the Earth's surface that are on the *axis* around which it spins **158**

positive charge: the charge on an object that has lost *electrons* **73–75**

positive terminal: the side of a *cell* or power supply that *electrons* move towards **56**

potential difference another name for *voltage*

power: how fast energy is transferred (or *work* is done); it is measured in units called *watts* or *kilowatts* **20–21, 39–41, 91**

pressure: this is the force on a certain area; pressure is measured in units called *pascals* **152–157**

protons: particles found in the *nucleus* of an *atom*; a proton has a *mass* of 1 unit and a *positive charge* (+1 unit) **134–137**

R

radiation: 1 energy that travels as *electromagnetic radiation*, including heat (thermal energy), which is *infrared* radiation **10–13, 16–17, 114–117, 120–129**
2 what *radioactive* substances give out (*emit*) **128–133**

radiation dose: a measure of how much harmful *radiation* a person's body receives in a period of time **128–129**

radio waves: long *wavelength electromagnetic radiation* that we use to carry radio and television programmes **120**

radioactive substances: substances that give out (*emit*) *alpha, beta* or *gamma radiation* **127–133, 136–138**

reflection: reflection occurs when *radiation* (or a *wave*) bounces back from something that it has hit **11, 96–97, 100, 102, 117**

refraction: refraction occurs when *radiation* (or a *wave*) changes direction when it crosses the boundary between two different substances; with water waves, this happens when the water changes depth **98–99, 101–103**

renewables: energy sources that are constantly being replaced and will not run out **25, 30–37**

repel, repulsion: the force that pushes magnetised or electrically charged objects apart **60–63, 73**

resistance: bulbs and other electrical components resist a current being pushed through them, so we say they have a resistance **85, 88–89**

resistors: these can be used in an electrical circuit to increase the *resistance* and reduce the current **89, 92**

S

satellites: objects that move in an *orbit* around the Earth or another *planet*; the Moon is a satellite of the Earth; there are also *artificial satellites* **166–167**

series circuit: parts of a circuit are connected in series if an electric current flows through each part one after the other **82, 85, 88–89**

solar cells: these transfer energy from the Sun's *radiation* directly as electricity **25, 34**

solar panels: these *absorb* energy from the Sun's *radiation* and transfer it as heat (thermal energy) **16–17**

spectrum: 1 visible spectrum – this is what you get when you split up white light into all the different colours from which it is made **112–113**
2 see *electromagnetic spectrum*

speed: the distance something travels in a period of time **146–147**

start-up time: how long it takes to start up a power station and get it generating electricity **29**

static electricity: electrical charges that stand still (when charges move you get an electric current) **72**

streamlined shape: a shape that produces very little *friction* when it moves through air or water **141**

sulphur dioxide: a gas that is produced when many *fuels* burn; it is one of the causes of *acid rain* **28**

symbols: a way of showing electrical components; they make it easy to draw circuit diagrams **90**

T

terminal velocity: the steady *speed* reached by a falling object when its *weight* is exactly balanced by *friction* **180–181**

total internal reflection: when all of a beam of light inside glass (or some other transparent substance) is *reflected* from the boundary between the glass and the air **118–119**

transformers: these are used to increase (step-up transformers) or reduce (step-down transformers) the *voltage* of an *a.c.* supply which is fed into them **58–59**

transmit, transmission: this occurs when a substance allows *waves* or *radiation* to pass through it **116–117**

turbine: this is made to turn by moving water, steam or wind; it transfers *kinetic* (movement) *energy* as its own *kinetic energy* **26, 30–33**

U

ultrasonics, ultrasound: sound *waves* which have a *frequency* that is too high to hear **110–111**

ultraviolet radiation: *electromagnetic radiation* with a *wavelength* shorter than that of violet light waves **114, 123, 126**

Units: we buy *mains* electricity in Units; 1 Unit is the same as 1 *kilowatt–hour* **21–23**

Universe: everything there is; it is made up of *billions* of *galaxies* **168–171**

uranium: a *fuel* used in nuclear power stations **26**

V

V: short for *volts*

vacuum: empty space **10**

vacuum flask: a container that has a *vacuum* between two walls to reduce heat transfer **13**

velocity: this is the *speed* of an object and its direction **174–175**

voltage: the 'push' of an electrical supply

voltmeter: this is used to measure *voltage* **82–83, 89**

volts: V for short; the 'push' of an electrical supply is measured in units called volts **56, 58, 82–83, 89**

W

W: short for *watts*

watts: power is measured in units called watts; 1 watt is 1 *joule* of energy transferred per second **20–21, 41**

wavelength: the distance between a point on a *wave* and the same point on the next *wave* **104, 115**

waves: evenly spaced out disturbances that carry energy from one place to another **102–109**

weight: the force of *gravity* on an object; it is measured in units called *newtons* **172–173**

wind farm: a lot of wind generators in the same place **33**

work: the energy transferred when a force is moved through a distance; work, like energy, is measured in units called *joules* **182**

X

X-rays: short *wavelength electromagnetic radiation*; X-rays pass through flesh but not through bone or metals **124, 127**